Micro Bionic

Radical Electronic Music & Sound Art in the 21st Century

THOMAS BEY WILLIAM BAILEY

A Belsona Books publication, MMXII

Second edition, 2012. Published by Belsona Books, Ltd.

Further information available at www.tbwb.net

Cover design by Thomas Bey William Bailey

Cover photograph of Dave Phillips by Randy Yau

ISBN-13: 978-0615736624
ISBN-10: 0615736629

For Rachael, obviously

Micro Bionic | contents

Preface To The Second Edition

I confess: the words *'revised and expanded edition,'* when I see them appended to the title of a new book, are ones that arouse more skepticism in me than excitement. This is because, in every medium where it is possible to revise or expand upon the original work, there have been great abuses of this concept that do not really 'expand' on the original in anything but cosmetic ways. To add insult to injury, the process of cosmetic revision is often done at the expense of other qualities that audiences found meaningful. Sci-fi fans, for example, will probably be familiar with one of the highest-grossing film franchises of all time, which had the audience-acclaimed features of its storyline altered so that its director could modernize it with superfluous CGI effects (making one wonder if the original work, now prey to the vicissitudes of its creator, would eventually morph into a kind of constantly revisable palimpsest.) Elsewhere, collectors of recorded music will surely have noted the multiple waves of questionably "definitive" album re-releases that hit the market, first during the compact disc bonanza and then again during the recording industry's mad dash to offer consumers something superior to those immaterial album copies that were being freely shared online. So, I know all too well that revisions are often seen as being the result of suspect motives: existing either as a salve for the creators' egos, or acting to propagate any number of false needs (particularly when an artist's muse is failing to deliver any convincingly new and original work.)

At the same time, I also feel that many creative artifacts do deserve a second life, when they aren't clearly irredeemable failures or fundamentally flawed designs resisting the best efforts to improve them. With seemingly nothing to stop me from reworking a flawed (and out-of-print) first edition of *Micro Bionic*, and everything to gain from this process, I feel that I owed it to friends and supporters to give them a better overall effort. The first edition was doomed by my signing with a fly-by-night publisher, and by the naïve expectation that this outfit would provide me with an editor, who would then collaborate with the starry-eyed "first time author" on a more coherent edition (rather than, as the case was, merely *adding* typographical errors to an otherwise 'raw' draft of the text.) So the rough-hewn quality of that first edition, in the end, owes itself entirely to mistakes in my own judgement. Having just returned from years of living overseas, with not as much of a grip on composing in my native language as I might have had otherwise, I should have been less hasty in my rush to get myself in print. Though the state of self-imposed panic turned out to be unwarranted, I felt at the time that various "windows of opportunity" were ready to slam shut all around me, thanks to an increasing number of geo-political situations that could explode at any moment and thus put my little educational enterprise on hold indefinitely. I began to think with the guerrilla mindset that it was better to err while acting than to deny any action for fear of erring. As a result of this 'impending apocalypse' bunker mentality, my would-be parting shot to the world turned out instead to be a warning shot, poorly aimed but heralding more 'precise hits' to come.

Since then, I've written much on the subject of the sonic arts and music, but have decided that - barring some unprecedented level of demand for what I do - my future book projects will no longer revolve exclusively around sonic culture. The "core" of what I wish to say on music and audio is now covered in my first two books and other scattered editorials. So my task now is mainly one of refinement, of acknowledging when my theses either continue to hold up or collapse, and of connecting this subject matter to a more holistic communicational project that takes all areas of human endeavor into account.

I do not indulge in any illusions that successive versions of the book will "wipe the slate clean" and make me appear more like a virtuoso writer. I imagine that both hard copies and 'unofficially released' digital copies of the first edition are still in circulation, and any attempt for me to make false claims as to the original contents of *Micro Bionic* will be rebuffed quickly and decisively. Admittedly, some of my attitudes relating to this book's subjects have changed to a significant degree since the first printing of this book, as keen readers will note from the exclusion of two entire chapters from the first edition, and the addition / expansion of others. My enthusiasm for some ideas and modes of implementation has increased, while enthusiasm for other phenomena has completely fallen away from me. This is to be expected of a culture that aspires to dynamism- these artists and their works are not static entities, and those who maintain a static opinion of these artists after they noticably reconstitute themselves are being intellectually dishonest, or perhaps seeking some social reward for their loyalty. Rigid, unthinking consistency is best avoided when dealing with a culture that is in a fairly constant state of flux.

The point of this second edition, then, is not to engage in mere reputation-saving exercises: be they historical revisionism, back-pedaling on "controversial" opinions, or even the release of a sort of "stopgap" transitional book to keep my name alive in the literary marketplace. Nor is it to make a sequel that "picks up where we left off" and downplays the importance of the prior discussions. The point of this revised book is to minimize the amount of unresolved issues or unanswered questions hovering around the original text- a process that will, in turn, maximize understanding of one goal that motivates most of my writing on the arts. That goal, simply stated, is to show that a creativity as self-determined as possible is essential to meaningful communication, and to positive changes in life quality on both a 'micro' and 'macro' level. I feel that, if a revised work makes progress towards that goal similar to what could be expected from a work that is "100% new" (whatever that means anymore), then that work should be issued without shame. If nothing else, it has more merit than a purportedly "100% new" product that only exists to shift attention away from the incomplete status of previous work.

If this version of the book brings my readership to a better understanding of their own relation to creative life than the previous version, I will gladly deal with any criticism that I may receive for suspected ulterior motives, or for any perceived form of inconsistency.

Introduction

Shibuya, Tokyo, January 2006: while on one of my routine, non-purposive walks up and down the Meiji Avenue, I take in the chilled hyper-modernism of the city while listening to the wild and abrasive abstractions of 'extreme computer musician' Peter Rehberg on a portable MP3 player. A singular, blank-faced and indifferent mass of human traffic along the sidewalks seems to share my non-purposive drift, even as they engage in an impressive, seemingly choreographed number of personal transactions, mobile phone conversations and communicative gestures. By contrast, the overdriven avalanche of digitally distorted sound pumps into my ear canals with a wild, near-death desperation. From this simplest of contrasts in stimuli, I begin to formulate a vague plan to compose a book about recent electronic music, which, in this period of gestation, will comment on the nearly eschatological hyper-modernism I notice around me in the city. At one point I entertain the idea of linking the newer types of electronic music extremity with the sensory extremities of architecture, but this idea - mercifully, given my contemporaneous lack of fluency in the world of architectural criticism - gets put on holdfor at least a few years.

A feverish enthusiasm to write a book on 'radical electronic music' comes to consume me, and for months I have no idea as to a possible thesis statement or cohesive argument to bind all the book's disparate items of inspiration together. Yet this rudderless feeling of *not knowing why I'm doing this* is, paradoxically, very encouraging. My interest in the type of music that informs this book came about in much the same way as the inspiration to write the book itself: it surreptitiously (one might say 'virally') invaded my consciousness and re-wired many perceptions of my lived environment before I even knew that it was doing so.

Still, in the beginning, I have few rigid guidelines other than to write without being too celebratory or too damning- without writing with either the absolute conviction of a fanatic, and without looking through the supposedly dispassionate microscope of that subset of cultural critics for whom sound analysis has to precede enjoyment. There is also the minefield of technological determism to avoid - in my readings and personal discussions on topics like techno, noise, and sound art, I have noticed listeners basing their opinions on these forms of music solely on the degree to which technology that animated the music, and discussing this factor to the detriment of any discussion about what life experiences, philosophies and external factors really informed that music. At the same time there was not, and still isn't, that much writing on this kind of music that didn't stray into academic obscurantism or thinly veiled attempts to prove how many records the respective authors had accumulated. I wanted to convey my excitement about this kind of music to an audience that, while not being spoon-fed and uninquisitive, had no patience for the rarified atmospheres and self-congratulatory, discursive muscle-flexing of elitists (either elite by means of academic credentials, or by the amount of money they had pumped back into the 'scene') who were hoping to remake the world in their authoritarian likenesses.

There were many individuals who, with varying degress of persuasive ability, did make me have second thoughts about foisting another music book onto the world. When my friend, the composer Zbigniew Karkowski, laughingly told me in conversation that "all writing about music is bullshit", I knew at this point that I had my work cut out for me, taking his aside as a direct challenge to pen something that did *not* fall into that unenviable category. So how to avoid this supposedly omnipresent "bullshit" factor? In Karkowski's reckoning (itself an upate of Schopenhauer's attitudes towards music)[1], music writing and reviews fail to accurately convey the illogical and spiritual feeling behind music, since the relative perception of that music from one listener to the next will always be too varied for any one writer's viewpoint to really encapsulate *all* of these subjective listener reactions. Music and sound can accurately simulate events, although their ability to conjure a perfect mental reproduction of one *specific* event is imperfect, given the divergence in memories, experiences, and personal prejudices of each individual listener.

Moreover, with music of the kind reviewed in this book - which relies on heavy amounts of abstraction and non-didactic techniques like pure noise and temporal / spatial distortions - the spectrum of subjective interpretations will probably be wider than ever. So, naturally, I decided to de-emphasize poetic descriptions of the music's visceral effect upon me (although some of this sneaks in here and there), instead suggesting ways in which these sound works are symptomatic or indicative of larger socio-cultural trends and problems. I especially hoped to convey that the spirit of interpretive flexibility animating this music is part of a larger movement towards de-centralization as a survival mechanism, especially as concerns more marginalized artists.

I coined the term *Micro Bionic* as the title of this book, because of the way in which the term neatly applies to this music's definitive features. While any utterance of the word "micro" will automatically cause some to think of its technological application, betraying the degree to which we are inundated with the computing technology of microprocessors, I use it here in a broader sense - it can just as easily apply to an apparently "minor" aesthetic phenomenon whose impact does not immediately register, yet can eventually command an influence equal to the bomb blasts of "major"

---

[1] For example, see his claim that "…music speaks not of things, but of pure weal and woe, which are the only realities for the *will*." *Essays and Aphorisms*, p. 162. Trans. R.J. Hollingdale. Penguin Books, New York, 2004.

culture. I am taken by the increasing amount of music which is characterized by superhuman intensity, speed, efficacy, etc., yet is produced with a bare minimum of physical exertion, sound equipment, and financial or material resources. In addition to these factors, makers of such music often operate using a tiny but adaptive cell structure for support, in comparison to the huge entourages marshaled by major record companies and entertainment conglomerates. A single person making this music might act as an entire record label, handling every aspect of the music from artwork design to recording to distribution. Again, it is a 'more than human' amount of responsibility for those single cells willing to take it all upon themselves- and many do so gladly.

On a less positive note, the audiences for much of this music remain in the 'micro' range compared to the millions of fans courted by conventional music entertainers. Even here, though, there are advantages to be found: these 'micro' niche markets be unusually resilient and can remain fiercely loyal to those who deliver them the goods, and are infinitely more participatory, often being inclined to spread the ideas of their favorite artists through music of their own making. Their numbers may be inferior, but they are a long-term and deeply entrenched support structure rather than a fickle, fleeting fanbase.

✚

"Micro bionic" as a musical genre will probably never make it into common parlance in the same way that zesty terms like "intelligent dance music" or Simon Reynolds' "post-rock" have become the coin of the realm. However, given the disappointingly limited set of artistic techniques that these broad labels apply to, I am not sure how much I really want to be a member of this genre-makers' club. As will become clear soon enough, the creative tendencies involving small-scale engagements with technology, popularity and personnel are far too diverse to be compressed into a single record store rack. The aspects of this material that could be refered to as "micro" are not purely ones of musical technique, social organization, or marketplace distribution - sometimes one of these factors comes into play, at other times the producers of this music oscillate between these different factors.

The subtitle of this book was another story altogether, one which could be misinterpreted as being contrary to the very aims of this book. So, before sending my mutant daughter of a creation out into the world to be judged (and hopefully liked) by all, I should make some cursory attempt at delineating the boundaries of these terms as I am personally using them.

"Radical?"

"Radical" is not a word that I use lightly, or as an indicator of fashionable, darkside cool (lest we forget the one-time popularity of the term as American "skate-punk" argot in the 1980s.) In a modern age when the actions of politicized, militant radicals have caused serious collateral damage (to borrow the sanitized military jargon meaning "mass murder") and swept thousands of innocent bystanders into bloody conflicts, and when desperate attempts to re-organize the world with such actions have caused innumerable disasters, a term like this seems as inappropriate and outdated as calling a guitar-wielding noise musician a "guitar terrorist." The equation of "radicalism" with political violence, on one end of the political spectrum or another, brings us back to this unfortunate linguistic trend of using too broad a descriptor for too narrow a set of activities.

One can be radically destructive *or* radically creative, and the difference between the two may come down to a question of intent. In the history of avant-garde music, activities like John Cage's visit to an anechoic chamber, wherein he learned that there is no such thing as pure biological silence (he claimed to hear the sounds of his own blood circulation within the chamber), have had radical effects on the nature of composition, to the point where it would be impossible to un-learn them. But the effect, in this case, was not something that was deliberately sought out or hoped for as a result. Many of the artists in this book simply "followed their own star" and resisted cultural mediation to such a degree that radical and irreversible results were achieved, even if those results were not the explicit, premeditated "mission" of those artists. John Duncan's description of his audio art as "psychic research" hints at such an openness to an indeterminacy of result and reaction. Like Cage's fable of the anechoic chamber, many of the discoveries outlined in this book have not had the radical and utopian effect of "changing the world" in the narrow sense of re-booting its socio-economic systems, but have revealed the way the world has more or less always been, even while this reality was obscured from our sensory perception in the age of mass media.

Does this all mean that I find politically radical artists to be of no importance? Far from it; yet I feel that radical culture and radical politics are not necessarily always joined at the hip, and that the former may more effectively transform reality than the other because, again, of this paradoxical de-emphasizing of intent and its accompanying openness to surprising conclusions. My own belief is that human history is a cyclical series of advancements and retreats, and that revolutionary overthrow of one *ancien régime* is more often than not followed by the ascendancy of another, either equally or more brutal and draconian than the previous one. I remain very suspicious of certain strains of revolutionary thought and their promises of a definite endpoint in human history - be it Apocalypse or Utopia - as well as their ignoring the fact that nature is ultimately indifferent to our efforts.

In a creative milieu where, more often than not, the revolutionary impulse and the "will to significance" is common, certain strains of creativity – like the "noise" music of Merzbow, or the unmediated swathes of natural sound recorded by Francisco López - are radical for their *refusal* to promise or herald human progress. Seeing things for "what they really are", or finding value in the way that things have always worked (rather than for what they may eventually become), has become one of the quintessential radical actions in an epoch where warring factions violently flail towards progress or change, only succeeding in creating something cosmetically different from the old order.

"21st Century?"

Right away, this is another term that is not going to be universally accepted: the "21st century" is an exclusive product of Western calendars and subsequent Western media domination, even though plenty of other timetables are still in existence and widely used. For a book that will try, from time to time, to convince that Western tradition isn't the only valid wellspring of creativity, it may seem preposterous to insist that we are all linked together by a common tradition of time-keeping that itself stems from our religious tradition. So "21st century" is admittedly an empty term in absence of anything that might point to the specific things *happening* now, rather than merely acknowledging that "now" itself.

The other time-marking musical terms on hand seemed equally vague and problematic. *Contemporary? Modern? "New Music"?* All of these terms seemed shot through with a "chronological snobbery" suggesting that the culture of the present is the only point in time worth investigating, or merely the best humanity is capable of since - as the argument goes - it represents a cumulation of all previous human efforts. In composing this book, I wanted to deal with music that certainly is happening or at least relevant at the time of writing, but which does not make chronological marking its exclusive or primary goal. That is to say, it is not oriented towards answering the question *when,* but towards answering other pertinent questions about modernity (particularly *why.*) I submit that a common factor of most interesting 21st century music is its refusal to deal only with that point in time which we can immediately perceive or engage in a tactile manner.

Much of the more interesting electronic music I've encountered has, if anything, a pronounced streak of *atavism* running through it: it brings submerged memories of the distant past – sometimes even a pre-rational or pre-human stage in our collective past - to the surface, in order to make more accurate projections about the future. (again, often without promising that the future will be a markedly more "progressive" time than the past.) "Back to the future," as it were. The same process can occur in reverse, of course, with state-of-the-art technology being used in an anti-progressive manner; breaking down the complex organizational structures and programmatic behaviors that are supposedly necessary for us to reach loftier plateaus of existence and understanding.

Also, a great deal of the music in this book comes from musicians who have begun their careers well before the 21st century began, yet are creating a body of work encapsulating the "big questions" that we now have to deal with. Many have been active since the 1980s or even 1970s, but are just now being recognized for their work, or have been creating work that projected those "big questions" into our ears before those questions ever became the topic *du jour*- or before those questions became amplified to a level of ineluctability that was distinctly "21st century."

In the end, the term "21st century", as used by this book, is just shorthand for the unique set of socio-cultural issues that have marked the years since 2000 in the Western common era. These include globalization of both market forces and of such countering forces as asymmetrical warfare / terrorism, and the numerous unpredictable factors which can come from having a globe saturated with humans as never before (e.g. a Malthusian catastrophe arising from scarcity of basic resources.) These include also the unparalleled amount of mankind now connected to the internet and with hourly access to personal computers, and all the issues which spin off from this situation: the glut of digital pornography and desire manufacturing, the increased experimentation and interaction with cultures outside of one's physical reach, the vast underground of peer-to-peer file sharing network users consuming huge amounts of audio-visual information against the wishes of copyright enforcers. Naturally, the 21st century is also marked by movements in revolt against any of these developments.

"Electronic Music?" "Sound Art?"

Electronic music and sound art are two more taxonomic terms contributing to our running theme of such overly broad terms signifying a narrow band of cultural activities. So my deployment of these terms should be clarified as well. Anyone with experience in the audio field will testify that virtually all music recorded or performed today incorporates some electronic element or another. We hardly think of the electric guitar or a turntable as an "electronic" instrument on par with a synthesizer or sampler, although both feature some component - the guitar's vibrating strings, and the vibrations of the turntable's stylus - which is amplified electronically. Even a completely un-effected human voice being heard over the radio involves the introduction of electronic equipment into the system. So, what exactly is so special about the selection of artists being recognized by this book?

In most cases, the artists who I've chosen to focus on in this book are ones who employ electronic tools not only as a means of advancing technically (enjoying increased fidelity, frequency range etc.), but also as a means of critiquing the human relationship with our steadily accumulating masses of consumer technology. That relationship is, as it has always been, fraught with tension - and if the sound surveyed in this book does not provide a satisfying resolution to that tension, then it should at least get us to think in a new way free from Manichean, absolutist opinions of technology (i.e., that it is inexorably "good" or "evil.") These artists generally do not occupy the extreme polarities of technophobia or technophilia; most of them simply work from the pragmatic standpoint of using whatever tools are available, without any concern for where they might fit into an eventual convergence of man and machine (or that hopelessly utopian replacement of humanity by artificial intelligence called the "Singularity" by the inventor Ray Kurzweil.)

When all is said and done, the artists herein have been selected because of their ability to seek unknowns in themselves and in an audience, rather than to merely proclaim known facts. The 'electronic music' in this book is made by individuals who are actively engaging in a kind of dialogue with their tools in order to answer questions that they would otherwise not know the answers to, as opposed to musicians and composers who believe these aforementioned 'big questions' - of the particular epoch, or life in general - have already been answered, thus using electronic devices and recording techniques as just a kind of ornamental flourish.

The same criteria could also be used for the examples of sound art listed in this book. This may be an even more contentious term than "electronic music," yet it is necessary to include since the distribution networks of sound art do not always perfectly overlap with those of radical electronic music, even though the boundaries are becoming more Gaussian-blurred by the day: sound art, owing to its frequent mixed-media presentation and its emphasis on being exhibited through public installations, occasionally differs from an electronic music which favors "static" media (compact discs, MP3s etc.) Even here, though, limited *objet d'art* editions of LPs and CDs have elevated the musical artifact to the level of a mixed-media presentation, giving listeners a tactile accompaniment- a small-scale *Gesamtkunstwerk* akin to a "private installation." Live performances are another story entirely - when the focus on the presence of a human performer is de-emphasized, and various combinations of sound-heavy sensory information take place of pride instead, are we dealing with a *concert* or an *installation*? The relative ease of one's own entry and exit from an installation, as compared to a concert, used to be the deciding factor, but these days concerts of electronic music – especially ones set up in environments not normally utilized as music venues - are less restrictive.

Whether electronically-assisted sound art is *synonymous* with electronic music is open to debate; and some of the rationales for deciding whether one is an electronic musician as opposed to a sound artist – such as adopting a "project name" for CD releases rather than using a given birth name - border on the irrelevant. Whatever yardstick we attempt to use for determining one's allegiance to electronic music or sound art, exceptions rise up to challenge the absolute validity of the rule. "Some, but not all" seems to be the answer to almost any inquiry we make about whether an electronic musician differs from or is equivalent to a sound artist. Therefore, claiming that this book was about "electronic music" *and* "sound art" at least allowed me to let readers draw their own personal conclusions from the many examples within, whereas a book about *either* "electronic music" or "sound art" would be insisting to readers that one or the other is more commercially viable, or perhaps more intellectually and emotionally stimulating - and none of this is easily quantifiable.

Et cetera...

Please note that the chapters in this book do not need to be read in sequential order, although they will occasionally refer back to one another- after a certain point much of the activity discussed did not happen in any linear historical sequence; many artists reached the same conclusions simultaneously within different geographic confines. To shamelessly borrow a concept from Gilles Deleuze and Félix Guattari's *Mille Plateaux,* the book could be seen as a kind of 'toolkit' with certain discussions and ideas being more useful to the individual reader than others. While I would recommend at least beginning with the opening chapter on Industrial music (which I feel puts a decent "primer coat" of paint onto this finished work) even this is not mandatory, and many readers may already be familiar with this brief 'pre-history' of 21st century musical tactics.

To borrow another statement from an influential book –in this case, Douglas Kahn and Gregory Whitehead's anthology *Wireless Imagination: Sound, Radio and The Avant-Garde,* these writings should not be taken as the "last word" on any of these musical phenomena. We are poised on the brink of technological and cultural developments that, while maybe not causing seismic disruptions in human nature, will change the sonic landscape more quickly than any of us can perfectly imagine or predict. Therefore, the *music* discussed here is not "the last word" either, and merely braces us for what may be even more unexpected and dynamic outbreaks of creative force. While finishing up this book I had the distinct, nagging feeling of packing a suitcase for a long journey and knowing that, despite my best efforts and notes to myself, some useful item or another would be forgotten- and even if I remembered it, it would probably put my suitcase over the weight limit enforced at the local airport and would force me to pay a heavy fine or haphazardly re-arrange all the items that I *had* remembered to pack.

With all this in mind, future volumes of this book would not be inconceivable, let alone dozens of other qualified reports on this subject. If this volume stimulates interest in conducting the research that would facilitate the writing of those future works, then my work here is done.

Resistance of the Cell:
Industrial Music vs. The "Control Machine"

At its simplest level, this book is an introduction to musicians and sound artists whose works reflect, and sometimes transcend, their temporal, spatial, and psychological boundaries. Making informed critiques of human nature and post-human development in this era is not as simple as it at first seems, though: such efforts are regularly challenged by an overwhelming amount of extraneous noise smothering unique and distinct signals with slick media flak. To build a convincing argument as to why these artists are successful in their activities, and worthy of further consideration, we first have to zoom out to the broadest possible view of our planet's condition, to see exactly what these constraints are which form the framework for their creative endeavors. At the moment, attempting a run-down of current events that would still be relevant at the time of this book's publication seems futile and downright silly, given the demented velocity at which these events are progressing. All the same, a very broad overview of the human condition at the opening of this millennium seems like a necessary formality here.

Much has been made of the so-called "population bomb" (or, in the words of 'Gaia Hypothesis' formulator James Lovelock, "*Disseminated Primatemaia*"), which lies at the epicenter of most 21st century crises. History shows that ideological disputes and feudal wars for the recognition of sovereignty would likely still rage on if our planet were at a tenth of its current population, but that is most definitely not the case now, and instead we have intensifying struggles over resource management, population dynamics, and wealth distribution- which in turn fuel the seemingly unquenchable fires of war, poverty and xenophobia. The biosphere seems incapable of sustaining a species that is doubling its numbers in record time, and debates about the scientific veracity of climate change pale in comparison to the fact that, even as natural disasters and warfare diminish our numbers significantly, we will re-populate at such a rate that the survivors of these tragedies will not even be able to enjoy the dubious reward of having more "breathing room."

To start this journey on such a grim note may seem counter-productive to some, but neither do we do ourselves any favors by denying the gravity of this situation. The shift in population dynamics alone, let alone the strain that a mushrooming population will have on the planet's resources, provides case enough for alarm. In developed countries that are widely believed to have "grown out of" their intense martial phase (see especially Western Europe and Japan) birth rates are dropping below replacement levels, and a significantly older population will be left to shape the future politics of those countries. In the meantime, a whole host of developing, increasingly militarized nations are growing rapidly in both population, ethno-nationalistic drive and material discontent, while maintaining a median age somewhere in the mid-20s. Impartial students of population dynamics are clearly not the only ones to seize on the possibility for disastrous conflict here, when an aging, shrinking, secular, post-martial world collides with a youthful, expanding, passionately religious, militaristic one.

The ultra-rightist, nationalistic parties of the developed countries are seizing on deeply ingrained phobias to up their recruitment efforts considerably, sensing that those contingencies in their countries who *are* still young and combative may be willing, in the face of immigration-related anxiety, to forget the past failures of fascist doctrine. The potential for such conflicts to explode in the streets and in cyberspace at any given moment has provided an easy rationale for local governments to increase their surveillance efforts, to disregard or discard numerous civil liberties, and to conveniently deploy more brutal methods of policing. Meanwhile, an immense military / industrial / prison complex turns the desire for security into a tremendously lucrative enterprise.

Entangling situations such as these are almost guaranteed to produce more intense artistic expression among those who can find the time for it. This is not to belittle those who, ill-equipped to find solutions for such catastrophes or lacking the stomach to aesthetically confront them, resort to more gentle, escapist or romantic modes of expression. Attempts to view more radical forms as the "over-writing" successors to previous aesthetic traditions are, more often than not, doomed to failure, and it is occasionally not even necessary to oppose them at all. Nor is the skepticism towards aesthetic transgression and confrontation solely the domain of cultural conservatives or reactionaries: thinkers like Herbert Marcuse also prefered a kind of traditionalist beauty to the aesthetic revolts such as Antonin Artaud's "theater of cruelty," stating "has not the audience [...] long since become familiar with the violent noises, cries, which are the daily equipment of the mass media, sports, highways, places of recreation? They do not break the oppressive familiarity with destruction; they reproduce it."[1]

I will not attempt to fully counter Marcuse's point here, but will partially rebut it by saying that different levels of aesthetic antagonism and abrasion are appropriate to different situations and contexts. This book will largely be concerned with engaging and - to borrow a therapeutic term - "working through" unresolved 21st century complexities with an artistic expression that does not forego some amount of transgressiveness, nor beat a temporary retreat from the issues until they become more tolerable.

So, with this in mind, we first turn to the colorfully named Genesis P. Orridge (née Neil Megson), one of the past century's most celebrated *and* reviled counter-cultural provocateurs, for some more opening thoughts on the present state of humanity:

> It seems to me that our species is in a multiple crisis. Ecologically we are the most efficient locusts ever known. Judging by our disinterest in the CONSEQUENCES of our actions, one might conclude we are also as stupid as locusts, in that we allow ourselves to be led down a locust path. Financially we are in the throes of hottest passion. Everyone is doing everyone else in a corporate parody of a bacchanalian orgy, complete with intrigues and perversions. We would do well to recall the last daze [sic] of Rome when everything was possible, and the sacred and profane unified in power.[2]

However, the 'locust swarm' effects of the population explosion are only one side of the rapidly unfolding story of the new millennium. It is indeed a "saturation society" where everything apparently needs to operate at the maximum possible level in order to remain useful for such an expansive global population, and the dissemination of information has been one of the few things capable of satiating the population's needs in a time of general scarcity. In fact, it has been so successful as to *surpass* the population's needs, with an increasing acknowledgement that information now comes down the pipeline at too quick a rate to even be properly digested. The obverse of our shared situation, in which an exponential multiplication of human numbers has meant an intensifying struggle for resource allocation and consumption, is the struggle to find real meaning within our surplus of information.

In/Formation: The 'Terror Guards' of Industrial

Genesis P. Orridge, as a founding member of Throbbing Gristle and consequently the musical genre known as Industrial music, is partially responsible for a good deal of the artists profiled in this book. While he[3] remains as controversial a figure today as in the Industrial heyday of the late 70s-early 80s (thanks to a recent proselytizing of 'pandrogeny', or the spiritual implications of hermaphroditic nature) his seminal group's influence on the current generation of sound producers can be perceived far and wide- from the 'extreme computer music' of the Austrian Mego record label to the paint-peeling synthetic pulse of the Finnish duo Pan

Sonic. Throbbing Gristle were, for a brief period, the flagship of a small but impressively varied fleet of sonic activists converging under the Industrial music banner: originally this applied only to the roster of Throbbing Gristle's Industrial Records label (TG, S.P.K., Cabaret Voltaire, Clock DVA, Monte Cazazza, and others) although the core group of 'original Industrialists' was expanded in the public consciousness somewhat with the publication of the Re/Search *Industrial Culture Handbook*: shamanistic metal drummer Z'ev, 'machine theater' collective Survival Research Laboratories and pure noise magus Boyd Rice were also named among the aggressive and prolific aggregate of multi-media artists that constituted the first Industrial wave.

Throbbing Gristle, before being recognized as the spearhead of Industrial music, were originally an outgrowth of an earlier multi-media art troupe called COUM Transmissions (named after a nonsense word heard in an out-of-body vision that P. Orridge experienced on a family drive through the countryside.) Capitalizing on the new thrust towards collaborative / group-based art dawning in the 1960s, which was embodied in Fluxus, correspondence art and elsewhere, COUM produced a wide-ranging body of work including sculptures built from recycled materials, film-making, guerrilla theater and (most relevant to their future incarnation as Throbbing Gristle) live, improvisational musical spectacles. Contemporary analogs could be found in performance troupes such as the Japanese Zero Dimension and Hi Red Center, or the Squat Theatre originating in Hungary (whose performance at the 1973 Open Theatre Festival in Wroclaw strikingly prefigured, in both content and subsequent reactions, the more confrontational moments in COUM's history.)[4] Nevertheless, COUM's eventual turn towards the musical arena would distinguish them from their peers in the realm of performance 'interventions' and 'happenings.'

The consciously anti-professional, willfully naïve and open participatory nature of the group's output is stylistically indebted to the other major rumblings of 20th century art based around a group identity - primarily Dada, Surrealism, Fluxus again, and Viennese Aktionism - infusing these mainly Continental movements with a more uniquely British vocabulary and sensibility. COUM activities were essentially a means of questioning and eliminating social divisions wherever possible: they were a-political and anti-materialistic, favoring direct experience and action as the real means to cultural dynamism and social change, in place of "official" art world's stockpiling and appraisal of static art objects. They were as populist as could be expected for the time, often bringing local petty criminals and groups such as the Hell's Angels into their orbit- a fact which heightened the police attention given to the collective, and eventually forced them to move from their native Hull to London in 1972.

In the 1970s performance art world, whose visual extremity and cathartic nature were embodied by pieces like Chris Burden's car-top crucifixion and Paul McCarthy's orgiastic and bathetic performances with food products, COUM were not an isolated curiosity. Yet their residence in a comparatively smaller nation than the United States, and their status as recipients of Arts Council funding there, arguably made them more notorious more quickly than either of these Stateside artists. All of the most potentially offensive aspects of COUM united into one raging current at *Prostitution,* the group's 1976 exhibit at the ICA- an exhibit with a three-fold significance. Firstly, it was intended as a retrospective / overview of COUM's work to date, then as a parting shot to the "official" art world, and thirdly, the exhibit at which the group would transition to its musical incarnation as Throbbing Gristle (TG's first official performance was at the *Prostitution* opening party.)

COUM, to their credit, had never participated in the kind of rarified culture that typified so much of the contemproaneous gallery art, in which creators were rarely on hand to discuss their creations or to interact with an 'audience' beyond dealers, curators, and prospective buyers. Each of the four COUM members who would become Throbbing Gristle were in agreement that music would provide more of an indelible imprint on the psyche of a younger, generally more diversified public. And just as COUM had attempted to wrest control of art from a limited establishment, Throbbing Gristle aimed to do the same with electronic music. The U.K. had a fascinating recent history of involvement with electronic music innovation, with such successes as Delia Darbyshire and the BBC Radiophonic Workshop- but again, it was largely confined to a hermetically-sealed studio atmosphere, not likely to be breached by untrained youth in desperate need of personal expression.

More than Throbbing Gristle's influence on the actual sonic structure of modern electronic music, though, the band's influence comes from the way they interacted with the information overload that was just beginning to manifest itself during their existence. The band's primary focus was the "information war" (as proposed by Marshall McLuhan in *The Medium Is The Message*) rather than, as many have supposed, the dehumanizing potential of factories. One of the most significant acts of the group, as a participant in this unconventional war, was to use audio-visual noise both as a means of producing physiological and psychic reactions; both as an aurally and physically perceptible phenomenon and as a disruptor of informational hegemony. "Noise" in the computerized, networked bureacracy has increasingly come to mean - as per media theorist Jussi Parikka - "[a] malicious [attempt] to disrupt and steal from the flow of confidential data,"[5] making the Industrial understanding of noise something of a harbinger of current "cyberwar" / "infowar" strategies of overloading informational circuits. Throbbing Gristle's heavy use of audible noise pointed to its being a sub-species of noise as it was seen in information-theoretical terms.

Meanwhile, the illumination of dehumanization through factory automation or rote labor was an approach which, though often assumed as the main goal of 'Industrial' music, had ample time to enter the public discourse well before the late 1970s. It was surely touched upon already by a number of politicized folk singers, Beat provocateurs and hippie collectives, to say nothing of the much earlier journalistic accounts provided by everyone from Friedrich Engels to Upton Sinclair. Thus the term "industrial" was a kind of misnomer to begin with, although later groups would adopt a more explicitly 'heavy industry' nomenclature and symbology rife with cogwheels, metallic clamor and lyrical allusions to hard labor (sometimes with nostalgic or erotic tinges, as in the case of much 'electronic body music' that followed the original Industrial wave.) Attributed to Throbbing Gristle cohort and like-minded San Francisco performance artist Monte Cazazza (who coined the slogan "Industrial Music for Industrial People"), the term was not so much an attempt to open the public's eyes to the bleakness of regimented factory life as it was a darkly humorous, ironic jab at the then-prevalent pop cultural desire for things to be 'real', spontaneous, or 'from the heart'- as opposed to centrally planned and manufactured by those with no interest in the spiritual qualities of the end product.

The slogan also hinted at a bitter irony inherent in contemporary culture: namely, that many artists of the day claiming to have a sincere, 'from the heart' product were, more often than not, partially or completely fabricated by the entertainment business. It took contrarian performance artists like Throbbing Gristle to actually *admit* to the degree of mechanization and reproduction which really took place in the commercial music world, and to be far more straightforward about their intentions than the rest of the 1970s musical elite. For people duped by the cult of *ersatz* authenticity, Industrial music was, on face value at least, a conscious inversion of supposed universal values of organic / natural living, liberal democracy and spiritual questing. The trends of 'branding,' and of increasing species homogeneity in attitude and appearance, were thrown back in the face of the public in an uncomfortable but irrefutable statement on the old 1960s subculture's powerlessness relative to the massive military-industrial complex. Distinct, flashy stage gear and flowing tresses were swapped for camouflage uniforms and short utilitarian haircuts, while some Industrial record albums came wrapped in interchangeable, artless packaging (sometimes bearing nothing other than a parody of a corporate logo and some descriptive text on a plain white background.)

The musical content, of course, was no less of a trend reversal. Lyrical poetry and rich metaphorical content was ditched in favor of lobotomized, spoken or shrieked accounts of desensitizing or traumatizing experiences (e.g. TG's "Hamburger Lady," inspired the horrors of a hospital burn ward.) Or, taking it one step further, the "vocals" on a track might be no more than an appropriated instructional tape meant to familiarize soldiers with the noises made by different types of artillery fire (e.g. "Weapon Training.") Sequenced or droning synthesizers, previously associated largely with the tech-positive pop songs of Kraftwerk or the romantic atmospherics of Tangerine Dream, spoke to more of an obsessive functionality in this context.[6] Metronomic, programmed rhythm-box beats and looped sound fragments rounded out the sonic program- serving to discipline and punish (one of Throbbing Gristle's signature songs is, indeed, titled "Discipline") rather than to warm and console.

Yet Industrial music was not a wholesale capitulation to, or endorsement of, superior forces of bureaucracy, war and mass production- far from it. It simply proposed a different way of conceptualizing and engaging these hostile powers: the 1968 generation's tactics of outright protest, street skirmishes and on-campus proclamation of anti-authoritarian positions were obsolete, if not downright foolhardy, especially when the authorities were now so huge and bloated as to be undermined in more subtle, stealthy ways. Though their gestures could be enjoyed on an aesthetic level, the bohemian drop-outs of the recent past had achieved all that they likely would with sit-ins, moratoriums and attempts to levitate the Pentagon: the proposed new youth subculture would be one composed of highly organized, paramilitary 'control agents' and (in a play on the initials T.G., as well as a nod to contemporary panics intiated by violent groups like the RAF [*Rote Armee Fraktion*] and *Brigate Rosse*) 'terror guards.' All of these individuals would, ideally, find some means of appropriating the establishment's most prized commodity in order to weaken or destroy it. Industrial culture therefore shifted the critique and cultural attack away from individual oppressive institutions and towards a force that was perceived as being common to them all. As Genesis P. Orridge suggested in 1980:

> Basically the power in this world rests with the people who have access to the most information and also control that information. Most of the paranoia concerned with politics is about what is really going on, what is secret, what we are not being told about...these [information] systems are very expensive and cumbersome, requiring capital equipment which can't be utilized the whole time. So to cover costs and keep equipment running, these systems have to be made available to the rest of us to keep them financially viable. That's why you can get access to cable TV, to computer time, instant printing and cassette recorders, even the mail, Polaroids too, and video...they develop these systems for their own reasons, but they are

so expensive they have to mass produce them to finance them. So we all get easier and easier ways to multiply our ideas and information, it's a parallel progression.[7]

Genesis' statements will almost certainly cause some to think of that most omnipresent example of the 'beating swords into ploughshares' strategy, the Internet.[8] In its earlier incarnation as the Arpanet, computer-to-computer communication over large distances was something only to be used in the event of fallout from a nuclear strike, while nowadays access to online communication is so integral to general communication, talk of Internet-disrupting emergency measures like "kill switches" seems as apocalyptic as the aforementioned nuclear war (at the very least, the plausibility of such measures is up for debate.)

While the gradual transformation of clandestine military technology into everyday consumer technology has certainly been empowering for many inquisitive and creative souls, this has not yet led to total counter-culture victory through re-appropriation of the nebulous "control machine's" information. While the Internet and all its attendant innovations have forced some governments and multi-national corporations into a position where - as GPO implies - they can be more easily monitored and criticized, the same has held true for those governing bodies' subjects. The potential for vacuuming up data about possible dissidents via cyberspace has now become so great as to make P-Orridge reassess the above opinion (which was, after all, voiced on the cusp of the 1980s) rotating it a full 180 degrees:

> I myself am absolutely on the side of an immense skeptical suspicion of the 'World Wide Web'. What a horrible title. Are we all the innocent little insects unwittingly trapped in a gluey binary Armageddon of telephone lines? Who is the spider? Well, control of course. Corporations, of course, increasingly insipid and acceleratingly effective bureaucratic governments.[9]

Genesis continues in even more damning terms:

> Mobility of labor is the capitalist dream, and computers realize the ultimate exploitative nightmare. All labor can now travel anywhere, without physically moving. Much cheaper and more efficient. Everything piped down a phone wire. Perfect! I don't think so. Count me out. I unplugged my modem ages ago. Best thing I ever did for my creative mind. Unplug yours too.[10]

Recent evidence shows an about-face on this issue: Genesis P. Orridge had a regularly updated online presence throughout the composition of this book, and elsewhere tempered his warnings on the Internet with gnostically-tinted suggestions that it could accelerate humanity's re-combination with the 'divine'. Still, another essay, circa 1998, better illuminates his personal fear of this medium's potential to turn humanity into a horrifically indistinct and pliant mass (also expanding on the opening statements about the population crisis):

> There may be an environmental issue here too. As the climate gets more and more unstable through the unrecyclable waste of our species of performing (and occasionally clever) rats, we will be forced to live in more and more controlled, indoor environments. What better solution than to have all the 'drone' workers at home. Out of the deadly rays cutting through the orgone. Out of the polluted air. Unable to see the ongoing death of nature. More and more content with virtuality, processed food. Infinite options of televisual, Internet experience and distraction. Even content to reduce their investment in direct sexuality. Thus slowly being weaned from the replication disaster that is biological breeding.[11]

Whether or not such a master plan exists has yet to be reliably documented, and possibly never will be. However, the trend towards making living environments more inorganic and bureacratically organized (and making this seem, ironically, like a 'natural' state of affairs) is a reality that cannot easily be ignored. This returns us again to the aforementioned shift in oppositional strategy from the days of machine-breaking and street fighting: the creative *raison d'être* of groups like Throbbing Gristle was the realization that the enforced greyness of bureacratic or managerial societies was not to be countered with the destruction or requisition of buildings and equipment, but with the of exposition of those persuasive techniques that conspired to make the bureacratic environment seem morally correct and desirable. Conveniently enough for a musical subculture that based much of its aesthetic upon reappropriation and mimesis, some of these behavior modification methods were already coded in musical form.

The Sound of Muzak / The Electronic Revolution

It is interesting to consider, despite having already mentioned that

Industrial music was not a pure critique of factory life, that the term "industrial music" was in use before the 1970s, and originally refered to a more functional style of music- a catalyzer of processes rather than a critique of them. That is to say, it refered to a style of music in which behavior modification, rather than aesthetic enhancement and environmental awareness, was the primary goal. The BBC program *Music While You Work,* broadcast from 1940 to 1967, was one of the first truly site-specific forms of broadcast music, as it was intended to be exclusively piped in to factories of the day. As Keith Jones notes, "The programme strived to be a show with a singular aim (of increasing industrial productivity) aimed at a particular (factory) environment" and was thus fairly novel for a radio medium that was "at that time rigorously concerned with broadcasting for an idealized domestic environment and listener."[12] It is possible to see this kind of music as both the natural enemy of the counter-cultural Industrial music and as a partial methodological inspiration, though the newer "industrial" style would eventually subvert the former style by removing it from its specific sites.

Here we are getting ahead of ourselves, though- in the new millennium, the sort of soft tyranny that Genesis predicts above is not being carried out purely by means of broadcast music or telecommunication, and the control of prevailing attitudes via communications media is supplemented by control on a more strictly neurological level. Whereas the computer-initiated information age of the 1990s may have simultaneously liberated and enslaved, so too did the boom in other emerging fields, such as behavior-modifying neuropharmacology. Pharmaceutical firms such as Novartis (formerly Ciba-Geigy), Pfizer, Eli Lilly and Glaxo Smith-Kline have become almost synonymous with mind control and 'social engineering' in circles of autonomous thinkers as millions upon millions of consumers have embraced their soporific products worldwide. Some saw the steady advancement of such 'social engineering,' anti-depressant chemicals as a godsend, and I will make no attempt to judge those who sought them out while suffering from severe emotional trauma. Yet other more skeptical individuals see them as little more than unnecessary 'cures' for universal human ailments that were meant to be experienced as a means to further personal evolution- in the case of anti-depressants like Prozac or Paxil, which release acceptable amounts of serotonin in brains starved of such, thus 'curing' sadness and nervous tensions, the question constantly arises: are these medicines simply a way to postpone public awareness of a disintegrating geo-political and environmental situation, rather than allowing the populace to be agitated into altering the situation themselves?

This is something worth considering, especially when one of the most effective soporific "drugs" is free and accessible twenty-four hours a day in the form of television (a medium whose major broadcasting networks are, incidentally, owned by conglomerates like General Electric, who elsewhere profit from war in their capacity as defense contractors.) As Neil Postman suggests in his 1986 jeremiad *Amusing Ourselves To Death*, the omniscient "Big Brother" of Orwell's *1984* can't feasibly exist in a world where normal individuals have an unprecedented amount of access to information- but a similar power could very well exist in a world where people are too drugged, pacified, and otherwise distracted through a deluge of entertainment media to even *attempt* uncovering the information detrimental to his activities. An inept governing body would have great ease in controlling its subjects when they mostly exist in comfortable mindsets free of emotional peaks or valleys, having absolutely *no* opinion on anything from ecological destruction to the failing educational system.

Not long ago, before either the advent of the Internet, 24-hour "news" networks, or the revolutions in neuropharmacology, this 'soft' social engineering within the Western world (as opposed to the 'hard' application of military and police force) still had to be largely carried out through the various forms of mass entertainment then on hand. Television, of course, has had a host of neurological effects comparable to those of mass-marketed pharmaceuticals- but, in the audio realm, perhaps no better example of "social engineering through entertainment" exists than the Muzak of the late 1970s and 1980s. The form (which is in fact a trademark of the Muzak Corporation) was the refinement of Wired Radio, a 1922 invention of the U.S. Signal Corps officer George Owen Squier. Squier was, in his turn, influenced by a techno-utopian novel of Edward Bellamy's - *Looking Backward (2000-1887)* - which featured an "industrial army" managing a socialist paradise brimming with instantaneous conveniences. Among these was a "musical telephone" that piped mood music into subscribers' homes, its emotional content varying in accordance with the human functions normally carried out during each portion of the day.

This feature of Bellamy's libertarian-socialist daydream would become a reality, at least, but in much less utopian post-industrial societies that - despite the impassioned protests of Muzak / easy listening apologists like Joseph Lanza[13] - would come to see it as a discomfiting banality. It was a music which, by today's music production standards, was laughably quaint and inoffensive- the characteristic muted horns, the subdued, even submerged flutes and the lightly-brushed percussion of Muzak melted together into an insidious beige soundscape; an aural tranquilizer meant to dull the alienating sensation of spending time in antiseptic offices or hospital waiting rooms. By contrast, such music would make previous manifestations of "industrial" or productivity-enhancing functional music (see especially Eric Coates' percolating *Music While You Work* theme) seem like a raucous joyride.

Whereas today's legally available tranquilizers aim to free the people from the wild, raging passions which define humanity, so too did Muzak attempt to strip all the emotional, soul-stirring 'peaks and troughs' from music and to replace them with something just 'human' enough not to unnerve people, but too vague to arouse the emotional surges inspired by conventional forms of music- passions which would be serious obstacles to meeting targeted quotas of production or consumption. Given its sole function as a spur to controlled activity, it was pitched to retailers and businesses as 'music to be heard but not listened to,' and thus listening itself became a kind of counter-productive activity incompatible with these other target activities. To achieve this passive mode of receiving the music's message, seemingly more emphasis was placed on the studio engineering of the music than the recordng of it Marc Almond, of the subversive synth-pop act Soft Cell, had the following to say on this subject:

> When I was doing the soundtrack for the film *Decoder* with [Genesis P. Orridge], we were doing some experiments with Muzak tapes, which we shouldn't have had but we got hold of, and we analysed them on a spectrum analyzer and the levels all stayed the same- just straight. With normal background music, the LEDs were just going up and down. Muzak is just straight across, it didn't move. Basically it's just totally compressed because it's music put together by scientists.[14]

Almond's claims are, in fact, borne out by Muzak's official literature; the recordings he mentions were also distributed as promotional LPs to prospective clients featuring written warnings that such albums "cannot be purchased at any price." As to the claim of the music as being 'scientifically' engineered, Lanza also notes promo album that demanded Muzak be understood as "a non-entertainment medium...employing rhythm, tempo, instrumentation etc., to scientifically-determined specifications."[15]

Muzak was, at one time, viewed as such an effective audio security blanket that it pitched itself to America's swelling network of fast food franchises and supermarkets as "the security system of the 1970s." This was a point not lost on Klaus Maeck, the Berlin-based owner of the 'Rip Off' punk record shop / distributor, and screenwriter for the aforementioned film, *Decoder*. In this illuminating 1983 film, which features Industrial culture mainstays Genesis P. Orridge and F.M. Einheit in acting roles (alongside a cameo by William Burroughs as the proprietor of a junk electronics store), Muzak represents the control machine which placates an entire city and keeps them completely focused on their leisure hours in 'H-Burger' franchises ("H" here being a wordplay on street slang for heroin.) Another amusing pun is in the movie's working title, *Burger Krieg* ('burger' being both the fast food favorite and the German word for 'citizen', thus punning on a meaning of 'civil war.') The film is a case study in what would eventually become the signature activity of Industrial music: manipulating and re-appropriating consumer technologies to effect media messages - especially those originally intended to have a behavior-modifying or pacifying effect - so that they will instead agitate individuals and once again stimulate them into a state of relatively free, non-compliant thought. As Klaus Maeck says:

> Being in the music business and participating in the punk and new wave explosion, I became more interested in music. Muzak was one thing that I found. Subliminal music to influence people's moods, to make them function better, or buy more. So my conclusion was similar to that of 'bands' like Throbbing Gristle; by turning around the motivation, by cutting up the sounds, by distorting them etc. one should be able to provoke different reactions. Make people puke instead of feeling well, make people disobey instead of following, provoke riots.[16]

Genesis P. Orridge (who had already dissolved Throbbing Gristle and transitioned to the Temple ov Psychick Youth / Psychic TV project by the time of *Decoder*'s filming), appears in the film in a clerical collar and is listed in the film's credits as *Höhepriester* [High Priest.] His filmic performance runs parallel with the chracter he created for himself within the Temple organization, a group which saw technological implements as merely an 'electronic age' means to carry out age-old magical awakenings, e.g. "[television] advertisements are structured in exactly the same way that rituals are, using mnemonic devices similar to the Qabalah...it is in the realm of tricking the subconscious into accepting the impossible that the traditional magician has always worked."[17] Besides acknowledging this spiritual repurposing of electronics, GPO also hints at the aggressive and tactical nature of Industrial music when he states, in a sermon-like monologue halfway through the film, that 'information is like a bank' and that it is the duty of inquiring minds to 'rob the bank' and to 'destroy everybody' who withholds free access to information. It's an unrepentant, easily-grasped sentiment, and one which at least identified a true enemy to be dealt with- it should come as no surprise that latter-day punk rockers' vague, scattershot injunction to "DESTROY," with no clear target in mind, has become a more suitable slogan to be mass-marketed on t-shirt designs than the ideas of the original Industrialists.

While Genesis P. Orridge, Throbbing Gristle and their ilk may have been among the first to present the 'information war' within a pop culture context, the anarchic writings of Beat author William S. Burroughs provided much of the raw schematic for these ideas in the first place.

Burroughs' *Electronic Revolution*, while one of his shortest texts, has also become one of the most widely cited and appreciated amongst members of the Industrial music community and its offshoots. This is due largely to its radical proposition that consumer electronic devices (in this particular instance, tape recorders) could be used as tools for sonic sorcery, empowering the otherwise disenfranchised through a sustained program of juxtaposing sharply contrasting information samples: pig squeals mixed with prayer calls, for example. This technique has been incorporated into the paranoiac drone of early Cabaret Voltaire and Clock DVA records, in the early voice experiments of Z'ev, and in countless others besides. *Electronic Revolution* not only offered practical examples for how anyone could short-circuit the "lines of association" laid down by the mass media, but also offered emboldening statements such as the following:

> No, 'They' are not God or super technicians from outer space. Just technicians operating with well-known equipment and using techniques that can be duplicated by anyone else who can buy and operate this equipment.[18]

Such blunt dismissals of impregnable authority were an exciting stimulus for the Industrial movement of the 1970s and 1980s. And, better yet, not only did the anti-authoritarian re-appropriation of technology 'level the playing field,' but in some cases, Burroughs insisted that it made the insurgent elements *more* powerful than their oppressors:

> You have an advantage which your opposing player does not have. He must conceal his manipulations. You are under no such necessity. In fact, you can advertise the fact that you are writing the news in advance and trying to make it happen by techniques which anybody can use. And that makes you NEWS. And TV personality as well, if you play it right. You want the widest possible circulation for your cut/up video tapes. Cut/up techniques could swamp the mass media with total illusion.[19]

Throbbing Gristle and company took the preceding advice and ran with it- layering sounds, images, and attitudes with surgical skill. It was helpful, of course, that the individual members came from very different disciplines, all with some direct connection to mass media or communications apparatus: Genesis P. Orridge was an expert on contemporary art movements, Peter "Sleazy" Christopherson was an accomplished graphic designer, Cosey Fanni Tutti had modeled for pornographic magazines, and Chris Carter was savvy with do-it-yourself electronics, stage lighting, and circuitry. Admittedly, no one in the band had any formal musical training (and most of the band even made a conscious decision to play the musical instrument they most hated), but the arsenal of non-musical maneuvers that they collectively developed made for something more resonant than much music of the day. Many of the new breed of Angry Young Men were willing to shake their fists at the all-enveloping communications media and information technology being used against them, but surprisingly few ever thought of using it as a weapon against itself.

To Have Done With The Judgment Of Punk

I'd heard The Damned, I'd heard The Clash, and I just thought they were rock crap- I was never interested in rock 'n roll. And Throbbing Gristle, although they used guitars, and bass, and originally drums, the whole aesthetic of it reflected the way my life was - I lived on really boring estates and [Royal Air Force] council blocks. What they put into their music lyrically and soundwise was so relevant to me, it blew punk out the window- it really did. They were confronting issues the other bands weren't doing...the other bands were being dressed by Jasper Conran, the clothes designer...The Clash were...and it was all clothes-oriented, and 'The London Scene,' and it was horrific. [Throbbing Gristle's] art was life, and life was art - there wasn't a difference."[20]

- John Balance of Coil

Industrial music had the misfortune to emerge concurrent with the UK punk rock scene. This led to occasional confusion of the former with the latter, and to an occasional complete indifference to Industrial efforts - or, more insulting to Industrial musicians, the claim that punk had "enabled" the very existence of Industrial music, and that punk was the populist umbrella movement under which all marginalized and antagonistic artists could now seek refuge.

This fallacy is easily dismissed, considering that the first wave of Industrial musicians had been experimenting with weird and spontaneous music since at least the early 1970s. In a cultural milieu as incestuous as British pop music, though, there was bound to be some crossover and cooperation between the genres from time to time - Peter Christopherson was responsible for some of the controversial shop window displays of

Vivienne Westwood and Malcolm McLaren's punk fashion boutique SEX (most notably a display in which it looked like a real punk rocker had been detonated, with his charred remains placed on display.) Both genres had a penchant for using archetypal symbols of totalitarian order to different ends: the punks donned swastika armbands and t-shirts, suggesting that they could regard even the greatest horrors of the 20th century with sneering apathy, and Throbbing Gristle utilized the lightning flash logo of Oswald Mosley's British Union Of Fascists, broadening that symbol's meaning of "action and unity" to a variety of other more personal contexts. Post-punk staples like Joy Division, by naming themselves after a Nazi brothel, and featuring old *Hitler Jugend* imagery as sleeve artwork, delved into this subject matter in yet more poignant detail, while their label (Factory) shared the austere design schemes and motivations of Throbbing Gristle's Industrial Records (Joy Division's frontman Ian Curtis was allegedly a close friend of Genesis P. Orridge.)

Of course, there were also the requisite concert bills shared by punks and Industrial musicians, which generated a full spectrum of reactions from forced ennui to all-out violence. So, several key differences between the two movements should also be noted, in spite of occasional efforts to link the two in their ultimate goals. Chiefly among these differences is the reactionary, Luddite panic that many - though certainly not all - of the nascent punks espoused in the face of new technology. Sound artist Francisco López noted the pitfalls inherent in this attitude when he stated:

> I once read an interview with [Clash guitarist] Joe Strummer, in which he was criticizing technology in music. He said something like 'I am a musician, I don't want to be a fucking computer operator'. Surprising to see he didn't realize about the fucking guitar operator in front of him.[21]

Peter Christopherson, when posed a question about the moral ambiguity of technology, also answers in a non-alarmist fashion that was disappointingly lacking in the punks of the time:

> I do not see a causal relationship between a hammer and playwright Joe Orton's boyfriend Kenneth Halliwell, who killed him with one. He could have used a rock... or even a pen. No matter what tools are available, it is still always the responsibility of us to use them wisely and generously, rather than to hurt others. If you are asking 'would the world be a better place without tanks and land mines?' the answer would obviously be yes, but this is an abstract and non-realistic question - we have them, just as we have

iPods and cell phones. Your question also infers that technology may inevitably lead to the destruction of mankind, but I believe that it is mankind itself (rather than technology) that will do this.[22]

Many punks regularly voiced their fears of automation and computerization in song (again, Joe Strummer can be cited here, with his acerbic shout of "*I-am-a-ro-bot!*" in "Remote Control," off of the debut Clash LP.) While prospects of being ground down by a post-industrial bureacracy were understandably unappealing for adventurous youth, these sentiments smacked more of the antithetical "hippie" consciousness than they might have cared to admit. Having written off tech-assisted performance as the province of show-boating "dinosaur rockers," they effectively cut themselves off from the possibility of personalizing technology, and using it as a critical tool in the more intimate performance environments that punks were relegated to. For its part, Industrial culture was a multi-media subculture from the outset (the pre-TG performance art collective COUM Transmissions referred to their happenings as 'transmedia', and de-emphasized artistic specialization), though the Industrial movement would often be judged purely on its merits as a musical genre.

Punk rock, for all its anarchist yearnings, did indeed build itself on a capitalistic rock'n roll chassis, and the act of supposedly beating straight society at its own game - earning "cash from chaos," as the slogan suggested - was never consummately anarchic. Punk concerts were still very much a means to selling records: on the whole they didn't manage to escape from the ironic cycle of making records to preserve a performance, then having a performance which is only successful insofar as it duplicates the record. Industrial performances, by contrast, were usually events which could not be replicated twice, which might have absolutely nothing in common with any pre-recorded work, and which replaced the usual technical skill exhibition expected of a music concert with a more generalized dissemination or critique of information. Which is not to say that Industrial events were tantamount to academic lectures- the sensory overload of these showcases comprised high volume ultrasound and sub-bass frequencies, high powered floodlights turned on the audience, disorienting collages of taped conversations or news feeds, home-built electronic devices emitting previously unheard types of modulation and oscillation, and also film backdrops of a disturbing or disorienting nature. It was a panoply of sights, sounds, and occasionally smells (Survival Research Laboratories are particularly famous for incorporating nausea-inducing compounds into their shows.) Unlike much other popular music, they struck on a physical *and* intellectual level- at their most potent, they assailed the body with high decibel blows while the brain attempted to decode the bizarre, scrambled crosstalk coming from multiple cassette machines.

The psychological effects of droning, continually escalating monotony were also put to use in place of traditional pop music's appeals to sentimentality. Despite the sheer unavoidable force of these presentations - something like a more brutal take on Warhol's 'Exploding Plastic Inevitable' concept - many period journalists and punk sympathizers walked away with the impression that it was no more than willful diletannte-ism from the perenially scorned "middle-class art students". Unfortunately for these critics, history has proven the inverse to be true- only one member of Throbbing Gristle had a formal art education (Peter Christopherson, at SUNY, Buffalo) whereas a disproportionate amount of the punks could boast of this.

However their respective educations were received, members of Throbbing Gristle were certainly "schooled" in the 20th century artistic avant-garde's accomplishments, having concretized or built upon the ideas of everyone from Kurt Schwitters to Günter Brus to John Cage. They had a vested interest in distilling these atavistic-progressive ideals into amplified music, at the time the most popular and immediate art medium. Yet most of the "art education" of these individuals was a matter of self-initiated questing after information, not a matter of formal training within an accredited institution. Many of the art-school educated punk rockers, who should have had a more thorough and applicable knowledge of experimental technique by dint of their education, were the first to run to the aid of musical tradition.

D.I.Y. Or Die

Another difference between the Industrialists and their musical contemporaries was the degree of autonomy with which they operated. Punk, again, owing to the relative ease with which the public could digest it in comparison to Industrial music, was given precedence over music which consumers didn't even have the technical vocabulary to describe - and today's nostalgic puff pieces on the punk era almost invariably celebrate how the punk movement re-asserted the right of the individual in society. Genesis P. Orridge, however, is quick to counter those who would give punks all the glory for a work that he was also instrumental in achieving, claiming (not unsentimentally) that "the difference between Punk and Throbbing Gristle was that Punk was trying to change the nature of Rock & Roll; Throbbing Gristle was trying to change the nature of music."[23]

Punk has, partially owing to the proselytizing efforts of Greil Marcus, been associated with the Situationist movement of Guy DeBord an incalculable number of times. In his "Theory Of The *Dérive* ", DeBord states:

> One can *dérive* alone, but all indications are that the most fruitful numerical arrangement consists of several small groups of two or three people who have reached the same level of awareness, since cross-checking these different groups' impressions makes it possible to arrive at more objective conclusions.[24]

The *dérive*, as per DeBord, translates to "drifting" and is an aimless walk or journey through an urban area, so as to break hold of routine patterns of movement and assign one's own 'psychogeographical' meaning to any given space- simply put, to control the spatial boundaries one finds oneself in, rather than to be controlled by them. Just like the Industrial employment of Burroughs' cut-up techniques using jarring tape collages, it was an attempt at negating control simply by refusing to believe that one park, building etc. had only one pre-set purpose. Some Industrial musicians, however, would probably disagree with DeBord's suggestion that small groups of people were the "most fruitful"- in fact, many Industrial musicians in the wake of the first TG-led wave operated using a 'lone wolf' cell structure that could initially be independent of any localized peer group or support network. While even the most radical and politically active punks, such as Crass, worked as a collective, individuals like Nigel Ayers (a.k.a. Nocturnal Emissions) would become one-man industries comprising pamphlet publishing, music production, graphic design and more. While the 'publishing' in question may have been just a matter of having access to a photocopy machine, and the 'graphic design' may have been little more than haphazardly cutting and pasting monochromatic images into maddening, cluttered montages, it was still a historically unprecedented level of autonomy for a single working class or middle class person to have - one which pre-dated the 'information consolidation' potential of Web pages by some 15 years. The process also did much to justify d.i.y. electronic artists' self-identifying as "projects" rather than as "bands" or some other term that had its provenance in pop music. While the term of course denoted the independent creation of products, it also (as G.H. Hovagimyan suggests) "Represent[ed] an intellectual shift away from simple object production and recognize[d] the investigatory nature of creating artwork."[25]

Individual cells in the early 1980s rose up in virtually every country where cheap mass-production techniques could be accessed by everyday consumers: there was Minus Delta T in Germany, Club Moral in Belgium, Merzbow in Japan, and a host of others- the TRAX organization in Italy also brought together these individual efforts and released their products using TRAX product numbers, yet never dictated content to any of their individual "units." In many cases, at least two of the above criteria for autonomous production were being taken care of by a single ambitious personality. The effect this had on culture as a whole - not particularly of an "Industrial" variety - cannot be overstated, because it meant finally having the opportunity to break free from whatever ossified ideology ruled one's lived environment. As the sound artist Trevor Wishart aptly states, "The democratisation of access to culture destroyed the private world of the avant-garde just as surely as the Fax machine helped defeat the anti-Gorbachev coup in Soviet Russia."[26] So, whether the fixed value system in one's immediate vicinity called itself radical or conservative, there were at least some means now to deny it its exclusivity of expression.

The processes of printing, layout, mail distribution etc. were just one part of the story, though- the actual recording of music had become, thanks to cheaper home recording devices and to highly versatile electronic instruments like the Korg MS-20 synthesizer, something which could be achieved in record time- without the anxiety of running up astronomical bills for studio time (provided a studio could even be found whose engineers would condescend to recording this kind of music), and without the need to get the consensus approval of a 'band' before one's musical visions could be realized. Waxing nostalgic over the revelatory introduction of new musical equipment, Moritz R. (of Germany's absurdist electro-pop group Der Plan, who developed concurrently with the British Industrial movement) states:

> A real watershed moment for me was an encounter with a machine: Pyrolator [a.ka. Kurt Dahlke, also of Der Plan] had a Korg MS-20. And I got a chance to play around with it a little. The thing looked like a little telephone switchboard. And if you wrangled with it long enough, it didn't sound like an instrument anymore, but like wind, water, a helicopter, or an air raid siren. And I had this definite feeling of 'finally, now I can make some music soon, too.' Without the MS-20 and a little bit of Japanese technology, none of that would have been able to transpire. From that point on, the whole development of music was also a technological development.[27]

The MS-20, as well as other period synthesizers such as the EMS Synthi A, were excellent tools for simulating or the sounds of the information war, or for casting them in a starker relief. The palette of electronic sounds produced by these instruments went beyond the confines of tonal music and reminded the listener of a great deal of other elements within the sonic landscape of the late 20th century: television static, automatic weapons, and humming of electric pylons being just a few examples that come to mind. Their ability to emulate deep percussive pulses also provided a convenient way to make rhythmic music without requiring a full battery of acoustic drums. New instruments such as these provided the perfect sonic component for a multi-media art form hellbent on becoming, as per one Throbbing Gristle review, "...a means to radicalize the listener into abandoning bourgeois romanticism for a realistic view of life."[28]

In situations where Industrial artists did resort to conventional instrumentation, it was often altered to the point of sacrilege. Boyd Rice's prepared 'roto-guitar' was modified to have an electric fan mounted over the bridge, a devious type of expanded technique that was at once the *ne plus ultra* of high volume electrified sound and a satirical jab at rock music's "amps to 11!" bravado ((Rice's early experiments with turntables also mark one of the first documented uses of that particular playback device as an instrument, outside of the *musique concréte* tradition.) Elsewhere, the 'wings' were sawed off of the guitar of Cosey Fanni Tutti, in order to make it more lightweight, portable and practical for use as a "ladies' guitar"- the placement of practical considerations before 'tradition for tradition's sake' seemed to offend almost as many serious music fans as Throbbing Gristle's unrepentantly harsh subject matter.

Elsewhere, Blixa Bargeld of the Berlin 'scrapheap music' ensemble Einstürzende Neubauten used sparse, rusted, and atonal guitar sounds as little more than a complement to his bandmates' primal pummeling on metallic implements. Both Bargeld and Fanni Tutti invested their talents into wringing irregular timbral qualities out of their instruments, an activity that took precedence over their melodic or harmonic use. In both cases, the wielders of the instruments probably had no knowledge of how to read or score sheet music, let alone the nimbleness of finger required to play the instrument properly- this in spite of the fallacious rock-'n-roll mantra that "anyone can play guitar".

The instrumental approach of Industrial music, then, depended on the primitivization of rock instruments, the innovative re-configuration of "non-instruments," and the use of electronics to portray the events of the lived present rather than those of the imagined future. This wider palette caused the results to be ignored by a frustrated music press, even being called "art" as a pejorative term- but it was a state of affairs which Genesis P. Orridge shrugged off by saying "in the end, music is popular culture and art is divine."[29]

New Collectivism

> Art is noble mission that demands fanaticism, and Laibach
> is an organism whose goals, life and means are higher - in
> their power and duration – than the goals, lives and means
> of its individual members.[30]

-Laibach

Industrial music did seem to return music to an exciting zero point where the only limitations on creation were the artist's own resourcefulness- yet, in a testament to the genre's fluid boundaries, the 'lone wolf' cell structure was not the only strategy embraced by all of its constituents. The leftist politics of the London metal-bashing group Test Dept., for example, demanded that strength in numbers be deployed against a corrupt and monolithic State: the individual names of the band's members were not widely known or listed on album credits, and their functions within the largely percussion-based ensemble were also assumed to be interchangeable. To do otherwise would have been a concession to the "star system" of popular music, in which a procession of nominally unique personalities supposedly performed a function (virtuosity with a musical instrument, athletic dancing skill) that could not be replicated or imitated by other mere mortals, making them objects onto which the masses could project fantasies about what *they* would do with such exclusive talents.

The end result of this is easy enough to see: a large-scale de-personalization brought about by the industrialization of common dreams. These dreams would be dictated to the masses by stars who stopped short of truly giving the masses the means to realize these dreams themselves. In a purely tactical sense, the development of a personality cult around the individual members of Test Dept. would also be foolish- groups agitating against a much more powerful State (Test Dept. supported the South Wales miners' strikes in the mid-80s, among other causes) can hardly afford to disclose their likely whereabouts or to offer up the same kind of candid personal details that pop musicians offer to appease their fans.

This collectivist take on Industrial was made more interesting when it headed East to Slovenia, to be taken up by an intellectually advanced group of artists known as Laibach. If Throbbing Gristle, with their camouflaged uniforms and homemade sonic weapons, appeared like partisan fighters aligned against a monolithic regime, then Laibach looked and sounded like the regime itself. Both groups proposed discipline as both an aesthetic and way of life, although Laibach did not share Throbbing Gristle's means of enlightening audiences through highly disorienting, bewildering Burroughsian music. Rather, their music switched out the elements which seemed to pride themselves on their alienating effects - e.g. the febrile, white noise 'wall of sound' - for 'militant classical' touches like sampled, soaring strings, horn fanfares and rolls of military snare. Industrial rhythms, vocal samples, and brooding electronics also figured into the picture, but were hardly the meat of the presentation itself.

In person, Laibach wore vintage uniforms with officers' caps and leather riding boots (even dressing like this on *all* public occasions for a brief period in the 1980s, sacrificing the entirety of their social lives to their performance.) Meawhile, Laibach adorned their concert stage with atavistic or nostalgic 'power' imagery such as antlers and cogwheels, but also Malevich crosses (a black symbol designed by the Russian 'Suprematist' artist, and visually more akin to the 'Red Cross' logo than the elongated Christian cross.) At least one swastika figured into the band's album cover artwork, but the irony of its use was lost on many: the swastika in question was appropriated from a design by anti-Nazi artist John Heartfield, and was formed from four interconnected hatchets. In its original context, the swastika warned of the conclusive effects that fascist ideology brought about- a brutal 'chopping down' of humanity. Yet Laibach refused to condescend to their audience by pointing out such things, allowing them to draw whatever conclusions they liked- and thus calling into question whether the artists were 'dictators' in the traditional sense of the word.

The band's name itself was the Germanized form of the Slovenian capital Ljubljana - just one out of many scandal-provoking points in the band's career - and they were, like Throbbing Gristle, originally an offshoot of a complex multi-media enterprise. The parent group of Laibach was NSK (short for *Neue Slowenische Kunst,* or New Slovenian Art.) NSK and Laibach were known for visual and audio works that were almost infuriating in their ambiguity, offering no clear explanations (public statements about the art tended to encrypt the meaning even further), and providing no explicit indications of the individual members' beliefs and ideals. Rather, this ambiguous presentation was used in a way that drew out the latent fanaticism and irrationality of the viewer / listener. The result was, as can be guessed, an art that set both fascists and socialists against them for blaspheming the icons of those respective political affiliations.

One early Zagreb concert, during which film footage of Yugoslav president Josip Broz Tito was superimposed onto pornographic film images, was abruptly curtailed by the police. Within June of the same year (1983), the group appeared on the nationally broadcast television program *TV Tednik* [TV Weekly], in a live interview with presenter Jure Pengov. Footage of the interview is now enshrined in the Modern Gallery of Ljubljana, and in it Laibach appeared like a paramilitary version of the British artists Gilbert & George (known for their comically flat, deadpan affectation and their habit of answering questions in unison.) Pengov goaded the band into making outrageous declamatory statements, while condemning their use of their former occupiers' German language (which figured into their name, lyrics, and poster art actions.) Although Laibach had been operating for a few years before the TV incident, only after the TV appearance would official censorship be directed at them: there was a 4-year ban on the usage of the name 'Laibach' (it was said that there was "no legal basis" for the name), which was said to needlessly stir painful memories of the nation's period of Nazi occupation. The incident could have been dismissed as a rude, punk-ish provocation for its own sake- yet, as NSK biographer Alexei Monroe writes, something was wrong with the picture:

> All the evidence necessary to condemn was present, except...Laibach's 'fascistic' statements actually sampled self-management texts [the social policy initiaited by Tito deputy Edvard Karelj], their uniforms were Yugoslav army fatigues, and so on. All the elements used to prove the group's guilt also 'prove' their innocence. This is the paradoxical position from which Laibach respond to the 'eternal question' about if they are really fascist: *'isn't it evident?'*[31]

The joke was, of course, that it was *not* evident, and that the longer Laibach stayed in the public eye, the more questions they raised, which again served to defend them against accusations of being tyrannical ideologues in the making - wouldn't people normally in this position have clearly comprehensible (if not completely pandering) manifestoes ready for the public to consume, in which they closed off all avenues of questioning? And what kind of self-assured 'totalitarians' would rely on a 'public relations strategy' of generating public debate, allowing the public opinion of them to freely oscillate from one misconception to the other?

Monroe is wise to note that the retro-fascistic elements utilized by Laibach - uniforms, banners, rigid discipline and Wagnerian symphonic triumphalism - are, paradoxically, the same elements which distance it from more modern (post World War II) emanations of fascism. Leading ultra-rightist politicians like Jean Marie LePen and David Duke have made it a habit to court mainstream respectability, opting for crisp business suits and jeans instead of military regalia, and insisting, at least publicly, that their followers claim power through the ballot box rather than through guerrilla actions and violent intimidation. While their speeches given to already 'converted' or 'awakened' racialists can still approach the fiery sloganeering of the Third Reich's leaders, their publicly voiced concern has shifted to more universally cherished institutions like the family unit, and towards tribal fragmentation of larger geographic territories - and thus away from the old imperialist concepts of *lebensraum* and *endlösung*.

Had Laibach employed a similar aesthetic at a time when the Nazis actually were ravaging Europe, their aims could hardly be viewed as anything but another rote exercise in heroic propaganda. As it stands, though, a Mosleyan "England Awake!" lightning flash being used on Throbbing Gristle regalia, or a Slovenian band singing martial anthems in German, actually manage to work *against* the post-war efforts to make fascist ideals palatable in the "politically correct" media landscape. Monroe suggests that, in such an overtly "PC" climate, the resurgence of archetypal fascist symbology is the *last* thing on the minds of neo-fascist organizers:

> ...these Germanic signifiers are, to those who have been exposed to the group's work, indelibly associated with the underground, taboo nature of Laibach, so it could be argued that Laibach's use of them takes them *away* from the boundaries of acceptability.[32]

Moreover, the musical content of Industrial itself does not sit well with the fascist political program. Even those who fail to do the minimal research on the alternative lifestyles of Industrial's founding fathers (see the homosexuality and drug use of William Burroughs, for starters) may have difficulty making any sense of the anarchic and asymmetrical sonic onslaught. As per Monroe:

> Fascism is, in practice, suspicious of - if not outright hostile to - avant-garde and experimental approaches to music or culture, and Nazi musicology always condemned atonal and avant-garde music. Fascism is also suspicious of ambiguity, contradiction and paradox, the elements that maintain uncertainty and suspicion around Laibach.[33]

Along with the above, the embrace of technology-driven music is, to many on the extreme right, another step into the abyss of decadence. This is puzzling, given the tendency of white supremacists in particular to boast of the white race's global lead in scientific and technological advancements, and the "reactionary modernism" that typified the domestic policies of the Axis powers. All the same, most fascistic music groups rely on a 'folkish' acoustic sound, on neo-classical composition, or guitar-based excursions into the now acceptably 'folkish' genres of punk and metal. The focus away from harmony, and into pure sonic texture, is too much of a theoretical leap for many ultra-right shock troops to make (the recent efforts in "National Socialist Black Metal" subculture notwithstanding.)

Laibach clearly shares with other Industrial artists the tendency towards explication of mass psychology and mass manipulation, and some of their own statements have been strikingly similar to the Burroughsian proclamations issued by groups like Cabaret Voltaire and Throbbing Girstle: the liner notes to their 1992 *Nato* album, for example, note how "in the *Kinderreich* [childrens' kingdom] mankind adds words together to make a sentence. As they learn the sentence, they learn order. Undo the sentence and you undo order. The sentence is a cell, the word a padlock on meaning."[34] All this notwithstanding, their critique of Industrial's leading lights has been anything but simple praise. Concerning Throbbing Gristle and their cohorts, Laibach say that

> The engagement of these groups, in terms of their programs, has remained at the level of romantic existentialism. LAIBACH [capitals in the original], on the other hand, stands in the midst of life and is pragmatic. Our motto is based in reality, truth, and life. From this standpoint, every comparison of LAIBACH with the specified groups is meaningless.[35]

In making this statement, Laibach are not alone: the quasi-mystical elements of Genesis P. Orridge's undertakings (especially his later efforts in Psychic TV) have alienated a number of would-be allies within the larger sphere of confrontational Industrial music. After the original formation of Throbbing Gristle dissolved, P. Orridge began to show a larger interest in the Promethean poses of rock gods who had, in his estimation, subverted the 'star system' of their time- delivering, as it were, a purely spiritual and transcendent musical content via the Trojan Horse of commercial music. To this end, Jim Morrison and Lou Reed were among the personalities most frequently channeled by P. Orridge in his Psychic TV project- unsurprising given his coming of age in the heady 1960s. In sharp contrast to such sincere efforts to carry on the would-be shamanistic tradition of these individuals, Laibach channeled archetypal rock gods of their own (The Beatles, Freddie Mercury of Queen) in order to expose the latent 'groupthink' and totalitarianism hidden behind their enticing aura of individuality. An act as simple as converting the lyrics of Queen's anthem "One Vision" into German, and retitling it as "*Geburt Einer Nation* [Birth of a Nation]" was enough to accomplish this. Hearing Mercury's optimistic/utopian lyrics twisted into *ein Fleisch, ein Blut, ein wahre Glaube* [one flesh, one blood, one true religion], and harnessed to a musical backdrop of marching rhythms, Wagnerian strings and uplifting brass, reveals the latent totalitarian obsession with "The One" and with central, outwardly radiating authority- slyly suggesting that the individualistic charisma of performers like Mercury is merely a catalyzer of collective and conformist spirit, rather than an exemplar to lead people to a greater sense of their own individuality.

'The impossibility of originality,' and consequently, individuality, is a theme returned to time and time again by Laibach- after hearing Laibach's militarized, highly de-personalized cover versions of famous pop songs (The Rolling Stones' 'Sympathy for the Devil', and the entirety of The Beatles' *Let It Be* album are also brought in for "historical revision" by Laibach) it is difficult to hear this music in the same way as before. At the very least, it is difficult to attend another arena concert, in which an artist's face or logo is replicated on a veritable sea of t-shirts and merchandise, and to *not* draw a parallel with the propaganda saturation of totalitarian political systems.

The existence of groups like Laibach and Test Dept. makes it more difficult to call Industrial a movement carried out exclusively by resourceful, isolated individuals- but neither the 'partisan' information warfare of Throbbing Gristle nor the 'regime' metaphor of Laibach constitute the sole, 'proper' form of Industrial culture. The two respective variants were developed to attack whatever manifestation of authoritarian control was most prevalent in the daily lives of the groups' members, with that control itself having a great plasticity from one lived environment to the next. In a managerial, post-industrial environment like the United Kingdom, it was more suitable for Throbbing Gristle to individualize the technological tools of conformity. In the socialist Yugoslavia of Tito, Laibach was required to adopt their extreme image in order to confront both the forces of Western cultural colonization *and* the false 'autonomy' forwarded by the Yugoslav authorities themselves. For all the ideological differences between the two factions, Laibach make statements about the nature of art that are remarkably similar to the above proclamations of Genesis P. Orridge:

> The aim of art is to give immortality to everyday practical behavior and work, which is necessary if life is to provide us with a ladder leading to divinity.[36]

"We Have Ways Of Making You Laugh"

Despite all the deathly serious socio-political issues which Industrial music was often mired in, it would be erroneous to say that it was without a sense of humor. All of the more respectable Industrial units, as opposed to the massed ranks of copyists and also-rans, seem to have cultivated this capacity- and not merely as a necessary release valve when the overall presentation became too oppressive, but as an essential component of the 'cultural camouflaging' technique. The degree to which this humor is effective, though, might depend on how great one's appreciation is for irony, or for recognizing the very fine line between a cleverly crafted parody and the "genuine article".

In this sense, Laibach again deserve special mention for making a caricature of totalitarian mystique so convincing - so much *more* marked by formal pomp and archaic nobility than real-life totalitarianism - that it becomes downright hilarious for those who notice the subtle distinctions. A good idea of this can be grasped by watching footage of the band's vintage live performances: the group's lead singer stands so stock-still, only occasionally tossing out a grandiose sweep of the arm, that anyone not already offended by the band's pseudo-'Nuremberg rally' stage set or seduced by the martial *sturm und drang* of the music will likely find this choreographed inaction to be a very funny negation of energetic, faux-shamanistic 'rock god' performance. At other points in the show, a pair of drummers at the front of the stage mime trumpet parts which are obviously being played on backing tape, and a lone woodcutter appears as an 'opening act'. The whole performance is so stripped of warmth and audience-performer rapport, the absurdity and sheer discomfort of the situation can force laughter where even a seasoned comedian couldn't. In the same way that groups like SPK turned floodlights on their audience to make them the 'focal point' of the performance, the more ridiculous elements of Laibach's performance made audience members the brunt of their joke: if the band's mock-militarism was something to laugh at, then even more laughable were the Third Reich nostalgics in the audience who convinced themselves this performance was a *real* fascistic political rally.

When not active in the public sphere through concert performance, Laibach were articulate interview subjects whose official statements nonetheless regularly contradicted each other, adding another level of humor to the proceedings. While referring to themselves in the 3rd person rather than the 1st, the band often flavored their speech with eloquent aphorisms and adopted a condescending tone that seemed, to the uninitiated majority, equally dismissive of everyone and everything. The humorous element to this aspect of their presentation was, in fact, its arch humorlessness itself: a stylistic extremity that, like the "uncompromising war on art" of the Soviet Constructivists[37], was so emphatic and agitational that it approached the braggadacio of the cartoonish characters in the professional wrestling business.

The band also seemed very cognizant of how such extremes were embedded in Western stereotypes of Slavic Easterners, and proceeded to amplify these stereotypical characteristics to an unreal extreme: these characteristics being coldness, incomprehensibility, and denunciation of individualism. Nowhere is this more evident than when Laibach calls into question the "problem" of humor itself, saying

> According to Darwin, *laughter* is an expression mostly common to idiots, and according to English psychologist M.W. Brody, it represents the concluding part of aggressive usurpation. It is well-known that the word *humor* springs from England and the English are proud of it; however, it is also well known that England has nothing left to laugh at. Its humor is a leftover of narcissoid hedonism, its weapon against the outer world and a proof of its pseudo-domination over the actual situation. In art, we appreciate humor that can't take a joke.[38]

Throbbing Gristle, meanwhile, milked a great deal of humor from the unlikely juxtapositions of tastes that they unironically enjoyed. For one, the band members were fascinated with the kitschy, light-hearted 'exotica' music of composers like Martin Denny and Les Baxter- a music associated more closely with wholesome, innocent leisure time in 1950s America than with the cruel realities of a crumbling, inward-turning British empire. Throbbing Gristle went so far as to be photographed in the "Hawaiian" outfits that characterized Denny's band, and the cover design for their *20 Jazz Funk Greats* album was also a case study in this kind of mimicry. According to P. Orridge, the record sleeve

> ...was drenched in ironic parody...we mimicked the print layout of Simon & Garfunkel as well, to give the impression of classic pop archetypes of design and consumer friendliness [...] The sickly pink lilac colour of the back sleeve was as close as we could get to Simon & Garfunkel's *Bookends* album.[39]

This was really not a humorous act in and of itself, and would be much less so for those who were not hamstrung by their expectations of cultural presentation. However, it becomes somewhat funnier when weighed against the actual musical output of the band. It is almost impossible for the casual listener to reconcile this with audio selections from the TG canon: see the harrowing audio suicide note "Weeping" or the viscous, sinister electronic fog of numbers like "Slug Bait." In this way, Industrial music used an aesthetic of irreconcilability to re-integrate the listener with life outside of those unrealistically smooth media transitions that seemed ever more "natural" to those inundated by them (i.e. the edits, 'wipe' effects and segues that were part and parcel of TV programming) In street-level reality, a moment of giddy laughter really could be followed a second later by one of terror or unexpected embarrassment, and vice versa.

Awkward moments of inter-personal contact were something that had to happen from time to time in order for individuals to understand if their life strategies were working or not, and Throbbing Gristle again set an example here by bypassing the rock club circuit and agreeing to perform virtually anywhere that would have them (one shining example being their riotous performance for an all-boys' boarding school.)

An advanced appreciation of pure mischief as a transformative tool would also be necessary to enjoy Industrial's more amusing side. Take, for example, NON's infamous 7" vinyl record [*Knife Ladder / Mode of Infection*] with multiple "center holes" bored into it by Boyd Rice, or Rice's vast back catalog of conceptual pranks- making obnoxious calls to radio call-in shows, placing a row of eggplants on spikes outside a shopping center, or presenting a skinned sheep's head to First Lady Betty Ford. Rice's propensity for criminal mischief eventually earned him a place of honor in the Re/Search publication *Pranks!*,[40] along with fellow Industrial culture alumnus Mark Pauline of Survival Research Laboratories. When confessing to the above actions, Rice makes a case for outlandish pranks being yet another way to dismantle the 'control machine'- a proposal that Re/Search interviewer Andrea Juno obviously lauds:

> [The police] know how to deal with real criminals, but somebody who puts eggplants on sticks- you're making a mockery of their social order, and that's worse than what most criminals are capable of doing. By doing something incomprehensible, you place yourself outside their magic, and then they lose control.[41]

A series of live radio showdowns with the evangelical talk show host Bob Larson have also provided a perfect glimpse into the eccentric Industrial sense of humor. Hoping to skewer Rice on air for his connections to the Church of Satan, and to spur him towards unleashing some mean-spirited tirades, precisely the opposite happens: Rice's unnerving calm and middle-American affability forces Larson into a series of audibly 'red-in-the-face' ranting fits. Although Rice quotes from Social Darwinist scribes like Ragnar Redbeard, scoffs at liberal humanism and generally comes off like a pop culture avatar of Oswald Spengler, he also admits a fondness for the bubblegum pop of Little Peggy March and invites his incensed host out for 'a beer' after being verbally pilloried by him for an hour (Larson gamely replies to the invitation with "make mine a Perrier".) Going by the simple comedic logic that the funniest things are the most unanticipated, this vintage show is funnier than the vast majority of contemporary *Saturday Night Live* sketches and the bludgeoning insistence of their comedic taglines - it is difficult to stifle a laugh when Rice's favoring of animal qualities over those of humans prompts Larson to angrily blurt *"Christ did not die...for a PLATYPUS!!!"*

Rice's 50/50 personality split between Nordic berserker and 'space age bachelor' is also another example of how Industrial culture's camouflaging techniques work not only to obscure the true intentions of their practitioner, but to *reveal* the true nature of an adversary: while Rice tempers his misanthropy with just enough ebullience to make himself seem likeable, his debate partner is reduced to an embittered, seething caricature of himself. The majority of on-air callers to the program even voice open support for Rice's fire-breathing ideals. Boyd Rice's method of enlightenment through enhanced irritation – also evident on his "playable at any speed" record of lock grooves (*Pagan Muzak)* - is not that far removed from the comic disruptions of period comedians like Andy Kaufmann, or from the tortuous boredom of select Warhol pieces. However, in the case of Rice and several others like him, there is a clear spiritual aim to even the most ridiculous of antics- Rice is a student of Gnosticism, citing the Gnostic deity Abraxas as a kind of tutelary divinity for his ability to "stand in two circles at once," or erase the fundamental contradictions arising from the duality inherent in human nature.

The glorification of quotidian artifacts is another humorous, occasionally agitating ploy used by the 'control agents' of Industrial culture - one of the most obvious cultural precedents for this being Marcel Duchamp's "readymades" or mundane, mostly unmodified modern objects which earn their elevated status merely because the artist (rather than the public or the critical community) wills it so. COUM Transmissions had, in fact, performed a piece entitled *Duchamp's Next Work* based upon Duchamp's 1913 exhibition of a bicycle wheel (the involved the wheels being 'played' by verious members of the group.)

Whereas Marcel Duchamp may have exhibited urinals and snow shovels 'as is,' with little extra embellishment beyond an artist's signature, Throbbing Gristle would elevate objects such as suitcases to the status of art commodities- such was the case when a full day's worth of live TG performances were packed into a suitcase on twenty-four individual cassettes. This shift towards such anonymous, utilitarian packaging was done spite of the demonstrated skill of Peter Christopherson as a designer of lush album sleeves (Christopherson was employed by the 'Hipgnosis' design firm, which provided covers for such progressive rock titans as Yes and Genesis.) Other artists, such as Berlin's Die Tödliche Doris (whose *Geniale Diletannten* movement could be seen as a German sister movement to Industrial), released a set of 2" records meant for playback within a talking doll's battery-powered voicebox (these were undoubtedly 'found' rather than manufactured at the band's request.) The constantly nagging refrain of "the medium is the message" is never far behind when such things are employed as the framing devices for the audio works within- the message, in this case, being that the age of mass production and, to some extent, of collectivist ideology, favors easily-directed human ciphers instead of a messy tangle of diversified individuals: hordes of briefcase-wielding businessmen heading off to work in sterile, climatized office buildings, while their children receive sage advice from such surrogate 'role models' as plastic dolls.

This concept is one that has recently come full-circle back to the 'recognized' art world, up from the grotto of Industrial culture: there is 'Young British Artist' Tracy Emin's Turner Prize-winning *My Bed*, a tableau whose inclusion of menstrual-stained underwear easily invites comparison to the infamous 'Prostitution' exhibit of COUM Transmissions in 1976, in which Cosey Fanni Tutti exhibited used tampons alongside the framed pages from pornographic magazines for which she modeled. Another pair of Turner Prize-winning artists, Jake and Dinos Chapman, largely constructed their panoramic war-scape *Hell* from untold numbers of toy figurines, either in Nazi uniform or naked and dismembered. The painstaking amount of time needed to assemble this piece, along with its panoramic style of composition, clearly removes it from the world of readymades, though its gallows humor places it firmly in a tradition previously occupied by artists such as Throbbing Gristle. Nothing seems so much like an extension of TG's presentation as a detail from *Hell*, in which an artillery-damaged McDonald's franchise becomes a scene of hideously orchestrated carnage and rape - temporarily inspiring pity for the inert plastic objects that are on hand to mime the conditions of extreme human suffering.

It's telling indeed, then, that the Chapmans would select TG as one of the star performers at the 2004 edition of the All Tomorrow's Parties festival, for which they acted as guest curators. This was initially one of a few select concerts played by a "reunited" Throbbing Gristle, before they eventually lapsed into full touring mode several years later in support of their *Thee Endless Knot* album (and were terminated irrevocably after Peter Christopherson's death in 2010.) Though the recognition of the group as having a meaning exceeding their own genre was belated, it did seem like a natural development to follow the pre-millenial "electronica" music boom, accompanied as it was by a fascination with obscured origins.

The 21st century reunion was nevertheless a strange anticlimax for a group that otherwise ceased to exist in 1981. In keeping with their career-long assessment of life's inexhaustible irony, the band had split up to *avoid* what seemed to be a coming breakthrough in commercial success and critical acclaim. In a fitting (although not pre-meditated) end to the Industrial era proper, the final record released in the 1980s by the band's Industrial Records imprint was not a Throbbing Gristle release, but *Nothing Here Now But The Recordings*, by none other than William Burroughs.

+

The idiom of Industrial music, as we'll see in later chapters, has since been consciously and unconsciously absorbed into the works of countless electronic musicians and performers (to say nothing of the other arts), but the real triumph of this music has always been its refusal to let records and live concerts be its sole cultural end product. This partially owes itself to the "intermedia" origins of the practice, which - as Ina Blom suggests - was "designed to cover those instances where the artist did not simply combine different artistic media, but worked against the grain of any categorical organisation by means of strategies of displacement."[42] Intermedia art's shift away from institutionally owned *space* to contested *environment* - which often meant the use of any public throughfare as a performance or exhibition stage - was very much embraced by Industrial music and culture. Though this practice has often been confused with multimedia (a misconception helped along by the type of audio-visual 'total experiences' mentioned earlier), its focus was more on those indefinable "spaces" of conduct and action in between the established modes of artistic production, rather than on the combination of those established modes.

Industrial musicians used music as a metaphor for a fully integrated lifestyle of radical autonomy and 'psychic self-defense'- unlike many other music-related subcultures, the music merely acted as the *frisson* to redirect the individual listeners' behavior, rather than claiming that attendance at a concert or ownership of a record was the absolute pinnacle of the cultural experience. The music was no more than the starting point in the struggle for realizing one's ideal self and hitherto unknown potentialities (which, of course, could be destructive just as well as creative) - and this made it potentially more effective than the claims of "power of rock 'n roll" evangelizing, i.e. that one's personal transformation *had* to involve further activity within the musical sphere. Andrew McKenzie, who has left his own mark on this musical aggregate through the gestures of his project The Hafler Trio, is worth quoting at length on the extra-institutional impact of Industrial music:

> At the time of the arising of all 'this stuff' (whichever label is put onto it), there was nothing. Worldwide, perhaps an audience of 3,000 - and that's a very generous estimate - people, most of whom were active in producing material themselves. Selling 1,000 copies of a record was a feat that was envied. But through it all, what emerged was a sort of movement - not in any organised form, or label, or name - but what was there was a blending and intermixing of film, music, literature, religion, art and many other things; something that really had not existed before. *This* was

what drove people on. It was the beginning of seeing *outside* of 'just making music', and the glimpsing of something greater. Now it is so that many people deny this now, but the artifacts contradict them, and indeed, their careers would not have come into being had it not been so.[43]

Musical genres and sub-genres come and go, but full-blown cultural movements tend to mutate in a rather tenacious matter, and refuse to die as easily as isolated musical trends. For this reason, it's fitting to close this chapter with some of the dialogue from one of Genesis P. Orridge's acknowledged 'foundation texts' (*Conversations with Marcel Duchamp*) - in which Duchamp defends the Surrealist movement in terms that could apply perfectly to the Industrial movement as well:

DUCHAMP: Fundamentally, the reason Surrealism survived is that it wasn't a school of painting. It isn't a school of visual art, like the others. It isn't an ordinary "ism," because it goes as far as philosophy, sociology, literature etc.

CABANNE: It was a state of mind.

DUCHAMP: It's like existentialism. There isn't any existential painting.

CABANNE: It's a question of behavior.

DUCHAMP: That's it.[44]

Whitehouse : Asceticists or Libertines?

Prologue: Resurgent *Rumori*

After the official dissolution of Throbbing Gristle in 1981, the chthonic beast known as Industrial music splintered into a variety of sub-genres, each of them expanding upon some key element of the founding quartet's radical agenda of cultural deprogramming. Not the least of these phenotypes were the follow-up projects formed by the actual members of TG themselves, although the influence of the factory foursome was, come the mid-'80s, just one piece in an increasingly complex puzzle of creative approaches. Newer artists at this time, already emancipated by TG's suggestion that it was the whole nature of music which needed re-assessing, and *not* just rock 'n roll, were free to tap the potentialities of non-linear noise, new technologies and a much broader palette of subject matter than courtship rituals. Few have ever succeeded on the same level as TG did- and despite the anarchic encouragement for others do whatever they pleased sound-wise, a certain amount of homogeneity and cloning was bound to become a contagion in the nascent genre.

One of the most heavily borrowed elements of the Throbbing Gristle program was the predilection for fetishizing the universally ugly, dutifully following Genet's sage advice *"to escape the horror, bury yourself in it"*. This particular quote was appropriated by Industrial arch-transgressor Monte Cazazza, a man who, with his sneering anti-music and faked snuff films, created more than his fair share of aesthetic horror for people to immerse themselves in. A survey of the young, restless, post-TG cadre of noisemakers shows that they largely did not have the same grounding in media theory or as varied an aesthetic sensibility as their forebears, and attempted to compensate with a pure lust for negation. This tendency is best exemplified by the exhausting sleeve notes of the New Blockaders 7" single *Epater Les Bourgeois*:

> Let us demolish these fetid blocks of security, of tradition, of certainty, of unquestioning worship...let us be murderors [sic] of the past! The obscene progression of regression shall be halted by us, The New Blockaders! Let us be anonymous. O brothers and sisters, let us work in subtle ways, and then at dawn our hour of glory shall come! Let us be chameleons, let us enter their ranks unnoticed...only attacks from behind ever succeed! Let us sever this parasite called history, it has nothing to do with us...this is the future! This is now![1]

The New Blockaders were not alone among the noise community in their insistence that the 'future,' whatever that was imagined to be, would come about by spontaneous, atavistic acts of destruction- although their official statements were some of the most hyperbolic (and consequently, some of the most entertaining). The New Blockaders would bolster their claims that "even anti-art is art...that is why we reject it!" with a shopping list of negation, again to be found on the notes to their *Epater...'* single. Sparing virtually no communications or entertainment apparatus, the Blockaders claim to be "anti-books, anti-newspapers, anti-magazines, anti-poetry, anti-music, anti-clubs, anti communications!",[2] then delivering the blackly funny *coup de grace:* "we will make anti-statements about everything....we will make a point of being pointless!"[3] It seemed that only the previous *enfants terribles* of the European art world, Throbbing Gristle's spiritual predecessors in the Viennese Aktionists, trumpeted nihilism to such all-pervasive levels: provocateurs like Otto Mühl stated that his 'ZOCK'[4] order "has no dread of chaos...rather it fears forgetting to annihilate something,"[5] and laid out a brusque 5-point plan for ZOCK culminating in blowing up the Earth from space, and the subsequent "attempt to cave in the universe". In 1963, Mühl would exclaim that "I can imagine nothing significant where nothing is sacrificed, destroyed, dismembered, burnt, pierced, tormented, harassed, tortured, massacred..,stabbed, destroyed, or annihilated,"[6] a statement so blunt that it cannot have helped him during the legal proceedings brought to bear on him later in his life.[7]

With such attitudes of cultural leveling running strongly through it, the rising noise underground of the '80s seemed to be heir apparent to the Italian Futurists of the 1920s, who, in a concerted effort to clear away the sentimental debris of history, exhibited plenty of their own destructive streaks. The open support that some noise-based acts voiced for the Futurists would not make it any easier for the new underground to repudiate claims that it glorified fascismas well- an allegation that dogged it throughout the genre's halcyon days of the 1980s. Whether they were aware of it or not, The New Blockaders were endorsing a type of 'rebuilding by leveling' which had led to the rise of fascism in the first place: take, for example, the actions of April 15, 1919, when the Italian socialist newspaper *Avanti!* had its offices and its communications apparatus (linotype machinery) wrecked by an unholy alliance of Futurists and *arditi* [the former frontline soldiers who would become so useful in furthering fascist policies of the '20s]. The poet / figurehead F.T. Marinetti and his Futurist coterie would become disillusioned with fascist politics soon enough, while Benito Mussolini would eventually seek an artistic movement that better combined Italian traditionalism with more progressive tendencies (and, of course, would find armed marauders like the *arditi* infinitely more useful in accomplishing his aims than the abstractions of poets and cultural theorists). Marinetti's true acceptance by the overlords of the fascist political system was also called into question when Hitler, hosting an exhibit of Nazi-denounced 'degenerate art' in 1938, included a selection of Italian Futurist works in the show.

Truth be told, though, Marinetti's influence on the noise movement, despite his founding of the Futurists and subsequent penning of *The Futurist Manifesto*, is not as widely felt today as that of another Futurist luminary, Luigi Russolo- and his own seminal manifesto *L'arte di Rumori* [The Art Of Noises.] No educational narrative on radical modern sound, let alone an assessment of post-Industrial musicians, can be totally complete without some acknowledgement of Russolo. His short but essential broadside against traditionalism is reverently quoted in at least one CD retrospective of post-Industrial sound (Z'ev's *One Foot In The Grave* compilation, released on Touch in 1991) and the number of sound artists now paying homage to Russolo, whether aware of it or not, is manifold. Marinetti's insistence that extreme violence was an aesthetic device (since, after all, life and art were indistinct concepts) was taken to heart by more than a few of the genre's more confrontational performers: early live performances could devolve into chaotic situations requiring police intervention, while the demanding physicality of performances by Z'ev and Einstürzende Neubauten localized this violence to within the performers' own bodies. Still, the credit for truly drafting up any kind of a sonic blueprint for a more apolitical kind of Futurist music belongs to Russolo (even though he does quote at length from Marinetti's battlefield poetry in *The Art Of Noises*.) And it is also worth noting that Russolo considered himself a Futurist painter with some novel ideas about music, not a trained musician or composer in any sense of the word- through this alone he has a special kinship with the 'non-specialist', artistically omnivorous tradition of Throbbing Gristle and beyond.

If nothing else from the Futurist history of polemics and agitations goes uncontested, it can't be denied their role in shaping the sound interfaces of the subsequent century: Rodney Payton confirms this by claiming their instrumental innovations were "the spiritual ancestors to the very latest synthesizers."[8] One quote from *The Art Of Noises* stands out as not only relevant to the makers of post-Industrial and noise music, but to many of the transient musicians of the 21st century who would attempt to compact a huge, dynamic sound into a small box operable by just a single person:

> It is hardly possible to consider the enormous mobilization of energy that a modern orchestra requires without concluding that the acoustic results are pitiful. Is there anything more ridiculous in the world than twenty men

slaving to increase the plaintive meowing of violins?[9]

It may have taken seven decades for a street-level, non-academic movement to finally create an economical live music more pleasing to Russolo's sensibilities- but with the post-Industrial avant-garde, Russolo's wishes were made flesh in a dramatic, unequivocal way. Giant stacks of amplification equipment were already *de rigeur* for the arena rock-n-roll of the 1970s, a fact that critic Lester Bangs attempted to make mirth of by "defending Richard Nixon's energy crisis of the time, which [Emerson, Lake and Palmer] flouted grossly with their truckloads of volume-enhancing, electricity wasting gear."[10] So it could be argued that the personnel required to prepare these lumbering dinosaurs for performance was at least equal to the 'mobilization of energy' spent on an orchestra in Russolo's day. An entourage of stagehands, instrument 'techs' and 'doctors', drivers, caterers and other assorted hangers-on, all arriving in town with extravagant contract rider demands, did not make for an economical music show. It would take the dawn of the digital age, and all its attendant innovations (ADAT machines, laptops etc.) before the ratio of human input to instrumental output could truly be maximized, but Russolo should still be lauded for his early attempts to help this process along. His co-invention of the *intonarumori,* which Payton alludes to above (i.e. waist-high acoustic boxes connected to bullhorns and operated by hand-cranks or electric buttons), was a step in the direction of making a transducer that didn't require either athleticism or extreme agility to operate. The *intonarumori* had only about a one-octave range, adjustable in tones or semi-tones, but 27 different types were created according to the type of sound they were meant to generate: there were howlers, cracklers, exploders, thunderers, crumplers etc. The instruments were built in collaboration with another painter, Ugo Piatti, confirming that Russolo was not the only artist looking to liberate organized sound from 'musicians'- reining music back into the organic whole of art and life.

Music For Monochrome Men

The voluntary termination of Throbbing Gristle in the early 1980s may have prevented the band from being pinned to the 'pop' status that it purported to abhor (at least until the group's 21st century reincarnation), but the template they created had already become quite useful to other marginalized individuals in dire need of catharsis. Genesis P. Orridge lamented the waning days of Throbbing Gristle, and the rise of their 'stereotypical Industrial fan', as follows:

> They wear Doctor Martens and military trousers and black
> leather jackets, semi-Nazi regalia, skinhead haircuts or
> black hair, they are mainly male. They make cassette tapes
> of their Industrial music, which are mostly just feedback,
> and they bemoan the non-existence of TG. They feel that
> we betrayed something wonderful.[11]

Other members of Throbbing Gristle would be less dismissive of their successors- both Cosey Fanni Tutti and Peter "Sleazy" Christopherson insisted that the 'scene' was formed out of (in Christopherson's reckoning) "the lack of a response by the music business to the changing needs of the audience"[12], rather than as a blanket emulation of TG. Still, P. Orridge continued, naming names this time:

> We'd left a rather unhealthy residue of people and ideas,
> albeit because people had chosen to misunderstand what
> we were saying. It got into this thing of who could shock
> each other the most, SPK doing videos of dead bodies
> [and] Whitehouse for example, who I instantly and totally
> despised. Making a hole for those people to crawl through
> was quite scary.[13]

The people who were 'instantly and totally despised' by P. Orridge are best described as 'power electronics' artists, the coinage of the 'totally despised' Whitehouse: this was a markedly sinister, cauterizing offshoot of Industrial music characterized by its apparent glorification of anti-social behavior, pathology, and the nihilistic fringe elements within post-industrial society, with no shortage of disregard for that society's plethora of sexual inhibitions. For the literary-minded music consumer, the 'power' prefix instantly brings to mind Friedrich Nietzsche's famous proclamation of the 'will to power'- and while no members of any power electronics act have attained any degree of political power, they did try to make good on attaining some of the more easily attainable qualities of Nietzsche's *übermensch*: liberal democratic and/or Christian values of humility and charity were mocked, while these systems' egalitarian trappings were unceremoniously swept aside- neither was there any place for, say, Rousseau's Enlightenment admission of the 'good in man'. The 'libertinage' of the Marquis DeSade was a vastly more influential idea from *that* period in European history (Juliette, the anti-heroine in Sade's similarly-titled novel, is even suspected to be a parody of Rousseau's heroine Julie.)

The songs of Throbbing Gristle, which covered every aspect of social deviance from voyeuristic obsession ("Persuasion,") to serial killing ("Urge To Kill," "Dead Ed") did give the power electronics generation a potent cocktail to imbibe- although, as Orridge has already touched upon, one of the intoxicating effects of this cocktail was a propensity for creating art totally devoid of subtlety and variance. Cheap cassette reproduction provided an outlet for the power electronics market to become immediately flooded with artists who reveled in Thanatos, discarding TG's concessions to popular music forms (subversive as they might have been), and unloading a deluge of recorded material onto a comparatively limited audience- it would not be unheard of for a housebound power electronics artist to release 5-10 tapes in a year to match a professional studio recording artist's single album. In this respect, at least, the patronizing declaration of "my week beats your year", on Lou Reed's feted noise album *Metal Machine Music*, held true. And while it may not have been intended as such, the endless underground flow of brutal power electronics releases was something of an indirect comment on such modern institutions as the evening news- could power electronics artists really be counted on to produce wildly varying and constantly innovative releases, in a culture whose mass media seemed to be either reflecting or initiating a state of social stagnation? Local news reports from the period were, by all accounts, virtually no different than the ones being broadcast now, with their blank, clinical assessments of extreme social mayhem and their inability to really convey any message more cogent than 'it's dangerous out there.' Much of the power electronics genre simply transposed the indifferent reportage of televised news onto an audio format, occasionally even using unaltered snatches of nightly news monologues to drive home the point of otherwise abstract and anonymous noise assaults. These noise assaults themselves were like the significantly more bloody-minded cousin of minimalist composition, featuring single notes on a synthesizer held down for indeterminate periods of time while being oscillated, modulated and tonally mangled. This would form the backdrop for similarly modulated, heavily effected shrieks, shouts and vocal tantrums, all coming together in an effort to simulate the deranged thought processes of an incurable sociopath.

Ironically, the most well-publicized mass slayers have shown a taste for music considerably gentler than power electronics- British serial killer Dennis 'Monochrome Man' Nilsen, to whom the *pièce de résistance* of power electronics (Whitehouse's 1983 LP *Right To Kill*) is dedicated, enjoyed more contemplative electronic music- Laurie Anderson's 'O Superman' in particular. Charles Manson, whose influence is felt in all areas of the post-industrial music community (his friendship with Boyd Rice of NON, and the inclusion of his song 'Always Is Always' on Psychic TV's *Dreams Less Sweet* LP are just two of the more obvious examples), has always preferred and even performed American folk music, and sharply refuted allegations that the influence of the Beatles influenced his 'Family' to kill- "*Bing Crosby* was my idol",[14] he protests.

For all its flirtation with the aesthetics of fascism and *lustmord* / thrill killing, the power electronics genre has turned out to be, on average, fairly conservative in the subjects it chooses to portray. One of the major shortcomings of the genre is its tendency to cherry-pick only those controversial subjects which have been firmly entrenched in the mass consciousness for generations: most power electronics bands would be just resourceful enough to dig up a Heinrich Himmler speech to use as an intro to one of their electrified acid baths, yet would sidestep the activities of the Croatian *Ustaše,* who revulsed even Himmler's elite S.S. troops with their gleeful throat-slitting contests. It also doesn't look as if any contemporary power electronics artists have delved into the grisly specifics of the more recent genocides in Bosnia, Rwanda, Darfur etc.- making one wonder if these purveyors of brutality truly have a sense of history beyond Anglophone and Western European spheres of influence (recent additions like Dominick Fernow's Vatican Shadow project are more informed by Middle Eastern despotism and political intrigue, but here they are the exception that proves the rule.) By wielding such utter predictability, there is a vast underground which sadly commits the cardinal sin of any subversive art movement: failing to move an audience beyond a purely neutral reaction when "provocation" is the intent (alternately, if the reactions are not neutral, their precise content is at least as predictable as the provocation itself.)

Yet we have to remember that this genre was effectively birthed by Whitehouse, a band that sent even Genesis P. Orridge reeling, and whose conspicuous absence in the academic treatments of "noise music"[15] (which will invariably mention Throbbing Gristle's own forays into transgressive art) invites intense speculation as to why the group is seen as canonical by other underground artists but not by the critical community. It is also interesting to consider those instances in which said group, upon making numerous stylistic and thematic transformations, is not allowed to adopt these changes without suspicion of ulterior motives (and if it seems I belabor this point for longer than necessary, it is because this intolerance of stylistic and thematic re-assessment applies to many other unfortunate artists besides the one under investigation.)

"Deliver The Goods...That People Want To Receive"

Whitehouse was formed on the cusp of the 1980s by a teenaged William Bennett, a soft-spoken, Edinburgh-based *bon vivant* and classically trained guitarist. The band's moniker was meant as an ironic jab at puritanical anti-pornography crusader Mary Whitehouse, who was unfortunate enough to share her surname with the particularly lowbrow

Whitehouse porn magazine. Bennett served a brief stint in the new wave outfit Essential Logic before the dawn of Industrial music sparked a musical reassessment- he envisioned a corrosive musical maelstrom that could "bludgeon audiences into submission." Before this dream could manifest itself, though, Bennett played guitar in a transitional group called Come, an angular 'garage electronics' combo matching Bennett's inventively skewed chord progressions with a jittery synthetic pulse (provided partially by Mute Records boss and Normal founder Daniel Miller, recording under a pseudonym.) While that band would sadly be relegated to a footnote in the annals of New Wave, their namesake was used as the label for releasing future Whitehouse records- under the 'Come Organisation' banner, there were nine Whitehouse albums released over a period of five years, as well as a house organ entitled *Kata* (from the Greek prefix meaning 'downward'.) The latter was a skeletal, but intriguing fanzine which mythologized the activities of Whitehouse and provided readers with some of the more interesting facts related to modernity's aberrant monsters and anti-heroes. As commonplace as such writing may be in the 'blogosphere' of the age, there are few other things to compare it with from that era- only Throbbing Gristle's *Industrial News* dispatch surfaces as an immediate point of comparison. Bennett's undeniable impatience with the shortcomings and of pop culture (and worse yet, the stylistic compromises of the 'underground') especially shows through in the *Kata* reviews section, where record reviews are more often than not venomous 2-sentence put-downs.

Whitehouse released the idiosyncratic *Birthdeath Experience* in 1980, unveiling their trademark sound of simple, pulverizing synthesizer bass tones, twinned with skull-shearing high frequencies bordering on ultrasonic. These were wrung out of otherwise unfashionable, unreliable instruments like the battery-powered EDP Wasp mini synthesizer. The act of listening to Whitehouse as a non-initiate (the author bought his first Whitehouse album on a more or less total whim, with no advance knowledge of the band's sound or intentions) is indeed an active one, not unlike driving by some horrific accident and attempting to create closure on the scenario by projecting a personal 'back story' onto the accident victims: the vague elements and buried clues hidden within the overall violent foundation of the early records almost force one to engage their imagination with it in order to endure it. Even in a music as LOUD and engulfing as this, little is merely handed to the listener with a satisfying explanation. And all of the above impressions occur *before* William Bennett's vocals kick in. His is one of the most immediately recognizable voices within the last several decades of recorded music: his signature being focused, crystalline screams rising and falling in a smooth arc over an extended number of measures. Sometimes these interlace with the electronics for novel timbral effects, or are supplemented with feedback generated by the close placement of dual microphones.

Whitehouse caught on quickly through a program of relentless releasing (their second album *Erector* was being recorded before the first had even begun to circulate), as well as the relative ease of getting in touch with the band- Bennett has stated that printing his contact address on the back of LP sleeves was, for the time, a publicity coup which surprisingly few others had thought of: even if no LP had been purchased, many might still write requesting further information. Total refusal to 'outsource' the Whitehouse sound as a tool to advance others' projects was another hallmark of the band: to this day, no Whitehouse pieces have been released on third parties' compilation albums, nor have they been used as incidental music for film scores- although numerous offers to do these things have come and gone.

This simple, but still novel promotional strategy brought many of the band's key players into its orbit. The 14-year old Philip Best, who ran away from home in order to attend a show by the band - and who used Whitehouse as the template for the similarly unyielding Consumer Electronics, the Iphar cassette label, and the magazine *Intolerance* - added synthesizer squall and eventually became an alternate lead vocalist. Another notable contact, from 1982 on, was Chicago writer Peter Sotos (still the band's most contentious point despite his departure in 2002), whose criticism of pornography and exploitative 'true crime' literature occupies a unique place in the literary netherworld.

Although a full overview of Sotos' work (much of it recycled into lyrics for Whitehouse songs) reveals a scything critique of mass media's hypocritical portrayal of predators and their victims, it is difficult for casual, piecemeal readers to see it as anything but sadistic pornography in and of itself. This is in spite of activities, such as Sotos' afterword written for a largely self-aggrandizing Ian Brady autobiography, which caused Sotos to run afoul of the author when this added commentary contradicted much of Brady's text. Nonetheless, Sotos' early '80s magazine *Pure*, printed during his studies at the Art Institute of Chicago, is especially hard to swallow given the mocking and condescending tone with which it treats abuse and murder victims- yet later efforts like *Parasite* begin to shift the critical ire from the victimized towards the shock dealers in the major media; they who attempt to cover the most prurient information in a thin veneer of morality, all the while presenting it as lurid entertainment. Sotos' Chicagoland environs provided a continually overflowing cup of such prurient material, being the stage for such storied acts of mayhem as the John Wayne Gacy murders and the McMartin preschool abuse case. The sustained media portrayal of the latter, in particular, did not escape Sotos' critique, and academic critics like Jennifer Wicke would concur that these events "allowed an astonishing social fixation on sexual acts and sexualized children's bodies to flow into public discourse unimpeded, in the guise of a repudiation of these acts."[16] Whatever his motivations, Sotos' stint as a Whitehouse contributor was severely overshadowed by his status as a convicted criminal: possession of a magazine featuring child pornography (photocopied for the 2nd issue of *Pure*) led to a controversial trial in which Sotos would become the first person in the U.S. to be charged with possession, rather than distribution of, such material.

Other early supporters did not carry with them Sotos' unenviable reputation, but would become well-known for their own musical confrontations nonetheless: these included surrealist-about-town Steven Stapleton of Nurse With Wound (whose vast archives of adventurous recorded music offered valuable inspiration to the similarly omnivorous Bennett), as well as the Hafler Trio's Andrew McKenzie.

Incidentally, it was both Stapleton and McKenzie who would aid Bennett in bringing his vision to a viewing public for the first time in 1982: both were participants in the first Whitehouse "live aktion", a more than subtle nod to the same Viennese Aktionism that had prefigured COUM Transmissions and Throbbing Gristle (an alternate contemporaneous meaning, at least in the late-1970s germination period of Industrial music, came from the terrorist activities of the German RAF [Rote Armee Fraktion], described as 'aktions' in their official communiqués.) While the public aktions of Nitsch, Mühl, Brus et. Al occasionally took the form of music performances or "psycho-motorik noise aktions," they were still grounded in an ethos of taking paintings beyond the 2-dimensional boundaries of the canvas- so 'body art' and irreverent misuse of raw materials (often confusing aktions with the less aggressive 'Happenings' of the 1960s) was the central component of the presentation, rather than the sound. For Whitehouse aktions, this formula was inverted- the jarring and unequivocal blasts of power electronics were the catalyst for the theatrical exhibitions of delighted rapport and utter hostility that rapidly unfolded between performer and audience. Only the effect on the viewing audience - involving an unpredictable mix of ecstatic convulsion and wildcat violence, some of it inflicted by audience members upon themselves - was the same between the two different takes on 'aktion' art.

The particulars of past live aktions are compiled in the band's official 'live aktion dossier' online. Such occurrences as *"Steve Stapleton gets arm cut after flying glass during Whitehouse performance / police raid in large numbers midway through 'Anal American' (many arrested in chaos) / Whitehouse manager Jordi Valls spends night at police station for barring access to police"* are cataloged in the dossier in a humorously understated way, beside other colorful attempts at audience participation like *"two guys with pants around their ankles make out near the front of the stage during performance"*. Also humorous was the band's former habit of (in the best Industrial tradition of camouflaging) disguising their sound during pre-concert soundchecks in an effort to convince wary promoters that they were a "Human

League"-style synth-pop band. Some individuals decided, however, that the joke had gone too far when, at a 1983 Newcastle performance, William Bennett *"lightly [slapped] a girl in the face in ritualistic fashion"*, subsequently causing a disinformation campaign to be launched against Whitehouse from another corner of the post-Industrial milieu. According to said campaign, the slap prompted a mass audience walkout and a decline in the number of U.K. record shops willing to stock their albums, although Bennett contends "the only knock-on effect was that the local Newcastle independent record store (sorry, can't recall its name) stopped selling our stuff."[17] Such inflation of minor offenses into universally recognized legends was not- and still is not- uncommon, prompting Andrew McKenzie to state that

> This is worthy of a book in itself. Truly. I seriously doubt that book will be written, unfortunately, as it would have the most effect. The problem is that we go into *Rashomon* territory - each with his own version. And that leads to useless and destructive insistences on 'proof'. History is gossip, and not facts, as someone wiser than I once said.[18]

The 'classic' Come Organisation period of the band lasted until 1985, when the band released its genre-defining *Great White Death* LP, played a pair of wildly successful live aktions in Spain, and subsequently claimed it had achieved all that was possible within the parameters of its chosen media. The official press release famously stated that Whitehouse's participants were now ready to turn to "a life of crime" in order to sate their appetites. This was, of course, one of many media-baiting proclamations accepted by the print media as gospel truth. The various performers in Whitehouse's milieu were notorious for such claims, and for exposing the tendency of people to believe practically anything they hear from a dubious 'authority' such as a performing artist: many people still believe, thanks to Steven Stapleton, that Aktionist artist Rudolf Schwarzkogler committed suicide by gradually slicing off his own penis- needless to say, an undocumented event easily disproved with minimal research. The sensationalism whirling around the band would be helped along further thanks to disinformation spread by bands unreceptive to their aesthetic.

Do You Believe In Rock 'n Roll?

Whitehouse is a project that will, in many reviews of the band's work, have some reference made to its inherent "darkness." This may be a slightly more apt descriptor than some others (especially when taking into account the considerable amount of art that uses literal or metaphorical "darkness" - or silence, or esotericism - as an interrogator of spirit.) Yet it is somewhat misleading in the contemporary pop-cultural sense, as the concept of "darkness" has been used as the heraldic banner of so many other music-based subcultures. To most latter-day industrial and Gothic rockers, for example, "dark" is merely subculture shorthand for a set of escapist leisure time activities, which involve an above average focus on paranormal subjects, and on either idealized times past or times yet to be realized (sometimes both occupying the same storyline- Japanese role-playing video games provide a fine encapsulation of this.) In other words, it is a subculture concerned more with fantasy and elaborate fictions than in, say, altering the social landscape through direct confrontation- very much a full 180-degree turn from the stoic, unromantic, survival-oriented atmosphere generated by the seminal Industrial groups, to say nothing of the atmospheres conjured by the music of Whitehouse.

Which is not to say that either culture is completely free of turgid cartoon caricatures, or that the more serious Industrialists are 100% committed to 'smashing the control machine' without occasionally looking over their shoulders in a moment of bittersweet nostalgia. Bennett is one of the more vocal opponents of such Industrial nostalgia, decrying the "1983 time warp" as no different from any other sentimentality for a bygone era of cultural production. His harshest criticisms seem reserved, though, for rock 'n roll orthodoxy:

> There's so much incredible amazing music in the world, why be so limiting? [Rock music is] a musical fast food chain. It's so horribly conservative, so co-opted (ever since Elvis and its mainstream marketing), so full of embarrassingly fake rebels, it's like seeing your dad at a disco. It's more than flogging a dead horse, there's nothing left to flog, and there's nothing left to flog it with.[19]

Whitehouse, although they have delineated the boundaries of musical extremity for over a quarter-century now (and have even curated a series of other artists' music [*"Extreme Music From..."*]), are more cautious about employment of the classifier 'extreme' (like 'dark,' another term which has been de-fanged through overuse). Bennett states that it supposes an outmost limit without stating in what direction an artist must travel to reach that limit. In the place of simple extremity, Bennett believes the band's success comes from working on levels "both esoteric and exoteric," with the aim that some will experience the band's music on a "purely visceral" level, while others encounter "unexperienced depths."[20]

Whitehouse also exists a world apart from musical scores, notation and the like, making Bennett hesitant to include Whitehouse in any grand tradition of outré musical development and averse to the terms (like 'improvisation') that have come to characterize any music too complex or alien in its structure to be immediately understood by the listener:

> The word 'improvisation' doesn't sit easily in my musical vocabulary, since I don't see what we do as part of an established musical language or culture. It reminds me as a teenager of reading interviews of rock bands 'writing' songs - as if they were sitting down in candlelight to compose with some music notation like Mozart or Beethoven might have done. It's more of a process of 'sculpture' from an internally represented idea, which then has to be transformed somehow into tangible sound. That's the challenge, and any number of ways are available to achieve that goal.[21]

Just as 'improvisation' is a kind of misnomer for the work of Whitehouse, so too is the term 'anti-music,' proclaimed with zeal by contemporaries like The New Blockaders. Bennett, who seemingly enjoys a much broader variety of music than many of his peers (he has written approvingly of everything from the work of John Coltrane and Magma to the giddy naiveté of Italo Disco), could hardly be called a spokesperson for the final destruction of the musical form. In fact, his recent downloadable mixes of African percussion ensembles point more to a desire to into Yet, as a confessed connoisseur of all the arts, he is happy to criticize *musicians* for their failure to present relevant work with a passable shelf life. He voices his disappointment with the bulk of modern musicians as such:

> So many musicians, at an early stage in their careers, will find themselves in a comfort zone where they no longer feel the need to come up with anything new, and will happily just sit back and do the retreads until the end, even when they're obviously failing. In the realms of literature and art for example, I see the fires burning bright into old age, even at times increasing in intensity. I'm not quite sure why that's the case, other than the theory that music attracts participants for a lot more reasons than the mere opportunity to create.[22]

Lest we forget, Whitehouse was partially formed as a reaction to what Bennett perceived as the quickly faded promise of The Sex Pistols, Throbbing Gristle, et. Al.: namely, as an attempt to nullify the perceived ironic poses of these artists with something of unmistakable, almost elemental, purity. Whitehouse, in sharp contrast to Throbbing Gristle, do not entertain any ideas of having a 'mission,' nor is public image an integral part of their work.

By the time Whitehouse's debut exploded onto the scene, the kind of single-minded sonic wrath it contained wasn't completely without precedent in the annals of electronic music. Gordon Mumma's *Megaton for William Burroughs* or Alvin Lucier's *Bird and Person Dyning* shared similar techniques of electronic swarming and 'feedback-as-instrument', respectively. Yet while these pieces are visceral in their own right, they still remain appreciated by a largely academic or formalist audience; their composers largely respected as theoreticians and innovators within this specialized community. Whitehouse, on the other hand, has earned a much more heterogeneous following throughout their existence (partially due to a strategy of playing at both conventional music venues and 'multi-use' spaces) and has guaranteed an equally mixed critical reception: Messrs. Mumma and Lucier, to this writer's knowledge, have never had death threats directed at venues where they were scheduled to perform, have never been physically attacked by militant feminists (or merely used as the stylistic benchmark against which to propose more acceptably '"feminine" forms of "noise")[23] and have been spared the endless string of chaotic incidents which once dogged Whitehouse's public appearances.

Psychopathia Sexualis

Due to their raw atonality and reliance on the poles of the frequency spectrum, the group has found more kindred spirits within the psycho-acoustic music and sound art communities than the more "mid-range friendly" sphere of alternative music, although both have admitted (with varying degrees of hesitation and enthusiasm) to borrowing components of Whitehouse's presentation. More left-field figures like Peter 'Pita' Rehberg and multi-disciplinary artist Russell Haswell have led the efforts in this respect, while Sonic Youth guitarist and relentless noise advocate Thurston Moore has also name-dropped the band on occasion (though this may be more an indication of Moore wishing to ingratiate himself with the Whitehouse fanbase than a concerted attempt to boost the band's popularity.)[24] Lastly, The band has marshaled an impressive array of cultural backers not associated with music - e.g. author Dennis Cooper.

Yet many of these artists are well aware of the band's notoriety, and are usually compelled to temper their admiration for Whitehouse's sound with an assortment of disclaimers and carefully worded rationales. Bennett's contrarian refusal to conform to accepted tenets of 'extreme' music has, in keeping with his own personal warnings, alienated many die-hard fans, though these losses have been compensated for by a newfound interest from the peripheries of the ever-fluid 'new media' world. This can be argued as an abrupt sea change in aesthetic tastes throughout the modern world, but it can also be argued that this change owes itself in part to Whitehouse's obstinacy. It would be difficult to conceive of William Bennett circa 1981 being invited for a sound art-themed lecture at CCA KitaKyuushuu, a cutting edge Japanese center for art and theory. Nor would the Whitehouse of 20 years ago be receiving honorable mentions in the 'digital musics' category of Austria's coveted Prix Ars Electronica contest (the nominated work in question being the 2003 release *Bird Seed*). Yet even in the latter example, a stereotype of Whitehouse as neo-fascist, misogynist thugs has persisted somewhat- *Haunted Weather* author and musicologist David Toop, on the Ars Electronica judges' panel for that year, allegedly threatened a walkout over this nomination. Speaking on this incident (where Whitehouse supporter Rehberg also served on the 'digital musics' judging panel), Bennett says that

> ARS Electronica's 'honorable mention' story ironically belies some of the outright board hostility from old-timers like David Toop. Having been thoroughly disenfranchised for so long, I take hostility as a perverse form of vindication, but it's true there's lately been some fantastic support from other quarters - and anyway, it works best not to let one's energy get affected by what people say, good or bad.[25]

Sound artist and bio-acoustic researcher Francisco López, another highly influential figure as far as his chosen fields are concerned, accurately exemplifies the cautious approach to the band:

> In the industrial culture, the term 'Industrial' was more related to an aesthetic of violence (images and references to genocide, murders, etc.) than [it was] to machines. The sex and violence discourse of Whitehouse, for example (so 'catchy' for many people), is absolutely uninteresting for me, whereas I always have found their sound work extremely appealing (and a true overlooked landmark in the experimental underground).[26]

No discussion of Whitehouse's influence could be complete by excising their sound from their thematic interests, though, and it is precisely this subject matter which has led to the inexhaustible hostilities aimed at the band, and their (only recently lifted) blackout on openly discussing their ideas on the air and in other public forums. Whitehouse texts have become something of a litmus test to see if one really adheres to the accommodating, "anything goes!" philosophy of the art world or not: they have been revered as holy writ by the type of genuine outcasts who hound imprisoned serial killers for correspondence and autographs, and in fact the Whitehouse albums of the '80s constitute some of the first ever items of serial killer memorabilia. In Whitehouse, prolific slayers and sadists like Dennis Nilsen, Peter Kürten, and Gilles des Rais all have their first-ever commercially released songs devoted to them, to say nothing of porn luminaries like Chuck Traynor (the band's *Great White Death* LP is largely inspired by *Deep Throat* actress Linda Lovelace's confessional biography *Ordeal*, based on her degradation at the hands of co-star Traynor.)

It was, in fact, Whitehouse's interest in human sexuality that set them apart from much of the Industrial and post-Industrial milieux, many of whom were quite contented with thorough examinations of overwhelming violence and despair, yet made uncomfortable by any mention whatsoever of carnal affairs. Electronic music practicioner-theorist Terre Thaemlitz, in the midst of an otherwise patronizing critique, nevertheless correctly identifies the situation at hand as they apply to the cutting edge of "electronica": "[it has] taken us into the bedroom studios of everyone and their father...and what sexless, empty bedrooms they tend to be."[27] Bennett, in his weblog, goes after this one-sided thematic approach as follows:

> It's noticeable that the legions of noise copycats are far more comfortable with murder and destruction, or just general total abstractness, than they are with filthy, explicit, juicy sex. It still amazes me now that, as a band within any genre, we seem to almost have an unchallenged monopoly on the use of the word 'cunt'. Well, the men don't know but the little girls do indeed understand.[28]

The reactions towards Whitehouse's flagrant sexuality shore up much of the latent, sex-related skittishness within modern 'progressive' cultures, though this is nothing new. Musical contemporaries such as the homosexual membership of Coil were laughably assumed to be "misogynist" for releasing records aimed at stimulating "male sexual energy," and even viewed with some suspicion for the incompatibility of their aggressive esotericism with an "official" gay culture. In a similar botched attempt to 'read between the lines,' Whitehouse were seen as lending their endorsement to cruel and abusive sex practices when they combined gender-neutral concepts in titles like 'Coitus', 'Total Sex', and 'On Top' with the lashing harshness of their music. Ironically, through this same juxtaposition of elements, the would-be titillating quality of the truly sinister entries in Whitehouse's catalog (see 'Rapemaster,' 'Tit Pulp' and 'Bloodfucking') is blunted somewhat: for most listeners, the Whitehouse sound is simply too alien to fit comfortably into any musical vocabulary of seduction and sexiness. Bennett's inimitable electro-shock vocals, for one, have little in common with the smooth whispered intimacy or pleading ululation of sexual 'come ons', and the instrumentation is as far removed as possible from the repetitive 4/4 pulse that is widely seen as being a simulation of coital rhythm.

The musical content, by standing outside comfortable carnal points of reference, hardly seems to lend any credence to the activities mentioned in the songs, nor do the songs feature the narrative elements that would identify them as "simulations" or documentary dramas. Combined with the sexual imperatives of Whitehouse's minimal lyric sheets (most 1980s Whitehouse pieces consist of about 5-6 lines of text) all this becomes something of a sonic 'double bind'- the more a listener consciously *tries* to become sexualized by an unfamiliar and unrepentantly vicious sound, the more he/she reveals the lack of desire to do something that must come naturally. The music is more complex than a quick scanning of lyrics will let on, and – like certain of Peter Sotos' writings - is something more than just an uncritical salute to those dominating individuals who leave a trail of broken victims in their wake. The disapproval hurled at Whitehouse for their supposed lionization of sexual predators, murderers etc. is, again, more appropriately directed at their sheepish imitators- and shows some inability on reviewers' part to separate propaganda from commentary. William Bennett clarifies his stance on the predator-victim dynamic in a 2004 interview by Johan Birgande on London's Resonance FM:

> *Birgande:* A major theme on the [*Cruise*] LP seems to be the world of women's magazines and obsessions with health and food. Is this album in any way a critique of that outlook? What [unintelligible] are you actually expressing that from? It's a very dark recording, isn't it?

> *Bennett:* A lot of bands that have tried to imitate Whitehouse, they focus on this very authoritarian element of this 'sadist', you know, this archetype sadist- but I think they're completely missing the point, because really all Whitehouse is about - and again, people might be surprised to hear this - is that it wouldn't work if there wasn't an incredible sensitivity to the people - in this case - suffering, and understanding them at their level. The understanding *is* at their level, it's not at the level of the person dishing out the punishment, or the treatment,

or...whatever. That's why it's so powerful, and that's why it can touch people- so...in this sense, I wouldn't call it a critique of the outlook, but it's exploring those vulnerabilities and those sensitivities to an extent where I think you can actually feel that, you can feel uncomfortable.[29]

This suggestion of empathy on Bennett's behalf - though it will almost definitely be dismissed out of hand by those predisposed to hate them - does seem borne out by some of th hitherto unmentioned literary influences upon the group. Rather than turning to someone like Simone de Beauvoir, who saw "[The Marquis de Sade] as an early anarchist, a precursor of Nietzsche and a martyr to libertarianism,"[30] it is Andrea Dworkin who is paradoxically endorsed by the group[31] as a compelling object of study (Dworkin, by contrast, blasted Sade as a writer in whom "the authentic equation is revealed: the power of the pornographer is the power of the rapist batterer is the power of the man."[32]) Though it is unwise to bind together the very different career trajectories of Sotos and Bennett, there seems to be a common admiration here for the furious extremity and complexity of Dworkinite writings. Her kinship to Sotos' pornography critiques is particularly strong in its suspicion of individuals who frame sexual self-degradation as "exploratory sexuality."

Peter Sotos, writing in his *Parasite* journal, also comes to the conclusion that Whitehouse's bluntest transgressions are in the imagination of the listener, rather than the stated intent of the creators:

> Whitehouse don't seek to comment on the need for an 'alternative,' just as they don't seek to comment on entertainment, or sadism, or man's inhumanity or hypocrisy, or sexual mores, morals or meanings. That erudite concerns and statements can be extracted from their work is in the motivations (however justified) of their fans. Whitehouse's concerns are their understanding of their tastes. And the band stands alone in their ability to apply these tastes without exploiting or mimicking them. Whitehouse remain as pure as their impulses. But their history and their reputation seems to be fostered largely by those who misunderstand it.

Yet, for a decent slice of the music press, none of these explanations have been particularly satisfactory. Whitehouse's music has been interpreted as a flat-out endorsement of violent compulsion, and has mobilized reviewers like John Gill to come to the rescue- writing a review for *Time Out* of the *Great White Death* LP (which is reproduced in the liner notes to that album's 1997 CD reissue), he seethes that "their output puts the lie to the 'ignore them and they'll go away theory', and I want to stop them. One individual tainted by their ideas is one far too many."[33]

For every John Gill, though, there is a counterweight, and maybe another listener whose opinions fall in some grey area between the extremes of repulsion and adoration- this diversity in reactions was, at one point, the stated objective of Whitehouse: *"the listeners of these records will always enjoy the most intense reactions of all, because they are the most repulsive records ever made"*. With this sentiment in mind, few people working in sound art hope for, let alone *advocate* outright polarization of their audience as Whitehouse does. Press releases for new Whitehouse releases often warn longtime supporters in advance of stylistic deviations, and most CDs on the band's post-Come Organisation record label, Susan Lawly, come printed with a stentorian inversion of the "play at maximum volume" disclaimer: *"warning: extreme electronic music- acquire with due caution"* (negative reviews like John Gill's are also included in the artwork for some albums, as a final warning and/or enticement to prospective listeners.) Indeed, William Bennett, as an interview subject, comes across to the uninformed as something of an anti-publicist for his own work, frankly stating that many people just will not have the ability to appreciate it. Yet he doesn't discourage adversity, stating that

> Polarization is desirable because it's more likely to make people reveal their true selves; it reveals more of their truth even if it says little about the work in question. While for some this is a wholly positive experience, for others it exposes the enemy in the mirror.[34]

Screams in Favor of De Sade

Since Whitehouse eludes most of the familiar musical points of reference, and their founder claims to find much music 'enjoyable, but not inspiring,' it's better to look for their roots in the literary realm: especially within the more scathing forms of socio-political satire, and written musings on the depths of human obsession and interpersonal manipulation. The aforementioned Marquis de Sade is the obvious starting point for understanding Whitehouse's breaches of lyrical 'no-go zones': a younger William Bennett saw a great many of his ideas fleshed out in the Grove Press translations of Sade, with their almost laughably exaggerated scenes of orgiastic sex and sacrificial violence, and their underlying premise that man is merely a more highly evolved animal with no real moral advantage over the rest of nature. From *Justine:* "No, there is no god,

Nature sufficeth unto herself; in no wise hath she need of an author."[35] Curiously for critics of Whitehouse's (and de Sade's) alleged misogyny, the latter was an author whose heroines, such as the imposing Madame de Clairwil, often tower over passive males in an atomization of the conflict between nature and supposedly 'superior' man- and while the lust-fueled transgressions committed by these women have little documented parallel in reality, literary critic Camille Paglia suggests that de Sade has built them up for another reason, i.e. "Sade has spectacularly enlarged the female character. The barbarism of Madame de Clairwil, orgasmically rending her victims limb from limb, is the sign of her greater *conceptual* power."[36]

20th-century admirers of de Sade, like the French philosopher, ethnographer and excommunicated Surrealist Georges Bataille, also figure into the Whitehouse pantheon. As for those books penned during Bennett's lifetime, Whitehouse's music sits comfortably alongside such works as Bret Easton Ellis' 1991 psycho-thriller *American Psycho,* his acidic satirical drama which binds together the twin 1980s obsessions of serial killing and vain, conspicuous yuppie consumption (those familiar with the novel's minutiae will notice it being referenced in Whitehouse tracks like "Now Is The Time" and "Asking For It"). The monomaniacal drive towards extremity of Ellis' anti-hero Patrick Bateman makes him an interesting character to interrogate lyrically, especially considering how his seemingly 'conflicting' obsessions in fact stem from the same source. As per Ruth Heyler, "commodity culture's pressure to stay in shape physically has become entwined in his feelings of tension regarding his sexuality and urge to kill. Nothing ever seems extreme enough, his excesses simply grow."[37]

J.G. Ballard's *Crash* and *The Atrocity Exhibition* are other possible influences, also for their exploratory quality in regards to obsession. Yet while almost nobody would confuse the above authors with the characters in their works, myriad elements of the listening public have assumed that Whitehouse are inseparable from their songs- that they truly aspire to be the heirs apparent to the bloody-minded legacy of Caligula and Nero, despite the very limited resources necessary to do this. William Bennett is not blind to this preconception, having occasionally launched Whitehouse performances with a 'thumbs up' salute and march inspired by Malcolm McDowell's film portrayal of the demented emperor Caligula (Current 93 frontman David Tibet, an occasional collaborator of the band, has also hailed Bennett as "an expert on Roman decadence.") However, the black humor of Bennett's Caligula poses, and indeed most of Whitehouse's lyrical content (to say nothing of their deliberately misleading and misinforming the gullible music press) are completely lost on a music audience which is used to having every aspect of their music rigorously dictated to them (note the shouts of *"why don't you stand up for what you believe in!"* on the vintage Whitehouse track 'Rock 'n Roll' - which bitingly parodies the inter-song banter bleated out by Kiss frontman Paul Stanley at live concerts.)

Stewart Home, author of *The Assault on Culture,* and perpetrator of numerous conceptual "Neoist" art pranks, seems like a natural enemy of Whitehouse given his somewhat utopian leanings, and indeed he is. With the 'violent sex' outrage perhaps covered too well by journalists like John Gill, Home instead goes after them because

> Whitehouse commodify terror and mass murder as an entertaining spectacle, and the consumption of this as 'art' mimics the fascist obliteration of private space. This tendency is manifested most obviously on the Whitehouse album *New Britain,* which features the tracks 'Movement 1982', 'Roman Strength', 'Will To Power', 'New Britain', 'Ravensbruck', 'Kriegserklarung', 'Viking Section' and 'Active Force'.[38]

Admittedly the alarmism and knee-jerk Situationist critique is disappointing coming from someone like Home, who seems to have a thorough knowledge of art's use in creating elaborate hoaxes, and its function of forcing Bennett's "enemy in the mirror" to reveal itself through self-righteous expression of moral outrage. Home's critique would have some weight to it, were it not for his own past dalliances in right-wing literature, but also for the fact that *New Britain* is an album packaged (like the similarly controversial *Buchenwald* LP) in a totally unadorned sleeve, with no published lyrics, nor anything even approaching the polemical in the musical content. Bennett's vocals throughout the 1982 release are disorienting, indecipherable shrieks modulated with numerous effects, audio Rorschach blots unlikely to stir the patriotic and nationalist sentiments common to garden-variety fascists. By the logic Home applies to this record - that song titles are necessarily a microcosm of one's ideology - should a listener to 'Mars, Bringer of War' from Holst's *Planets* suite interpret this as an encouragement to make war rather than as a representative or symbolic portrayal?

Within this context, it is also interesting to compare the Home's comments on these LPs with the assumed intentions of Maurizio Bianchi's [a.k.a. MB] 1981 LP Symphony For a Genocide, originally released by Nigel Ayers' Sterile Records and re-released by numerous parties, including the label of the Basque anti-fascist Mattin. Though, again, it is a sonically vague and non-didactic recording on the surface, Ayers (incidentally, a colleague of Home's) claims that "from early correspondence with Maurizio, I took *Symphony For a Genocide* as intended as a metaphor referring to the Auschwitz Orchestra playing for their lives, and as sympathetic to the victims of Nazism."[39] It is odd that, without this personal correspondence available to us, we are meant to take both the 'fascism' of *Buchenwald / New Britain* and the 'anti-fascism' of *Symphony For a Genocide* as givens. Further digging into this subject reveals that local 'scene' rivalries have much to do with the campaign to determine which artists' efforts are ethically sound.

If the fear here was of Whitehouse gaining 'converts' and becoming an agitational force aligned with the New Right, a quick survey of Whitehouse interviews over the years shows that winning converts is the last thing on their minds, a stance that again takes us back to their formative influences. As Bataille says of Sade, "His characters do not speak to man in general, as literature does even in the apparent discretion of the private journal. If they speak at all, it is to someone of their own kind."[40] Bataille is also careful to note that de Sade wrote one of his most incendiary works from a lowly victim position: his excessive *120 Nights of Sodom*, though it has a wealthy, aristocratic quartet of fiends at the center of its erotic atrocities, was written by a victim of overzealous state prosecution (De Sade was held under lock and key after narrowly escaping the death sentence for sodomy.) Bataille suggests that the character of that particular manuscript came from de Sade's desire to judge those who had meted out the harsh punishment for this trivial crime, and to "[sit] in judgement on the man who condemned him, upon God, and generally upon the limits set to ardent sensuality."[41] This theory is enforced by de Beauvoir's research on the subject, as she also cites the vengeful letter written to his wife from prison ("I'll wager you imagined you were working wonders in reducing me to agonising abstinence from the sins of the flesh. Well! [...] you've made me create phantoms which I must bring to life."[42])

Sade, writing the bulk of his influential work in this condition, could not have honestly believed that his fantasies would come true in his own lifetime. In the same way, the accusations that Whitehouse wanted to use their music as a sort of recruiting tool to attain fascistic power must be treated skeptically, as is the accusation that they may have been actual initiators of 'ultraviolence' in their free time. One has to wonder how deliriously stupid a criminal, in any frame of mind, would have to be in order to telegraph his desires for pathological behavior in such a visible profession. Only recently, within certain enclaves of the 'gangsta' rap genre and the Black Metal underground, have recording artists been able to use a genuine life of crime as a P.R. boost for their careers as entertainers. Otherwise, the number of historical precedents for the 'killer entertainer' archetype is slim. Shoko Asahara and Charles Manson, to wit, were both cult leaders whose ideologies influenced highly publicized murders, and they were self-styled musicians as well- yet their music contains no overt references to their planned actions[43], or celebrations of the same.

The Second Coming

The 1990s, defined by a desperate and flailing need to provide closure on every touchy issue of the foregoing century, were almost guaranteed to spawn a sideshow industry of theatrical extremism as a caricature of those issues. The American daytime talk show circuit became one such release valve for those helpless to explain or adapt to the pre-millenial spasms of genocide, technological instability (the 'Y2K bug'), the ongoing decline in work ethic and 'value for money', *ad nauseam.* Just the first few years of the decade alone provide a whole cornucopia of lurid examples: on TV staples like *The Jerry Springer Show* and *Geraldo,* America's raging id was trotted out before it in the guise of 'shock rock' mainstay G.G. Allin, who appeared on stage clad in jockstrap, crudely etched prison tattoos and *Wehrmacht* helmet to hurl all the anticipated affronts at "the pigs" while boasting of raping female fans at his concerts and heaving his freshly deposited fecal matter at gaping onlookers as a holy "communion" (his body was, after all, the "rock-n-roll temple" in his estimation).

The eager nosedive of so-called 'trash TV' into the world of *panem et circenses* was only the most obvious exponent of all this: the world of underground print media was also rife with its pariahs of 'extreme' culture. Mike Diana, a Florida cartoonist and elementary school janitor known for his amateur comic *Boiled Angel,* was taken to court and placed on a 3-year probation in which he was banned from further cartooning. Diana's ghoulish depictions of sexual molestation and blood-soaked sacrilege may not have even registered a blip on the radar had one *Boiled Angel* not been discovered at the scene of a Floridian murder, but whatever the case, the unalloyed ugliness of his child molestation scenarios made him the temporary face of the cyclical 'freedom of expression' debate. Elsewhere, the lacerating, Portland-based 'zine scribe and satirist Jim Goad, in a misfired attempt to throw the self-congratulatory, disaffected edginess of his own readers back in their faces, published a 'rape'-themed issue of his journal *Answer Me!.* The cases of Diana and Goad, among other cases involving less artistically-inclined criminals, finally pushed the envelope to the point where America's aggressive moralists took up sexual abuse as their new *cause célèbre,* having so dramatically failed in their hunt for "Satanic covens" in the 1980s.

The California-based pornography industry, naturally, also responded to - and eventually epitomized - the 'provocative is better' media trend of the 1990s by inventing (or at least mainstreaming) whole new genres of product. These newer sub-genres were based less and less on goofy depictions of consensual love-making and more and more on sexual endurance tests with mobs of faceless, grunting males servicing a single 'actress', or showcases of freakishly huge (to the point of useless) genitalia, and decidedly un-sexy encounters with robotic 'fucking machines'. Meanwhile the industry, beyond the reach of the czars of political correctness, resurrected all the available ethnic and cultural stereotypes in order to give an extra shot of naughtiness to their program of titillation through degradation. All that remained, after exhausting every conceivable kink and fetish, was to attain digital market saturation via the Internet- a cakewalk if ever there was one. The 24-hour omnipresence of porn has only recently led to critical backlash, collective guilty 'soul-searching', and a parallel recovery industry aided by porn experts such as Luke Ford outing it as "fast food for the soul," and by author Pamela Paul writing well-intentioned but inconclusive jeremiads on the subject of porn addiction (e.g. *Pornified*). The fast food comparison was an apt one, anyway, since both the food service and porn industries, from the 1990s onward, habitually introduced new products that baited consumers with the word "extreme" as an enticement to buy.

As one-dimensional and prurient as 90s-style extremism may have been, though, too many of its emissaries confused its unique prurience for transformative power. Performers like G.G. Allin were an extension of the entertainment tradition of the carnival geek show, not the simultaneously horrific and introspective "abreaction plays" of the Viennese Aktionists. Both attendance at a G.G. Allin show or at a Hermann Nitsch aktion carried with it risks to one's physical or psychological well-being, and while both the participants in Nitsch's blood orgies and in Allin's scatological mayhem have claimed them to be epiphanies, it was Allin who reflected his era while the Aktionists transcended theirs. Allin's self-immolating antics merely reflected the very 1990s trend towards accepting any and all superlatives as worthy of attention, if not respect- at the very least, he elicited gasps betraying a sense of simultaneous disgust and awe.

With becoming the most outrageous performer ever (the "public animal #1") as his stated agenda, Allin limited himself to a situation where he would be defined solely by his interaction with a public, whereas the Aktionists often performed their art as a clandestine ritual, behind closed doors and with no corresponding documentation other than whispered hearsay or a few photographs. In this sense, Whitehouse is much closer in spirit to the Aktionists: both their *Right to Kill and Psychopathia Sexualis* LPs, after being pressed in near-private editions, have been refused re-issue on the grounds that being made available to a larger public would nullify their impact (a fact that has, maybe inevitably, led to the interminable bootlegging and digital file-sharing of these items.) And despite the occasionally charismatic stage presence of both Whitehouse and the Aktionist performers, both have down-played the relevance of their public personae as being secondary to the understanding of their art: both the direct intensity of a William Bennett scream and of a Günter Brus self-mutilation had a mediumistic quality to them, relinquishing power and even accepting a role as 'lightning rod' rather than imagining themselves as the centripetal force Allin must have thought himself to be. Whitehouse's entrance into the 1990s was - though certainly timely in this regard - more than just an attempt to capitalize on the growing acceptance of 'shock' techniques, or to make a bid for influential status in the new circus of excess- but their continued existence did illuminate the hollowness at the heart of the extremist gestures perpetuated by Generation X, and the inverse relationship between their empty embrace of shock tactics and a knowledge of what truly ignited humanity's more furious passions.

When Whitehouse resumed record-releasing activity in the 1990s, this time releasing their material under their Susan Lawly imprint, they joined forces with Chicago's highly articulate and highly irascible Steve Albini- a producer and independent music journalist known throughout Chicago just as much for his willful belligerence as for the superb quality of his studio recordings, and particularly for his encyclopedic knowledge of microphone techniques. Press updates of Albini's musical activities virtually always contained some variation on the begrudging sentiment "love him or hate him, he gets the job done", along with acknowledgements that he never aborted any of his promises, despite his apparent bottomless cynicism.

Despite Albini's firm grounding in the rock world, the two had overlapping interests that shouldn't be ignored. During his tenure as the frontman of the scathing post-punk combo Big Black, Albini's subject matter for songs could be every bit as difficult as those guiding Whitehouse's songs- perhaps not as terse and with much more of a narrative element, but still not at all recommended for the willfully oblivious. Like Whitehouse, Big Black commits the grievous sin of stripping the fantasy element from stylized "darkness": take as an example "Jordan, Minnesota" off Big Black's *Atomizer* LP, which could almost qualify as a rock revision of certain Whitehouse numbers. If you were to excerpt just the last, rhythm-free 90 seconds or so of "Jordan..." the parallels would become even more clear: the stinging, quivering guitar feedback drawn out over an extended period, the distressed vocals that sound eerily like a desperate plea and a spat order at once. This is to say nothing of *Atomizer's* lyrical strip-mining of all possible forms of social decay: topics such as post-traumatic stress and the sexual thrill of arson all become grist for Steve Albini's topical mill, making one wonder why *Atomizer* and its companion pieces never met with quite the same indignant protests as Whitehouse's releases. The liner notes to this album include, among the self-effacing notes about malfunctioning equipment and the string of obscure in-jokes, an Albini-penned statement that sounds like a Stateside approximation of Bennett: *"Our interests in death, force and domination can change the way we think. Make us seek out new forms of 'entertainment.' Ever been in a slaughterhouse?"* One last parallel worth noting: both Big Black and the Come Organization-era Whitehouse dissolved at a time when they felt they were at their creative peak, and had reached some satisfactory level of completion.

With Albini fine-tuning the band's sound, Whitehouse embarked on a far more idiosyncratic creative phase than before. The enveloping intimacy that is Albini's trademark makes some of the mid-90s pieces exude a sense of genuine claustrophobia: the small room sound of the album centerpiece "Quality Time," for example, highlighting the sparse electrical crackles and the spastic, wounded nature of Bennett's vocal, is profoundly uncomfortable, almost cinematic in its evocative ability- the impatience, frustration and burning need of the track's narrator is a world away from easy portrayals of invincible libertines churned out by the bands generated in Whitehouse's wake.

Elsewhere, the epic length (12 minute) "Halogen" features a lush introduction by way of interlacing feedback 'solos,' low-volume snatches of confectionery Thai pop music buried beneath a rolling noise tumult, unexpected interjections of silence, and a hyper-animated William Bennett shrieking lyrics that are direct and unsettling even without clearly discernible meaning. The voice anchoring these pieces is one that may itself be vulnerable to forces beyond its understanding, simultaneously victimizer and victimized. At least, without any obvious references as to the track's inspiration, this is one conclusion we can reach. This kind of perceptual ambiguity is what, once and for all, demarcates the boundaries between Whitehouse and the other musical shock merchants so typical of the era. That the aforementioned recordings of Whitehouse come packaged in stereotypically 'cute', airbrushed doll artwork by Trevor Brown only heightens the inability of critics or casual music consumers to "pin down" the intent of these songs.

Whitehouse circa the mid-late 1990s was an outfit that truly has absorbed the major lessons of the avant-garde without having ever been absorbed by the avant-garde establishment in turn- but this, too, would change over time (one portent of the band's arrival in this territory is a page at the prestigious *UbuWeb*, topped with a graphic of Bennett's muse Yoko Ono, that offers the 1984 Whitehouse LP *Dedicated to Peter Kürten* for download.)[44]

Animal Response Technicians

The 21st century incarnation of Whitehouse was not only an anomaly in the world of noise and power electronics, but in much of the sound art world, period. Their newer, heavily digitized sound provided an object lesson in dynamic tension, keeping pace with the mind-warping computer chaos of the Mego and Fals.ch rosters (though accompanied by the expected cries of "Judas!" from the analog purists.) The sharp, ceaseless harangues of the William Bennett / Philip Best vocal duo defied the listener to fixate attention on anything other than their hectoring voices: the 1980s lyrics of the band are mere thumbnail sketches compared to these lengthy, oddly worded analysand's assessments. To this end, the 'new' Whitehouse benefited from incorporating the techniques of linguistic pseudo-sciences such as Scientology auditing and neuro-linguistic programming (NLP) into the mix, with vague hints of *est*[45] in Bennett's demand for the listener to "Get It!" (from "Dyad," on the 2007 CD *Racket*.) The new lyrical approach seemed geared, as such, to reassessing the ability of each individual word to severely alter listeners' emotional states and subsequent behavioral patterns.

NLP, in particular, is an esoteric subject that has gone surprisingly unnoticed by a post-Industrial music milieu otherwise interested in the politics and poetics of language being used as a tool of influence. The practice has roots in the thought of radical thinkers like Gregory Bateson and Noam Chomsky, and the enthusiasm with which the often adversarial forces of advertising / marketing have greeted NLP, compared with the frosty reception of typically libertarian skeptics towards its non-verifiable claims, is a discussion-worthy subject of its own. An editorial in *The Journal of Marketing Communications*, for example, notes that NLP founders "[Richard] Bandler and [John] Grinder concurred that human beings create representations of the world in which they live through internal coding via their sensory representational systems. Therefore, a consideration of these modalities is not only highly relevant for advertisers, but of significant importance."[46] *Total Quality Management & Business Excellence* chimes in as well, boasting "there are exciting times ahead for practicing NLP in organizations."[47]

Academia has kept its distance from the subject, though. The few academics to treat NLP are not remiss in wondering why NLP's "controversy" regarding "a certain reputation as a 'manipulative' approach" does not "make it more, rather than less, attractive to research attention."[48] Again, the practice's partial origins in Ericksonian hypnotherapy are at fault, though the loss of academia is the gain of the performing artists under discussion here (Bennett has professed a keen interest in stage hypnosis.) Some of the NLP-derived word games within the lyrics of Whitehouse's later records include intentional grammatical errors (referring to listeners as "*the* you") and overloading conscious attention with imagery too obscure to process: mentions of "the chlorine gargoyle," "the chickenskin swim," or "the Alice pill you snatch from the blind evolutionary drift" all stand out as phrases in need of 'Googling' to be clarified somehwat. By the logic of NLP, the alluring ambiguity of such verbal play 'frees' the unconscious as the conscious mind is busy decoding and trying to personalize the more puzzling references.

Another noteworthy point is that NLP operates on a rather optimistic premise, i.e. *"there is no failure...only feedback,"*[49] suggesting that the meaning of any communication is the response generated by it, not the intial content of the communication itself. This is a striking parallel to what William Bennett has been saying throughout the years about his audiences' reactions 'completing' the band's artwork: "art has the capacity for any reaction," he claims, "and unlike the 'real world', isn't constricted to achieving certain specific responses."[50]

However, the therapeutic, nurturing, "no wrong answer" nature of NLP is not the only usage that Whitehouse explores. Rather, the kinship with 'magical' thinking and hypnosis (and the fact that NLP operates under no professional code of ethics) is highlighted in the monologues of dirge-like Whitehouse songs like "Philosophy"; which utilizes a particularly sadistic NLP 'pattern' aimed at reducing a lover to a state of complete, hopeless dependency. Other tracks, like "Dumping The Fucking Rubbish" (appearing on the *Asceticists 2006* CD and reprised on the following year's *Racket*), are based on the method of Scientology auditing, firing off a fusillade of highly personal questions at a patient: *"is sex boring to your body? Is sex degrading to your body? Does some body withhold sex from you? Invalidate you sexually?"* etc. Delivered in Philip Best's lucid and disgusted bark, rather than in the languid tones of an apparently sympathetic auditor, these inquiries are revealed as having a potential beyond that of merely "clearing" patients (condescendingly referred to as "pre-clears") of their deeply-ingrained complexes: namely, that of entertaining the questioner at the patient's expense.

In what philosopher John Gray refers to as the 'entertainment economy' of the 21st century's affluent nations, the role of auditors and other pseudo-psychiatric professions will come to the fore in order to stave off the numbing feelings of lifestyle dissatisfaction and *affluenza*. As he theorizes, with the increased demand for professionals to eradicate the anxiety exclusive to this age, there will likely be an increase in more unsavory personalities entering the field: the newer material of Whitehouse offers a striking and frightening view of what can be expected from such emotional wreckers, psychiatric charlatans and self-styled 'gurus': just as Peter Sotos' writings exposed mass media's sham sympathy for (and secondary wounding of) the archetypal victim, the contemporary Whitehouse recordings seem to suggest the potential for various therapeutic techniques to reinforce the common master-slave dichotomy. Then again, the ringing intensity of the sound and the merciless interrogative style of the vocals could be the means with which to carry out an unorthodox kind of abreactive therapy- shocking patients into a more desirable existence.

Meanwhile, all of this experimentation with complicated, multi-threaded linguistic data has not diluted Bennett's interest in the transformative nature of simple profanity. Very much a 'renaissance man' of swearing, a lingering, clenched-teeth *'cunt'* or *'fuck'* in Bennett's hands assumes a potency that it hasn't had in years of terminally dumbed-down culture, in which the latter word is used to fill virtually every grammatical function. Bennett suggests that

> There's a real art to being a good swearer. It's a tightly nuanced balance between timing, the unexpected, intonation, and a special intent that betrays a subtext ranging from mischief, to hard sincerity, to anger, to seduction, or perhaps to irony. And above all, I feel it's important that there's a comforting sense of you being given permission not only to say 'fuck' or 'cunt' back, but also to engage in actions that might otherwise not be appropriate.[51]

It is a curious world that Whitehouse inhabits: one in which an innocuous phrase like "do you see that door over there" becomes an emotionally crippling NLP pattern, while well-placed vulgarities are used to liberate. Yet it is a world that is, more and more, very close to the actual truth of reality.

New Asceticism

> One of the best things that ever happened to me was getting burgled, it happens to people all the time, it's a miserable fucking experience, you just want to kill the people. They took everything I had, absolutely everything, video equipment, records, the whole collection, stereo, the whole lot. That was the best thing that ever happened to me because suddenly I realised that - and I don't want to sound too spiritual or religious, it's nothing to do with that - I was no longer tied down by my possessions. I thought I can now do whatever I want. The month before, we'd done a concert in Barcelona and had such a great time. Fuck it. I'm going to move to Barcelona. OK, I've got no money, no possessions or anything, but I'm just going to

get on the next plane and go to Barcelona. Which is exactly what I did. And it was the best thing that ever happened to me.[52]

-William Bennett

"Minimalism" is an idiom generally associated with conceptual maturity within the art world, but has decidedly more negative connotations in consumer parlance, especially as regards music. People conditioned to life in today's information-saturated, hyper-materialistic (yet nonetheless recession-prone) societies can harbor severe anxiety over seeing some product or service not used in the most economical way possible. So, calling a CD release 'minimalist' often implies that people are not getting what they truly deserve from the music, and that the artists themselves are carelessly squandering a golden opportunity at making a definitive statement- with so many billions of people wishing for just one chance to immortalize their ideas and opinions within a well-marketed physical product, an act like leaving one-minute silences between the songs on a vinyl LP is seen as some type of artistic dereliction of duty (said act was a staple of the earlier Come Organization Whitehouse records.) Along these lines, listeners have complained of paying for full length Whitehouse CDs (at import prices, no less) which contain less than 40 minutes of music, when twice that amount is possible. It is a grievance similar to criticizing a painter for leaving blank patches of canvas in a painting, or worse yet, relegating musicians to the role of urban planners who must make every nook and cranny of a lived environment conform to a specific functionality. This shows a woeful misunderstanding of not only music, but of art in general, which has historically used 'negative space' to provide contrast between compositional elements, or to allow the full absorption of one idea before moving onto the next.

Hungering for an inexhaustible all-you-can-eat buffet of all possible sounds betrays a childish desire to be pandered to, and artists who do this pandering can lessen their relevance dramatically, if not careful. 'Breakcore' producers such as Kid 606 and Venetian Snares, who both admire Whitehouse's unflinching intensity and align themselves with Whitehouse associates like Trevor Brown, are capable of dazzling audio fireworks and entertaining bouts of beat-driven fury- but in the end it becomes difficult to ascribe anything buy a self-referential meaning to their virtuosic displays. In the worst scenarios the music eventually becomes, like a caffeine-based drink that also dehydrates the body, more fatiguing than energizing.

Commercial music since the 1970s has seen an increasing number of electrified virtuosi 'fill' sonic space with as many possible notes per second- digital beat music often just replaces the flurry of notes with a mashed-up flurry of more generalized 'sound events' (distorted rhythms, movie dialogue samples, spasmodically shifting synthesizer patterns). Track and album titles brim with in-joke references to the equipment used to make the records, as well as with sarcastic references to the pop culture also heavily sampled in order to make the final product. Whether this is a comment, like Throbbing Gristle's more overloaded pieces, on the 'culture of congestion', or just a matter of hobbyists dabbling with a potpourri of electronic musical forms, is debatable (although personally I suspect this music is symptomatic of the 'culture of congestion' rather than a criticism of it- and the producers of this music look like they quite enjoy blasting it from PA systems all over the world.) One thing that is clear, though, is that it is the polar opposite of Whitehouse's approach: one in which willful denial of expectations, rather than fulfillment of them, leads to greater rewards. With this approach comes a dismissal of the technophilia hard-wired into "extreme electronic" forms like breakcore. As Bennett says:

> I'm only interested in results. It's not about equipment or technology, it's about music, and its success will be measured by how people emotionally respond to it, now and tomorrow. Since we anyway obsessively and self-consciously work outside the established musical traditions and templates, we can easily and effortlessly transcend any raging contemporary music technology debate.[53]

Elaborating on this statement somewhat, Bennett references a 2010 *Wire* editorial promoting the Ableton Live music software suite, dismissing "the effusive praise implied that the software is granting some kind of newfound creative freedom, if not independence, to its users...the same arguments could have been, and indeed were, applied to the invention of the mechanical piano; that which enslaves us was once promised to set us free."[54]

Feeling perhaps that associations with minimalism carry too much baggage with them, Bennett has proposed 'asceticist' as a better qualifier for his sound: in his estimation, this word refers to a conscious, disciplined stripping away of talents that one can otherwise capably utilize, in order to reduce an experience - of listening, performing, etc.- to only its most essential components. In a way, this has always been a component of Bennett's approach, given the abrupt leap from tonal, guitar-based music to the more textural electronic style, and now to the dominantly percussive style of his Cut Hands project.

The 'minimalist' designation also seems to smell a bit too much of what Henry Flynt (who was ironically responsible for much of this culture, due to his associations with Tony Conrad and LaMonte Young) derided as 'serious culture'. In short, this was a Euro-centric, academic compositional style placing too much emphasis on the importance of handing down precepts from master to pupil, rather than on the nurturing personal, revelatory examination. Bennett's asceticism is more vivid, and pan-cultural in a refreshingly un-patronizing way: the final (to date) Whitehouse releases *Racket* and *Asceticists 2006* are loaded with rattling, tactile samples of West African percussive instrumentation (e.g. djembes, ksings, doundouns) employed in such a way as to perfectly integrate with the 'lead instruments' of voice, spiky computerized feedback and queasy time-stretched abstractions. The resulting hybrid form of 'Afro Noise' has since turned into a personalized transfer of energy from traditional sources, though Bennett cautions against placing it within any sort of 'world music' context: "I always tend to work, on a conscious level at least, within my own microcosm - if the semantic difference can even be made, [the music] is 'Afro' rather than 'African', because I'm certainly not claiming to be respecting any specific cultural traditions, yet am exclusively employing instruments from that part of the world (mostly Ghanaian actually); beyond that with regards to electronic implementation, I've applied a few strict rules (e.g. no use of loops.)"[55]

It should be clarified that the religious association with 'asceticism' - of withdrawing from the worldly to contemplate the divine in solitude - is not the one proposed by the essentially atheistic Bennett. At the same time, Bennett is not exactly a Diogenes figure - that enigmatic Greek philosopher so often associated with asceticism. He harbors no illusions that he can improve mankind morally, though there are other similarities with the Cynic philosopher, such as a cosmopolitan sensibility and enjoyment of quality enabled by reduced dependency on material goods. Criticism of humanity's valuing the institution over the individual is another trait shared by Bennett and the 'dog philosopher', and Bennett has been especially damning of those collectivist ideals that, though portraying themselves as secular, still carry with them the eschatological fervor of religion. From the medieval Brethren of the Free Spirit to the various strains of Marxism, the numerous utopian social movements over the ages have downplayed the issue of inextricability from nature while suggesting that new forms of technological progress (such as automation) would make human labor unnecessary. *Ergo*, there would eventually be a permanent state of play with no checks on human desire- we should easily be able to see where this attitude has resulted in unprecedented environmental devastation, while replicating the 'end time' / 'paradise on earth' fantasies of the supposedly discarded religions. The denial of the 'savior' complex - be it salvation by mechaincal automation, or the earthly incarnation of divinity - is at the epicenter of Bennett's asceticism, as is the exhilirating personal responsibility that this denial would entail.

Looking back on Whitehouse's whole body of work, it now seems more obvious that the shift into asceticism is not a recent 'awakening' on behalf of Bennett and his collaborators, but a thread which ran through their music all along, and has now beeclarified as part of a larger life strategy. Reduction to the non-ornamental essentials of a form is nothing new in the musical field - ask any Tuvan throat singer or Tibetan monk - but rarely has such music been used outside of a religious context, and in the service of brutally personal inquiry. Whitehouse's legacy is the creation of music appealing to *both* ascetics and libertines - who, united in their rejection of the assorted collective 'lowest common denominators', and their adoption of an almost unattainable higher standard, may have more in common than we think.

Re-Launching the Dream Weapon:
Considering Coil

Introduction: That Ole Post-Industrial Magic

The real art communicates before it is understood, it contains the knowledge that all men once had, a knowledge that today is unfortunately often ignored and forgotten. I believe that our life is magical in its essence. The working of magic is a series of actions bringing intention into focus. It's a conscious and active participation in transformation between cause and effect. We know that everything we've ever done and do is intentional, and every intentional act is a Magical act. Not understanding it means human life as a journey from nowhere to nowhere.

-Zbigniew Karkowski[1]

The distinction between musician and nonmusician-which separates the group from the speech of the sorceror-undoubtedly represents one of the very first divisions of labor, one of the very first social differentiations in the history of humanity, even predating the social hierarchy. Shaman, doctor, musician. He is one of society's first gazes upon itself, he is one of the first catalyzers of violence and myth.

-Jacques Attali[2]

The Bard's curse is supposed to be able to blight crops and bowl over crooked politicians. The Bard is not just another imagemonger: the Bard, the shaman-poet, wields power. When the Bard pays attention, even wild animals come 'round to snuff at the psychic overflow.
-Hakim Bey[3]

The post-industrial age, obsessed as it is with the narrative of exponentially unfolding technical progress (and the curious notion that this goes hand in hand with the ascent of ethical progress), seems to have a special allergy to the word "magic." Nowadays, "magical thinking" is mostly a pejorative term that connotes not a beneficial seduction or entrancement, but rather a kind of languid, unproductive daydreaming: a hope that good things will come to the dreamer from wishing alone, and with no additional effort made to attain these things (no classical hermetic art now referred to as magic has ever promoted this type of "magical thinking", but I digress.) Even when "magic" is utilized in a positive manner, it is now used in a way that de-fangs or domesticates it: surely we've all seen some television commercial or another in which a stereotypical homekeeper claims that the latest kitchen cleanser works *"like magic!"*

Meanwhile, in the loftier academic strongholds of philosophical and scientific inquiry, the term is either used in a cautiously complementary fashion, with a host of disclaimers or qualifiers, or used in an apologetic way when suddenly realizing how perilously close its *raison d'être* comes to the emancipatory aims of 'post-modern' or 'post-structuralist' theory. Take, for example, the cultural critic Brian Massumi, who, when compelled to define his use of the term "transcendental empiricism," gives us something of a 'parental advisory' warning before driving us any further: "Giordano Bruno had a word for something like an incorporeal materialism that is *even more troubling* [emphasis added]: magic."[4] Massumi then calms our fears by stating that "...the distance between Bruno and our modernity (or postmodernity) is narrowed by his definition of magic as the 'alloying of knowledge and the will to power to act'"[5], which in turn "authorizes a pragmatic understanding of magic."[6] Still, it leaves us wondering, what exactly *is* so troubling about magic?

Apparently, there's nothing very troubling about it if it is simply called by some other name. With just a casual bit of searching through the post-modern marketplace of ideas, we find a healthy amount of concepts synonymous with 'magic,' yet refusing to name that particular devil while playing his game. The Slovene philosopher Slavoj Žižek, for example, is often praised on the back jackets of his books as a "master of counter-intuitive thinking." More interestingly, the philosophers Gilles Deleuze and Félix Guattari, in their challenge to Freud (*Anti-Oedipus*), famously spoke of 'libidinal flows' or eroticized desires that did not bind themselves to specific bodily targets, yet seemed to permeate everything. This, despite its greater acceptance by academia, is not entirely dissimilar from the attitudes of someone like the magically-minded artist Austin Osman Spare[7], whose "...intention was pan-sexual, transcendental, and androgynous in that he claimed he was '...all sex.'"[8] One Deleuze acolyte, the theorist-practicioner artist Joseph Nechvatal, unearths further correspondences between Spare's trance-induced painting and the going concerns of 'post-structuralist' thinkers:

Spare's relevance here is to be found in his interests in the loss of subjectivity, as experienced in sexual transport and sexual fantasies, interests which now dovetail into our interests in the philosophical loss of sovereignty typical of the disembodied finesse when encountered in virtual space.[9]

At any rate, it is definitely not by accident that Spare's working methods found their way into the Industrial music counterculture - originally through the efforts of Genesis P. Orridge, but handled more gracefully by the late John Balance of Coil, who we will be introduced to in short order. As such, it was one of the first art movements of the late 20th century to view radically "anti-passive" use of then-new consumer electronics (read: "unintended" uses) as a way of achieving exactly what Giordano Bruno has outlined above. The musicians mentioned were, if nothing else, cognizant of the way that "libidinal flows" were manipulated, misrepresented, or outright monopolized by humanity's greedier representatives, and how re-capturing them was crucial to psychic wellbeing. The genius of these musicians was to realize how a society enraptured by technical progress was not immune to appeals to its irrationality, so long as those appeals came clothed in the comfortably 'rational' circuitry and wiring of the present day.

If magic really is just a 'will to power' as Bruno described it, then maybe the present toxicity of the term stems from a distrust or *ressentiment* of those who now wield it most effectively. And there can be no doubt that magico-religious principles have, even in the modern age, been used to cynically exploit masses of impressionable beings - whether that exploitation was done by means of infusing powerful archetypal symbols into rousing oratory, or into television programming. The special feature of many post-Industrial musicians, then, has been their acknowledgement that simply ceding this controlling power to exploitative authorities would gladden their hearts immensely, and that it was time to reclaim these tools for their own use.

Historical record also shows that, without those actions that went beyond mere need and utility, present civilization may not have even existed. Speaking on the infamous cave paintings at Lascaux, historian Lewis Mumford proposes that, if the art was "...only an incidental by-product of magic, did it not nevertheless exert a special magic of its own, which drew men back to the scene of this first triumphant expression?"[10] In other words, these uninhabited ritual centers became the germ of the modern city-based civilization: they were containers for the "social and religious impulses that conspired to draw men finally into cities, where all the original feelings of awe, reverence, pride, and joy would be further magnified by art, and multiplied by the number of responsive participants."[11] So, there we have it: acts of magic not seen as the enemy of technical innovation, but as the very spur of that innovation. The alchemists' futile search for the Philosopher's Stone may have never yielded the secret to immortality, yet in the process of badly aiming for the farthest star, they did lay some of the foundations for inorganic chemistry.

Form And Function

The Industrial music of post-Throbbing Gristle groups like Coil, among its other innovations, placed emphasis on making music that was completed by some active involvement on the listener's behalf. In the past I have described various post-Industrial music configurations as "functional music", out of pure journalistic convenience, but now I realize that this was far too vague a term. After all, being entertained, and passing time at one's workplace or during a dull commute without becoming agitated are the functions of pop music, as banal and utilitarian as they may be to the thinkers and dreamers toeing society's margins. So, more properly, "functional music" might be that which is (as per researcher Keith Jones) "evaluated primarily by [its]...capacity to impact upon worker output, rather than by its aesthetic or 'artistic' value."[12] Seen in this way, both the calculated peppiness of "music while you work" and the particularly esoteric or hermetic strain of post-Industrial music are "functional." However, they differ in that the former attempts to make mechanized routine more tolerable, and the latter attempts to make radical breaks with that routine.

So perhaps it's more accurate to divide the musical sphere into two 'active' and 'passive' hemispheres - or more accurately, *activating* and *pacifying* - rather than making functionality and aestheticism the criteria for division. On one hand there is 'active' music which requires the listener to complete its work through some heightened mental focus, or with a physical activity like shutting off all the lights in the room, re-positioning the speakers that the music is coming from, or maybe manipulating one record by hand as a second record plays by itself (to be sure, the vastly expanding world of dance music fits into the "activating" hemisphere as well.) That remainder of music that requires no input on the part of the listener, or a negligible amount of mental processing, could then be called pacifying, as in the case of the Muzak discussed in the first chapter.

The concept of pacifying music, or music for 'leisure listening' only, is a comparatively recent one when we go back to the pre-human roots of the song form: birdsong has always been used as a means of marking territory, or as a device for attracting mates. The success rate of these short musical phrases to make their point was very closely tied to a bird's survival, and the furthering of its species. Numerous ethnomusicologists also theorize that the first primitive, human song forms had a function of communicating with neighboring tribes. But even as the variety and amount of passive music has exploded since the dawn of sound recording, the functions of 'active' music have multiplied to the point where its best examples achieve an elegant, uncanny synchronization of the senses.

It was the functional and 'activating' turn of electronic music that endeared it to a nascent esoteric underground within the Occident, one whose aggregated rituals and symbolic actions seemed to aim at Deleuze & Guattari's "heterogenesis," or a process whereby the "othering" nature of chaos is acknowledged as the revitalizing force in an aesthetically and morally stagnant world. Varying degrees of sentience were attributed to this chaos by the underground culture, with some approaching it as a divinity to be invoked (some within the 'Chaos Magick' community even believed that the chaos gods populating H.P. Lovecraft's fictional universe were speaking through him unawares), and others seeing it as a Deleuzo-Guattarian 'plane of immanence.'

Accepting chaos as a benefactor was an act that, in theory, would seem to generate untold different strains of cultural behavior. However, one unfortunate consequence of this acceptance was the outright evangelizing of destructive forces as being those most representative of "chaos", or the uncritical acceptance that anything inverting the popular consensus on morality and ethics was a change for the better. So 'power electronics', free-form distortion, and unyielding death drive became valuable tools for many post-Industrial performers to clarify their outcast role in society. For many others associated with the Industrial genre, though, this was not enough - such exercises in unbridled extremity tended to shore up the parochial nature of the performers, and their susceptibility to sheer frustration, more often than not. As per Throbbing Gristle's Peter Christopherson, "it's only a culture with a long history of decadence and decay that has a need for music that strikes that particular chord. In Thailand, for example, people mainly like to have fun, so really only appreciate music that answers or assists in that need."[13]

Many of the artists associated with the esoteric wing of Industrial culture set out to become like the 'sorcerors' in Attali's above assertion or the 'Bards' of Hakim Bey, though not all managed to transcend their status as downtrodden, disgruntled citizens with an unorthodox way of articulating their grievances against modernity. And for what it's worth, many of these unorthodox techniques supposedly 'exclusive' to the new breed of dark electronics manipulators had already been employed by individuals worlds away from their (anti) social circles: Afro-futurist composer Sun Ra is a noteworthy example here, having incorporated cyclones of synthesizer violence into his work already in the mid-1960s, and having used sheet metal resonance (normally seen as the of hallmark of 'ritual Industrial' music) as a central feature of his 1965 album *Strange Strings*. Even the themes of eschatology, death, and stereotypically 'evil' iconography (see the *Fireside Chat With Lucifer* LP) were deeply woven into his music, albeit in a more generalized and less 'site-specific' way than in Industrial music.

Perhaps a greater dilemma concerning the esoteric Industrial music of the 1980s was the fact that many of its representatives *epitomized* the modernity they intended to diametrically oppose. Considering that many of these specimens were steeped in the transgressive *vamachara Tantra* or 'Left Hand Path' lore of Aleister Crowley - the Victorian age's "wickedest man in the world"- it is unsurprising that they would become late-20th century avatars, in this respect. As Hugh Urban writes, "Crowley is a remarkable reflection of the era in which he was born. On the one hand, he deliberately set out to overthrow all established values; on the other, he merely expressed the darker underside or 'secret life' of the Victorian world in which he was raised"[14] (the same could easily be said of Freud, Crowley's contemporary.) In this same way, much esoteric Industrial art was an aesthetic mutation of late 20th century concerns rather than its wholesale rejection. The "taboos" of self-realization that the 80s subculture flaunted with its "modern primitive" forms of tattooing and piercing could certainly shock (as the ludicrous Operation Spanner[15] attests to), yet the increasing materialism of this era suggests that theirs was a competing manifestation of indulgence - despite the underground's Crowleyan blasphemies against the Church, monastic self-denial was hardly the order of the day.

There were, of course, other formative influences on the scene besides Crowley - individuals who ignored the glamorous and self-aggrandizing elements of ceremonial pomp in order to concentrate more fully on the fundamentals of the creative ritual. In doing so, they may have lost the seductive power of the 'secret' (and were in fact more intent on the public exposition of secrets than upon finding the proper aspirants to entrust with them.) However, the works of these influences more elegantly achieved the esoteric-scientific symbiosis discussed earlier in this chapter.

Rubbing Out The Word

> ...and, as I point out, the montage method is much closer to the actual facts of perception than representational painting. So, that's it- life *is* a cut-up, every time you walk down the street or even look out the window, your consciousness is cut by random factors. And it was a

question of bringing that back into writing.[16]

-William Burroughs

While the 'war universe' of William Burroughs may have provided Industrial culture with much of its insurgent tactical apparatus, his luminary status could not have been accomplished without the aid of his long-time friend and associate, Brion Gysin- who in turn influenced the underground's embrace of alchemical process art, while bridging a gap between the European avant garde and the more loosely-defined of cast of characters evolving out of Industrial music. Sound artists as diverse as Throbbing Gristle, Carl Michael von Hausswolff, and the concrete poet Henri Chopin (who published Gysin's poetry in his magazine *Ou*) have adapted works or key concepts of Gysin's to suit their own needs. At the very least, Gysin deserves credit as the co-author, along with Burroughs, of the now omnipresent 'cut-up' writing techniques - with his declaration of 'poets don't own words', Gysin validated this new enterprise of forming magical narratives out of randomly chosen, de-assembled and then re-assembled texts.

It was an idea that was dismissed as "plumbing" by Samuel Beckett (when Burroughs relayed to him that he was fusing Beckett's texts with sliced excerpts of the *Herald Tribune*), looked upon with ambivalence by even staunch Burroughs supporters like Gregory Corso, and wasn't entirely without precedent in modern art (see Marcel Duchamp's exhibition of four separate texts placed within a square, or Tristan Tzara's Dada poem composed from paper scraps pulled out of a hat). It has also been argued that *all* writing is essentially "cut-up," given that all writing is a composite of diverse sources and mental images- and, with this in mind, skeptical minds could ask why it was necessary to engage in this activity another time. Gysin and Burroughs believed that having writers engage in this process on their own was remarkably different in its effects than merely accepting writing as another form of montage; that "the exposure to both the product and the process of this technique aims to remind the cutter-reader (because reading is also inevitably a process of cutting-up) that the word is not what it seems."[17] Or, as Nathan Moore suggests, the word "is not what it *is* [italics mine]"[18] - the words on a page were never anything but representations, and cutting them up was to deny them their 'secret' power of ordering the world. New "meaningless" recombinations of words could then be steered towards the pure affect or sensory impact that Gysin and Burroughs already felt existed within painting.

Though the written word was clearly the focus of the 'cut-up' technique, its ability to be at once critical, revelatory and transformational endeared it to a good deal of culture working with means other than textual or linguistic ones. The musical 'sampling virus' of artists such as John Oswald and Christian Marclay, for one, put the basic cut-up principle to devastating, often hilarious effect by stripping well-known musical quotations of their original context and re-configuring them to serve the artist's own ideological ends. The text cut-up was a necessary step towards using the products of broadcast media as just another 'musical' material, and reconfiguring them to have more of an affective power than a dictatorial one, or to focus on potentialities rather than inevitabilities and creation rather than communication. It was a fact already understood by Throbbing Gristle and eventually carried over into Coil by common member Peter Christopherson. Meanwhile, the basic theory of the cut-up also allowed for simple communications devices (shortwave radio, satellite TV feeds) to be re-interpreted, with a built-in degree of serendipity, as musical instruments when their informational feeds were modified by modern studio editing techniques.

Brion Gysin's appeal to the current crop of avant-garde musicians and sound artists lay in his natural, non-trained (yet not "dilettante"-ish) expressive ability, and also in his ability to distribute creativity across the entire artistic spectrum: to adopt an ecumenical anti-professionalism more suitable for personal questing, in which art and "normal" life both work towards the same ends of continual subjective transformation. Though never experimenting with music himself (outside of some recordings that feature his speaking voice complemented with musical instrumentation), Gysin was certainly well capable of expounding on the transcendental power of music, especially the tornadic musical frenzy he encountered in the Moroccan hill country of Jajouka. Yet his infatuation with it only served to fuel his other creative endeavors - concrete poetry, painting - rather than to divert energy from them. Put in Gysin's own words:

> ...ecstatic dancing to the secret brotherhoods is [in Morocco] a form of psychic hygiene. You know your music when you hear it one day. You fall into line and dance when you pay the piper...inevitably something of all this is evident in what I do in the arts I practice.[19]

Gysin was born in Buckinghamshire to Swiss parents in 1916, with his father dying in the battle of the Somme before he was one year of age. Numerous relocations would occur, taking him to New York, Kansas City, Edmonton, and finally back to England where he began publishing poetry at the highly-regarded Downside school (despite his studies there, Gysin taught himself painting and had no formal training in the arts.) His early status as a child without a country perhaps informed the de-centralizing nature of his life work, and would encourage him to become involved with the Surrealist group in the 1930s. After the war, and after garnering a

Fulbright fellowship for his studies on the history of slavery, Gysin eventually settled in Tangier and became a restaurateur- spending one of the most fruitful periods of his life in an environment where, as he claims, magical phenomena were a daily occurrence and an accepted fact of life. Unfortunately, this often manifested itself in the form of 'curses' personally directed at him: once a mysterious packet addressed to the "Djinn of smoke" was discovered in his restaurant, The 1,001 Nights. Among other things, the talismanic packet bore an unmistakable silhouette of Gysin himself, and an inscription "may Massa Brahim depart from this house, as smoke departs from this chimney." A few days after receiving the cryptic message, Gysin had a falling out with his financial backer, and was effectively through with the restaurant business - a result he saw as testifying to the potency of the curse.

In spite of demonstrable technical genius, Gysin was by no means perfect. He was beset by a tendency to weave intricate, paranoiac conspiracy theories when the public and the modern art vanguard (including Surrealist figurehead André Breton) showed indifference to his art. A mean misogynist streak may also prevent some students of Gysin from completely identifying with him. Both of the two counter-productive energies crash together when Gysin suggests "…The reason I'm a flop is that I don't have a really potent built-in widow as a wife, working for my success morning noon and night. Just what Gala did for Dali all those years. While he was producing, she was on the phone setting prices and arranging dinner parties."[20]

Yet, even with such embittered quotes attributable to him, Gysin's work still provides one of the best templates for new and revelatory sound art (and we can safely concede that few practicing artists are ethically infallible, anyway.) Gysin's methodology is one in which the term "experimental" art truly means art in which the creators have certain clear intentions yet no advanced knowledge of the results, or rather the "experimental" quality derives from uncertainty over the work's reception and an openness to unintended consequences. This, I submit, is a better way to conceive of "experimentalism" than the bastardized catch-all term applied to anything too 'weird' for the tastes of the *zeitgeist*. Certain of Gysin's artistic imprints - such as his gently chiding poetry recital voice, and the whirling micro-organisms created by his fluid synthesis of Arabic and Japanese calligraphy (some Japanese-language skills were acquired when he was drafted into the U.S. army), - are signature elements obviously coming from years of refinement, keeping his art from ever sinking into the anonymity that most would-be "experimental" artists inhabit, voluntarily or involuntarily. All the same, Gysin achieved his most striking results by surrendering some part of the creative process to the whims of unknown entities. Commenting on his own relation to this form of experimentalism, Peter Christopherson says:

I never really know what 'x' is until I get there, so the process of reaching 'x' is always, in a way, the result of happy accidents. The tools nowadays (software in particular) are so complex that chance and randomness are always part of the process. For me the artistic process is ALWAYS a matter of ceding to another entity (not ceding control, exactly, but guidance for sure)- but what it is, or from where that comes, I can't describe.[21]

One of Gysin's most curious contributions to the luminous art underworld was not his poetry or painting, but a stroboscopic light device called the Dreamachine, intended as a drug-free hallucinatory aide which could be used indefinitely with no physiological side effects. Conceived with intentions similar to those of multi-disciplinary artist Tony Conrad - whose film *Flicker* "puts viewers in intense contact with their own retinas, and with some of the ways in which eyes and brain interact when stimulated by different rhythms of light and dark"[22] - the Dreamachine was an attempt to inculcate a threshold experience in users who might not otherwise have the means or mobility to do so. "Threshold experience" was, incidentally, a choice of words that would eventually make its way into the Coil lexicon (their vanity label and Web presence was, for some time, refered to as "Threshold House," while variants of the term itself featured in interviews with the band.) In providing a novel sort of cinematic experience, both *Flicker* and the Dreamachine were part of a new category of 20th century artwork that, as per Deleuze, "can replace the film stock, in a virtual film which now only goes on in the head, behind the pupils."[23]

The Dreamachine was little more than a paper cylinder a few feet high (though other materials such as copper have been used) mounted on top of a turntable spinning at 78rpm, and with geometrically arranged slits cut in the cylinder, through which the light of a single 100-watt bulb would filter and fall upon a viewer's closed eyelids. Unlike other proto-scientific or pseudo-scientific inventions adopted by the counterculture (see Wilhelm Reich's Orgone box in particular), the Dreamachine was built on sound mathematical principles, mapped out by the mathematician Ian Sommerville, which would cause the light to flicker at a rate of 8-13 pulses per second, thus stimulating the optical nerve and simulating alpha rhythms in a viewer's brain. Varying accounts of the device's efficacy exist, as well as a host of unfounded urban legends (such as its contributing role in the shotgun suicide of alt-rocker Kurt Cobain)- but at the very least, it accomplishes the goal of being 'the first artwork to be viewed with your eyes closed'.

Panoramic dream visions or no, the colorful barrage of light that falls upon the viewer's eyelids is an alternatingly relaxing and stimulating thing to behold. With some meditative persistence, a hypnagogic state can occur where viewers begin to fish distinct images out of this ocean of strobing color, producing filmic sequences like those found in dreams, but without dreams' tendency to be totally forgotten upon waking. Gysin's enthusiasm for this device was great: its potential to liberate people from preset patterns of thought and action would have dwarfed anything accomplished by, say, the Situationists, and he once felt that mass-produced dreamachines could replace the television as the central fixture in the modern home. Despite the dreamachine's status as an icon of counter-cultural ingenuity, and a limited number of manufacturers, this would never came to pass, though- for reasons that the reader can probably surmise. Whatever the case, the dreamachine was like a 'kinetic art' attempt at realizing the same goals of the cut-up: bypassing waking consciousness in order to make artwork / life more vibrant, honest and revelatory. Like the shamanistic Tibetan practice of *chöd*, which attempted to destroy the ego by surrendering the body to the demons lurking in a charnel ground at night, these techniques forewent academic study and encouraged direct engagement with unknown (even hostile) forces as an alternative or supplement to conscious thought and reasoning.

Perhaps returning the favor to the younger generation he had helped to inspire, Brion Gysin recommended Throbbing Gristle's largely improvised live record *Heathen Earth* as, outside of his beloved Moroccan trance music, the ideal music for viewing the device. Gysin acolytes The Hafler Trio and Psychic TV would, in turn, record a CD with the intention of being used as dreamachine backing music, while numerous lesser-known tributes and soundtracks exist.

To say Brion Gysin deserves sole credit for drafting the blueprint of 21st-century counter-cultural expansion would be false, but he has more concretely embodied its principles and methods than most of his 20th century contemporaries. By ejecting the quasi-Luddite fear of technology as a block on spiritual progress, and by merely becoming a 'doer' rather than a recorder of events, Gysin certainly lit a bright and mesmerizing torch to pass on to those working in other artistic media. Only a few were truly ready to have it handed off to them- although one of the willing recipients, Coil, ran with it to places maybe not even imagined by Gysin himself.

Dark Start

The musical project Coil was founded in 1982 by the late Geoff Rushton, who would become better known by his *nom de guerre*, John

Balance (spelled 'Jhonn Balance' in later years). A connoisseur of Throbbing Gristle, fanzine publisher (*Stabmental*), and all-around omnivore regarding any kind of esoteric information, Balance eventually took to music as a means of reconciling his celestial aspirations with the mundane realities of his youth: having grown up on RAF base camps in Germany and having been unceremoniously shuttled from one school (and consequently, formative social environment) to another, the then-Geoff Rushton suffered through an isolated youth made more uniquely strange by unexplained hallucinations and visitations - some hellish and some angelic. Claiming to have been partially "raised by mushrooms," the preteen Balance experimented intensely with psychedelics before having even sipped an alcoholic beverage, and was likewise inclined at an early age towards such sidereal activities as projecting himself into schoolmates' heads. Apparently well-read and seasoned beyond anyone in his immediate peer group, it seemed unlikely that Rushton would fade into the background scenery without first delivering some missives from the parallel universe he inhabited - and so it happened when his fanzine writing put him into contact with Peter 'Sleazy' Christopherson. Christopherson, 7 years Balance's senior, describes his own background relative to his partner's:

> I did not have much spiritual awareness before the age of 10, when my parents decided to send me to a Quaker co-educational boarding school - rather than the tougher and more posh school I was previously destined for. I guess they reckoned (correctly) that I needed a gentler 'alternative' approach to my education. At Ackworth all the pupils attended Quaker meetings, during which one sits in silence and anyone (in theory) can stand up and contribute thoughts or ideas to the meeting. Learning the ability to sit quietly with one's thoughts, for an hour or so, is a great and wonderful gift - everything else flows from there.

Although history will likely remember him for his Coil work first and foremost, John Balance contributed to a number of like-minded projects before his flagship project crystallized: Vagina Dentata Organ, Cultural Amnesia, and Current 93 early contributions from him. While still in Geoff Rushton guise, Balance was also able to make good on his Throbbing Gristle fandom by participating in Psychic TV, alongside TG's Peter Christopherson and Genesis P-Orridge. That band's 1983 LP *Dreams Less Sweet* still stands as a high watermark of post-Industrial culture's eclectic abilities: the quintessential 'cult' album, it was recorded in Zucarelli holophonic sound and features such subversive gems as a choirboy recital of Charles Manson's "Always is Always," and words from the final sermon of Jim Jones (prior to the mass suicide of his followers in Guyana) set against a lilting backdrop of 1960s pop. The incarnation of Psychic TV during Balance's involvement was a musical collective whose main aim was to examine and parody the power structure and indoctrination methods of such cults, and of more "professional" religious organizations as well (it was pitched by P-Orridge as the musical propaganda wing of his TOPY or 'Temple ov Psychick Youth').

Picking up more or less where Throbbing Gristle left off, early 80s Psychic TV was an iconoclastic hybrid dedicated to the Burroughsian rallying cry of *conflict creates energy.* The music itself was a mixture of the arcane and the futuristic (or 'techgnostic,' to borrow the term from Erik Davis), aesthetically linking the historical and the speculative. It was moored by paganistic / ritual drumming, cut-up tape collages almost identical to those of TG, and a many-hued tapestry of electronic effects. Balance's most visible role within Psychic TV performances was as a performer on Chapman Stick bass: a versatile stringed instrument whose strings could be either tapped, plucked, or slapped- in Balance's hands it was used to generate a distinctive combination of wolfish growl and keening feedback.

Ideologically, the band promoted overt sexuality and ecstatic noise as a means to destroying pre-set systems of social control - going so far as to suggest that exposure to certain types of noise could alter one's own genetic code. Seeing the orgasm as a concentration of psychic energy or a "self-reprogramming", TOPY was very much an heir to esoteric groups like Crowley's *Ordo Templi Orientis* and the Process Church, although Genesis P. Orridge insists upon a key difference ("TOPY did away with obfuscation and deliberate theatricality, and made public the 'secret of all ages,' while publicly confessing that sex magick was central to our contemporary occult way of life.")[24] A certain initiation ritual involved combining three bodily fluids (blood, semen and saliva) and mailing them to TOPY. It was a wry poke at religious sacraments that was bought hook, line, and sinker by some of PTV's more humor-impaired fans and also by (tragically for the group) the voracious, sensationalist news media. Although Balance would come to strongly disagree with Psychic TV's emphasis on the collective rather than the individual as creativity's driving force, the inclination towards the orgasmic would be retained for use in Coil- sometimes manifesting itself in more pronounced or more sublime ways than what Psychic TV had suggested.

The departure of Balance and Christopherson from Psychic TV marked the beginnings of Coil proper, as well as a long cooling of relations with Genesis P. Orridge. Both parties would fire shots across one another's bow in the years to come, with P. Orridge even blaming the Christopherson family's influence (Peter Christopherson's father was a former Cambridge professor granted a knighthood) for the infamous early 90s police raids on his home, and his subsequent tabloid status as "the most evil man in Britain."

Fortunately for Coil, their decided emphasis was on building and refining their own work rather than on dismantling another's, and there would come to be a pronounced difference between the musical apprenticeship in PTV and the Coil project proper. Most significantly was Coil's emphasis of the aforementioned Austin Spare within their personal pantheon, an artist whom John Balance praised for his ability to visualize the strange mutability of the myriad life forms: "all of the Janus-headed, multi-faced, theriomorphic swarms which proliferate in "Spare's paintings threaten to break out of their world and spill into ours."[25] It was this emphasis on mutability and evolutionary uncertainty as a desirable, if not outright erotic state, that arguably made the group's regular shifts in musical style and attitude seem more organically "right" than jarring.

With this in mind, the project name Coil was itself chosen by Balance for its seemingly inexhaustible multiplicity of meanings - just an association with DNA coils on its own would be loaded with such meaning, provided their role in the development all cellular life. Spiral galaxies are another point of reference, as are coiled serpents of wisdom, hypno-spirals and coiled electrical inductors providing opposition to changing or varying currents. Choosing a project name with apparent connectivity to everything was only the first step towards the group's larger project of revealing the hidden order within, and arising from, chaos.

Because of its breathtakingly unpredictable and varied body of musical work - not merely its fraternity with other key artists - Coil remains one of the most celebrated acts in the post-Industrial scene. Their *ouevre* has ranged from hedonistic dance music to multi-layered synaesthetic sound art pieces, with numerous stylistic deviations in between. The main reason for this may be that Coil has incorporated a far greater number of cultural (read: not only 'musical') influences into its eclectic mix than is normally expected of popular musicians. A single credits page of the booklet accompanying the an album from the group's *Black Light District* alias serves as a perfect introduction to Coil's theoretical and artistic alliances - the literary anarchism of William Burroughs and Hakim Bey rests alongside the eschatological 'singularity' theories and "DMT elves" of Terence McKenna. The gay camp film aesthetics of director Bruce LaBruce are acknowledged in the same space with the sidereal painting of, again, Austin Osman Spare. Other influences not mentioned on this list are no less important to Coil's output, such as the eternal drone of LaMonte Young, Karlheinz Stockhausen with his hymns to 'Pluramon,' or Angus MacLise's solar invocations and transposition of Eastern *mantra* onto electronic instrumentation. From this collective pool of influences and cultural memes came Coil's ability to shape-shift without seeming as if they'd gotten stuck in mid-transformation. Yet Coil is more than the sum of its parts: it is the confrontation and reconciliation between highly personal experience and this canon of underground ideas that makes Coil what it is; making for its richest sonic moments. Coil's Occidental origins, for one, are never completely subsumed by their interest in bringing together the globe's occult currents into a unified whole.

In spite of the group's apparent *élan vital,* though, it is surprising how much contemporary commenting upon the band has dealt exclusively with their treatment of "darkness." As we will see, such concerns are not entirely unfounded, especially given the proclamation of *out of light cometh darkness* on their *Love's Secret Domain* LP. However, I submit that this is not an attempt on the band's part to outdo its Industrial music peers in the realm of morbidity, but an acknowledgement of both actual and metaphorical darkness as an "illuminator of spirit." The darkness inhabited by Coil is like the *yami* used as the raw material for the theatrical works of Tatsumi Hijikata and Juurou Kara - as critic David Goodman saw it, "an endlessly repeating, constantly changing form of time" where "things are not orderly or predictable, but as innumerable and conflicting as words and images."[26] Put another way, the group uses its engagement with dark matter in the same way that J.G. Ballard suggested of the Renaissance, e.g. "the Italians had the right idea...most of their paintings were in dimly lit churches, unclean and difficult to see. As a result, the Renaissance lasted for centuries."[27] So - if, in spite of its vibrant eclecticism, much of the band's work seems to have a sinister or "dark" tinge, it is because, by their own admission, darkness - and not the pallid orange glow of endless columns of streetlights - is necessary to see the stars.

Various Panics

With this last realization in mind, it seems natural that Coil's music treats both the lofty sophistication of spiritual ideals and the rapidly decaying world born out of unchecked or unthinking materialism. They have made no secret of their disgust with the pervasive 'quantity over quality' aspect of modernity, shielding themselves with defensive mottos such as *"avoid that which is everywhere"*, while counseling the depressed to take a *"deep-rest"* in natural surroundings before relying on mass-produced panaceas. The indomitable, cyclical flux of nature is held up by Coil as being superior to humanity's constant striving towards definite endpoints and landmarks in 'progress', and to this end they have (like Brion Gysin before them) used the Greek nature god Pan as a sort of patron saint. Pop culture aficionados will also be familiar with Brian Jones' album *The Pipes*

Of Pan At Jajouka (an encounter between Jones and Gysin in Morocco ended with the latter finding the former to be an arrogant, self-absorbed dilettante.) A biography of Pan in Harris & Platzner's *Classic Mythology* applies strikingly well to the music of Coil:

> Like nature itself, Pan creates both beauty and terror: with the seven-reed *syrinx* (panpipe), he produces enchanting music; he is also the source of unreasoning fear (panic) that can unexpectedly freeze the human heart. With his horns, hairy shanks, cloven hooves and lustful energy, Pan becomes in postclassical times a model for the physical shape of the Christian devil.[28]

On the jacket of Coil's *Scatology* LP, there is a short text with the header *'I summon little Pan; not dead'* penned by John Balance, which outlines the beneficial possibilities of Pan's 'unreasoning fear':

> We are great believers in the redeeming powers of Kaos [sic] and confusion. Panic is about the deliberate nurturing of states of mind usually regarded as dangerous or insane. Using fear as a key, as a spur, as a catalyst to crystallize and inspire. It is about performing surgery on yourself - psychic surgery - in order to restore the whole being, complete with the aspects that sanitized society attempts to wrench from your existence…a murder in reverse.[29]

This is the preparatory text for an intense piece of guitar feedback, feral singing and mechanized Linn drum machine rhythms also entitled 'Panic'- the condition known by the ancient Greeks as *panikon deima*. The track is one of the more immediately recognizable tracks on the original 1984 release of *Scatology*, which was the band's earliest long-playing attempt at reconciling the profane with the divine. As the band discovered to their dismay earlier, with the release of a one-sided EP [*How To Destroy Angels*] intended "for the accumulation of male sexual energy" not everyone within the alternative culture, let alone the cultural mainstream, was immediately or entirely sympathetic to their methods of 'psychic surgery'. In fact, the very reference to male sexuality was, laughably enough, condemned as a 'misogynist' statement by some parties- the fact that Coil was a group of homosexual artists must not have been readily apparent. Such misinterpretation - if not outright alarmist fear - of the band's mere acknowledgement of what they were places them in a niche also occupied by contemporary artists and countrymen Gilbert & George, whose own comments on their work neatly mirror the *How To Destroy Angels* 'controversy'. From an interview with the subcultural journal *Rapid*

Eye:

> *RE:* One PC criticism of your work is that you don't include women in your work.
>
> GILBERT: We are not politically correct.
>
> GEORGE: Perhaps *too* politically correct. Actually we don't get much criticism from feminists, except the feminazis in America who hate gay men. Modern feminists should agree with us that we are not exploiting women. It became interesting because all over the world people started asking us about women. They never ask Anthony Caro about women. But we know nothing about women. Most other artists have used women's images for centuries, the art world is run by men.
>
> *RE:* So, you're not objectifying women in any way...
>
> GEORGE: Also, men are the sex women are the most interested in. The moment you exclude something in art it becomes important to people. We didn't even think about it.[30]

Never ones to capitulate or to let misinformed critics have the final say in anything, though, Coil merely upped the stakes - the packaging of the neo-Surrealist opus *Scatology* was graced by numerous blasphemies against the guardians of 'acceptable' sexuality and social mores. There's an excerpt of a pornographic story swiped from the pages of one *Mr. S.M.* magazine, tales of drug-induced religious visions, the obligatory Charles Manson quote, an excerpt from *The Selfish Gene* (Richard Dawkins' pioneering work on natural selection, and the origin of the 'meme' concept), references to "the clap- both the action and the affliction" and a confession by Salvador Dali that moments of defecation give him the divine inspiration necessary for his 'paranoia-critical' method.

All of this intellectually charged, defiantly heretical text is anchored into place by a 'black sun' logo, an alchemical symbol that clarifies Coil's intentions of transforming base material (read: 'shit') into gold, and is also a symbol which bears a strong resemblance to the 8-pointed 'chaos star', another motif heavily used by the band. From the simultaneously clumsy and grandiose opening instrumental "Ubu Noir", to the crumbling and apocalyptic *denouement* "Cathedral In Flames", *Scatology* masterfully combines sonic elements both crude and refined, drawing uncomfortable parallels between the ethereal atmospherics of the church and the reverberations of the sewer. Murky production on some tracks meshes with moments of crystalline sonic clarity. Heraldic, regal brass parts collide into atonal flare-ups from guitar and John Balance's Chapman Stick. Numerous samples (played on a then state-of-the-art Fairlight CMI music computer) strive to harmonize with the unique tonal vocabulary - e.g. disruptive howls, slurs and choirboy flourishes - of Balance's vocals. The execution of this LP would be an unmitigated disaster in the hands of others, but the group (abetted significantly by guest arranger J.G. Thirlwell) draws on a knowledge of both cinematic and ritual methods of creation in order to pull it off.

The aesthetic inaugurated by Coil on this album would come to be Coil's career-long *modus operandi*, despite their aforementioned tendency to continually re-assess their inventory of techniques - in a way, it is a fulfillment of the much-touted Dionysian and Apollonian fusion promised by rock music, but scarcely delivered. Coil convert Ian Penman, writing in *Wire* magazine, suggests that Coil's success lies in their refusal to embrace only the cosmetic or seductive aspects of occultism, hoping that audiences will not call them on their bluff. Upon visiting the group, he writes:

> If Coil were more archly / laxly rock'n roll, I would doubtless be received in some be-scarfed den, black candles burning, tattoos all on show: all the surface paraphernalia. Such dilletantism probably explains why rock's would be diabolists have come to such grief- why they usually emerge hurt and chastened by the experience. Stubborn ego clings on to contaminate the work, which fails to progress any further than dark-knight affectation.[31]

If the music itself isn't sufficient to drive home the point, there is one final visual reminder in the *Sctalogy* packaging of Coil's 'post-industrial alchemist' intentions. An iconic black and white photo on the record's inner sleeve, taken by Lawrence Watson, depicts Peter Christopherson and John Balance in a pastoral English setting, where the sight of cherubic Balance with darkened eyes and a frost-white sheaf of hair contrasts with a heavily soiled, wild-eyed Christopherson (whose filth-smeared presence is made even more unsettling by his proper business attire.)

Scatology was one of the most coherent explorations of the Burroughs / Gysin aesthetic yet converted into audio form - a fact not lost on the poet and Burroughs associate John Giorno, who, in 1985, included the band on his Giorno Poetry Systems LP *A Diamond Hidden in the Mouth of a Corpse*. Yet even as Coil trumpeted the news of their iconoclastic existence to all adventurous enough to listen, death was not far behind - with the AIDS menace taking a personal toll on those close to the band, the post-*Scatology* phase of Coil meditated on death in a way perhaps too intense to be correctly interpreted by an ill-equipped music / 'alternative' press. Shortly after their first LP release, Coil issued a crushingly spare, sorrowful cover of Soft Cell's "Tainted Love" (itself a cover version of Gloria Jones' Northern Soul ballad of the same name.) The song is practically an *a capella* turn by Balance, save for some tolling bells and orchestral hits - it vampirizes the beat-driven energy of the original until only an elegiac core of sound remains. The harrowing visions of its accompanying video clip were so unusual for that medium at the time, that they were taken to be a sick bit of *schadenfreude* concocted for the band's personal amusement. The threats and denouncements from gay activist groups would, in their refusal to go beyond surface level impressions, ironically equal the hue and cry raised by the conservative agents of morality who once called Throbbing Gristle the 'wreckers of civilisation'. For all the outrage, though, the record would eventually be recognized for what it was - the first real AIDS benefit record released by any artistic entity, underground or mainstream.[32]

With the stark tone thusly set, the next full-length effort by Coil - *Horse Rotorvator* - was a brutal Coil-ification of the classical tone poem, a haunting song cycle produced astonishingly well with only an independent label's budget to work with. The album carried lyrical warnings such as *"you get eaten alive by the perfect lover"* and *"you must realize…that everyone changes, and everything dies"*, staring down inevitable doom in a way that, thankfully, eschewed fashionable Goth teases and aimless, maudlin moping.

The inspiration for the album's title and cover imagery came from an IRA assault on a marching parade, a gory and surreal incident which resulted in horse carnage flying at the assembled spectators. The historical significance of this gruesome event was then overlaid by one of Balance's characteristic visions- of the Four Horsemen of the Apocalypse using the jawbones of their horses as a ghastly tilling device. The very lifeblood of the record is death, as well as the events leading up to and following it. From a lush musing on the filmmaker Pasolini's death at the hands of a rent boy, to a cover version of Leonard Cohen's "Who by Fire," *Horse Rotorvator* hardly blinks in the face of its unpleasant, yet all-enveloping subject matter. Its symphonic, cinematic allure is tempered with heavy doses of percussive battering and acidic Industrial squall - exemplified most disturbingly on the short 'bridge' of layered, terrified tape voices contained on "Blood From the Air". Slinky 'crime jazz' (again supplied by Jim 'Foetus' Thirlwell) and strange snatches of distended brass only seem to reinforce the orchestral portions of the album, rather than distracting from them. In yet another grand stroke of irony, the LP finds Coil, as a musical entity, in full bloom even as they contemplate their extermination. Having mastered the application of the 'cut up' theory to music, the result was a professional product which, were it a conventional motion picture rather than one of the 'audio only' variety, would have been marketed as an epic tragedy rather than as an intellectual oddity.

Side Effects of Life

Throughout the 1980s, Coil had never made any concerted attempts to draw attention to their own artist personae, but rather to the energies their music was liberating and transfering. It made perfect sense, then, that the next incarnation of the group would be involved with a subculture based on similar premises. By the dawn of the 1990s, the 'rave' party culture had built itself upon the dissolution of "performer" and "audience" in favor of a different social model, in which the DJ was (originally, anyway) no more than a conduit for energy that informed the audience's interactions. This smiley-faced and often pill-besotted rave culture promised a new communal, utopian current (Hakim Bey's much-referenced 'temporary autonomous zone'), and brought with it a massive upsurge in the amount of ecstatic electronic music available on the market - but precious little of it attempted to, as Coil did, highlight the continuity between the contemporaneous 'eternal present' of rave culture and its shamanic ancestry. Coil's forays into this scene were very much an attempt at embodying Terence McKenna's "archaic revival," in which (as per Ben Neill) "the emerging electronic media and connectivity art would assume a role similar to its position in pre-literate societies."[33] To *"see the future leaking through...see the person who once was you"* - as John Balance sang on the proto-'trip-hop' track 'Windowpane' - was a necessary supplement to the technological ecstasy of the moment.

Techno producers of the late 80s and early 90s were initially refreshing for their willingness to operate in complete anonymity in order to further the cause, but too often were limited in the life experience The rave community did indeed pride itself on youthful exuberance: it rejected the inevitable by-products of adult social life such as alcohol consumption, taking a "lest ye become as a child, ye may not enter the kingdom of Heaven" approach that favored pure light and sound over the prizes (marriage, home ownership, job promotions) occasionally found along the way during the phased march into the oblivion of conformity. The movement also seemed to be grasping at a more pure kind of spirituality than what was on offer in the urban (and suburban) sprawls of England and America: a church which served to temporarily pacify the unrest created by poor government and myriad socio-economic inequalities, rather than to offer any lasting, transcendent experience. As with the majority of television and print media, its non-spiritual motive of performing social "damage control" were becoming insipid and transparent to even wet-behind-the-ears club kids, who sought to build their own euphoric tribal movement from scratch.

Along these lines, the noted psychologist Stanislav Grof (whose psychedelic research was too often given a 'back seat' to that of the more media-savvy Dr. Timothy Leary) sums up the hopes of urban rave culture with an account of his first LSD-assisted self-analysis:

> Even in the most dramatic and convincing depths of the [LSD] experience, I saw the irony and paradox of the situation. The Divine had manifested itself and had taken over my life in a modern laboratory, in the middle of a serious scientific experiment, conducted in a Communist country with a substance produced in the test tube of a 20th-century chemist.[34]

John Balance would come to empathize with the rave culture's acceptance of Grof's 'paradoxical' situation as a natural development, and would identify with the youth movement 's replacing some of the pastoral escapism of hippies with the street-smart "suss" of the punks. This bass-driven Never-Never-Land could clearly have its merits, yet the sum total inexperience of ravers meant that their visceral music was rarely informed by intellectual rigor or by tested methodology.

It is difficult to bring judgement down on those who did not have the economic means to, say, travel abroad or to cultivate specialized skills whose application required years to learn. The worst exponents of the scene, though, got by solely on knowing the right passwords to the clubhouse and waving all the right emblems, while either willfully or inadvertently ignoring the 'science' in the colorful science fiction they were weaving. The ideologues of previous counter-cultures made cameo appearances as the 'grand old men' of pharmaceutical and cybernetic questing, but it cannot be easily verified that ravers took anything from their beat-assisted monologues beyond a kind of 'parental endorsement' of their activities. If it seemed that Coil forgave much of the scene's naiveté, it was perhaps because they noticed a continuity between the new culture's variety of ecstatic dancing and the ancient kind romanticized by Brion Gysin in Morocco. John Balance described his initial positivity towards the rave as follows:

> When [dancing] happens properly, it's a liberation...and I've had a lot of revelations on it, I completely conquered my fear of death. I have a disturbing faith in human nature actually, now....maybe I am deluded (laughs). Before I thought that the universe was sick, and that people were sick...and I've seen that it doesn't have to be that way.[35]

Despite having conquered this fear of death, Coil injected their so-called "dance" album (*Love's Secret Domain*) with touches of unease and theriomorphic menace, conjuring up a disco populated by Austin Spare's strange fluid organisms. Among these flourishes were incantations lifted from William Blake (see the quotes of Blake's *The Sick Rose* on the album's title track), and an especially subversive style of sampling and vocalization that did what few bedroom techno producers dared to do: leavening the rolling technoid bliss with admissions of fragility and (in direct contrast to the psychedelic egotism often embraced by 'instant gratification' youth drug cultures) the seeming indifference of the universe to see any individual organism as its center. *"Man has given a false importance to death"*, intones a genteel, sampled voice over tight piston-pumping rhythms and ambient swells - *"every animal, plant, or man that dies adds to nature's compost heap"*.

Meanwhile, hitherto unexplored sonic juxtapositions mark the record as another link in Coil's chain of unpredictable releases: 'Teenage Lightning' makes use of vocoder-aided voices and over Latin rhythms and flamenco guitar, while one of the few recordings to successfully combine throaty didgeridoo and robotic Roland drum patterns pops up elsewhere. A gorgeous string arrangement even surfaces as an interlude between slabs of electronic mayhem. Impossible to pigeonhole as a "techno" album, it is really an example of 'Coil' becoming a category of music unto itself.

Despite its purely technical innovations, the record has achieved an over-simplified reputation that places it in a category no less restrictive, i.e. "drug music." The track 'Windowpane' of course references the LSD variant of the same name, while the acronym spelled out by the three words in the album title will be obvious to just about anyone (as will the acronym contained in the "Answers Come In Dreams" remix of the strobe-lit dancefloor masterpiece 'The Snow.') This may seem to come into conflict with the Coil slogan of 'music to take in place of drugs' adopted later, yet the band's chemical enhancement during this period was no trifling thing either. John Balance recalls:

> ...we started [Love's Secret Domain] in January '87, and then in February '87 we went out to a club, and it took us six months to recover from that visit, and we had to start again. Each time we do some recording, we tend to get involved in, uh, mind-altering experiences of one kind or another, and our minds are so altered that when we come to record again, it means something different.[36]

Chemically guided recording sessions were apparently the norm for the 'LSD' era - Peter Christopherson claims that "we made the studio sacred and then blasphemed it" - although this was to be the apex of Coil's experimentation with chemical intake, as Balance confesses:

> Personally I found that the path of excess leads to the palace of excess, and to insecurity, neuroses, a profound disillusionment with almost everything, and an insurmountable depression. I have never been one to do things by halves, and I have suffered as a consequence of my youthful adventures with the Left-Hand Paths.[37]

If Balance harbors some regrets for his dissipation into narcotic limbo, he is especially embittered about the side effects of the legally sanctioned pharmaceuticals meant as an alternative: "I wish I had never gone onto antidepressants. They were a nightmare to come off of and my doctor, along with nearly all the medical industry, seems to want people *on* the fucking things."[38] Echoing Balance's thoughts on these subjects, Christopherson states:

> I am not a fan of the pharmaceutical industry, and do not recommend un-informed acceptance of advice by it, or by the medical profession in general, especially when it comes to soporifics. I don't think the trend towards popularity (or rejection) of drug use is very culturally or artistically important. People who repetitively use cocaine or Ecstasy for example, are not learning anything or creating anything original, they are just burning themselves up, and causing uncontrolled flows of money that bring about all kinds of damage to economies - and hence uninvolved people - around the world. On the other hand, I do believe the use of some psychedelics can open doors for artists to new perceptions that could impact our destiny.[39]

Christopherson's attitude towards soporifics extends to the musical variety as well, which may mark the distinction between the industry-sanctioned varieties of dance music and *Love's Secret Domain:* by Christopherson's reckoning, the former was intended to reduce thought, while the latter was meant to encourage it as an adjunct to rhythm-fueled physical rapture.

Wounded Galaxies Tap at the Window

By the mid 1990s, it was becoming obvious that - as Tactile's John Everall notices in a personal appreciation of the band - not *that* much was new underneath the black sun: recent notable innovations, like Scanner's blurring of private and public space with recordings of pirated phone conversations, were eerily similar to the audio voyeurism of Peter Christopherson's street recordings for Throbbing Gristle and Coil. Rising electronic artists of the time, like producer / sci-fi writer / cultural theorist DJ Spooky (a.k.a. Paul Miller) were able to perform regional variants on what Coil had done- in Miller's case, melding a distinctly Afro-American futurism and mytho-poetic approach with cross-generational collaboration involving monumental figures like Iannis Xenakis.

Positive developments also occurred in the ambient music realm, where projects like Mick Harris' Scorn took the rhythmic structures of hip-hop and dub reggae, and had them sucked into some negative universe, inverting the bland 'chill out' nature of much ambient music into an unnerving sensibility of heightened tension and premonition. Scorn was, incidentally, one of the chosen few to be graced with a Coil remix of their work, and also one of many such projects to be saddled with the silly "isolationist ambient" designation - a scene shadowed in no small part by Coil, who were proving to be increasingly influential despite genuine reclusivity. In fact, Coil were fast becoming the toast of the entire electronic music spectrum, forging bonds with the likes of Industrial dance heartthrob Trent Reznor as well as asymmetrical beat scientists Aphex Twin and Autechre - they were now the perennial act that everyone had heard *of* but never actually heard (a fact that owed itself partially to the World Serpent distribution network's habit of charging exorbitant import prices for their records and compact discs, which also had a tendency to quickly go out of print.) Meanwhile, as the 1990s electronica boom upgraded to a full-blown glut, more and more musicians took to the wholesale re-think of mass media apparatus, as if Industrial culture had not happened at all: with a new breed of musicians seemingly hellbent on providing a Cliff's Notes version of the lessons already taught by artists like Coil, the only option for them was to once again divorce themselves from the fleeting, the temporal- and, in the case of their ELpH project, from terrestrial communication itself.

When Coil titled the double-10" record set by their pseudonymous project ELpH as *Worship The Glitch*, few probably could have predicted that "glitch" would become the watchword for a whole genre of pre-millenial electronic music using the breakdown of technology as its primary 'instrument'. The existence of technology presupposes the existence of accidents, although, as this singular form of music shows, not all those accidents have to be synonymous with catastrophes.

In retrospect, *Worship The Glitch* may have had the misfortune of being released in the same year as Oval's landmark *94 Diskont* album on the Mille Plateaux label - Oval's Markus Popp is, to the present, one of the names most commonly associated with "glitch" as a method and cultural movement. Popp's basic approach was to create woozy and melancholic instrumentals from montaging the music contained on scratched CDs (a habit which he eventually tired of, going on to make purely 'hands off', generative music with his *Oval Process* software.) While it is tempting to draw parallels between both Oval and Coil for their refusal to be the heroic 'protagonists' of their own music, and to let a certain degree of 'the unknown' filter through, the two do not share a common *raison d'être*- much of Coil's work has been predicated on something like Crowley's motto *"the method of science - the aim of religion,"* while Markus Popp humbly shrugs to *Haunted Weather* author David Toop "I just want to make a contemporary statement."[40]

As Popp was laying out a new theory of user interfaces, Coil claimed to be sensing extra-terrestrial presences in their musical equipment, seized with a feeling that other entities were 'playing through' them at those times when certain functions of their electronic gear seemed to be malfunctioning in ways that were more unexpected than the malfunctions themseles. The exact nature of the equipment and its faults is vague, even clandestine - although Christopherson hints in one interview about being intrigued by the sound of an Eventide harmonizer choking up. All the same, the results are suitably otherworldly, with highly disorienting panning effects and odd changes in the audio's depth of field predominating. Flitting high-frequency sounds zoom in and out with a Doppler effect added, and overall the pieces feel not so much like 'songs' as inter-species attempts at bridging a vast communicative gulf: they needle away at one's perception in the same way a Morse code transmission might, before abruptly ending. One track entitled 'Opium Hum' is especially beautiful in its peculiarity; the buffering function of some digital studio tool failing as a mournful alien melody taxes the machine's available memory. If *Worship The Glitch* is not regarded as one of the 'canonical' Coil albums, it is definitely one of the most intriguing and unusual. And given the enthusiasm of mentors William Burroughs and Karlheinz Stockhausen (an 'honorary member' of Coil) for reaching into space and eventually ridding mankind of his terrestrial shackles, the ELpH project carries on a grand *kosmische* tradition of sorts.

The last ELpH recording to date is their contribution to Raster / Noton label's award-winning "20 minutes to 2000" series of mini-CDs, meant to usher in the new millenium. Titled *Zwölf* (a polyglot play on words, with the German being *elf* being 'eleven' and *zwölf* being 'twelve'), the musical content is something like a protracted alien birdsong combined with the droning sound of a malevolent artificial intelligence learning how to hate. In light of the terrifying birth pangs that have so far characterized the new millenium, it is especially eerie to speculate about the music being characterized by a celestial being with foreknowledge of things to come. Or, it could just be Coil having a laugh at the expense of those inclined to make these connections: Coil, after all, did not recognize the authority of the Gregorian calendar and consequently did not view the rollover into the year 2000 as a 'new era' in human history.

Drones and Lunacy: Some Cures For Time

> The idea behind the drone state of mind is that, by using my sound environments, you can set up a pattern of harmonically related impulses. The environments are created with harmonically related sine waves that produce periodic composite sound waves. The resulting impulses make a periodic composite waveform that flows through the ear, and is relayed through the neurons and up to the cerebral cortex where, if it's a constant sound, these patterns become continuous [...] If you have this drone state of mind as a point of reference, the mind then should be able to take elaborate flights of the imagination to faraway and very specialized places that it has probably never been to before.[41]

- LaMonte Young

As Coil inched closer towards an arbitrary place-marker in human history, they likewise ignored the trend towards hyper-complexity that ran roughshod over the ecology. With new cultural fusions sprouting from the sidewalks of Tokyo and New York on an almost weekly basis (to say nothing of cyberspace) an accelerated groping for a collective cultural identity was taking place - but the result was, more often than not, an inconsistent rag-bag eclecticism or a profound lack of cognitive and spiritual depth. Style tribes and micro-variations in design and musical expression came and went with depressing regularity. Unprecedented access to satellite broadcasting, the internet and mobile telephony only seemed to reinforce people's ability to 'say nothing loudly,' often overshadowing the valuable role it could and did play in connecting marginalized peoples from around the globe. Meanwhile, whistle-blowing media theorists like 'dromology' expert Paul Virilio became more in demand to make sense of the reckless velocity at which all this was happening. The latter offered no soothing panegyrics, and in fact did much to contribute to the millenial sense of apocalyptic finality, likening the "emergence of global information networks" to "the frontier veloctiy of electromagnetic waves [...] hitting the wall that stands at the limit of acceleration."[42]

Coil did not necessarily 'pull the plug' on the self-intensifying enjoyment of all things new, shiny and convenient (as evinced by Christopherson's endorsements for products like Apple computers and Ableton Live music production software.) However, they did step far enough outside of the madding crowd so as to not be as dramatically affected by it. One obvious step was to flee London's oppressive atmosphere of CCTV cameras and general paranoia for the relative comfort of the seaside. Another was to strip their music to the bone so radically that it inverted the common ratio of *content* to *message*: rather than composing pluralistic mash-ups which showcased prodigious editing skill, Coil began to rely on the simplest aural artifacts to open gateways onto inner and outer space.

An approach based on stern minimalism or drone could manifest itself in a number of ways, as Coil antecedent LaMonte Young had already demonstrated with his "theater of eternal music". One face of Coil's drone-based period was the bracing *Constant Shallowness Leads to Evil*, one of the harsher examples of their 'trial by music' phase. Movements with titles like 'Lowest Common Abominator' and 'Freebase Chakra' coalesce into a banishing / purification rite carried out primarily with analog synthesizers and vicious electronic distortion; a cyclical instrumental assault on those citizens of the 'global village' whose misuse of everything from drugs to laptop computers has caused them to devolve rather than to gain any higher realization of themselves: *"color, sound...oblivion"* Balance growls in an apparent indictment of uninformed hyper-stimulation and easy access. In a blatant mockery of the instructional labels carried on bottles of prescription painkillers, the CD also includes a warning not to use while operating heavy machinery or driving.

The compositions on *Constant Shallowness...* would end up becoming (along with the occasional "classic" like "Blood From The Air") the rough schematic for the music on the first-ever Coil concert tour, which compounded the wrathfulness of that release with 15-minute fusillades of strobe light, huge video projections of wheeling, polymorphic, *yantra*-like symbols, and torrential rains of electronic noise. The band members were outfitted in costumes that gave them the appearance of institutionalized lunatics escaped from some prison spacecraft orbiting the Earth: Balance looked especially unsettling in a reflective designer straitjacket with blood dripping from his shaven temples, an effect that would likely have impressed even such celebrated theatrical madmen as Antonin Artaud. Needless to say, this aura was lessened none when Balance hurled objects at a 'thunder sheet' in the midst of a free-form electronic tsunami, or hurled screams and shouts at the bewildered spectators: it is difficult to tell from hearsay and video evidence alone if this 'concert-as-exorcism' routine was more physically draining for the performers or the audience.

Whereas *Constant Shallowness… exorcised*, the two volumes of *Musick To Play In The Dark* healed using a new 'lunar' technique: dubbed 'moon musick' by the band, the two volumes (released in 1999 and 2000) are among Coil's most critically acclaimed material, weaving together more divergent strands of unmistakably 'personal' material in two discs than most recording artists will achieve in the span of a career. Subject matter for songs ranges from Balance's taking stock of his unwanted obsessions ("Paranoid Inlay"), to more alien interventions ("Tiny Golden Books"), and the musical composition follows suit: twittering machines formed from digitized clicks and pops, alien birdcalls, lonesome refrains played on an Optigan 'optical organ', every conceivable tone color of analog synthesizer from sepia-toned to glimmering silver. On the lunar devotional ("Batwings- A Limnal Hymn"), Balance - like the admitted inspiration Robert Wyatt on his *Rock Bottom* LP - sings in a language of his own invention over a palpable sequence of four smoothly descending tones. And even as Balance whispers "the key to joy is disobedience" beneath the synthesized tumbling of glass beads that opens the track, there is a remarkable restraint to it all.

The release of these albums also gave Balance a personal platform from which to discuss ideas related to the earth's sole natural satellite: he advocated returning to the Mayan calendar and its thirteen-moon cycle (as well as its inclusion of a single 'nameless' day in the calendar year), and decried all forms of light pollution. The latter was one thing that largely went unnoticed by the Jeremiahs of global warming given the most 'face time' in the media, who focused their energies on recycling plastics and reducing carbon dioxide emissions. Balance, in contrast, was an avid campaigner for reducing the amount of artificial lighting, claiming that it actually made people in populous cities less secure (what car thief, as the logic went, would try to steal a vehicle he couldn't even see in the first place?). The function of darkness was, for Balance, analogous to the enforced silence Christopherson experienced during his schooling at Ackworth - a necessary screen upon which to project one's inner thoughts and to confront them; a feature of antiquity that had been forgotten even during the trance-dancing sessions of the 'archaic revival.' Balance, seeing the need for total artifical illumination as an outgrowth of evangelical Christians' metaphorical 'lighting up the world' with the Gospel, saw this as one particularly negative byproduct of humans' severing themselves from respect towards natural virtues.

Just as the black sun symbol embodied certain aspects of Coil's *Gesamtkunstwerk* early on, the monad glyph of John Dee - English occultist and advisor to Queen Elizabeth - was the symbol emblazoned on the Coil banner during their final creative phase. Dee was famous for his use of mirrors as 'scrying stones', an activity which would be taken up in the Beat Hotel of 1959 by Brion Gysin and William Burroughs, who hoped to see past incarnations of themselves during brutally prolonged mirror-gazing sessions. The monad symbol, introduced in Dee's work *Monas Hieroglyphica*, does the same for the late-period Coil: used frequently in live projections during the band's concerts, in promotional photography, and appearing also on the artwork of the *Time Machines* release, the symbol unifies all the raging currents which have run through Coil over the years. If nothing else, two of its component parts (a solar symbol and a lunar crescent) hint at the types of stylistic and philosophical reconciliation they would attempt in their final years.

Also included in this glyph is the astrological symbol for Jupiter, indistinguishable from modern 'first aid' and medical crosses, and a wavering line of fire beneath that. Dee himself never fully disclosed the ultimate significance of this hieroglyph, and his writings on it were seen merely as an introduction to a more detailed description that he would give when coming face to face with adepts. It takes on a deeper meaning, as with all Coil's symbology, when applied to the sounds on the *Time Machines* release - this release is comprised of four electronic drones spread over a similar number of tracks, which in themselves conform to the musical definition of a monad (a single note or pitch). These four tones, which span almost the entire 74 minutes of the compact disc, have been designed by the group "to facilitate travel through time." To aid this process, the album comes with a set of four image stickers, each one printed with one of the four component parts of the Dee glyph on a brightly colored background. The images, as deceptively simple as the sounds on the album, combine hermetic knowledge with modern pharmacological science. Beneath each one of the brightly colored images, the name of a powerful, if sometimes obscure, hallucinogen is written: DMT, psilocybin, DOET (a.k.a. Hecate) and Telepathine. Printed on the inner sleeve of the album is the slogan *persistence is all*, which would seem at first to be a gentle warning insulating listeners against disappointment - obviously there will be those who expect instant 'mind-blowing' gratification and immediate time-warping effects. Viewed in light of Coil's past influences (*Perdurabo* or 'I will persevere' was another magical motto of Aleister Crowley), it is a further attempt to re-introduce such ideals into an era short on patience and long on insubstantial distractions.

The last of Coil's more "conceptual" releases was realized in 2004 - a triple CD and DVD box set entitled *ANS*. All the enclosed audio works were performed on the monstrous photoelectric synthesizer of the same name, built by scientist Evgeny Murzin, kept at Moscow State University and named in honor of the ecstatic Russian Symbolist composer Aleksandr Nikolai Scriabin (1872-1915). Scriabin was known, like Coil, for a rich tonal vocabulary and for his immersion in the pantheistic and the esoteric - his connections to Madame Blavatsky's Theosophist circle being one prime example of this. His enthusiasm for the apocalyptic also shone through in his unfinished composition *Mysterium*, a symphonic work performed to be by an orchestra in an Indian temple and basically intended to usher in the end of time. His *Poem of Ecstacy* was another philosophically-informed symphonic work meant to spur on the triumph of the (artistic) will, while his interest in synesthesia led to the scoring of works for the *clavier à lumières*, the 'color organ' developed exclusively for the performance of his *Prometheus: The Poem of Fire*.

As the keyboard of the *clavier à lumières* was played, colors corresponding to the notation were meant to be projected onto a screen in the concert hall - it was this basic concept that inspired the construction of the ANS unit, and which attracted composers like Edward Artemiev and Alfred Schnittke to have a go at utilizing the machine's uniquely spectral sounds. When handed over to Coil, the results are supple and singular as could be expected - the set of DVD visuals by Christopherson attempts to add the synesthetic component to a program similar to the one inaugurated on *Time Machines*: a lengthy yet effective immersion into a pool of slowly moving, concentric electronic ripples, which tame the raging mental flux and allow one to omit needless thoughts. The music's neutralizing of intensified emotions and mental narratives, and its attempted exploration of the non-cognitive world of the senses, place it in a tradition alongside projects such as LaMonte Young and Marian Zazeela's *Dream House* installation. The latter aimed at becoming a "fluid, variable environment...which appears to contain self-luminous colored bodies freely suspended in an atmosphere of continually moving calligraphic strokes,"[43] and the *ANS* discs seem to have a similar environment-building exercise at their core. That is to say, they challenge the common misperception of minimalism as an emptier or annihilator of space.

+

With just one major career compromise, it seems that Coil could have easily slipped into wider acceptance, joining the ranks of artists like Matmos and Björk on the short list of the mainstream's tolerated eccentrics. As it stood, though, one major element of their presentation always seemed to interfere. They were too firmly rooted in queer culture for the heterosexual Industrial and 'dark ambient' orthodoxy. They were too taken with the hermetic for those trying to make their abstract electronic music complement more strictly polemical concerns. They were too fond of the redemptive qualities of abrasion, and too familiar with the coordinates of Burroughs' "war universe" (announcing early on that *"the price of existence is eternal warfare"*)[44] to sit well with more pacifistic, or at least, pacific neo-pagan communities. If a quick browsing of online CD reviews is anything to go by, projects as diverse as *How To Destroy Angels* and *Time Machines* tended to infuriate as much as they illuminated. When representatives of the major league media came knocking, proceedings were not always marked by enmity, but nevertheless managed to kill the band with kindness: one wince-inducing BBC documentary lauds the band for being like "lovely aunties" while giving the impression that the many-faceted band has a library composed of nothing but musty grimoires and well-thumbed Crowley books.

Happily for their die-hard listeners (and a skimming of Coil-related internet message boards over their lifetime indicates that there may be no other kind of Coil listener), no perceptibly major creative compromise was ever made. The same talents that Peter Christopherson applied towards programming Coil's equipment and overseeing their albums' sleeve design were also funneled into various lucrative day jobs, such as the direction of occasionally award-winning music videos for a host of industry names, and even for the composition of advertising jingles (a selection of such was made available as a single track on Coil's *Unnatural History III* compilation.) These activities allowed Coil to achieve an enviable level of creative autonomy, despite having to simultaneously weather the typical accusations of having one foot planted in the consumer mainstream and one in the underground. As unromantic as these gigs might have been to the more starstruck and idealistic Coil followers, their regular presence finally allowed Coil to sever connections with deadbeat record labels and distributors, and allowed the world to 'come to them,' as it were - by the end of their career, Coil was selling their material almost exclusively (and by all appearances, not unprofitably) through mail order.

Some items in the Coil mail order catalog were also of such an intimate nature that stocking them in retail outlets seemed out of the question: there was the special "trauma edition" of *Musick To Play In The Dark 2* smeared with Balance's blood after a psychotic episode, and "beast boxes" of the Coil live *oeuvre* hand-painted in an ectoplasmic fashion. Perpetuated partially by the mania of the band's own fans, and partly by the band's own desire to 'bless' their final product, raising them from lowly merchandise to functional totems, each new release seemed to have a corresponding *objet d'art* edition. With this in mind, keeping a complete record of the band's discography is a perplexing hobby that one enters into at his or her own risk.

Coil's success, whatever level it may have ultimately ascended to, was curtailed when John Balance died of injuries sustained from a fall in autumn of 2004. Some subsequent efforts (e.g. 2005's *Ape of Naples* release and 2007's *The New Backwards*) would be possible thanks to a decent number of previously recorded Balance vocals, yet Coil's status as a musical partnership was effectively ended. In light of Balance's erratic mental health and relapses into heavy drinking, along with a string of lyrical predictions, all this seemed sadly inevitable: Balance sang that *"most accidents occur at home"* (he was home at the time) on one of the final Coil tracks, and *the* final Coil track to be performed live was "Going Up"- a re-working of the popular *Are You Being Served?* theme which, when associated with Coil, was almost certain to be taken as a musing on death or dissipation into the ether. The original song's quirky cataloging of material goods, recited while ascending a department store elevator, seemed to be recontextualized as the shedding of material commitments accompanying death - the last in a series of trying purifications.

In his final few years, John Balance's vascillating dispositions gave rise to a host of apocryphal tales, vengeful gossip, and the requisite clever winks about how he failed to live up to his stage name - it is difficult to sift the truth out from the well-crafted smear jobs, although one believable proposition is the psychic toll that the 'live' Coil era took on the often hesitant artist. Not all of Coil's live performances lived up to the grueling standard set by the *Constant Shallowness...* shows, in fact Coil concerts - as their recordings might suggest - served up a full complement of stylistic variations, from sweet nocturnal balladry to demonic noise avalanche. Yet the amount of psychic energy expended by the enigmatic vocalist was perhaps out of proportion to what audiences actually perceived - few people, let alone people with the sensitivity and awareness of a John Balance, transition smoothly from lengthy periods of enforced solitude into a public arena as demanding as that of the concert tour business. Balance's terminal discomfort underscored the difference between Coil and those who cleave to music for purely financial and egotistical reasons - the pressures would result in a few Balance-less Coil performances (at high-profile events like Toronto's Mutek festival) and in the end of Balance's relationship to Christopherson as a life partner.

Christopherson would eventually, like Gysin, cut himself off from the paranoiac fundamentalism of West, and 'go native' in a culture in which he claimed daily life was intertwined with magical happenings. His relocation to Bangkok also provided a necessary reprieve from recent trauma- in a 2006 interview, he states:

> At the time - Spring 2004 - living alone with Geff (who was going though a 'bad patch' - screaming, passing out on the rocks, pissing and shitting the bed etc) in the cold and draughty North Tower building, with the rain beating in from the sea onto cracked windowpanes with bits of Geff's hair in the glass where he had smashed his head against them, it was a comforting fantasy for me to imagine a different life where I was waited on hand and foot by beautiful brown skinned houseboys, who would do

anything I asked of them, and take care of my every need...[45]

As a Bangkok resident, Christopherson had access to, and documented, deeply ingrained aspects of Thai culture rarely seen by Western eyes - one such example is his film of the GinJae festival, in which entranced youths submit to acts of ritual bodily piercing in order to ward off evil spirits. His one-off musical project The Threshold House Boys' Choir remains as the soundtrack to such, fittingly enough, threshold moments. Christopherson eventually came to identify himself as a Buddhist, because "the basic tenets and precepts seem to make the most sense to me - but also because I cannot help being moved by the passion that even the sleaziest or unlikeliest of street boys has for [Buddhist] spirituality."[46]

Christopherson would remain busy until the end maintaining Coil's vast back catalog, which was meant to be converted to BluRay format by the first printing of this book, though the equally daunting *Colour, Sound, Oblivion* live DVD archive would be as far as this re-appraisal effort went. Meanwhile, Christopherson joined in a limited number of engagements with the newly re-formed Throbbing Gristle, as well as forming an electronic duo with Ivan Pavlov (SoiSong), and generally cultivating a Pan-infused creativity spanning nearly all the available electronic media.

If the growing number of 'tech-gnostics' prove to be among the 'winners' who write history, then the work of Christopherson, Balance and valued accomplices will be spoken of in the same breath as that of ambitious mages like Kenneth Anger or Harry Smith. That is to say, works which use all available methods to unveil the contradictions of human existence, and to aid personal advancement by acknowledging and reconciling them. Reflecting on his part in this ongoing struggle, Christopherson concludes, "I certainly feel that the music of Coil was 'informed', and reacting to, as yet unfulfilled & inevitable events...if we were able to lighten our own load, and in doing so, perform a similar service for others then it was worthwhile."[47] Having died in his sleep in November of 2010, Christopherson himself is no longer available to hear from those who did have their loads lightened. However, Coil's work still beckons for new listeners who, in spite of Austin Spare's caution that "the price of identity is suffering," still prefer the pain of developing new identity over that of enduring a stagnant reality.

Electro-vegetarianism:
An abridged history of Merzbow

It's an early hour of the morning within the futuristic, jet-black citadel on Osaka's Dotonbori River known as Kirin Plaza. The imposing black fang of a building is often given over to multi-level art exhibitions and live performances, courtesy of the Kirin beverage company's generously deep pockets. The theme for the day, from 11p.m. on to 5 a.m., has been 'Op Trance', a lively celebration of optical art's convergence with modern sound art. It seems like a fairly foolproof concept, given the high amount of synesthetic crossover between the two scenes: the deep striations, concentric circles and other serialized patterns favored by 'Op' artists, along with the fearless deployment of intense brightness and contrast, mesh neatly with the hyperesthesiac methods of the post-digital sound arts milieu. The crisp syncopations and circular, generative sounds being emitted by the host of DJs and laptop-wranglers on hand at Op Trance is a near-perfect compliment to the retina-blasting visual exhibits - among them an entire floor painted in fuschia and lime-green faux camouflage - and multiple sets of strobe-emitting goggles.

In this context, a performance by Merzbow, the Japanese noise scene's ambassador to the world, seems both appropriate and unusual at the same time. It's appropriate in the sense that Masami Akita, Merzbow's guiding force, is a cultural polymath who certainly knows and appreciates the relevance of Op art in the grand scheme of things. For one, stunning Op artworks grace the covers of multiple Merzbow products: there's the almost mouth-watering procession of undulating black and silver waves on the cover of his *Pulse Demon* CD, and the engraved, foil-stamped pond ripples of the similarly-minded *Mercurated*, to cite just a pair of examples. In spite of all this, it seems somewhat strange that a sound project named in honor of Dada artist Kurt Schwitters' infamous junk monuments would find a kinship with the more structured and geometric parameters of Op art. However, there are similarities if one looks beyond the assumed rigidity of the respective schools' working methods: the true unifying factor between Op art and Akita's often formless torrents of sound is not to be found in their respective production techniques, but in the undeniable multi-sensory impact and perceptual warping brought about by the results. Just as selected Op pieces 'breathe' and undulate under concentrated viewing, an equally concentrated sensory encounter with Merzbow's noise can bring about aural hallucinations and ephemera that are not included on the recordings proper.

Merzbow's concert at the Kirin Plaza certainly delivers the goods as described above, despite him having to follow a succession of crowd-pleasing techno DJs, who are milking the usual 4/4 tempos and wavering, arpeggiated basslines. The clinically calm, poker-faced Akita, with a few gentle brushes of his fingers against the track-pad of his G3 laptop, proceeds to turn the generously loud house P.A. into a set of blaring rocket thrusters. The sweat-soaked audience, already pliant, submissive, and dehydrated after hours of dancing in close quarters, can do nothing but sit back and have their remaining defenses stripped away by the steadily multiplying swells of chthonic sound. A seductive loop of sub-bass frequencies opens the set and then, after a few minutes, in comes the familiar rush of white noise: a bracing sensation that brings to mind the single-minded, relentless determination of mechanical and natural processes alike, bypassing the clumsy ambiguities of human endeavor. It is like a chorus of jackhammers vying for attention with the roar of a nearby waterfall: a perfect aural summation of the conflict between post-modern man and primordial nature.

In the most immersive moments, this sound's effect is that of reaching ecstasy through negation - and by Akita's own admission, the music of Merzbow is inspired by negating all but the most intense motifs of popular music, then systematically piling them one on top of the other. This applies especially to popular music already inclined towards psychedelia or altered states: the rainbow feedback of Jimi Hendrix' guitar denuded of its reassuring melodic structures, or the Dionysian proclivities of Jim Morrison minus the cod poetry and rambling monologues. Along these lines, touches as unexpected as the 'fuzz organ' of Soft Machine's Mike Ratledge also provide partial inspiration. The side that Merzbow personally takes in the 'man vs. nature' conflict will be disclosed soon enough - but for the moment, as the P.A. speakers throb and shiver under Akita's withering assault, none of this really seems to matter. To attempt any analysis of the sound while still in the thick of it seems totally counterproductive - better to let the cascade of beneficial abrasions just wash over you, and see what comes of it later.

+

As one of the most immediately recognizable names in the Japanese underground and the global market for alternative music, Merzbow takes its name from Swiss Dada artist Kurt Schwitters' monuments of discarded objects known as *Merzbau* ['Merz building']. The *Merz* from which these buildings were constructed bears an orthographic similarity to the French *merde* [shit], likening things such as used bus tickets and trampled newspapers to a kind of fecal matter 'excreted' by the urban landscape. The deliberate misspelling of the German text, at this early stage of this overview, already points to the sound unit's propensity for constructive confusion - with the German *bau* 'mistakenly' rendered as the English homonym *bow,* the mental image is transformed from that of a standing structure to, say, the "bow" being both a weapon and a formal gesture. That these meanings are nothing but the author's subjective interpretation (which also detects very Japanese historical resonances within both types of "bow") does not take away from the cleverness of Merzbow's feigned linguistic ignorance: the mutated English constructions, derisively referred to as *Engrish,* evince a kind of Surrealist 'evolution through error' that allow for an international language of commerce to instead become a tool of personal amusement and enlightenment. Using communicative incomprehensibility (read: 'useless noise') as the basis for new forms is a key concept for Merzbow, and many of his fellow travelers.

Yet before this is discussed in depth, at least some biographical thumbnail sketching needs to be done. Akita's project has existed in some form or another since 1979, following several stints as a drummer for cover bands (one specializing in the Frank Zappa and Captain Beefheart repertoire, and another treating the classics of Hendrix, Cream and Led Zeppelin.) Around this time Akita met original Merzbow partner Kiyoshi Mizutani, with whom Akita added free improvisations to the more anticipated rock 'n roll gestures. The signature sound described in the paragraphs above wasn't arrived at until the mid-1980s, and only by the 1990s was there enough of an international infrastructure to really make Merzbow a household name. The names Masami Akita and Merzbow are now, however, virtually synonymous: the ironically soft-spoken, tranquil man, with his obsidian mane of long, straight hair and wire-frame glasses, has been the only constant member of Merzbow from its inception to the present day. Others have come and gone - most notably Mizutani and fellow multi-disciplinary artist / journalist Reiko Azuma. A host of collaborators have also participated with Akita in that staple of underground communications, the 'split' release- with an album or single side given over to each artist.

Akita has been a prolific writer on the arts, music, erotica, esoterica, and modern architecture, with articles on emerging subculture appearing in publications like *SM Sniper, Studio Voice* and *Fool's Mate* (a hip alternative monthly throughout the 1970s and 1980s, but now almost exclusively devoted to the goofy spectacle of 'visual *kei'*- an ultra-androgynous strain of heavy metal-inflected Japanese pop). His development of the Merzbow aesthetic ran parallel with a series of investigative books that catalog a vast amount of subculture and counterculture. Books such as *Scum Culture, The Anagram of Perversity, Terminal Body Play* and, of course, *Noise War* helpfully explain and 'collect in one place' the most hermetic types of music, sex practice and autonomous creativity to a fairly conservative (but not always close-minded) Japanese audience. For those who are interested, the Tokyo publisher Seikyusha has the majority of these available in lavishly designed hardback editions.

Akita's books, in terms of their subject matter, feature a generous amount of overlap with other influential subculture journals of the 1980s and 1990s - see especially the *RE/Search* and *Rapid Eye* collections. Akita's books function more as an information service, or outright advocacy of imaginative exploration, than as cultural criticism- a fact which separates him somewhat from colleague Masaya Nakahara (of noise-oriented unit Violent Onsen Geisha), who is known within Japan primarily for his work as a film and culture critic. This is not to belittle his writing efforts, though: the process of distilling such a massive amount of information in the pre-internet days did require a high level of dedication. Still, Akita's books are published exclusively in Japanese, and even his growing number of paintings and photographs are not widely exhibited. It is the Merzbow sound which has made the most visceral impact on those willing to receive it, and it is that to which we now turn our attention.

Antimonument

What still keeps that vitality, even if passive, may be primitive art or the art created after Impressionism. These are things in which either, due to skillful application of the paint, the deception of the material had not quite succeeded, or else, like Pointillist or Fauvist, those pictures in which the materials, although used to reproduce nature, could not be murdered after all. Today, however, they are no longer able to call up deep emotion in us. They already belong to a world of the past. Yet what is interesting in this respect is the novel beauty to be found in works of art and architecture of the past which have changed their appearance due to the damage of time or destruction by disasters in the course of the centuries. This is described as the beauty of decay, but is it not perhaps that beauty which material assumes when it is freed from artificial make-up and reveals its original characteristics? The fact that the ruins receive us warmly and kindly after all, and that they attract us with their cracks and flaking surfaces, could this not really be a sign of the material taking revenge, having recaptured its original life?

- Jiro Yoshizawa, *The Gutai Manifesto*[1]

While Akita's writing was, prior to his focus on animal rights issues, mainly a straightforward journalistic investigation of controversial material, Merzbow's sound was steeped in severe abstraction and willful derangement from the outset. The earliest Merzbow releases were made available on his 'Lowest Music And Arts' label, which morphed eventually into the more internationally minded 'ZSF Produkt' (featuring non-Merzbow contributions from the likes of Controlled Bleeding, Kapotte Muziek, The Haters and domestic stalwarts like KK Null). While fans of "real music" will likely disagree, these early ventures into the netherworld of home cassette production and mail art were some of the most radically uncompromising outlets for independent Japanese music since the URC [Underground Record Club] soundtracked the 1968-1969 student revolution at Tokyo University. Unlike URC, though, both the "Lowest..." and ZSF labels mainly steered clear of any political soapbox, allowing the albums' autonomous distribution, utilitarian artwork and ragingly loud, coarse contents to speak for themselves about what kind of lifestyle the artists might prefer in place of the present system.

This is not to say that Akita's work can't be situated within the history of local counterculture, though, as certain of his works and pronouncements cleave close to those of the original post-War 'Anti Art' practicioners like Genpei Akasegawa, an individual who caused a great public scandal in 1963 by creating monochrome facsimiles of the 1,000-yen note and distributing it as a humorous means of announcing an upcoming exhibition. Despite Akasegawa's refering to himself as a *musansha* or 'proletarian,' Reiko Tomii notes that Akasegawa was "never a Communist or ideological activist," and was more notable for "his ironic and sober observation of the way power operates in real-life contexts."[2] Both Akita and Akasegawa (as suggested by supporter and *manga* critic Junzo Ishiko) have worked from a Bataillean tradition of liberation through transgression, a tradition that also brings them into the orbit of Tatsumi Hijikata, originator of the *ankoku butoh* or 'dance of darkness.' Critics inspired by Akasegawa's circle, and the agitators within it, refered to Anti Art actions as a "descent to the mundane [*nichijou-sei*]", a process that allowed for relationships to everyday objects to be re-imagined (e.g. the sacralization of trivial objects) and for the power of the modern State to be disrupted as a result. Such processes are integral to Merzbow's work, whether he intends for them to be part of this artistic lineage or not.

Early Merzbow outings were fittingly described as 'assemblages,' and had more in common with the elusive compositional maneuvers of *musique concrète* than with the electro-metallic overdrive of contemporary Merzbow. The finished products were not just 'assemblages' in the musical sense, but in the theoretical sense as well, calling on the ideas, attitudes, and code words of virtually any 20th-century anti-establishment art movement fortunate enough to have survived total obscurity. Coupled with this ecumenical approach to the underground, Merzbow recordings cover a full spectrum of thematic interests, some of which seem perfectly relatable to the audio contents, and some which seem almost arbitrarily chosen. In parsing the album cover designs of these for clues, Marc Behrens notices a distinctly "Japanese motif":

> *Batztoutai* (1986) - [also] a Japanese military hero in the Russo-Japanese War[3] - has an obscured chrysanthemum blossom on the cover. *Antimonument* (1986) has the image of Ise Shrine, the shrine of the Imperial family, along with geometric shapes, and *Ecobondage* (1987) has slight resemblances to Japanese calligraphy. In addition to these, there is the title of the 1989 cassette *Crocidura dsi Nezumi*- the name of a Japanese shaman-rat that feeds upon the stomachs of men.[4]

Akita, though articulate when interviewed, does not hint at any polemical or subversive use of this kind of imagery, tempting as it may be to ascribe fixed meanings to it. Rather, as Behrens suggests, "these hints of Japanese culture are only important if you consider that it's all about Akita creating an 'information mix' out of various cultural sources."[5]

Merzbow from this mid-1980s period was built up from a florid sonic vocabulary of scrapes, clangs, thuds, sandpaper-y abrasion and muffled explosions, all treated with varying levels of delay, distortion and reverb. Radio broadcasts and disembodied voices from tapes, all coming under the Merzbow blowtorch in some devious way or another, also added texture and colorful confusion (not necessarily context or commentary.) Imagine if Luigi Russolo and his compatriots were given free rein to use the subway stations of New York City, Tokyo or Berlin as recording venues on a nightly basis - they might have come up with something similar in spirit. Persistent listening to this music will be rewarded by amusing visions of garbage cans being overturned and dragged through the street, motor vehicles running amok, or maybe even a situation like the kind driving J.G. Ballard's novel *High Rise* - affluent apartment complex dwellers throwing social convention to the wind, joyously resorting to primal nature while fighting petty battles for elevators and vandalizing 'enemy' building floors.

There is little regimentation in sight on these recordings - instead there is a strong feeling that constructive labor has been totally abolished in favor of meaningless play, an atavistic view of artifice, and the building of new communication methods from scratch. Another ineluctable feature of this approach is Merzbow's insistent, occasionally maddening use of brief tape loops (later in his career, similar sound particles would be looped with sound editing software): Merzbow has used these to a significantly greater degree than his peers, and to different ends than what might be expected of a similar practice within the bounds of, say, electronic dance music. Instead of insinuating or enforcing a sense of perfect automated order, these metronomical repetitions are subsumed by the yet more persistent chaos circling around them, and succeed only in creating a knowing mockery of that order.

It is too easy, given the amount of similarly motivated music that now exists, not to see the personal risk that Akita and his peers took in following this path, and to underestimate the pervasiveness of the local cultural conservatism that it challenges. Urbanized Japan has, from the time of its post-War economic miracle onwards, put in more man-hours in its offices, factories, and laboratories than any other 1st world country save South Korea and the U.S. This diligence has been powered by a sense of national obligation, with philosophical and moral roots in the Confucianism that was solidified and enforced during the country's feudal era. As a result, critiques based on Japan's materialism have been typically seen as an affront to its national spirit rather than as cautions against universal qualities of greed and shortsightedness: this was the case when the failed *coup* attempt of novelist Yukio Mishima, intended to incite the Self-Defense Forces to reinstitute the sovereignty of the Emperor, was blasted by then Prime Minister Sato as "scandalous behaviour on the part of an eminent writer...[that] might tarnish the reputation of the country founded on economic prosperity."[6] Within this milieu, where economic prosperity was being seen as an inevitable phase of a people's spiritual destiny, subcultural activities and hobbies have typically been seen as a distracting nuisance, rather than as an extension of mainstream free market activity into more specialized or 'niche' markets. Though a consumer-oriented society, it has been one highly critical of individualism, with the disapproval falling particularly hard on the 'youth culture' seen as being most susceptible to this tendency. As Sharon Kinsella writes, "[individualism] has provoked approximately the same degree of condescension and loathing among sections of the Japanese intelligentsia as far-Left political parties and factions, symbolizing the threat of communism, have provoked in the United States and the United Kingdom."[7]

Indeed, most of the currently existing Japanese subcultures are refered to using the oft-derisive term *minikomi* ["mini-communications"], which separates them from the mainstream *masukomi* ["mass communications"] and makes these subcultures' smallness, rather than any of their innovations or aspirations, their defining feature. These subcultures, which can be anything from amateur *manga* clubs to gaming circles, are seen as not having any serious perspectives on social or philosophical concerns. This fact arguably keeps them from being associated with the more agitational *anguro* ["underground"] movement that involves Merzbow, yet it does not make them any less free from policing, surveillance, and the general suspicion (well known to American teenagers) that initially harmless acts of deviance may be a "slippery slope" towards complete abandonment of one's moral compass and civic responsibility.

Sharon Kinsella, in her study of Japanese subculture, mentions one such group meant to prevent access to this "slippery slope," the *Seishounen Taisaku Honbu* ["youth policy unit"], which "[was] established precisely to monitor the recurring tendency of youth to take fantastical departures from the ideals of Japanese culture."[8] There is at least one major precedent for the type of "slippery slope" moral panic that can arise suddenly in Japan, and effectively implicate all members of that subculture in the criminal activity that was engaged in by a few members - or even one member - of that subculture. Tsutomu "the *otaku* murderer" Miyazaki, who abducted, murdered, sexually violated and (in one case) cannibalized four young girls between August 1988 and July 1989, became the unwitting emblem for the perceived perversity of *manga* subculture when press visitors to his apartment discovered "his bedroom was crammed with a large collection of girls' *manga*, rorikon[9] *manga*, animation videos, a variety of soft pornographic *manga*, and a smaller collection of academic analyses of contemporary youth and girls' culture."[10]

In such an environment, where truly spontaneous acts are looked upon as counter-productive (one Public Security Regulation in Japan even bans stopping on the street for short periods of time without police permission), it is easy to see where this kind of sound could be amazingly cathartic for those Japanese citizens who can overcome the local news blackout on subcultural reportage. Of course, an argument could be made that this sounds no different than the noisy Japanese public works projects that often last until the small hours of the morning - but these 'assemblages' are really animated by a different spirit, and are noticably different from these other sonic phenomena, not only because of the additional studio effects included on the Merzbow tracks. The combination of anarchic improvisation and occasional *detournement*-style documentary exercises (like the sound of rain-slicked streets recorded on the track 'Asagaya in Rain') suggests that Merzbow is re-wiring the psycho-geography of the city or opening certain spaces up to new functions other than the ones assigned to them. It is an audio documentary example of what Jonathan Raban called the *hard city* (its built / material fabric) competing against the *soft city*, or the individualized interpretation of surroundings that exists within the experience of each urban dweller.

As the quote above from the *Gutai* movement's founder Yoshizawa (who are sometimes unfairly likened to a 1950s Japanese approximation of Dada) suggests, early tape-era Merzbow music hummed with the sound of raw materials re-asserting themselves and being revived as instruments of chaos. In this sense, Merzbow music could be seen as much more optimistic than many in the underground tape-trading communities or "extreme culture" curators have perceived it to be. Such communities were occasionally overrun by glum and obsessive Whitehouse copyists, atrocity tourists, or dealers in ultra-rightist shock tactics, and were not exactly repositories for positive thinking- but it is difficult to see Merzbow's re-appropriation of raw material as anything but a joyous refusal to just let a piece of scrap metal remain a dead byproduct of an impersonal, unsympathetic environment.

Space Metallizer

In relating a capsule history of Merzbow to the Japanese counter-culture magazine *Dice Talk,* Akita confesses that he performed virtually no concerts throughout the 80s, focusing instead on studio works. This was owing not so much to a complete lack of underground performance venues, but because of a reluctance on Akita's part to perform noise in a setting that required heavy doses of rock 'n roll charisma (and, really, would *you* expect dazzling showmanship from someone who regularly includes the caveat 'recorded at bedroom, Tokyo' in his albums' liner notes?) The live concert moratorium was rectified by a 1988 tour of Russia, resulting in one amusing two-date engagement where Merzbow was deemed to be "too loud" and had to return for the 2nd concert using only acoustic instrumentation like balalaika (documentation of this exists, if one can find it, on the *I'm Proud By Rank Of The Workers- Live in Khabarovsk CCCP* LP). Next came a 1989 tour of Europe, where Akita has returned time and time again in order to offset the Japanese mass media's apparent indifference to his work. During the first of his European tours, Akita confesses to having his back turned away from the audience most of the time, adopting what he calls a "dis-human" posture and placidly tending to an array of tabletop electronic devices. Early supporters, like Frans de Waard of the Dutch Staaplaat and Korm Plastics organizations, still speak fondly of these early diplomatic visits by Akita, but it would take the dawn of the 1990s for Merzbow to truly 'put the pedal to the metal,' as it were, and to craft the distinct sound that, live or on record, would slice energetically through the malaise of that era.

If Merzbow's intensified *musique concrète* period brings to mind *High Rise,* then what follows it is - to invoke the name of Ballard's other infamous 1970s novel - pure "*Crash.*" The Merzbow of the early-mid 1990s is marked by a feverish, orgasmic fascination with mechanized destruction and meltdown; the sound of impact drawn out to the kind of interminable length normally reserved for sacred rites. Like the stylistic variations that went before it, this model of Merzbow uses utilitarian means to erode away at the very bedrock of utility and purposefulness: an amplified electric shaver is just one example of this ethic, as is a comical strap-on device that looks like a cheese grater festooned with spring coils. A pulsing and frequency-sweeping EMS analog synth is also a regular staple of this newer annex to the *Merzbau*, which swallows space in a way not previously felt by the project's recordings. This period of Merzbow was also remarkable for Akita's dramatic surge in output (on which, more in a moment), a fact that noise theorist Paul Hegarty points to as "arguably largely as a result of the development of affordable digital technology."[11] This claim can be countered by examining period photos and album texts that show Akita still favoring analog technology, e.g. the notes on the *Metalvelodrome* 4-disc set that proudly proclaim "no synthesizer or MIDI sampler." Another argument is simply that the obduracy of the 1980s post-industrial underground had led to a fair increase in CD labels and distribution nodes, allowing Akita to accelerate an ambitious program that he had already begun when participating in the Cassette Culture networks of that era.

Akita was arguably the first artist to experiment with this exact style of electronic music on the Japanese archipelago - Western antecedents include John Duncan (whose shortwave radio experiments on his LP *Riot* helped to encourage the Tokyo noise faction forming around Merzbow), Boyd Rice, The New Blockaders, Z'ev, Maurizio Bianchi and Whitehouse. In Tokyo's rival commercial city of Osaka, Hanatarash and Hijokaidan also began experimenting with marked destructive tendencies in their music, and with the re-appropriation of urban junk as both a means *and* an end. However, Merzbow in *Crash* mode is not identical to any of the above artists: his noise flow tends to heat a room rather than chill it, as Maurizio Bianchi's desolate noise would. His sound favors ultra-high frequencies and bruising low-end like Whitehouse, yet ejects the hectoring vocal style and the amoral explorations of sociopathy. He massages numerous metal implements as Z'ev would, although with more of an emphasis on electronic amplification and less of an emphasis on shamanistic physical exertion. In short, the mish-mash of noise elements shows that Akita has not lost his talent for scavenging, and therefore his upgrade to a music of pure distortion, engulfing all aural space available, is a natural progression rather than a radical 're-think' or change of plans. Not unlike the characters in Shinya Tsukamoto's 1989 cult film *Tetsuo*, who gradually become grotesque flesh-metal hybrids in the weirdest Kafka-esque manner (and who come to love their horrific plight), it sounds as if Akita's noise-making junk has ceased to be a removable *extension* of the body, and has now grafted itself directly onto the flesh, becoming indistinguishable from organic material. Akita must have had this idea in mind when he dubbed the lo-fi, street-level clique of noise artists developing around him 'expanded noisehands'. Thought processes themselves turn metallic and Merzbow's world becomes a flame-belching, high-velocity surrealist landscape the likes of which Max Ernst and friends would have been proud to help construct. Track / album titles like *Artificial Invagination, Flesh Metal Orgasm, Locomotive Breath* and *Electric Salad* give cues as to the lurching chimeras and monstrosities to be found within this new world.

The temptation to refer to this subconscious scrap yard stocked with razor-edged sounds as "noise" is overwhelming, and even people with a vested interest in marketing it may never call it anything but that (some also prefer the quirky ethnocentric term *Japanoise* when dealing with Merzbow.) However, while it's certainly tempting to assume this is term is purely the creation of ethnographers and journalists, part of the blame for the "noise" genre does lie with some of its own membership, particularly the small clique of musicians that frequented the Kyoto "free music" coffeehouse Drugstore. This was a venue that, like much else that typifies post-industrial "micro" subcultures, garnered a long-term influence that far outweighed its short-term obscurity (David Novak notes that Drugstore "only existed for a few years, operated on an almost random schedule, and had a maximum capacity of less than twenty.")[12] The remote, unheated space survived on donations from regular patrons - thus skirting the need to apply for a business license - and was known as much for the eclecticism of its record collection as for the happily absurdist actions that would take place there, such as making an impromptu performance by applying contact microphones to the *nabe* pot in which communal meals were served.

The core of patron-supporters at Drugstore included Hide Fujiwara (Ultra Bide), Junko & Jojo Hiroshige (Hijokaidan), and Toshiji Mikawa (Hijokaidan / Incapacitants), and it was the latter who Novak points to as the actual originator of noise as a local genre:

> Before becoming a description for their own sounds, 'Noise' was an assignation for off-the-map sounds: *henna* ['strange'] records, so extreme-sounding that they escaped generic categories of music. According to [Shojiro] Ishibashi, the term was introduced by Hijokaidan member Mikawa Toshiji, who always referred to his favourite strange records as 'Noise' regardless of their original generic context.[13]

As Ishibashi puts it, "whatever [Mikawa] liked" became "noise" regardless of its tonal features, and this included not only groups that are now associated with like noise 'label' (e.g. Whitehouse and the Nihilist Spasm Band) but also those who are associated with a much different artistic lineage (e.g. Karlheinz Stockhausen.) When Mikawa uses this criterion of atypicality to determine what can be called "noise", his opinion may jar with scholars who try to define this music by non-sonic criteria such as its ideological content, or by the host of psychosomatic effects it produces. Yet his widely applicable definition has gained arguably as much currency as any other, and is still adhered to by a few music retailers and artists to this day. By this reckoning, noise was merely "extreme sound," but a type of rapturous incomprehensibility.

Indeed, the challenge to comprehensibility that comes from the velocity and layering of sound events is as integral to Merzbow-style noise as the high volume of playback. It moves at too quick and too intense a pace for most languages to adequately describe, but it can clearly be seen as structured music by people with the patience to surf the incoming waves of stimuli and to fish certain *leitmotifs* out of the churning sea of apparent chaos. Listening to Merzbow today, it is easy to forget that once things like Ornette Coleman's free group improvisations, or John Coltrane's final creative phase, were considered the pinnacle of "noise" because they strayed from 19th-century Western conventions of tonality and rhythm (again, earning them the "noise" sobriquet because of the unfamiliarity of the communicative gestures rather than because of their total volume.) Even jazz in its more tonal and rhythmic forms was once grating to the ears of the fundamentally-minded: the legendary mentor to Al Qaeda, Sayyid Qutb, visited the post-World War II U.S. and, when defining jazz as "a type of music invented by Blacks to please their primitive tendencies and desire for noise,"[14] hinted at the cultural relativity and almost frustrating, subjective elasticity of noise as a concept - to say nothing of the assumption that only the degenerates of any given culture would find "noise" enjoyable.

The term "noise" is likely to dog Merzbow for much longer than it did the free jazz vanguard, if for no other reason because the source materials of the sound are not conventional acoustic instruments, and could be seen as having tenuous connections to 'human' expressiveness. It seems that, on a whole, the closer one gets to the organically familiar, the lesser the risk of being denounced as noise - and in this hierarchy, the modulation and processing of phenomena like radio interference is much more trying, much more 'noisy' than even the most atonal, off-kilter, and high-volume horn section- the human 'warmth' of the brass trumps that of radio static, no matter how ingenuously it is transformed into musical material. The deft manipulation of electrical processes, for most, has less of an emotional resonance than sounds generated by the interaction of human hands with an acoustic instrument. This may owe itself to what Michael Pedersen calls the different orders of "sound surrogacy", or ease of identifying sound sources and the physical causes of sounds: whereas "first order" surrogacy refers to sounds that leave no doubt as to their origins, the "sound sources and causes behind Merzbow's noise drones can be difficult to identify and would therefore often be places in the third orders, or even in the remote surrogacy orders."[15]

However, there is another theory regarding the perception of noise that does not involve a technological leap, but an alteration of perception that came from a different means of quantifying sound. For the German media theorist Friedrich Kittler,

> ...the fundamental change in the conception of music and sounds has nothing to do with the sounds of the industrial age or the emergence of the era of the machine, but everything to do with the fact that sound itself became something else. When sound became frequency, all sounds became equal; the conception of frequency undermines the privileged and distinctive status of written music and changes the concept of sound and music altogether.[16]

Kittler's theory is compelling, yet perhaps arrived too late: the seminal artists of the modern "noise" genre, the Italian Futurists, had long ago proudly claimed the term for themselves in their own manifestoes, and irrevocably associated it with their celebration of technology, particularly the velocity of new machines. Their romantic re-envisioning of the urban landscape itself as a sort of massive concert hall was one of the first steps towards electronic music as we now know it, though - despite their place on the "sound surrogacy" scale relative to practicioners of non-electronic avant-garde music - they did share some common goals with the latter. Sun Ra biographer John F. Szwed, discussing the link between the European avant-garde and the later American upsurge of free jazz, states that "Noise, they contended, was richer in harmonics than pure sound; and if audiences failed to understand that, they should be trained through concentrated listening to hear the musicality of noise and understand its emotional effect."[17]

Having noted all of these directions from which to approach the "noise" conundrum (and the seeming impossibility of completely reconciling them), it might be worth, at last, considering Akita's view on the subject. Speaking on the subjectivity of noise, Akita has no problem dismissing the old canard that noise is just any form of persistent, unpleasant sound- by this dead simple logic, "most pop music is noise to me," he claims.

Pornoise

Akita has likened his music to being, in concordance with the name of his first micro-label, 'the lowest form of music', just as pornography is generally considered the lowest form of visual art in a technocratic society. Much of this lowness is owed to its purely representational aspect, its supposed inability to engage the spirit or critical faculties, and the fact that even the most artful embellishments within porn will likely be ignored in favor of its functional use as a stand-in for a sexual partner. But before investigation into this aspect of Akita's work is taken further, the Japanese perception of pornography, and its contrast with Western views on the same, should be clarified somewhat.

Distribution of pornographic literature in Japan (primarily magazines and comics) is far more widespread, extending to the most banal convenience stores- there has not yet been anything in Japan approaching the campaign of Western feminist firebrands (Andrea Dworkin, Catharine MacKinnon et. al.) to lobby for these items' removal from such omnipresent shops, on the grounds that they exploit and terrorize women. Distribution of titillating and prurient material extends, in the larger cities, even to the front doorstep of one's home: I can hardly remember, during my residence in Osaka, many days that did *not* see my mail slot being stuffed with the infamous 'pink *chirashi*' or soft-porn promotional flyers for innocuously-named sex businesses like 'aesthetic salons' and 'delivery health'.

Although the distribution of pornography to retailers is less regulated in Japan, the content of the actual materials are more highly scrutinized by the censor's eye (apparently overriding the Japanese Constitution's Article 21, which flatly states that "no censorship shall be maintained"): shots of penetration are not allowed without being covered by *bokashi* (a digital 'mosaic' or other blurring / obscuring element.) In such a climate, legal debates that ended years ago in the West are just now being resolved in Japan: Takashi Asai, the head of Tokyo's Uplink publishing concern, became the subject of a landmark "obscenity or art?" ruling that favored the latter: he was finally granted legal permission to publish a book of black and white Robert Mapplethorpe photographs, featuring male frontal nudity, as of February 2008. An editorial in *The Economist* magazine attempts to shore up the bizarre incongruity of calling Mapplethorpe's work obscene when traditional art in Japan dealt with this subject matter at least four centuries ago: specifically "woodblock prints from the 17th century, called *shunga,* depict penises the size of battering rams."[18]

Amazingly for 'adult' magazines, certain words are even printed in an incomplete, censored form- the word *manko* [vagina] normally has the middle of its three written characters replaced with a hollow circle akin to the dashes or asterisks used to mask profanity in English texts (although, like those bowdlerized texts, it will be perfectly evident to any adult reader what the 'mystery' word is.) A quick glance at Article 175 of Japan's penal code will shore up the vagaries and multiple possible interpretations of Japanese obscenity law, which seems to be very inconsistently enforced. Fictional pornographic scenarios are also required by the censors' board to have a 'socially redeeming' or even moral message. The above variables have all combined to make for some of the most bizarre erotic entertainment on record: *anime* cult favorites of the 'erotic horror' genre, like *La Blue Girl* and *Urutsukudoji,* have arisen out of a social climate where sex scenarios have to be outlandish and transgressive enough to compensate for the disappointment engendered by the *bokashi* - so, enter animated sex with hermaphroditic demons, or even scenes of would-be rape with a "moralistic" ending (e.g. animated scenes in which the attackers are magically incinerated by their prey prior to climax.) Akita himself has commented on the fetishistic subcultures that have sprung up as an unintended consequence of the *bokashi* and the related attempts to preserve standards of decency within porn: "the mosaics, which cover the genitals, imply this attitude - largely particular to the Japanese - to sex. For example, female genitalia are generally a fetish. In addition, the number of fanatical adherents of the 'Lolita Complex' is growing, because - as children have no pubic hair - their genitals are not censored. Males in the media tend to be boys...[and] these are not necessarily political subjects (in the sense of elections, etc.)"[19]

All this aside, there does not seem to be a monolithic attitude towards the erotic or "ero" media: participation in the production of Japanese porn is also not seen as an instant ticket to social disgrace, nor are porn actresses and models always assumed to be on the receiving end of organized criminal exploitation (despite the undeniable involvement of local crime syndicates in all sectors of carnal entertainment.) The sound artist (and one-time Akita associate) John Duncan, in conversation with the author, recalled at least one incident where a well-known female racecar driver worked on the set of an unorthodox erotic film of his. This side detour into porn acting was not seen, as it might be elsewhere, as a careless discarding of the status gained by her racing success, or as a desperate means of maintaining the spotlight on herself - it was, by all accounts, something done willingly and enthusiastically, for personal reasons that had little to do with public image. Some notable female participants within the *noizu-kei* have themselves contributed to the various "ero" industries, including Junko Hiroshige of Hijokaidan Mayuko Hino of C.C.C.C. (the latter's dual role as live electronics manipulator and pornographic actress has caused her, on occasion, to be seen as a Japanese analog to Throbbing Gristle's

Cosey Fanni Tutti.)[20] Still, accusations hold that Merzbow is tilling a starkly chauvinistic field by attaching his work to the male-oriented porn world, and by lending his sounds to, for example, *harakiri* fetish films.[21] Akita offers up the following defense of his interests, invoking Jung and Wilhelm Reich in the process:

> ...pornography is the unconsciousness of sex. So, Noise is the unconsciousness of music. It's completely misunderstood if Merzbow is music for men. Merzbow is not male or female. Merzbow is erotic like a car crash can be related to genital intercourse. The sound of Merzbow is like Orgone energy - the color of shiny silver.[22]

It is not the continually cresting and falling tidal wave of mainstream Japanese porn which holds Akita's interest, though- although he has regularly used pornographic images in his mail-art style collages (and had a series of recordings tellingly entitled *Pornoise*), the porn images were just another element in the assessment of mass communications debris: in their crudely xeroxed, discolored form, isolated from the glossy sheen of their parent media, this imagery could hardly be seen as titillating- if that did happen, it was perhaps a case of the viewer's visual hierarchy favoring female nudes over the other abstractions gracing Akita's cover collages, rather than the creator's sole intent (the nude flesh on display in Akita's cassette artwork has, for example, also been overlaid with grids, halftone patterns or other visual devices.) The apex of Akita's interest in extreme eroticism was his interest in *kinbaku-bi*, the Japanese art of rope bondage extant as an art form since the Edo Period (1603-1868). Not always viewed as high art or as a form of sexual stimulus, it was originally a form of punishment by public humiliation, and was also a residue of the country's astonishingly bloody *Sengoku* [Warring States] era. Not until the eccentric 19th-century reign of Emperor Meiji would rope bondage become a subject worthy of artistic portraiture, as exemplified by Edo-period painter Seiu Itou. Nowadays it is a vital visual component of the Japanese arts underground; 'extreme' *manga* artists such as Suehiro Maruo (known in the music subculture for his works gracing the covers of John Zorn's Naked City albums) have used this imagery to stunning effect when combined with a social realist illustrative style. Akita warns, though, that his use of *kinbaku* imagery - connected as it is with deep emotional and historical resonances - is not something intended as a careless 'shock tactic', and more work goes into these particular images than has gone into the use of 'found' pornography. In contrast with the anonymity of those images, Akita has photographed *kinbaku* images by himself and maintained personal relationships with both the bound models and their binders.

As Akita was once fond of reminding interviewers, Kurt Schwitters' maxim of "everything erotic, everywhere erotic" has helped to legitimize both the visual and sonic methods of Merzbow - the 'descent to the mundane' which is simultaneously the acknowledgement that any object can grant an epiphany, from the hemp rope of the bondage practitioner to the discarded, dog-eared magazine found in the waste receptacle of a Tokyo subway station. And although Akita's project name may owe itself to Kurt Schwitters, there are clearly other thinkers lodged in his personal pantheon- thinkers who paint eroticism and carnality in even more vivid hues. Like his contemporaries in Whitehouse, Akita made no secret of his fondness for French philosopher Georges Bataille: one Merzbow release, *Music For The Dead Man 2*, is a soundtrack for Dutch filmmaker Ian Kerkhof's film treatment of the Bataille story *Madame Edwarda*. In some respects, Akita's championing of Bataille's ideals dovetails into his fondness for Kurt Schwitters- both individuals, in their respective media, seem to believe that transgressive acts can provide a gateway to the sacred. Just as Schwitters elevated scraps of debris and other base materials to high art, Bataille favored the paganistic means of reaching divinity through 'impure' actions. Both Schwitters' and Akita's refusal to become dejected by the scum of their immediate surroundings (in Akita's case, the defoliated sprawl of Tokyo) recalls Bataille's thoughts on the origins of eroticism- namely, that eroticism lies in the "certainty of doing wrong." Some statements by Carl Jung's protégé Aniela Jaffé strengthen the philosophical link between Schwitters' artwork and Bataille's theory of sacred transgression, claiming that

> Schwitters' exaltation of the grossest material to the rank of art, to a 'cathedral' (in which the rubbish would leave no room for a human being) faithfully followed the old alchemical tenet according to which the sought-for precious object is to be found in filth.[23]

Bataille's theory of transgression was, given the time and place of his own investigations, necessarily aimed at Christian religious precepts. However, in the non-Christian yet clearly conformist environs of Akita's Japan, the Bataillean species of transgressive behavior still have plenty of targets to aim at (Pedersen identifies these as "the magical, extreme violence, sex that does not aim at reproduction, insanity and generally prohibited behaviour.")[24]

The Million Record Man

Pornography thrives through its promises of inexhaustibility - an endless procession of interchangeable bodies willingly participating in an endless number of sexual scenarios; an illusion of constant sexual diversity and infinite virtual sex partners offered in place of committal or monogamous relationships. And if none of these fantasies ever do manifest themselves in reality, the internet has at least created a situation where these fantasies can be projected *ad infinitum* - with some 12% of the internet given over to porn (and growing), it can safely be said that more exists than can ever be consumed in the lifetime of the most die-hard, lusty aficionado. Given Masami Akita's fascination with pornography's role in the grand scheme of both *masukomi* and *minikomi*, it would seem natural that he mimic pornography's 'unlimited supply' with one of his own.

Akita's breakneck pace of releasing records, with only miniscule stylistic deviations from one to the next, has few other obvious parallels in the mass media world besides the production of pornographic films and magazines - and given that the majority of the design / layout work, recording, mixing etc. is handled solely by Akita, the Merzbow assembly line almost makes the distribution of porn products seem lagging in comparison. The Merzbow discography, next to Sun Ra's, is one of the most extensive in the history of recorded sound, providing a rich variety of choices for casual consumers and continually frustrating the efforts of completists / elitists.

Within this unprecedented discography, release formats run the gamut from the older hand-copied cassettes with photo-copied (again, often pornographic) inserts to conventional mass-produced CDs, with a host of *objet d'art* anomalies in between (e.g. 7" acetates in crudely stitched-together vinyl bags.) The liner notes for the Merzbow 'remix' CD *Scumtron* list - for the year 1996 alone - six 7" records, one 10" record, one double 10" record, one LP-only release, and 13 full CDs (two of which are more than one disc's worth of material.) Go back to 1983 on this same list, and the grand total of releases stamped with the Merzbow insignia comes to *sixty-nine* - but this is really one of the more *conservative* estimates of Merzbow's output, considering that it doesn't take into account the dozens of self-released cassettes, on the 'ZSF Produkt' imprint, that were Merzbow's stock in trade throughout the 1980s. It also omits Merzbow's frequent contributions to various-artist compilations, works that featured Masami Akita in a capacity other than the 'main' performer in Merzbow (e.g. his frequent earlier collaborations with KK Null), and the non-Merzbow cassette releases issued on ZSF Produkt by other respected 'tape underground' artists. Nor does it include two of the most dramatically ambitious releases in the canon of commercially available music: the overwhelming fifty-CD retrospective "Merzbox", or, more amusingly, the Merzbow CD sealed into the CD player of a Mercedes car.

The latter item has been, like most things that happen without a clear precedent, hotly debated as to whether it exists or not. Many have written the Merz-mobile off as a quirky urban legend, or as a viral meme intended to expose and ridicule the cosiderable monomania of noise collectors. Still others are amused just by the *possibility* that something so pregnant with meaning and / or comic potential could exist. The conflicting Merz-mobile legends are best laid to rest by Anders, boss of the Swedish 'Releasing Eskimo' record label, as follows:

> A while ago I had a Mercedes 230 that I didn't drive much. The police told me that I had to move it or they'd tow it away. Well, I didn't want to keep it and I didn't have anywhere to store it so I decided to use it for something else. I rigged the car's CD player with our latest release of Merzbow's "Noise Embryo" CD so that the music started when the car was turned on and it was impossible to turn it off. I put it up for sale as an extremely limited edition of the "Noise Embryo" CD but no one ever bought it, and in the end the car broke down. So we took out the CD and got rid of the car. Now I'm thinking about if it's possible to release a record in a Boeing 747...[25]

The existence of a 'Merz-mobile' would seem to confirm a gnawing suspicion about his gargantuan *ouevre*, namely that Akita's unmitigated onslaught of releases is a cynical statement on the nature of commerce and the insatiable lust for constant novelty - *the more you have, the more you want* - which is again seen most vividly in digital porn consumption, but certainly applies to any other number of consumer goods. Critic Nick Smith suggests that this cynically humorous approach is endemic to the entire "noise" genre, wherein "noise flaunts the absurdity of its condition, exagerrating its commodification to call attention to the swindle at work."[26] Elsewhere, a positive Merzbow review in *Wire* magazine (where Akita unsurprisingly remains one of the most heavily-reviewed artists) applauds this approach: "say, is that a 50 cd Merzbow box set in your pocket, or are you just pleased to be erecting a monumental indictment of the music business?"[27] Alternately, the avalanche of recordings is an extension of the Schwitters aesthetic to which Akita is partially indebted: like Schwitters' original *Merzbau*, Akita appears determined to view his recorded output as a single continual life's work that will only reach a satisfactory finished state when the artist himself terminates. He has stated repeatedly that "Merzbow is me," hinting at the fact that the furious releasing will probably only conclude with own his death.

However, to many of his critics, Akita's recognition of his own mortality, and his subsequent effort to construct a dual shrine to his self and his influences, are no justification for the hyperactivity that has become his trademark. An *AllMusic* review of the *Merzbox* typifies the type of criticism that sees Akita's work purely as a "freakshow" entertainment more concerned with some Olympian level of achievement than with aesthetic progression:

> Does Akita honestly believe that these two full days of unedited noodling are worth a serious listen? Is he toying with gullible listeners? Is the ultimate conclusion he wants us to reach that, in the end, after enough time, all music sounds like the same old processed crap? It will never be possible to understand his intentions. When all is said and done, though, the *Merzbox* belongs in *Ripley's Believe It or Not*, and not in your record collection.[28]

Interestingly, this review's attempt at forcing the noise audience to "face the music" - i.e. to admit that is in denial about the degree to which it *really* enjoys the aural qualities of such work - is not exclusive to pop-cultural critique. While it is understandable that mainstream music consumers would steer clear of Merzbow's furious sonic scourging, he has not yet earned across-the-board approval within the more limited sphere of the avant-garde, either. Within many of the same organs that sing Merzbow's praises, contradicting voices rise up to bring him back down to earth, sounding as harsh or occasionally harsher than the perplexed reviews issuing from pop music journals. In the same issue of *Wire* featuring the above praise for the *Merzbox*, critic Biba Kopf scoffs that "[Merzbow's] discography is way out of proportion to the slim idea it contains," and that "his imagined cultural transgression is like that of salarymen who read SM comics while rubbing themselves against women on crowded Tokyo trains"[29] (interestingly, in this column, Kopf seems quite contented to invoke Western stereotypes of excess Japanese perversity while simultaneously decrying "the myth of Japanese extremism"- but that's neither here nor there.)

Some of Merzbow's most severe critics are, of course, the guardians of "authenticity", that most sacrosanct of artistic attributes which has already been battered away at by Marcel Duchamp's toilet, Andy Warhol's Brillo boxes, Damien Hirst's formaldehyde-soaked shark, Genpei Akasegawa's 1,000-yen notes, and much more besides. The "authenticity" schoolmarms not only echo complaints like Biba Kopf's (that Merzbow's huge body of work is an exercise in naked self-indulgence), but accuse Akita of plundering the idea bank of the most influential 20th-century art movements without adding any real substance of his own.

In the eyes of the harshest Merzbow detractors, he is little more than a glorified "piggyback artist" of the kind who would add his own amateurish, clumsy brushstrokes to a reproduction of a universally recognized masterwork - a charlatan who swipes the artistic lexicon of previous innovators and uses their key terms as seductive ciphers, operating in the same way that a flashy corporate logo might work. However, Akita has never professed to be an 'originator' of anything in spite of what his many record labels' press releases may say about him; even in his self-penned 1996 book *Noise War* there is but a single mention of his own activities among the discussions of other seminal Industrial and noise artists, and of artists perhaps less relevant or meritworthy than himself. If Akita fancies himself as anything, it is perhaps as a "safe deposit box" guarding the more relevant facets of 20th-century subculture in a largely unappreciative, culturally conservative, and hostile world, keeping this knowledge on ice until some cataclysm ushers in a future world that may be able to understand it better.

Among the items re-appropriated by Merzbow are, of course, the project's namesake itself, taken from Kurt Schwitters' tendency towards ennobling random detritus. The Viennese Aktionists (specifically Otto Mühl) get their customary nod with references to noise performance as being "material action". The Pop art canon is also picked over, with works such as Tom Wesselman's *Great American Nude* being used as album titles, or 'superstars' from Warhol's Silver Factory being used as the 'subject matter' for songs (see "International Velvet", B-side to one of Merzbow's *Pornoise* series of cassettes.) Would-be Warhol assassin Valerie Solanas even gets sucked into the Merz-vortex, as Akita wittily changes her S.C.U.M. ("Society for Cutting Up Men") into "Scissors for Cutting Up Merzbow". Other references in Akita's name game are slightly more obscure, such as the track title "HGL Made A Race For The Last Brain", a knowing wink directed at exploitation film director Herschell Gordon Lewis. The more celebrated exponents of home turf counter-culture from the 1960s onward (see experimental filmmaker Shuji Terayama, or the ruggedly independent Tohoku folk singer Kan Mikami) are conspicuously absent from this roll call, echoing the tendency of post-Industrial sound artists to consistently reach beyond their native shores for flashpoints of inspiration: Zurich Dada and American celluloid sleaze fit Merzbow's research agenda just as comfortably as Tibetan Buddhist ritual or Balinese gamelan have done for European artists.

It is tempting for the anti-Merzbow constituency to write off the 'name dropping' titles as the self-conscious intellectual preening of a fine arts graduate from Tokyo's Tamagawa University. Indeed, Nick Smith implicates Akita in such activity when insisting "noise advertises its relation to the history of modern art as if to grease its cultural acceptance and pre-empt charges of vapid meaninglessness" (Smith also adds the "popular musicians have also used this ploy to add high-brow meaning to club music.")[30] However, there may be more practical reasons for the frequent cultural namechecking in his works, which should at least also be considered until Akita's "vapid meaningless" can be decisively proven. Certainly Akita could merely take the route of his colleague, the sound artist Francisco López, and leave titling out of the equation altogether- but unlike López' ongoing project of 'absolute music,' Merzbow's cultural references act as signposts which show how hopelessly cluttered and confusing the mass media landscape has become, while at the same time showing how vibrant and varied the counter-culture has remained in spite of it all - providing listeners a rough guide to the triumph of the imagination, as it were.

The jury is still out on the ultimate usefulness or relevance of Merzbow's endless record-releasing project, and will likely remain so: it is simple enough for some to dismiss claims that his creations are insincere and therefore inauthentic. As we have seen, 'pure' noise has existed as a style well before the first releases of Merzbow, but this alone hardly disqualifies Merzbow from authenticity. The preoccupation with being 'the first' to do something (therefore being more 'authentic' than any future protégés) should not always dictate how sincere an artist's intentions are, and it is likewise foolish to believe that the originator of a style or technique deserves a career-long salute from critics on the strength of this "early bird" status.

Theater of (Anti) Cruelty

Vegetarian though he may be, Akita has a conspicuously omnivorous musical diet, and the giant musical output on his behalf is a distillation of these varied tastes - everything from free jazz to Brazilian psych / space rock group Modulo 1,000 to minimal techno has colored one aspect or another of the Merzbow maelstrom. In fact, a listing of Akita's favorite records on the Essence label's website points at musical influences far removed from the realms of Industrial music and power electronics: King Crimson, Deep Purple and Black Sabbath all emerge as clear favorites. This eclecticism, though it might appear to contradict the methodology of noise, is in fact highly compatible with it: David Novak (following from Toshiji Mikawa's definition of "noise") has pointed to noise as being an "anti-generic" genre, a classification that I might expand upon by noting the similarly diverse tastes of Akita's peers in the noise underground. Everywhere one turns in these subterranean environs, we can find artists whose engagement with noise seems to be a matter of fusing all their myriad tastes into one overwhelming totality of sound - an activity that is quite different from using noise to wipe out or deny these influences. Although Akita has stuck mainly to live performances of his own material, a Merzbow DJ set would have to be one of the more eclectic ones on the face of the planet, his fanaticism for musical archiving, and for mildly proselytizing the value of 'unsung' heroes becomes more interesting when seen as part of a larger program of preservation.

Along these same preservational lines, Akita has - for over a decade now - devoted much of his output to ecological issues and to confronting the reality of a brutally scarred Gaia. There is a sub-category of Merzbow releases that are released in tribute to either favorite musical acts or adored animals, and in both cases there is a genuine desire on Akita's part to become more than just a rank -and-file noise agitator, but to act as a militant ecologist preserving sounds, concepts, and hopefully even whole living organisms. Curiously, Merzbow is not a participant in the 'acoustic ecology' movement that uses audio recording to - among other things - catalog bio-acoustic noises and to critique the relationship of humanity to the biosphere. Also, given the sheer enthusiasm that Akita has since shown for preserving terrestrial biodiversity, it is noteworthy that he makes very limited use of field recordings. In fact, as Paul Hegarty points out, the 2001 Merzbow release *Frog* is a standout in the Merz-catalog for this very fact,[31] while also noting that the mutation and expansion of the characteristic frog noises is a sort of technique to place nature again beyond man's comprehension (and thus, control.)

The urgency of this particular mission requires an aesthetic framework that will effectively convey that urgency, and so Akita's magnified bloodstream of noise is just as suited to this campaign as it was to parodying or *detourne*-ing the hyper-materialist 'scum of the city.' Merzbow's noise is just elastic and abstract enough that the addition of one extra signifier - let's say, in this case, a sampled bird call - can completely re-wire the noise machine, upgrading it from its role as Orgone generator to that of an alarm warning against the unsustainable abuse of the ecology. This heightened concern for *la terre* comes concurrently with a switch to a purely digital recording format (Akita now works mainly with computers and the more noise-friendly applications such as Max/MSP). Despite the needless protests from the analog cult, the digitized sound is very much a seamless integration with his older material, not the imagined betrayal of Bob Dylan 'going electric' - this holds especially true on recordings in which snatches of analog-era Merzbow appear to be digitally sampled, carrying over the practice of xenochrony that informed earlier Merzbow works like the *S.C.U.M.* LP. The newer computerized work also has the advantage of using the entire audible frequency range from 20Hz to 20kHz (as John LaTartara has discovered while viewing spectograms of certain Merzbow tracks.)[32] Like the red-tinted subtitles that scroll across the bottom of the television screen during hourly news reports, warning of changes to the current 'terror alert' or other critical issues, Merzbow's 'digital-era' noise is relentless and practically dares one to *not* feel like the genuine threat level has been raised.

The wild sonic vision of Merzbow, as we've seen, is not just an affront to conservative Japanese aesthetics and 'harmony at any cost' social customs - it is also a splash of acid in the face of condescending foreign Japan-o-philes, who delight in reducing modern Japanese life to a set of cutesy consumerist signifiers, or envisioning the buzzing modern Japanese landscape as a harmless video game made flesh. Though he is no ambassador for the culture of Hello Kitty and other neotenous cartoon characters, Akita fits into the general pattern established by the post-War *anguro* culture: that is to say, less opposed to Japanese tradition than to Japan's drive to become appreciated as a world power. While previous manifestations of 20th century art, e.g. *butoh,* celebrated the concept of transitory beauty or *mono no aware* [lit. 'the sadness of things'] that typified the Heian era's (794-1185) classic literature, Merzbow has become concerned with the transitory nature of things for a different reason altogether. That is to say, he has become concerned with the mutually assured destruction that will result from treating all organic life as raw material to serve humanity.

This involves personal sacrifices that may not be immediately apparent: by dint of his diet alone (Akita is an avowed vegan and 'straight-edger'), he has already excluded himself from the majority of Japanese social life, which invariably revolves around meat-eating and alcohol consumption. There is, arguably, a greater pressure in Japan than in the West to eat meat and consume heavy volumes of alcohol, which arises partially out of a post-War phobia of appearing destitute - as the logic goes, the only 'sensible' person who would resort to a vegetable diet would be someone without the income to pay for meat dishes.

The floating abstraction of Merzbow's sound has, until this turn towards ecological concerns, been open to interpretation, and has shunned the sociopolitical in favor of a more personal quest to (again, partly owing to Schwitters' and Bataille's influences) find an erotic charge in the most mundane materials. Merzbow's anarchic approach originally made no intellectual demands on listeners other than that they listen in the first place. But now the older, open-ended Merzbow has indeed been supplanted by a newer incarnation with a proper mission: raising awareness of animal rights, and of the increasingly suicidal reign of anthropocentrism, also called 'speciesism' by *Animal Liberation* author Peter Singer. At least one of Singer's thesis points – that the "greatest good for the greatest number" ideal of utilitarianism should be applied to animals as well as humans - has had some definite influence on post-Industrial music culture, with compilation LPs such as *Devastate to Liberate* promoting the agenda of the Animal Liberation Front, and with several musicians crossing over from endorsement into activism: Tactile member and Coil associate John Everall is one of the more recent cases of a member of this scene being arrested for animal liberation guerilla tactics. Akita has not been as militant (as far as I know), but has been involved in a number of street protests coordinated with the PETA [People for the Ethical Treatment of Animals] campaign against "Kentucky Fried Cruelty," and has stated on occasion how he wishes to use his music as a weapon to counter the noise pollution generated by swarms of Tokyo residents, also hoping that the music's inherent rage and severity would serve as a reminder to humans of their destructive potential. This applies not to the destructive potential of modern warfare, but also to the haughty assumption that nature can replenish itself at a rate equal to the rate of humans' conspicuous consumption.

Straw Dogs author John Gray has referred to mankind as *Homo Rapiens* in said work, a designation that Akita would likely agree with. Gray sharply dismisses the possibility that humanity will ever completely subjugate its host body Earth, though, suggesting that "the biosphere is older and stronger than [humans] will ever be"[33], or, even more damningly, that "either the Earth's self-regulating mechanisms will make the planet less hospitable for humans, or the side effects of their own activities will cut short the current growth in their numbers."[34] Biologists such as Reg Morrison have also noted that human fertility will follow a natural curve instead of continuing to double interminably: actually taking a nosedive once its collective metabolism adjusts to a more resource-poor environment, and following the examples set by other prolific species (including rats, a comparison which agitated misanthropes have made many a time). This is a happy ending of sorts for biophiliacs, although it side-steps the gruesome realities involved in getting to that endpoint: with humans being an extremely tenacious species, environmental stress will manifest itself in numerous wars over raw materials, extending even to raw materials as fundamental and 'given' as water. Inability to combat new strains of disease, evolving quicker than the antibiotics tailored to fight against them, would be another grim inevitability leading to a population crash. The true tragedy of all this, though, is not that prolific population will lead to a terrifying de-population, but that human arrogance will accelerate the inevitability of all this. Fellow vegan sound artist Dave Phillips, who claims to have been on hand at the concert event where Akita experienced his vegan 'epiphany' (an event at the Red Rose in London, alongside the New Blockaders), describes the situation as such:

> Many humans act as if they are elevated, but to think or feel that is just dumb. Humans definitely have qualities that are well worth exploring, but to think we should only

consider ourselves, our values and our goals and to put everything else secondary is a way of perceiving and dealing with things that definitely lacks perspective. C'mon, we know we are seriously dangerous, for ourselves and for all around us. We are (or might be) incredible beings, but might is not right. The ways humans perceive things, the value we give to things, are not the only ways that exist to do so, nor that we ultimately exist in. We're all in this together and there's more to 'gain'/learn than what is generally proposed. As well as asking ourselves what we really want, we should also question what really matters and what is involved.[35]

Phillips' insistence that humanity is not elevated above the animal kingdom is not the unfounded, eccentric opinion of someone on the radical fringe of the arts, but a growing consensus among students of animal behavior, in particular animals' communicative mechanisms. The most recent issue of National Geographic, as of the first edition of this writing, cataloged a number of incidences in which animals have learned communicative behavior supposedly exclusive to humans: an African gray parrot forming neologisms when it doesn't know the English word for an object, border collies that will 'fetch' a photographic representation of an object when the real object cannot be found, and bottlenose dolphins who will exhibit individualized, spontaneous behavior when being given a command to 'create.' Such discoveries lead University of Florida researcher Clive Wynne to conclude that "we're glimpsing intelligence throughout the animal kingdom, which is what we should expect. It's a bush, not a single-trunk tree with a line leading only to us."[36] Other animal researchers, like the primatologist Frans de Waal, have claimed that culture -learned behavior patterns passed from one generation to another by means other than genetic ones- is not an exclusive human property either. De Waal's books Chimpanzee Politics and The Ape and the Sushi Master are revelations in this regard, and in the former he suggests that the unfocused nature of human perception is to blame for the assumed lack of intelligence in animals, not any actual failure on animals' part. Claiming that "initially we only see what we recognize" when observing animals, In describing the learning process associated with studying chimp behavior, De Waal uses a metaphor of chess:

> Someone who knows nothing about chess and who watches a game between two players will not be aware of the tension on the board. Even if the watcher stays for an hour, he or she will have great difficulty in accurately reproducing the state of play on another board. A grand

master, on the other hand, would grasp and memorize the position of every piece in one concentrated glance of a few seconds. This is not a difference of memory, but of perception. Whereas to the uninitiated the positions of the chess pieces are unrelated, the initiated attach great importance to them and see how they threaten and cover each other. It is easy to remember something with a structure than a chaotic jumble. [37]

De Waal goes on to explain how this is the guiding principle behind Gestalt perception, in which the 'larger picture' is greater than the sum of its individual parts. To people like Akita, attempting to observe this 'larger picture' has landed him in Japanese zoos and aquariums, where the suffering and psychological stress of captive animals - in particular, several varieties of seal - has struck him as being too close to its human equivalent for comfort.

So where exactly does Merzbow's biophilia fit into his previous examinations of, among other things, ritual bondage and urban 'scum' culture? It's possible that, having mapped out the limits of human behavior so thoroughly in multiple media, Akita has simply done all he can to provide illustrative examples of the human condition using humanity itself- and, in the best Bataille tradition, has come to the conclusion that man is little better than animal life in its basic impulses and needs. So the logical progression from this point seems to be a shift in subject matter towards the 'source' itself- towards that which humanity has unsuccessfully attempted to estrange itself from. The non-linear nature of Akita's noise has always hinted at the fact that the man/nature rift is less wide than guardians of progress-at-any-cost would like it to be- and his past interest in *kinbaku-ki* hints at this.

Akita's documentation of ritual bondage is not an admission that cruelty is the guiding force in nature, but that human social hierarchies based on wealth and lineage are inherently flawed in comparison to natural hierarchies based on strength and aptitude. These natural hierarchies have not disappeared from modern human behavior- they have just been absorbed into ritual or behaviors like sado-masochistic practice; into private ceremonies which distill the dull, aesthetically blank control and subservience of work-a-day urban life into one compacted threshold experience, in order to 'burn it out' of one's system. Here is a practice which, depending on the personal desires of the participants, voids the privileges of wealth, social standing, and gender as well (remember that many of de Sade's most avid 'libertines' were female.) The man who gives 'masochism' its name, Leopold von Sacher-Masoch, declares that "it is possible to love really only that which stands above us,"[38] suggesting a yearning towards a more natural ordering of things.

For, try as it may, humanity can't seem to achieve a total dominance of nature - as the *Homo Rapiens* suggested by John Gray, it is a parasitic body who can only claim victory by means that would destroy it as well.

If nothing else, Akita seems to be, for the first time in a while, preaching to an audience that is not entirely converted to his stance. The audience for noise is less homogeneous in its ideological makeup than might seem otherwise; covering both sides of the left-right political divide, and comprising everything from dyed-in-the-wool nihilists to cautiously optimistic 'peaceniks' with a slightly more pronounced flair for aesthetic aggression than their musical forbears. Perhaps knowing that many members of his audience closer to the 'nihilist' end of the spectrum are more likely to behave in a cynically wasteful, solipsistic manner, Akita has taken a risk in declaring himself to be otherwise: he has re-tooled his presentation and somewhat lessened its ability to be appreciated in a completely subjective way. Reviews for recent Merzbow releases, as can be expected, have been decidedly mixed. But again, this is in keeping with Merzbow's (and indeed, most "noise" artists') desire to confront an audience rather than placate them. It was Georges Bataille, after all, who claimed that he preferred to discuss the Marquis DeSade only with people who were revolted by him.

In Akita's 2005 book *Watashi no Saishoku Seikatsu* [My Cruelty-Free Life], he states that, while vegetarians and vegans are very much ostracized in the modern social landscape, there is a long tradition of vegetarianism and anti-cruelty within Japan- and vegetarianism / anti-cruelty mandated by the highest levels of government, no less. Akita makes a case for Japan's history as being, until recently, a fastidiously vegetarian one: in the concluding chapter of his book, he writes that successive emperors from the 7th century onward (beginning with the emperor Tenmu) went so far as to make official decrees banning meat consumption. One reason for this injunction, originally, was human utility rather than a pure consideration of 'animal rights': otherwise useful animals could not be squandered for purposes of eating. Of the five main animals listed in the ban, horses provided transportation, cattle were used for plowing the fields, dogs served as trusty alarm systems and security guards, and roosters had a knack for telling time. Monkeys served no particular use, but nonetheless resembled humans and were thus off limits.

Although this ban was limited to the cultivation period of April through September, hunting and other acts persisted- so in the 5th year of Tenmu's rule, the *houjoue* or 'order to release live animals' was initiated: this decree was largely influenced by Tenmu's Buddhist faith (curiously, a Merzbow CD entitled *Merzbuddha* is part of Akita's expanding laptop-composed, 'pro-animal' canon, as is a 6-disc juggernaut entitled *Houjoue*.) The ban on slaughter of animals for consumption purposes would be tested during a famine in the year 737, under the emperor Shoumu's rule, although it was not repealed- and a ban on rice wine consumption was tacked on as well. The war-ravaged *Sengoku* period, with its increased need for animals to be mobilized to the various fighting fronts, would bring another blow to humane treatment of animals, as an inevitable side effect of the widespread human slaughter that characterized the age. Then in 1549, Francis Xavier would introduce Christianity to the archipelago, temporarily popularizing the custom of meat eating, although carnivorism ironically became one of the reasons cited for the subsequent ban and vicious crackdown on the faith. Over a century later, the cruel treatment of dogs in some regions could net one the death penalty, thanks to the edicts of the "dog shogun" Tokugawa Tsunayoshi (Tsunayoshi also gained some notoriety for, during times of austerity, feeding his dogs fresh fish at taxpayers' expense).

Western influence would make a resurgence, however, with the appearance of Commodore Perry's black ships during the era of the Tokugawa shogunate, and culminating in the opening of the first Japanese-owned beef vendors in the 1860s. All that remained for a full transition was for Emperor Meiji, upon restoring Japan to Imperial rule, to lift the previous bans in an attempt at promoting a synthesis with the Western powers (although this was not done without some angered protest). It was one of the many concessions that would earn Meiji foreign accolades like the English Order of the Garter, but would have the Japanese population viewing him as a reckless appeaser. Meat eating would then become especially prominent among the modernizing military, despite the advice of noted military doctor Sagen Ishizuka to the contrary. From the dawn of Japan as a legitimate world power, to the post-war American occupation, straight through to the present day, no attempt at a government order on par with Tsunayoshi's actions, or the *houjoue* of Emperor Tenmu, has ever been established.

Akita concludes *Watashi no Saishoiku Seikatsu* with a heartfelt wish for his native country to return to the days in which meat consumption was seen as a barbaric act, and throughout the book he establishes himself as a gentle and compassionate soul- again, quite a surprise for those expecting a one-dimensional, brutish cartoon character. Akita's tenderness also says something for the malleability of pure noise as a medium- while some continue to use it solely as a metaphor for power and authority, Akita now uses it as either a defensive weapon / a digital deterrent or as the avenging 'voice' of his beloved, yet grievously wounded, flora and fauna. If he can find a way to foist the unhinged rage of his pro-animal rights music on the pedestrian populace as well, he may yet have a chance to win some new converts to his cause.

+

Despite the chorus of groans arising from reviewers who must review yet another Merzbow release without attempting to use the words 'extreme' or 'harsh', the ongoing career of Merzbow has succeeded in a rare coup: broadening his appeal while restraining himself to a tried-and-tested set of techniques and ideals. Merzbow has provoked debate at an international level, about all of the themes he has trafficked in - and yet the very existence of this debate, and his status as a polarizing artist, has served to confirm the potency of his creative approach. Within the Merzbow camp there are now refugees from 'old school' Industrial music, electro-acoustic researchers, death metal denizens, militant vegans, psychedelic eclectics, fetishists and still more indefinable shades of culture - all united and inspired by the core defining feature of this music. To wit: radical autonomy combined with heightened levels of persistence in the face of "micro" popularity, and with a refusal to make any ancillary concerns beyond the ideas themselves the focal point of the work. The *Merzbox* did not appear overnight, nor distribution deals with virtually every outlet that stocks outré music, nor the opportunity for presenting his art in every conceivable venue from smoke-filled Osaka basements to sterile, hyper-modern galleries and museums. But these things did finally come to pass, and not by squabbling endlessly about the intricacies of musical equipment, by taking refuge in the shielding conformity of a musical 'scene,' by trading in ethno-cultural stereotypes, or by trying to cover up the lack of conceptual rigor with a media-friendly public persona. The things that have 'made' Merzbow are important, as they are the things which will continue to animate the uncompromising art of this century- no matter how complex its entanglements or how brutal its tragedies.

Mash Communication
(and Other Symptoms of the Sampling Virus)

During much of the previous decade spent living abroad - prior to my un-triumphant return to the United States - I had no television in my home. I can hardly say I regret the decision. The perpetually rotating cast of eccentrics that found their way to my Czech *panelak* apartment more than compensated for whatever talk show deficiency I might have been experiencing, and occasionally did their best to liven up my surroundings with intimate "action" sequences (as was the case when a heavily drunk friend-of-a-friend, assuming that my being born in the U.S. made me complicit in starting the Iraq War, took several haymaker swings at my head and thankfully missed before being forced out of the building.) While in Japan, I had hardly enough domestic space to accommodate such colorful and violent characters, but still found it unnecessary to keep a TV on hand for surrogate "company." I learned that merely sitting on a raised concrete slab outside of a major train station, for a length of no more than 10 minutes, could provide more entertaining variations in audio-visual data than the majority of television programming could. In a culture that seems constantly on the move from one functional node of the city to another, any slight withdrawal from the purposeful swim can be illuminating.

Speaking of withdrawal: when I returned to the land of my birth (which, for all its many many flaws, was not accusing me of complicity in violent geo-political catastrophes) one effect of my prolonged absence from television's staged realities was a kind of nausea. Upon seeing it again, the hyper visual editing that I had been ignoring for years seemed to come at me with a redoubled aggression and insistence, to the point where I found it infinitely more relaxing (if not more invested with an element of surprise) to watch the TV channel which hosted live, closed circuit camera footage from my apartment building's lobby. I was initially bothered by the fact that, while I took pride in being able to handle the most chaotically collaged forms of electronic music, I was repelled by this same effect being applied to the medium of television. Yet it didn't take me long to realize why this was the case, and why this didn't reflect some deep denial over aesthetic consistency: it was not the technical aspect of this presentation that irritated me, but the arrogance inherent in its content.

In blasting out vividly distorted sequences of unrelated or abstract images, these slick promotional clips and trailers seemed very confident in the fact that they were having the "last laugh" on the "industrial" culture that previously used this technique of data overload as a de-programming, de-standardizing device. Upping the ante by adding all kinds of blatantly digital "grunge" (or what might be called "pre-stressing" in the garment business), it had to be admitted that this noisy visual style of advertising knows what it is doing, and is particularly cognizant of the thrill that audiences get from the feeling they are tuning in or decoding some clandestine transmission.

The fact is, though, that TV advertising's *re*-re-appropriation of a prior counter-cultural reappropriation is not the last word in anything so much as it is another stage in a reciprocal struggle (and we can wonder if it is even the "latest" phase at this point.) Students of Deleuze & Guattari would call this back-and-forth shifting between contexts a cycle of deterritorialization and reterritorialization, in which "territories do not refer only to geographical or physical entities, but also to mental, psychical and cultural territories (ecologies in later Guattarian vocabulary.")[1] Whether one subscribes to these theories or no, this struggle over the value and meaning of "cultural remixing" is itself an epiphenomenon nested within the larger phenomenon of "culture war." And while some cultural producers - identifying themselves with one mode of resistance or another - have proudly declared themselves as "guerrilla" mixers, the romanticized language of partisan fighting does not really apply anymore. The leveled playing field presented by networked digital culture has, in this "non-kinetic" mode of battle, led to a peculiar dual mimesis in which state authorities and insurgents will each appropriate the others' communicative modes: for example, the Chinese government's "50 Cent Party" takes to Internet comment boards wearing the mantle of "unaffiliated" concerned citizens, while weblogs and YouTube videos can be developed that falsely purport to be the "official voice" of policing agencies. Presuming that this war is being fought primarily on grounds of greater autonomy or greater regulation, which "side" has the upper hand? It is a question that cannot be answered without first surveying some of the more celebrated and controversy-courting manifestations of reappropriated and collaged culture.

Audio vérité

It is painfully easy to take a defeatist stance in a culture where virtually any creative content can be made to endorse products or politics inimical to its creators. A number of different strategies exist, though, for making music that cannot be put in the service of commercial imperatives. Sound artists like Francisco López, CM von Hausswolff, Sachiko M. and Mika Vainio have so far avoided representation by commercial factors, with sound works of such demanding nature and elemental purity that it would seem absurd to harness them to the quaint, inoffensive 'lower-case' or 'Helvetica' culture[2] of most corporate advertising. The same could be said for their quieter counterparts- Roel Meelkop, Bernhard Günter and others. Anything is possible, but for the moment it seems like their works invite listeners into a world where minimum sonic output will serve a maximum of needs, from study aid to spiritual reflection- it is a concept far from the reach of the 'vertically integrated' corporate world, and its strategy of planned obsolescence.

Another method of resistance - one which has seen many precedents throughout the history of collage art - comes courtesy of the defiant groups of so-called "culture jammers" who use the raw materials of corporate advertising culture and mass entertainment either against them or without regard for these materials' officially designated use (this group includes Negativland, The Tape Beatles, John Oswald and a host of others.) The distinctive feature of their work is the simultaneous consumption of communications media and *production* of new media using that same material, a strategy that opens up onto numerous different stylistic avenues. Whether the end result is irreverent entertainment, scathing commentary or some form of transcendence, their methodology usually shares many of the same creative features- as per the Tape Beatles' Lloyd Dunn:

> It is sort of an empowering act, as far as I'm concerned, to take this stuff that sort of comes out of the pipes like running water...using it as an ingredient in a recipe that we've come up with on our own...and taking what we consider to be meaningful, telling bits, putting them in a new context 'makes them strange'- it estranges the listener from those bits that they're very familiar with, and puts them under a microscope so that they can be examined in a kind of weird mixture of objectivity and subjectivity.[3]

Groups like the Tape Beatles used a large archive of video images as well as audio to re-shape the media landscape, often smashing together the otherwise neutral and inoffensive imagery of big businesses to shore up their banality and shallowness (the Tape Beatles' parent organization 'Public Works Productions' also hints at the corporate ideal of banality as an indicator of progress.) Elsewhere, the 90s phenomenon Electronic Broadcast Network built their multi-media works on the energetic and rhythmic chassis of techno and hip-hop (genres which, of course, already relied heavily on montage as a method.) The video component of their work was a discolored and retina-frying barrage of multiple screens synced to the time signatures of their music, with the speeches of all-too-familiar political figures and heads of state being contorted into absurd proclamations. One EBN staple was a clip of George Bush Sr. mouthing the chorus to Queen's "We Will Rock You" in the Oval Office, while other prominent newscasters had their nightly monologues seamlessly edited to encourage slavish submission to mind control.

Ignoring the merits and drawbacks of video montage for now, the audio collage has been used with to a greater degree by insurrectionary elements in society. Forms like the *musique concrète* of Pierre Schaeffer took a bold step by using audio montage of natural and non-notated sounds as early as the 1940s, but explicit socio-political content in sampling would not come about until later. One example of this, from the European continent, is *Preislied* [Song of Praise], the 1972 *Hörspiel* [radio play] of Paul Wühr. *Preislied*, as described by radio historian Gregory Whitehead, was an a-musical collage work pieced together from various German citizens' statements of approval for their nation, however:

> ...when these positive expressions are isolated from their original context, grouped thematically, and arranged by inflection, the effect is profoundly critical. By separating individual words and sentence fragments from their usual fluid context, by listening to the concern latent in the hesitation and aggressive inflection, by allowing the original voices to recombine according to principles transparent only in the language as raw material, Wühr uncovers a discordant malaise beneath the superficial harmony of everyday praise.[4]

The use of the sample and the sampling collage as critical, interrogative audio weapons really came into its own with Industrial culture: Cabaret Voltaire set the template for many less imaginative industrial dance bands by marrying breakdance electro-funk with histrionic evangelists, while Throbbing Gristle's tape collages created a hyperbolic yet oddly convincing portrait of coercive, controlling behavior and its omnipresence in all areas of modern life. Early Psychic TV built upon this research by collaging *un*controlled, unmediated sound events - recordings of wolf howls and orgasmic climaxes - in an attempt to bypass the superego and obliterate inherited conceptions of 'self.' The Catalan artist Jordi Valls (a.ka. Vagina Dentata Organ), closely associated with PTV, dealt with much of the same material. From roughly the same era, the anarchist collective Crass had the 'Thatchergate' tapes attributed to them: a collaged conversation between Ronald Reagan and Margaret Thatcher that seemed to present the two leaders as supporting an all-out nuclear war, and which was deemed convincing enough to cause a media panic before it was revealed as a hoax.

+

In parsing this history of radical audio collage (and "appropriation" by extension), it is worth considering more of the avant-garde attitudes towards the collaging practice that pre-date the somewhat "media-centric" version we experience now. Lautreamont's proto-Surrealist classic *Les Chants de Maldoror*, with its celebrated "fortuitous encounter of a sewing machine and an umbrella on a dissecting table," was something of a defining moment for literature and eventually the whole of the arts - Renato Poggioli has pointed to the "fortuitous encounter" as a method in itself that thrived upon "the jostling of mutually repugnant objects [...] to symbolize the absurd complexity of the psyche."[5] Further down the road, the Surrealist fascination with the *wunderkammer* or "curiosity cabinets" of Renaissance Europe inspired projects like Max Ernst's *Histoire Naturelle*, itself a kind of ode to the endless recombinant potential of nature (Ernst speaks here of mutations like "feather-flowers" and the "circumflex medusa.")[6] The Surrealists were also, I submit, informed by a Darwinian optimism about the continuity and malleability of organic life - a belief in the potential of hitherto inconceivable organisms - more than by a pure desire for amusing perversity. The Surrealist campaign for greater automatism, via Ernst and other representatives, had to admit that the regenerative biosphere was the ultimate "automatic" artwork. In focusing on nature as such, this seemed to be a necessary companion piece to the cultural heterogeneity favored in the ethnographic exploration of fellow Surrealists such as Georges Bataille and Michel Leiris.

Given the lengthy history of the radical "sampling" methodology, it is strange to consider how long it took for this to be applied to television, if even in the way that was introduced at the beginning of this chapter. On one hand, this is not surprising, since - as Tim Wu notes - "unlike the telephone, radio, the Internet, and other technologies, electronic television in America simply skipped any amateur or noncommercial phase."[7] This lineage does much to explain why experimental and even irrational uses were found for these other media, while the emerging U.S. counterculture tended to avoid television. So, on one hand, this focus away from video information was not completely an extension of the 1960s youth counterculture's desire to have its 'own' media (underground newspapers, underground radio, rock 'n roll records) which were distinct from the one-way, non-responsive television enjoyed by their elders. Access to television studios was severely limited, and the censorious 'standards and practices' of that day would excise any kind of social commentary from new programs whose initial premise met with interest from network officials. Another reason for the cultural shift towards audio collage was the time-consuming nature of video production and editing, and the speed at which social and political events were occuring relative to this laborious process: by the time a group of artists could compose a masterful work of superimposition like the kind the seen in Kenneth Anger's films, current events might have dramatically changed. In short, film and television were not yet the media that would lend themselves well to broadcasting urgent, time-sensitive messages from the underground.

Bite Back

The Californian "culture jamming" group Negativland, active in some form or another since 1979, has come to exemplify much of what is now taken for granted within the digital cultures of appropriation and audio sample collage: with their unparalleled obsessiveness relating to media manipulation, and their near-total focus on media sampling as musical raw material, they have come to exemplify the novel situation in which "the consumer is at once consumer and producer."[8] That is to say, they refuse to see any incoming transmission or recording as a finalized product, but as mutable material for new works. In doing so, they have run afoul of U.S. copyright law numerous times, but have more importantly spotlit the hypocrisy of those who claim exclusive access to the tools of manipulative or opinion-guiding techniques of audio-visual editing. Negativland's singular focus throughout their history has been the exposition of manufactured media realities. Having achieved this, the band also provides an object lesson in the creation of counter-realities, and hints at the overall level of commitment that needs to be maintained if one wishes to make this type of psychological warfare into art. Put simply, their aim is to increase awareness of the "dissecting table" that is necessary to organize the meeting between the umbrella and sewing machine.

Consider, as an example, the exhausting 3-hour show offered by their 2000 *True / False* tour: a stimulus festival served up by an indistinct team of white-suited technicians whose racks of gear were camouflaged by similarly white sheets (although these had an aesthetic value on their own, they were used as a video projection surface as well.) Their set featured such anomalies as a maudlin folk song dedicated to a favorite brand of lime soda, advertising detritus layered on top of polished heavy metal loops, and a kind of audience 'sing-along' using lyrics recited from the text appearing on an overhead projector. During a lengthy instrumental segment, the band's mysterious master of intercepted communications, 'The Weatherman,' appears via TV screen to rant about blighted urban America, while a pulsating bass groove moors his surreal storytelling into place. All told, the show would be a comic masterpiece if not for the effect of having the brain hammered with one out-of-context advertisement or pop music quotation after another: such a congested presentation gives you the deflating feeling that you have wasted much of your life learning and regurgitating pop culture trivia or performing equally needless, automatic actions.

Negativland's cultre jamming practice - taken from the radio context in which "jamming" is a deliberate increase in the ratio of noise to signal - is at once a counter-narrative and a surrealistic entertainment, with both these effects arising from a different type of reappropriation, namely that of using tranmission and playback tools also as compositional tools. Despite the seeming novelty of this action, Negativland are part of a long tradition of wrenching consumer electronics from their intended uses. Home entertainment playback devices, like record turntables, were re-envisioned in pieces like John Cage's 1939 composition *Imaginary Landscape No. 1* as tools to be manipulated and not merely 'heard.' Fluxus artists like Milan Knizak showed similar tendencies- see his short *Broken Music Composition* built from the sound of broken records pieced back together in new configurations (pre-dating the CD 'glitch' techniques of Oval by four decades.) Nam Jun Paik, also an artist associated with Fluxus, regularly used television sets as artistic building blocks for his sculptures- one of which is, appropriately enough, an American flag composed of 70 monitors (*Video Flag.*)

A strong desire to cut television off from its role as the temple of consumer culture, and to use it as a more introspective tool of inquiry, also shows through in pieces like Paik's *I Ching TV*. In his video collage piece *Suite (242)*, a narrator invites the viewer to participate in a ritual which will reconfigure the television as a meditative device: turning the TV screen towards the wall, then tuning the box to a dead channel while cranking the volume of the white noise louder, and dimming the lights in the room- all in a concerted effort to "find out what television has to say to us, from the other side."[9] This was a practice that would be encouraged by members of the Temple ov Psychick Youth and by their musical counterparts Psychic TV, who - echoing Paik's 'monitor sculptures' - would arrange television sets on stage in the antenna-like shape of their "Psychick cross" logo. The politicized hip-hop act Disposable Heroes of Hiphoprisy did the same in the early 1990s, with a Christian cross formed from TVs appearing as a motif in their video for "Television: The Drug Of A Nation," hinting at a different, and more sinister kind of television deification.

Negativland, however, have eschewed the spiritual elements, adopting a more pragmatic view of what their work will ultimately accomplish, but also noting (in an echo of our opening discussion) the corporate / state media's advanced ability to recuperate any kind of 'alternative' dialogue back into its hegemonic power structure:

> In Negativland, we understand that those who create
> culture for distribution by the corporate dream machine

have no effect on how they operate. Even when work is criticizing the machine that is consuming the work, you will not notice even a hiccup in response. In fact, such work is often welcomed because it proves the machine is the pillar of free expression in a democratic society that it claims to be.[10]

In other words, even the most virulent forms of protest can be re-packaged as entertainment. One 1967 incident on the *Smothers Brothers Comedy Hour* illustrates this scenario perfectly: the 'hippie' act Buffalo Springfield had been booked to perform their protest song "For What It's Worth" on the program, although the numerous cutaways and comedic interruptions during the performance of the song ruined its ability to be taken on face value. As Aniko Bodroghkozy describes it,

> [Buffalo Springfield singer Stephen Stills]' comments about police power weighing down on the rebellious young, and the generational gulf created by the war in Vietnam, were obliterated by the manner in which the lyrics were illustrated. For those already familiar and aligned with Stills' sentiments, the meanings of the song were still available despite the comic intrusions. For audience members who did not know the song and its political implications, the cutaways may have made the material politically meaningless.[11]

Curiously, in spite of such manipulations, Bodroghkozy suggests that there has been a steady increase in anti-establishment or anti-corporatist programming on television since the 1960s. For one, she notes that "businessmen were consistently disparaged and demonized in the aftermath of the 1960s,"[12] citing *Dallas* character J.R. Ewing in this regard. Bodroghkozy also claims that, even in the right-wing revival of the 1980s, shows taking a politically conservative tack "...ended up being a ratings loser, if the project even got past the development stage."[13] The 1990s and 2000s naturally sealed the deal with the massive popularity of irony-laden, liberal-leaning cartoon shows like *The Simpsons* on the Fox network, but network television was far from being a stimulus for genuinely radical modes of thinking: television transmissions were still, after all, a split narrative of the "main" content and advertising, with the latter's share of overall broadcasting time increasing significantly over the years. If assembled skillfully enough, the messages contained in advertising could easily neutralize whatever morals were contained in the programming proper.

Meanwhile, the 24-hour news networks of the 21st century present cultural upheaval in a kind of "info-tainment" format, so framed with slick graphics and high-tech effects, that the raw events themselves appear to have been fictionalized or dramatized. The utterly trivial (like a celebrity's 'coming out' or drunken escapades) can be projected as something of world-shattering importance, and matters of world-shattering importance can be downgraded to passing irritations.

To this end, the 'sound bite' (which will hereafter refer to short clips of audio as well as video with an audio component) is still the most deadly arrow in the mass-media quiver. Its power to falsely imply new contexts not intended by the original speech has been used with an efficacy that can, in the space of a few seconds, destroy or discredit political campaigns, cultural movements, and academic careers that have taken years to build. So, unsurprisingly, the sound bite is also the main weapon in Negativland's acute counter-strike on mass media's disingeneuous play with contexts and meanings - the group's best pieces are built from dozens at a time. Just as the merged governmental-corporate media has co-opted 'alternative' ideals and diluted them into fashion statements and purely cosmetic concerns, the dominant icons of mainstream media have been by re-designed by Negativland as something else entirely. By isolating select moments from countless audio and video recordings, and pairing them with 'leaked' recordings of badly behaving celebrities or intercepted private communications, all kinds of things become possible: a well-loved radio announcer is unmasked as a cynical and vulgar egomaniac, leaders of obscure religious cults alternatingly lend their endorsement to MTV stars and damn them to the eternal pit of hell, *Sound of Music* star Julie Andrews joyously sings that "girls with blue whiskers, tied up with noodles" are one of her "favorite things."

Triumph of the 'Stupid'

Perhaps Negativland's first major success in turning the mass media against itself was the track "Christianity is Stupid" off of their 1987 *Escape from Noise* LP. This would soon become the fuse for a deviously executed media hoax that would raise the bar for all future attempts at 'culture jamming,' exposing the gullibility and manufactured hysteria hard-wired into mass media, especially the carefully edited 'infotainment' of nightly news broadcasts.

The original song samples liberally from a 1971 Christian propaganda film entitled *If Footmen Tire You, What Will Horses Do?*, which illustrates a nightmare scenario of American takeover by Communist forces that will happen if the country does not experience a full-scale Christian "revival". Of course, a land invasion of the well-defended U.S. was hardly feasible during the Cold War period, but that is beside the point. The exasperated narrator of ...*Footmen*, a reedy-voiced Southern Baptist preacher named Estus Pirkle, becomes fodder for Negativland in a most unequivocal way when his doom-and-gloom pronouncements are snatched from the original context of the film, and set against a backdrop of thudding industrialized rock.

In the original film, Pirkle narrates a scenario in which beleaguered Christians are forced by their Soviet captors to sit around a campfire "from 5 o'clock in the morning...to 10 o'clock at night" endlessly chanting "Christianity is stupid...Communism is good...*give up!*" Negativland removes this selected quote from its surrounding narrative framework, reducing Pirkle's message to the exact opposite of what it wished to convey: in song form, its defeatist message is more like the kind of 'Tokyo Rose' broadcast used to puncture American troops' morale in wartime. Of course, on one level it is a poke at the terrified bunker mentality that is adopted by the evangelical Christian movement even when it is, in reality, doing quite well in its recruitment and fund-raising efforts. More importantly, though, it is also a comment on the power of the "blurb" or "sound bite" to severely alter a speaker's original intentions, harmonizing them with whatever pre-scripted template that the mainstream media is presently using. And if the original manipulation of the Pirkle footage was not illustrative enough of this tendency, it was taken even further in Negativland's live concerts of the time: hearing Pirkle's alarmist message re-edited to say "*Christianity is...Communism!*" takes the content to even loftier plateaus of subversion.

Pirkle's exasperated quote is just one in a staggering catalog of alternately chilling and laugh-out-loud appropriations collaged together with surgical skill- a skill that, given the effort and timing involved in selecting individual samples from an ocean of recorded and broadcast sound, can capably be called virtuosity. The band also has a special talent for unearthing the confidential: much of the sampled material in Negativland's *oeuvre* was clearly *not* intended by its originators to be publically available, to say nothing of being in the "public domain". Try, for starters, a pirated recording of the legendary American 'top 40' radio DJ Casey Kasem, as he unleashes a breathtaking torrent of profanity on one of his aides in the studio sound booth: upon receiving an earnest request to dedicate a song on air to the deceased dog of a listener, an audibly enraged Kasem rants venomously about the impossibility of segueing into this dedication from a "fucking up-tempo number". The Kasem rant has been left intact, largely unedited, because in this case it 'speaks for itself'- Kasem tells us all we need to know about the hot-tempered control freak which occasionally lurks behind his public façade of avuncular likeability (to his credit, however, Kasem allowed the resulting Negativland recordings to remain in circulation in the spirit of free speech.)

This straight, uninterrupted playing of a sampled source may be the exception in Negativland's sampling campaign: for every Kasem rant there is something like the piece "O.J. and his Personal Trainer Kill Ron And Nicole." This is built on samples from an actual O.J. Simpson exercise videotape, in which the ex-football star and widely suspected wife murderer good-naturedly chats with his personal fitness trainer about his blood circulation: "...getting the blood flowing," as it were. This is set against a backdrop of screams and other violent sound effects. It is the kind of stuff that easily provokes lawsuits over defamation of character, and Negativland did take a definite risk with this kind of presentation- but first more about their work itself before the consequences of that work come to the fore.

The true *coup de grâce* of Negativland's "Christianity is Stupid" came not with its inclusion on the *Escape From Noise* LP, but with the subsequent usage of the song in a carefully staged, tragicomic media hoax. In the beginning, this was not a simple one-off prank, but a means of releasing the band from some unwanted obligations: *Escape From Noise* had, somewhat unexpectedly, gained the band an attentive following in the alternative music world. Even an independent record label like SST, to which Negativland was signed at the time, would have wanted to convert this popularity into a concert tour- an option which, according to Negativland's Mark Hosler, was an impossibility for the band:

> ...we had to cancel the tour [because] we weren't going to make money; we couldn't afford to take time off from our jobs and lose money. One member of the group suggested that we think of a more interesting reason why we can't tour, and so we put out a bogus press release saying that we were being investigated by federal authorities, because of a possible connection between the song 'Christianity is Stupid' and a quadruple ax murder in Rochester, Minnesota. A few fanzines came out that reported it, and then a magazine in California called *BAM* wrote about it, and it just started to snowball. Then KPIX, which is a CBS News affiliate here in the San Francisco Bay Area, picked up on the *BAM* article, came to our studio and interviewed us. After that ran on TV, the *San Francisco Chronicle* saw the KPIX news broadcast and then *they* wanted to write about it, and at a certain point we decided that it was turning into something where we were going to be guilty of this gratuitous exploitation. There was no way to ever get around that, but it was turning into that more and more, so we then decided that the best thing to do was to

make a record out of it that explained what had really happened: how we had lied.[14]

Although the influence of "Christianity is Stupid" on the aforementioned murder was a concoction of the band, the murder itself was a real incident plucked from the headlines of the day: a 16-year old Rochester teenager named David Brom had indeed murdered every member of his immediate family, allegedly over religious disagreements (which, as the hoax went, were amplified to the breaking point when "Christianity…" sent Brom over the edge.) The 'religious argument' angle of the hoax was included as a nod to the media's then current, pseudo-scientific obsession with backwards messages and subliminals included on popular music recordings. One such element in the 1980s news cycle was the allegation that, upon hearing the message *"do it!"* subliminally encoded in the track "Better By You, Better Than Me" from Judas Priest's *Stained Class* album, Nevada teenager Ray Belknap killed himself with a 12-gauge shotgun. In the ensuing trial over subliminal content, the issue of Belknap's troubled relations with his family, and his general mental instability, were predictably downplayed by the prosecution (although Judas Priest's defense attorneys certainly made them an issue, as can be seen in the documentary film *Dream Deceivers*).

Although Judas Priest was on trial and the family of Belknap was not, the family did have to acknowledge some factors that would put their son 'at risk' of committing suicide upon hearing such an apparently neutral message as *"do it"* (the audio of which was heard as having completely different content by listeners who had not already had those words suggested to them.) According to *Skeptical Enquirer* writer Timothy E. Moore, both Belknap and his friend Ray Vance, who seriously disfigured himself in an attempt to commit suicide alongside his friend,

> …felt socially alienated; they were emotionally distressed, often depressed, and impulsive. Vance once broke another student's jaw in a fight at school. Both had a history of drug abuse, petty crime, school failure, and unemployment. Family backgrounds were violent and punitive. Belknap had attempted suicide before and had expressed suicidal intentions. Just prior to the shootings, Belknap gave out some of his Christmas presents early and indicated a desire for his sister to name her baby after him if anything happened to him. Most of these factors were mentioned by the judge in his final ruling. They were included "reluctantly" to show that the deceased were at high suicide risk (see Litman and Farberow 1994.)[15]

Furthermore, Moore (who was a witness at the trial) writes that the effectiveness of subliminal messages has never been proven in any rigorous study:

> There is not now, nor has there ever been, any reliable empirical evidence that subliminal stimulation can produce anything other than fairly brief and relatively inconsequential reactions. Further, there is no evidence whatsoever that subliminal directives can compel compliance, and no such evidence was presented at the trial. Perhaps with the help of the defendants' experts, the judge came to realize that subliminal directives do not have the influence attributed to them by the plaintiffs. A more thorough grasp of the issue might have yielded a summary judgment, thereby precluding a long and expensive trial.16

Finally, it should be mentioned that the placement of such a hidden message by a professional music group would be a reckless career move. As Judas Priest vocalist Rob Halford intimated, what band with serious aspirations towards making money in the entertainment business would want to liquidate its own fanbase by ordering them (subliminally or otherwise) to kill themselves?

Although the Judas Priest trial would not take place until 1990, it was precisely this climate of poorly researched, sensationalistic reportage that spawned the 'David Brom' element of Negativland's scam. Negativland's Don Joyce suggests that the "Christianity..." hoax was so successful in its critique of media that it was revelatory even to the band. The group had always been reasonably suspicious about the actual degree of truth contained in mass communications, but had even their own expectations shattered by reporters' willingness to accept Negativland's bogus press release as a legitimate news source: "We found out that journalists *routinely* do not check sources, they simply re-print, cannibalize and copy what's been written elsewhere in the news, which *they* believe when *they* read it. And it's so routine it's frightening."[17]

Meanwhile, "Christianity is Stupid" made a 21st-century comeback of sorts, in a media climate once again obsessed with the violent fringes of religiosity: to coincide with the release of Mel Gibson's gore-soaked film *The Passion of the Christ* ("the most violent film I have ever seen" according to film critic Roger Ebert)[18], Negativland used "Christianity..." as the soundtrack for a video collage *The Mashin' of the Christ* composed almost entirely of films - *Passion* and others - depicting Christ's flogging and crucifixion. In doing so, the band was in clear violation of the Digital Millenium Copyright Act (DMCA): the film used to edit *Mashin...*, since it was obtained around the same time as the movie's actual theatrical release, would have been an illegal decrypted copy, and the DMCA states that it would be illegal to use this material even in the making of collage art. Nevertheless, the *Mashin...* video was still in heavy circulation on the Internet as of the original draft of this writing, and was even uploaded to peer-to-peer file sharing networks by some mischievous subversives who convinced downloaders that it was a full version of Gibson's *Passion* film.

The Copyright Fence

Unfortunately for them, Negativland will not be remembered only as the band that pulled off the grand *Helter Stupid* performance almost without a hitch, but as the band which engaged in a financially and emotionally draining legal battle with Island Records- at the time the record label of the platinum-selling Dublin rock heroes U2. The saga began with the 'leaked' Casey Kasem radio rehearsal mentioned above, in which the disc jockey goes into a fit of pique when being forced to read out the names of the U2 band members on air- *"these guys are from England, and who gives a shit!"* is Kasem's famous explosion (made extra humorous by the fact that, moments before in the same recording, Kasem had correctly identified the band as being from Dublin, Ireland.) Despite some foolish public relations moves made on behalf of Negativland's contemporaneous label (SST released a t-shirt featuring a "KILL BONO" design), the record featuring Kasem's 'contribution' (titled, conveniently enough, *U2*) was more concerned with the ambiguity and limitations of broadcast language than it was a direct attack on said band. In fact, the record featured a number of other samples which obscured the record's exact message and made it something of a potpourri of then-current Negativland concerns: it featured more samples of anti-rock 'n roll evangelists railing against the power of "the beat" to erode morals, clumsy threats seemingly delivered over citizens' band radio, and comparitively sober voices cutting through the insanity to lecture on the history of vulgarity in broadcast media. Nevertheless, this was not enough for Island's lawyers, who saw their content as the primary taregt of attack, serving Negativland with a lawsuit before even issuing a 'cease and desist' order.

Initially, the objection from Island Records came as a result of the *U2* EP's cover art being a "deceptive" use of their property: a viewer's visual hierarchy might cause them to think it was indeed a new U2 album, since the word 'Negativland' appeared on the cover in much smaller print than the blaring 'U2' (which was also placed above the word 'Negativland.') In addition to featuring the letter U and the number 2 in a bold typeface spanning the album cover, the artwork also featured a graphic of a

Lockheed U2 spy plane (a visual pun whose meaning was initially lost on Island's legal watchdogs.) As Negativland and their sympathizers have noted, it was ironic that the name of a well-known Lockheed product was being appropriated, even "trademarked," by a world-renowned rock band with no protest from the plane's manufacturers. The EP *did* feature liberal sampling of U2's smash hit "I Still Haven't Found What I'm Looking For," with one version of the song replacing Bono's lyrics of romantic longing with a laughably awkward and obsessive stream-of-consciousness monologue from the nasal-voiced, hectoring 'Weatherman.' This would be discovered by the Island team soon enough, but in the meantime, there was the controversial cover to deal with. On this issue, Don Joyce says "we would have changed the cover if they'd asked us to, but they never did. They never even asked about that. They just had this sledgehammer approach which is based on being so big and so rich that no one can fight them."[19]

Negativland's near-destruction at the hands of Island's legal team turned them into unwitting spokespeople for the concept of fair use and copyright law. The band has been especially acute in its condemnation of entertainment conglomerates, like Disney, who rise to prominence in very much the same way that Negativland did: by tossing aside the myth of 'originality' and creating new works that may be indistinguishable from previous works, at least in certain aspects.

Don Joyce features in a short film entitled *Mickey & Me*, which details the case of a video store owner being served with a $110 million lawsuit by the Disney corporation, merely for the act of making theatrical trailers for Disney films available on his store's website- an act which was, in essence, *promoting* Disney product. Disney's strong-arm legal attempts to have complete control over their properties (Mickey Mouse, Donald Duck etc.) are shown as being hypocritical in light of Disney's own numerous appropriations: *Snow White*, though falsely assumed by some to be a Disney original, was simply an animated re-hash of an earlier silent film, which was itself inspired by a Grimm Brothers fairy tale. *Steamboat Willie*, the legendary 1928 Mickey Mouse cartoon (and the first cartoon to feature both a musical soundtrack and sound effects), was revealed as a structural parody of Buster Keaton's short film *Steamboat Bill Jr*. Professor Lawrence Lessig of Stanford Law School, also featuring in *Mickey & Me*, capably summarizes the ethical quandaries (and ultimate agenda) involved in such multi-media megacorps' criticism of those artists who make use of the same re-appropriating tactics:

> Was *Steamboat Willie* theft of Buster Keaton's *Steamboat Bill*? I think the answer's got to be 'no, it wasn't.' Yet, the freedom to make *Steamboat Willie*, which was the core behind Mickey Mouse, would be denied today if anyone

tried to take a Disney character and make an equivalent takeoff, and produce a new line of creativity on the basis of that. Now that's to show, you know, one argument in this is the argument about hypocrisy. What justification is there for this radical expansion in the ability of the past to control the future, when so much of the greatest part of the past was made in a context where creators before *it* were not able to control it?[20]

American copyright law can seem maddeningly selective when parodies of the *Steamboat Willie* variety are involved. Shervin Rezaie notes that a parody often meets the criteria for legal acceptability since the "original work used is the subject of the commentary," whereas "with regards to satire, something other than the original work is the subject of the commentary [...] satire is not sufficiently transformative because the original work is simply used as a vehicle to make miscellaneous commentary."[21] Much of Negativland's work lies in a grey area between these two poles, considering that they often - within the same song - offer commentary on "original" works and yet also make miscellaneous commentary: as hinted at before, their "special radio edit mix" of "I Still Haven't Found What I'm Looking For" mixes a "cheesy" note-for-note synthesizer reworking of U2's original track overlaid with unrelated thoughts on broadcasting and recording speech codes, along with numerous sound events whose precise meaning could be quite subjective. The objections to satirical content seem to be grounded in a fear that the transformative use of the work will somehow "upstage" the original property within the marketplace of ideas- superseding it in popularity and meaning. It is an objection that is not purely based upon competition for financial rewards: in an age where more and more parodic or satirical work is made available at no cost by its digitally networked producers, this marketplace of ideas re-emerges as the main battleground for this issue.

On the topic of legal troubles arising from unclassifiability as either parody or satire, the trials of Canadian 'plunderphonics' godfather John Oswald should not go unnoted either. Like the *U2* ep, John Oswald's 1989 *Plunderphonic* CD, an independent release, caught the attention of the record label lobby group CRIA [Canadian Recording Industry Association] through a cover which mimicked the design of Michael Jackson's *Bad*- the head and leather jacket of Jackson, from the original *Bad* LP, were placed onto the body of a naked white female model. According to Oswald, some 6,000 copies of the original album leaked (and one of these may fetch you a 4-figure dollar sum, if you own one)[22], but all the rest were unceremoniously crushed, along with the master recordings. In no way, though, did Oswald ever attempt to convince listeners that the music on the 'banned' *Plunderphonic* CD was his own creation from start to finish: he has gone so far as to list all the sources he has sampled on his releases, using the credits in the same way that the writer of a research paper would use bibliographical notes. For his song titles, Oswald also delights in soldering together the names of appropriated musicians in order to form *portmanteau* such as "R.E.M.T.V. Hammercamp" and "Marianne Faith No Morissey" (see his release *Plexure* on the Avant label for a full listing of these Frankenstein monsters.) Another game involves using the names of the original artists and making them into anagrams for the listener to decipher: Michael Jackson becomes "Alien Chasm Jock," James Brown becomes "Jem Snowbar," and Bing Crosby becomes "Gibbons Cry." Oswald's mischievous practice (the original *Plunderphonic* album cover notwithstanding) also has its visual equivalent in sound artist Christian Marclay's *Body Mix* series of collages, which take unmodified original LP album covers and overlay them at key points so as to create aberrant pop-rock monstrosities from conjoined body parts.

Oswald's work, while it has met with the same controversy as Negativland's, and also uses dense masses of manipulated samples as its raw material, largely ignores the topical content that animates Negativland discs. Although one of the seminal pieces of this genre - Oswald's 1975 piece *Power* - combines the bludgeoning rock of Led Zeppelin with (you guessed it) an equally intense revivalist preacher, his later Plunderphonic works have passed on the chance to criticize crass TV entertainment, consumerism, and militant forms of religiosity. Unlike Negativland, Oswald composed his most talked-about pieces by himself with a digital audio editor, and did not make the occasional forays into mimicking 'real' pop song format with conventional instrumentation (although Oswald was a capable sax improviser on the side.) The aforementioned concept of 'making strange' figures heavily within the music, which, despite a preponderance of humorous content, can also delve into the realm of the haunting and beautiful (this is especially evident on later discs released under Oswald's birth name rather than the Plunderphonic moniker.) While it's hard to repress instinctual laughter upon hearing Oswald loop James Brown's grunts and elated shrieks into the realm of physical impossibility, there are moments of bliss, as well- like when Michael Jackson's "Bad" is given some kind of Gaussian blurring treatment, reducing the Quincy Jones dance-funk concoction into a narcotic haze of stuttering voices and brittle rhythms. It is an obvious bit of computer processing magic, but is no less captivating because of it.

Here, too, Christian Marclay pops up as a point of comparison: in this case for his fêted art object *Record Without A Cover*. A thick haze of disorientation hangs over this crafty audio montage of samples from $1 bargain bin records, and not just because the record - as suggested by its title - was meant to become dirtied and rapidly degraded upon purchase, gradually absorbing new audio ephemera (pops, crackles etc.) into the original mix. Like Oswald, Marclay tantalizes the listener with the sound of vaguely familiar "made strange"- the record's obscured and fouled sound snippets capably disrupt the mental filing processes of popular music junkies, especially those who are too concerned with "who-did-what-when" musical trivia to enjoy audio artefacts at a more pre-rational sensory level- and as odd as it may seem, *Record Without a Cover* is (for this author anyway) a genuinely pleasant listening experience on its own merits.

The broad usage of the quasi-legal audio sample, as both an aesthetic device and as a lucid form of socio-political commentary, now figures into the work of an expanding number of artists: the anarchic, often contrarian "irritainment" of Negativland and Messrs. Marclay and Oswald was also yanked into the new millennium by Stock, Hausen & Walkman (a blatant re-rappropriative pun on the Stock, Aitken & Waterman pop music assembly line- Andrew Sharpley and Matt Wand are the 'civilian' names of the band's twin sample-wranglers.) Stock, Hausen & Walkman's release of a record entitled *Buy Me / Sue Me* would seem like a subtle hint that the ongoing drama swirling around copyright law was beginning to supersede musical content (in this record's case, the 'musical content' was limited to 42 locked grooves, each one containing a different voicing of the word "me" repeated *ad inifinitum*.) More detrimental than the legal tug-of-war over sampling, though, may be what happens when these adversarial forces of hyper-commerce *embrace* it as a means of creative conduct, replacing the acumen of more critical artists with the desultory "throw something against the wall and see if it sticks" quality which is its hallmark.

Good Jammer, Bad Jammer?

> The process of replication functions even in cases in which the intent is critical, or the identification is made with a non-conformist model; anti-conformism creates a norm for replication, and in repetition music is no longer anything more than a detour on the road to ideological normalization.[23]

> -Jacques Attali

These ad people thought it would be really cool to hire Negativland. They wanted to give us their ads to cut up and do things with, and mock them and manipulate and do our Negativland 'thing' to. Since they were offering us a lot of money - $25,000 or so - both Don and myself immediately thought, 'Wow, we'd like that money, that sounds great. Is this an opportunity we could do something with?' Because over the years when weird things have happened to us, like when we've gotten in trouble, we've looked at these things as opportunities, not problems. In this case, my brain was doing the same thing: 'Can we somehow subvert these guys and do something interesting with this, and turn the tables on them?' And what I then realized was, 'Wait a minute, they called us because they want me to be thinking exactly what I'm thinking right now! That's what they want the ad to be.' So then I realized that we'd been had, we were fucked. There wasn't any way you could out-think them.[24]

-Mark Hosler

As suggested by Hosler above, the artistic technique that was once a gesture of defiance from the corporate feudalists' downtrodden serfs has been absorbed back into their "regularly scheduled program," to borrow the well-known television station announcement. The aesthetic of irreverent re-appropriation and "guerrilla remixing" has successfully wormed its way into a mainstream Western culture which has embraced irony and self-reference as 'hip', 'cool' marketing tools for generations now. In the U.K. and U.S., the coveted youth demographic of 18-35 years' age has, since the 1990s, favored consumer products which re-package familiar iconography in a manner more in keeping with the younger generation's post-modern questioning of cultural absolutes, and in keeping with their occasional dives into pure cynicism. Film comedies, especially those coming out of Hollywood, aim to court this market with 'spoof' movies featuring little more than a visual mash-up of characters and situations from dozens of other recently released films. During the writing of this chapter's original draft, the directors Jason Friedberg and Aaron Seltzer, famous for this gratuitous brand of entertainment, have parlayed another one of these films *(Meet The Spartans)* into an $18 million box office opening.[25]

Considering the legal troubles which have dogged Negativland, John Oswald and numerous other artists for their satirical use of popular songs - and given the fact that the Friedberg / Seltzer productions cleaver closer to the aformentioned legal definition of satire than parody - it seems puzzling that their comedic films, whose very lifeblood and narrative substance is formed by chaining together exaggerated reenactments of moments from other popular films, are given the 'green light' to exist. Theirs is a formula popular enough with the 'booboisie' so derided by Mencken, but they have also sustained a firestorm of criticism. Of a previous Friedberg and Seltzer production, *Onion* critic Nathan Rabin encapsulates the confusion surrounding these 'spoof' films' existence: "Is it enough to simply place a familiar pop-culture phenomenon into an unfamiliar context? Can contemporary comedy be reduced to the simple equation 'pop-culture reference + slapstick violence or scatology = hilarity?'"[26] So far, the answer seems to be a resounding 'yes' in a culturally cannibalistic America.

The popularity of the postmodern re-appropriation aesthetic is also evident in the youth fashion and design industries, where the turn of the millennium has been marked by a deep suspicion of imagery that appears sincerely happy or unashamedly positive- the assumption is that most, if not all, prosperity in 1st-world cultures must be either superficial or ill-gotten. So, these images, when employed, should therefore be worn in a 'critical' manner or should be combined with other paraphernalia that diffuses their meaning. For example, a cute, pastel-colored t-shirt from a popular cartoon franchise like Hello Kitty or My Little Pony combined with the more violent and monochromatic imagery of punk rock bondage gear. The skull and crossbones, once the heraldry of outlaw motorcycle gangs, has become the neutralized or "cute-ified" visual anchor for a thousand and one Etsy.com offerings, being knitted into brightly colored socks, scarves, mittens and other clothing items. As could be guessed by such re-appropriations of imagery previously associated with outlaw orders like the Hells' Angels, this mixing and matching of cultural signifiers from all over the map extends to the realm of the spiritual, and crosses class divisions as well: crucifix pendants being worn by people with no allegiance to Christianity, Celtic knots combined with Taoist icons, or cheaply made, mesh-backed truckers' caps worn with expensive designer jeans. Other unmistakable signifiers of class, like cans of the cheap, poor-quality 'working class beer' Pabst Blue Ribbon, are thrown into the mix as fashion *accoutrements.* The above styles, popularized by leisure culture magazines like *Vice,* show what can happen when re-appropriation is abused: in this case, mockery of the working poor (read: "rednecks") by the well-funded, youthful elite of districts like Williamsburg in Brooklyn, or Chicago's Wicker Park neighborhood.

Advertisement-laden magazines like *Vice,* in their early "noughties" heyday, tended to visually sample the culture of the (usually non-urban) American underclass, pulling it into the glossy world of high fashion. Sampling - be it the textual sampling of a Burroughs / Gysin cut-up, the visual icon sampling of a Heartfield anti-fascist collage, or a Negativland sound work - may have radical origins in challenging the *status quo* or dominant order and pinpointing its structural weaknesses. However, despite its avant-garde lineage, there has never really been any real 'safeguard' on the practice that would prevent it from being used in the service of that same existing order.

Having already noted how groups like Negativland have good fun at the expense of their cultural and ethical enemies, it also seems hypocritical to suggest that the problem here was *Vice's* adoption of the same agonistic means of enjoyment. Rather, the problem was one of the non-commital "having it both ways" pose of the "ironic PBR drinker" and all the other manifestations of ironic, mashed-up fashion or design: the producers and consumers of these images could at one moment point to their use as a self-deflating proof that all trends and styles are equally transient and pointless, and the next moment could return to enthusiastically trumpeting "x" appropriation as the latest unmissable trend. I believe that their brand of cultural appropriation is not a harmlessly chaotic game of just "trying something to see what happens," as this might imply taking some responsibility for whatever does happen. Rather, it is disingenuousness marked by a deflection of responsibility onto "popular culture" itself, as if popular culture were an immutable force that resists all attempts at altering its form and functionality. Negativland, whatever else one may think of them, have at least taken the more constructive route of refusing that we are inextricable from mass culture.

Certainly, these developments did not go unnoticed, themselves coming in for a strong dose of satirical mockery. The limitations of the post-modern youth culture blender to create meaningful discourse was at the center of Chris Morris' and Charlie Brooker's TV comedy mini-series *Nathan Barley* (Brooker's titular character is inspired in no small part by the success of pseudo-anonymous South London graffiti artist Banksy, whose work Brooker calls "imbecilic daubings" and "vague, pseudo-subversive preaching").[27] The show's anti-hero, a parentally funded, would-be subversive (in his own self-congratulatory words, a "self-facilitating media node"), runs a calculatedly offensive website called 'Trashbat,' which he uses to broadcast meaningless acts of cruelty online. His enslavement to social climbing and material acquisition causes him to worship superfluousness in the most idiotic ways (e.g. wielding a mobile phone equipped with "scratchable" MP3 mini turntable decks), and he seems incapable of seeing any uses for mass media beyond social grooming and perverse, ironic entertainment. When Barley's roommate Claire, a video journalist with an eye towards social activism, attempts to show him her documentary film footage of a of a 'junkie choir,' Barley immediately assumes that the film is meant to ridicule the sincerity of the choir members.

A poignant fact within this satire is that some of Barley's antics are almost indistinguishable from the acclaimed artist Banksy's brand of culture jamming, showing the possibility for such antics to be quickly "reterritorialized." A flyer for a Trashbat dance party features disturbing images of detainees at the Guantánamo Bay prison, mimicking a stunt in which Banksy snuck a dummy in Guantánamo prisoner garb into Disneyland. In another sequence, the 'splash page' of Barley's Trashbat site features an image of a police officer slitting his wrists, which is a carbon copy of Banksy stencil design. When not directly referencing Banksy, Barley still finds other ways to shock for its own sake: he delights in self-promotional pseudo-profundities such as *"Trashbat is…two people leaping from the Twin Towers…and they're fucking on the way down!"*

In addition to its implied condemnation of Banksy, the program fixes its sights on *Vice* magazine as well: the fictional magazine *Sugar Ape* in *Nathan Barley* lampoons the real-life tendency of *Vice* to "remix" atrocity and to cope with social crises by trivializing them[28] (one episode prominently features a *Sugar Ape* special issue entitled 'The Vice Issue,' whose centerpiece is a fashion shoot featuring female models pretending to be beneath the age of consent, who are then placed in sexually compromising positions.) The use of sampling and re-appropriation has become, in the hands of fictional "*faux*hemians" like Barley and his real life equivalents, a valuable tool in triumphally declaring that 'nothing is sacred,' even though such a proclamation ignores the existence of belief systems beyond the boundaries of the 1st world (even *within* the 1st world this is far from a blanket truth.) If anything, the tendency of privileged "media nodes" to marginalize and misrepresent has only encouraged more violent retaliatory actions from those who wish to re-sanctify their environment: the 21st century has already seen the declaration of a global war which essentially pits the sacred ideals of the de-centralized globalist order (read: 'freedom') against the cultural conservatism of local ethno-states and theocracies.

Banksy himself cannot be nearly as grating as the Brooker / Morris TV caricature, although he hints at the efforts of overground culture to absorb his work by boasting that "Nike have offered me mad money for doing stuff."[29] He has also been commissioned to design an album cover for Brit-pop sensations Blur, while courting the attention of mega-stars like Brad Pitt. Nevertheless, his art, as portrayed in catalogs like *Existencilism*, shows a pronounced disrespect for authority: columns of riot police with smiley face logos inserted beneath their visors, rats wielding detonator devices and other wrecking equipment, London Tower guards relieving themselves on city walls in plain sight (in a somewhat contradictory and regrettable move, Banksy has also stenciled his name onto helpless farm animals.) His art shares many of the same goals with copyright-flaunting forms of underground electronic music, while presenting a form of publicly viewable art that requires no admission price. However, Banksy runs into trouble when making statements that smack of absolutism: see his poorly considered axiomatic saying *"there are no exceptions to the rule that everyone thinks they're an exception to the rules,"* or his not infrequent claims that "all cops are 'x'" or "all artists are 'x.'" It is this kind of heavy-handedness and ideological inflexibility which leads eventually to new dissent-smashing political systems, as one *Guardian* reader points out:

> Banksy's political attitude is actually deeply conservative, because it assumes most of us are zombies who need to be 'shocked and awed' into a new consciousness through 'radical' juxtapositions of symbols. The parallels between the proponents of 'subvertising' and 'culture jamming' and the American neoconservatives are telling. We just see the shadows on the wall; only they can see the truth.[30]

Similarly, the perceived overzealousness of Negativland's consciousness-raising campaign has caused them to be seen as artists too foucsed on "waking up" a braindead populace to notice those instances in which audiences are already "awake." Frans de Waard, formerly employed at the Dutch Staalplaat shop and record distributor, claims that "Negativland came to Staalplaat for distributing ther [*Dispepsi*] CD, and the only thing [Mark Hosler] was interested in was getting it on the market to cause to trouble with Pepsi. And he was convinced people in Europe would care about that very much. I told him nobody cares what they drink, [and] I'd rather hear good music."[31]

Banksy brings us back to the music world via his alliance with the hip-hop producer and 'mash-up' artist Brian "Dangermouse" Burton, with whom he initiated a project criticizing the debutante heiress Paris Hilton: copies of her ill-fated debut CD were purchased from record stores throughout the U.K., then replaced in store bins after the original artwork had been defaced, and song titles had been altered to comment on Hilton's 'celebrity for the sake of celebrity.' Dangermouse had previously gained notoriety (and a 'cease and desist' order from EMI) through his release of *The Grey Album*, the formative 'binary mash-up' album that mixed together the vocals from hip-hop artist Jay-Z's *The Black Album* with the Beatles' *White Album* as the "backing band." Though Jay-Z had cleared his "a capella" tracks for use in remixes (part of a growing trend in club music that also sees techno producers offering stripped-down "tool" versions of their single releases for use in DJ mixes), the surviving Beatles did not offer consent, and hence the cease and desist order. Bizarrely, though, EMI offered Dangermouse a sort of backdoor entry into major label success after denying him sales of the *Grey Album* (he was invited to join in on the sample-heavy *Demon Days* album by the Gorillaz supergroup.)

The *Grey Album*, widely mourned as an album that would have been the "hit of the year" if not for the intransigence of EMI's lawyers, brought the re-appropriation debate to a plateau of publicity not yet experienced by the seasoned "jammers" in Negativland or People Like Us: as Mickey Valley notes, it was even "taken as politically empowering because it offer[ed] insight into the site of polysemic cultural production/consumption as the reworking of 'top-down' history."[32] While the record was an occasionally humorous exercise (and one which even inspired a sequel mixing together both the 'black albums' of Jay-Z and Metallica), it is questionable what kind of artistic statement it hopes to make. It is perfectly fine as entertainment, but attempting to read a deeper meaning into it will not always yield profound revelations. Many graffiti artists mobilize with no other agenda than just alleviating the stifling boredom and visual monotony of the city, or enjoying the element of danger that comes from defying the surveillance state. Likewise, many mash-up producers want little more than to have a laugh and invite others in on the fun.

As such, much of the academic discussion about these artists' confirming Roland Barthes' "the death of the author" is a projection of academicians' own agendas onto the artists, many of whom simply trade in the "problematic" role of the author for that of another role earning the censure of critical theorists- the virtuoso performer. When it is admiringly noted, for example, that Girl Talk's Greg Gillis "samples over 300 songs per album"[33] and that he formerly moonlighted as a biomedical engineer, there can be no doubt that his above-average level of ambition is seen as deriving from a kind of "mad genius." Many artists working in this idiom are indeed reluctant to concede that they have no distinguishing ability, and do believe they can reclaim originality, individuality, and virtuosity by resorting to more demanding collaging methods or by fusing contrasting sampled materials in such a way that their fusion seems completely "natural". In this style built on home studio construction rather than live performance, the musical criteria for virtuoso talent have changed from memorization and performing dexterity to skill in reconciling contrasts and maintaining the element of surprise.

Yet, to add another layer of complexity to this thumbnail sketch of the practice, the mash-up or culture jam is also regularly lauded as being the province of the inspired amateur. These forms place a technique which was once the exclusive domain of the avant-garde into the hands of a younger and less professional group of creators than ever before, who have newer ways of skirting the edicts of the corporate music industry: even artists in the hip-hop and post-industrial genres had to deal with studios, record pressing plants and printers where their work could be refused (or, perhaps, where the contents might be scrutinized by RIAA officials.) Not so with the mash-up generation: with Internet distribution and home CD-r duplication as a possible (and widely utilized) method, they can reach thousands of listeners before the full weight of copyright law comes down upon them- if their activities are traceable by the law. Mark Hosler admits to enjoying music of the genre, though:

> There are thousands of 13-year-olds all over England who are taking their PCs and iMacs and they're just dragging little sound files one on top of another to make new songs. It's very punk rock. It's great. You don't have to know how to play anything at all. Also what's interesting is that it seems to have no political, cultural critique in it whatsoever; it's just about making some funny thing you can dance to. A couple years ago on the 'True/False' Tour, I used a ZZ Top song played at the same time as Julie Andrews singing the theme from *The Sound of Music*, and made it work, and it was really funny. It's a very satisfying thing to pull off.[34]

Vicki Bennett, of the loosely allied sampling outfit People Like Us, seconds this opinion by likening the amateurism of the scene to "folk art" (e.g. "Making collage and working with found imagery and sound is very much the natural folk art way of working, for they are the tools of the modern times.")[35] However, much folk art has always dealt with the yearning for unattainable Olympian heights out of the reach of the "folk," and in present-day America this still means the romance of pop celebrity. It can be argued that some mash-ups do much more to entrench the cult of personality surrounding entertainers than they do to expose them as pre-fabricated 'one-man brands', much in the same way that celebrity-obsessed satire like the *South Park* animated series (and yes, the Friedberg / Seltzer movies) sustain public interest in these brands. This theory is proved in part by, again, the popularity of Dangermouse as a 'legitimate' producer now recording 'real' tracks sanctioned by the record industry (Burton also graduated to become half of the platinum-selling hip-hop act Gnarls Barkley alongside Cee Lo Green.)

Other mash-up technicians are unashamed about their creations' use as a celebration of (or even a 'love letter' to) the original mega-star, and as a "what if…" fantasy of an aesthetic fusion that would probably be outside the musical range, contractual obligations, or just personal tastes of that object of desire. Kid 606 is known for his love of sonic grit and self-destructing, clattering synthetic beats, as well as a love of harsh and confrontational musical genres such as Industrial and grindcore- even with such a pedigree, his use of vocal tracks from eccentric R+B artist Missy Elliot in a mash-up seemed like not like an attempt to demean Elliot's work, but a wish for an alternate universe in which both artists reside on the same artistic and commercial plateau.

The unorthodox yet respectful tone of Kid 606's mash-up is perceptibly different from the types of "metamusic" experiments engaged in by V/VM. Their *Sick Love* CD from 2000, for example, is not so much a mash-up as an outright defacement of the source material in question: the disc's contents are popular love songs from the past three decades which, rather than being sampled or layered atop other musical materials, are played straight through from beginning to end while digital pitch-shifting, de-tuning, and distorting effects are applied to the otherwise un-edited original tracks. V/VM also changes the titles of the originals to include puns on meat and animal butchery[36]: it is a practice the band has applied to other discs in its catalog, and which none-too-subtly dials up the counter-cultural association of "pigs" with greed and with the police forces that monitor deviation from an unreflective and greedy lifestyle.

For every confrontational commando unit like V/VM, though, there is a sympathetic figure like Jason Forrest who "does not share V/VM's contemptuous approach to pop culture"[37] and claims that "I think my music is really sincere...there's no 'isn't this funny' kind of gesture involved. If there's a rock riff, it's a rock riff that I really love. The Go-Gos song I use is just a fucking great Go-Gos song."[38] Again, Vicki Bennett provides a voice of assent, insisting that "I never use anything [in my music] that I don't like. It is always paying homage to it. It is a celebration of the content. It is finding ties between things that are disparate and incongruous, showing that everything is actually the same, because I really do believe that."[39]

One has to wonder if the respectful tone that these artists take towards their "raw materials" saves them, in the end, from otherwise highly probable cease-and-desist actions. The case of Dangermouse's eventual sponsorship by EMI has already been noted here, while Vicki Bennett's focus on tribute rather than subversion caused her to be one of the few recording artists with complete access to the BBC television archives. Meanwhile, Forrest, who records as Donna Summer, has not yet been called upon to stop using the name of the 'real' disco diva Summer on his records. It either suggests that Forrest has been keeping too low of a profile to be discovered by the guardians of intellectual property, or it marks an interesting sea change in the attitude of the record industry that so mercilessly descended on Negativland for their *U2* record. With the substantial decrease in major record label profits rising from illegal music file-sharing networks, perhaps the powers that be have turned their attention elsewhere for now, perceiving free downloading and distribution of their product as much more of a threat than people like Forrest and Bennett (who, after all, are paying homage to their product and providing "free advertising" to markets otherwise indifferent to this product- a lesson that even Disney may soon take to heart.)

The question also remains as to how much "everything is actually the same" in terms of hierarchical positioning: whether it be a hierarchy of musical styles, of instrumental content (the dictates of the human voice versus the audio data transmitted by other musical instruments), or of the cultures that are made to "clash" in order to give mash-ups their particular "shock of the new." So, by reading too much of a tech-utopian and egalitarian mission into this music, various critical theorists have already done much to shoot themselves in the foot. For example, post-modern critic Philip Gunderson conveniently ignores Burton's own statements on the ludic motivations of *The Grey Album* (which he admits was mainly a kind of self-challenge or "more of a statement of what you could do with sampl[ing] alone"[40]) in order to assign a "Communist" rationale for his work[41]- a motivation which is somewhat more difficult to ascribe in the wake of Burton's rise as a (presumably well-paid) major label remixer and producer.

So what, after all is said and done, is the mash-up really good for? The audio *wunderkammer* of the mash-up is no more and no less than an art of the possible- it sketches the outline of different forms moreso than it actually acts as a form unto itself. And, like other 'transitional' or 'meta-genre' forms of electronic music ("glitch," "noise" etc.), the real merit of the mash-up lies only partially in the realm of either simple hedonism or some egalitarian program of "freeing information." Instead, it might be better to consider the form as the catalyst for negotiations on what is truly worth preserving in media culture.

Smashed Holograms and Endless Grains

Although the sample bombardment of the new mash-up generation is effective in generating diverse reactions (many of them already touched upon in this chapter), it is not now nor has it ever been the only "game in town" as far as a criticism-by-sampler is concerned. In the era of quasi-legal music downloading, it is only a matter of time before the pioneering efforts of such artists will be surpassed by even more mind-boggling paeans to hyper-complexity. Still, neither the net amount of sound consumed by an individual nor the amount of sonic material put in their mash-up stew will always translate into a solid understanding of that sound's potentiality and implicit meaning. Techno-cultural professor and sonic activist Bob Ostertag, who has built a large portion of his career on sampling (and who has released a few CDs on Negativland's Seeland label), suggests an alternate method:

I think the way I approach sampling technology is…how do I say it…for a lot of folks, the way they approach it is to sample everything and then put it in a blender. I've never been interested in that- for me it's always been a question of really thinking very carefully about what I wanted to sample, and finding one thing- not finding a hundred or a thousand things, but finding *one thing* that was meaningful to me, and not using sampling to decontextualize that or to rip it out of its native environment and make it into something else, but to do the opposite. To use the sampling to 'blow it up', to allow people to get inside of it or confront it in a way that they hadn't confronted it before. My piece *Sooner Or Later* would be a good example of that. For that I made a whole hour of music out of just this little sample of this boy burying his father. All those samples were taken from works that I had real connections to in real life- I spent several years in El Salvador during the war there, and made the recording of *Sooner or Later* out of that. To me that's the antithesis of the way that sampling has mostly been used…you go out and sample a million things, the whole world and then you blend that world into one mix. I wanted to do the exact opposite- taking one thing and blowing it up so that it became a whole world in itself.[42]

This technique, although highly divergent from the sample barrage of Negativland or John Oswald's plunderphonics, offers an equally valid statement, and an equally essential counterweight to mass media's inexhaustible supply of contradictory, transitory messages and images. Ostertag's work *Sooner or Later* is one of, as can be assumed from the description above, uncomfortable intimacy. In a media culture that has been conditioned to see the burial scenario described by Ostertag side-to-side on television with, say, reportage on a college basketball game and updates on the stock market, it is potentially mind-altering to be suddenly immersed in an emotionally intense experience at such a microscopic level. The same effect is accomplished in Ostertag's piece *Burns Like Fire*, which zeroes in on explosive split-second fragments of voices of street ambience during gay riots in San Francisco, looping the selected sound samples or freezing them in place. Some would argue that these edits ruin the 'you-are-there' documentary effect that would be accomplished by an unedited street recording (available elsewhere through the work of audio documentarians like Christopher DeLaurenti), since they place the recorder in the role of an intrusive narrator, somewhat like a roving TV news anchor. But in this case, the edits do not work in an intrusive way-rather, they have a complimentary, contrapuntal effect of casting the unaltered sounds in starker relief and thus heightening their impact. In their own manner, they act like a highly abstract Greek chorus: with their rippling and echoing effects they summarize all that has gone before, in both a verbal and non-verbal manner.

Far removed from Ostertag's activism, yet retaining some of the same working methods, other artists have seized upon the intimacy conjured by envelopment in a single, isolated sound, and have used this to further more hermetic or mystical ends. Jordi Valls' Vagina Dentata Organ recordings, each one mercilessly focused on a single sound sensation (of human orgasm, wolves' growling, or revving motorcycles) utilizes the tactic of the sound 'becoming the world of the listener' as a kind of religious indoctrination- perhaps a modern update of the interpretation of unaccompanied drumbeats as a spirit vehicle (as Mircea Eliade notes, the Altaic shamans considered this instrument the "shaman's horse.")[43] Organized religions, as well, have tended towards a heavy degree of sonic repetition in their rituals, in order to make a distinction between the disordered chaos of the natural / material world and the Apollonian clarity of the faith. This concept seems to lie at the heart of Valls' recordings, which are unrepentantly ascetic and repetitive, elevating the isolated sample to a function as a totem; a 'power focusing' tool. Valls' Psychic TV collaborator Genesis P. Orridge also sees the advent of electronic music sampling in grandiose mystical terms:

> It can be said, for me at least, that the transformational implications inherent in sampling, looping, cutting-up and/or thereafter re-assembling both found data materials and infinite combinations of site specific sounds, is as probably equivalent to, and as socially significant and profound as, the popularization and mass proselytisation of LSD and the splitting of the atom. All three involve the cutting-up of the essential 'matter' of science, religion and language; the basic, potential inhibiting, cornerstones of what has been coined- our contemporary 'dominator' culture.[44]

When referring to sampling's ability to contain worlds within a small 'bite' of information, P. Orridge uses the analogy of the 'smashed hologram': when the projection surface of a holographic image is smashed, the same image will be replicated as a perfect whole on each individual 'splinter' of the original surface. Expanding on this idea, P. Orridge states that

> It has always been my personal contention that if we take,

for example, a SPLINTER of JOHN LENNON [capitals in the original], that that same splinter will in a very real manner, contain within it everything that John Lennon ever experienced; everything that John Lennon ever said, composed, wrote, drew, expressed; everyone that ever knew John Lennon and the sum total of all and any of those interactions; everyone who ever heard, read, thought of, saw, reacted to John Lennon or anything remotely connected with John Lennon; the specific time zone, calendar date that it theoretically resided in; and every past, present and/or future combination of any or all of the above.[45]

San Francisco multi-media artist Ken Sitz, while not approaching the poeticism of P. Orridge's 'smashed hologram' analogy, also likens sampling to being a device which breaks up long periods of stagnation and forces cultural evolution. According to Sitz, sampling does not bring about sudden, revelatory disruptions in patterns of behavior, but works incrementally to erode away at these patterns:

The way culture evolves is just like how DNA evolves or mutates- regardless [of] how quickly it changes, it's based on material that existed before. An accumulation process of small incremental changes can produce sudden 'discontinuities' like the collapse of the Eastern Bloc or the Berlin Wall coming down.[46]

Echoes of Sitz' suggestions can be heard in a 2004 CD by Leif Elggren, *The Cobblestone is the Weapon of the Proletariat,* in which samples of a single stone, being thrown once in a Stockholm street, become all the raw material needed for 10 album tracks' worth of supple electronic humming, sputtering and sawtooth noises. Elggren's method here has more in common with magic than with the hard sciences mentioned above: it is an alchemically altered sample used as a 'wishing machine' to bring about cultural change and empowerment. It may be a bit of a stretch to presume that a carefully chosen sound bite, in the right context, can become a faultless virtual copy of a person, place, or event. What can be done, though, is for the sample to re-intensify experiences and mental associations that have been dulled and rendered as one-dimensional, bringing these sensations as close as possible to the realm of the tactile.

Certain electronic composition techniques also give the isolated sample an opportunity to bloom into a total sonic atmosphere, to become a sound world of its own. The technique of granular synthesis is one prominent example of this, and it should not go unnoticed that granular synthesis was first proposed by the Hungarian inventor of holography, Dennis Gabor (although Gabor's discovery has taken a back seat to the subsequent re-discovery of the technique by Iannis Xenakis in the 1970s.) Granular synthesis uses the 'grain' as its basic sound unit (this can be any electronic tone or sample typically of a 5-50 millisecond duration), layering these miniscule particles on top of each other while shifting playback speed and phase.

Microsound author and *Computer Music Journal* editor Curtis Roads (generally credited as the first composer to develop a granular synthesis engine) has demonstrated the ability to form mesmerizing 'clouds' of sound from layering individual grains, which are controlled by the musician in a half random / half deterministic fashion: in other words, the frequency of a grain's waveform can be randomized, but only within an upper and lower limit set by the musician or composer. As with mash-ups, which can be either simple pairings of two incongruous elements or hyper-detailed collages generated from hundreds of minute pop song samples, the results differ in accordance with the atoms of material that are selected for granulation. And, sure enough, this technique is just as applicable to appropriated segments of popular music as it is to the eternal "public domain" of pure sinusoidal tones.

Granular synthesis really needs to be heard to be fully grasped, but, in any case, it is an indication of sampling culture's full potential to swallow entire worlds of data and reconstitute them in a form that bears no resemblance to what came before it. When a simple cough or sneeze can be stretched into a seamless oceanic drone, or broken down into a cluster of distinct pointillist sounds before returning to its original form it is - at the very least - another vivid demonstration of how we can use the materials of the mundane in order to transcend it. Roland Barthes once wrote an essay entitled *The Grain of the Voice*, in which he proposed that the whole body of a performer can be contained in that performer's voice - with granular synthesis and other novel forms of sample transformation, we now have an opportunity to put this theory to the test; to see if one's sampled voice, or any highly personal sound information, can still retain its original identity while going under the surgical knife of granulation effects. The same question can be asked of this material that is asked of other forms of digital sample-based music- is this a destructive process, or an additive one? A third option is that the former process can bring about the latter, as Jasper Johns suggested in his encomium for Marcel Duchamp: "He declared he wanted to kill art ('for myself'), but his persistent attempts to destroy frames of reference altered our thinking, established new units of thought, 'a new thought for that object."[47]

Sampling contagion

There is something worth noting about the new musical vocabulary that has been brought into being by granular synthesis and related techniques: the distinct units of sampled sound, given their perceived smallness, are often refered to using micro-biological terms (e.g. sonic materials refered to as "cells" rather than as "tones.") As such, discussion over the creation of electronic music has become loaded with allusions to genetic material - much like those voiced by Sitz above - while the musical creation process itself has been re-imagined as a kind of phylogenetic process, like the Surrealists' fantastic mutations engineered at a much more fundamental level.

With the micro-biological metaphor in play, it would only be a matter of time before the release and distribution of such music was seen in terms that modified the cellular metaphor with a gloss of insurrectionary activity: it was seen as a "sampling virus." The term as used here is traceable to Otomo Yoshihide, the Tokyo-based improviser who, in his former group Ground Zero, gave Japan some of its more vibrant and hectic sample collage work. Refering to his home studio as a "6-mat virus factory" [Japanese apartments are measured in the number of *tatami* mats covering the floor, with 6 being an average size], his 1993 CD on Australia's Extreme label, *The Night Before the Death of the Sampling Virus*, recalled William Burroughs' proclamation in *The Job* that another "cellular" unit of creation - "the word" - was a viral phenomenon.

Indeed, it was the culture of speculative and experimental fiction that, long before "cyber-security" experts appeared on the scene, introduced the public to "viruses'" potential spread through silicon rather than carbon. Long before their popularity solidified as weapons for state cyberwarriors and anti-state agitators alike, there where cultural anticipations such as the novels in William Gibson's "sprawl trilogy,"[48] from which the term "cyberspace" largely derives. Cyberneticist W. Grey Walter also refered to processes of subjective transformation as ocurring 'virally' (in his 1956 novel *The Curve of the Snowflake)*, while the first known reference to a malicious, self-replicating computer program as a "virus" was in David Gerrold's 1972 sci-fi novel *When HARLIE Was One* (although the fictional self-replicator in this book was simply named VIRUS, and did not refer to a distinct category of computer programs.) Though it is difficult to attribute the currency of the term exclusively to Gerrold's work, especially when considering how many people are likely to relate an undetectable and deleterious agent within the body to a similar agent within manmade systems, it nonentheless remains the common vernacular expression for a damaging and usually clandestine transmission of computer code.

For Burroughs, linguistic communication was mainly a parasitic force: language was a form of communication that handed cultural presets down from a few authoritative voices to an exponentially increasing number of parroting ventriloquist dummies. The source could, however, be attacked through the deliberate re-arrangement of messages, since "the word" invaded at an unconscious level, and becoming conscious of it – or making the word 'concrete'- was the key to regaining control over one's own evolutionary process. One merely had to be cognizant that a parasitic infestation was happening in the first place, which for many would be the most difficult first step towards future realizations- much of what has happened within "mash-up" culture and digital sampling has been about creating a parallel to the self-replicating and mimetic forces already transmitting the "word virus" through the major communications media. It is especially telling that, some three decades after Burroughs first refered to language in this manner, "viral advertising" has become an ubiquitous watchword of global marketing that appears to spread over digital networks without any coercion or direction on the behalf of a master controller (false as this assumption may be in some cases.) Unlike this form of "viral" communication, however, the culture of sampling and media re-mixing does not need to conform to any expectations of public taste or to any restrictions on "acceptable" output- This is a crucial distinction, and one that may ensure the "sampling virus" continues to evolve, always staying one step ahead of the vaccine.

Beyond the Valley of the *Falsch*:
Mego (and Friends) Revitalize "Computer Music"

Prelude: "A Viennese Tragedy"[1]

21st-century Vienna is an idyllic, smoothly functioning capital of a couple million residents, where a *U-Bahn* train can whisk you across the Danube with no more than a 5-minute wait between trains, shuttling you from St. Stephen's cathedral to the ultra-modern austerity of the city's diplomatic hub, 'UN city'. The city's past as an imperial epicenter of musical significance hardly needs to be recounted here- the titanically looming, archetypal figures of Beethoven, Mozart and Schubert are still never far from any informed discussion of Viennese cultural history, even if they hardly figure into the current discussion. What may be more relevant is the occasional flash of concentrated eccentricity which arises in opposition to the city's conservatism: sitting side by side with more traditional homes, you can find the undulating, children's storybook architectural novelties of Friedrich Hundertwasser, built around a unique biomorphic design and his personal maxim of "the straight line is Godless." During the reign of the embattled, ultra-rightist Austrian Freedom Party chairman Jörg Haider, the eye-popping façade of the Viennese *Hundertwasserhaus* could also be seen with draped in banners bearing anti-Haider slogans.

Sadly for Vienna, some of its more well-known cultural exports are also its most patently ridiculous- take the late Johann 'Falco' Hölcel, for example, whose unnerving bilingual synth-funk was once described as "...obnoxiously patronizing attempts at African-American lingo, accents and music, sung in a constipated gurgle as appealing as hearing someone vomit outside your window."[2]

Luckily, though, any small amount of scraping beneath the surface of commercially viable Viennese culture will reveal things much more gripping, albeit reserved for the brave (and even Falco, prior to his ascendancy to cocaine-pop stardom, was once a bassist in Drahdiwaberl, the media theorist Stefan Weber's humorous and controversy-courting socio-political rock spectacle.) As it is situated at the horizon which separates Western Europe from the still misunderstood and under-explored "East," Vienna has been blessed with relative "creative freedom and verve...undogged by the territorial back-biting of a larger and more competitive city like London."[3] Where the world's design and lifestyle industries are concerned, Vienna is priveleged to be a key point on a network but not "*the* place to be", thus providing both the freedom to work without being watched by the eyes of the world and the ability to quickly access those geographical nodes more recognizable as proving grounds of global culture.

It is ironic, then, that such conditions would occasionally give rise to local subcultural movements that could, in terms of singularity and extremity, outclass their peers in these other "proving grounds." If you should find yourself walking through the city's world-renowned Museum Quarter, ignore for a moment the generous selection of elegant 18th-century architecture and the enticements to see Gustav Klimt's glittering Art Nouveau pieces, and make a straight line for the charcoal-colored futurist facade of the Museum Moderner Kunst (MOMUK), which houses a permanent collection of artifacts from the Viennese Aktionists in its basement. The illuminating archive of Aktionist films, photographs, texts and art objects circumscribes this group of artists that often used the body as just another form of 'material' in their works. This was an act that took the "action painting" of Jackson Pollock to a hitherto unrealized extreme, projecting the violence associated with this painting technique into theatrical situations that were psychic self-interrogations as much as they were performances. This merger of cultural production and purgation involved such superlative acts as self-mutilation by razor blade, lying blindfolded and passive beneath a cascade of animal blood, or exposing hidden or silenced bodily processes. All of this had a very sacrificial aspect to it, as Aktionist Hermann Nitsch was careful to point out in both word and deed (drama critic Herbert Blau points out that the Catholic Nitsch "in one early event, not quite ready for being nailed to the Cross, had himself impaled on a wall in Otto Mühl's apartment."[4])

The Aktionist artists sacrificed their flesh, sanity, and societal reputations so that the spectator could achieve some degree of individuation without submitting to the same level of trauma (although numerous 'participatory' *aktions* did integrate audiences into the ritual as well.) As for the aforementioned social reputations, arrests and police interference played no small part in the Aktionist story, especially after the infamous *Kunst und Revolution* event of June 1968- for which Günter Brus earned the maximum allowable penalty for acts of public indecency.

Originally a loose gathering of writers, poets, performers and painters, the Aktionist movement was eventually whittled down to four main personalities in the public eye: Hermann Nitsch, Günter Brus, Rudolf Schwarzkogler, and Otto Mühl. Nothing has really come along since to supplant their reputation as the most transgressive artists on the European continent, although the number of 'honorable mentions' has been significant. Unlike the Surrealists and other movements which had to occasionally go along with the demands of a megalomaniac 'leader' (Andre Breton in this case), the Aktionists were mainly a de-centralized group, united in aesthetic and method but completing a good deal of work while independent from each other. A thorough exploration of the body's malleability was used to completely different ends by each: Nitsch used orgiastic encounters with flesh, blood, and cathartic noise for religious / transcendental purposes, while Mühl's work - significantly less informed by religious iconography - argued the case for perverts as they who "reveal society's vulnerable points." Elsewhere, the elusive, esoteric and comparitively withdrawn Schwarzkogler used the overwhelming and synesthetic nature of his work to achieve an Apollonian clarity and to annihilate base urges. On a side note, the Aktionist-affiliated philosopher Oswald Wiener (who lectured at *Kunst und Revolution*, among other events) has written prolifically on the subject of artificial intelligence.

Those searching for an explanation for the Aktionists' directness would do well to start with those artists' early brushes with death: Otto Mühl experienced his as a teenaged soldier fighting on the western front with the Wehrmacht, and particularly in the incomparable 'Battle of the Bulge' under Gerd von Rundstedt's command (135 of his comrades were reportedly numbered among the 85,000 German dead.) Hermann Nitsch, being Mühl's junior by 13 years, was far too young for frontline combat, but he recalls the bombing of Vienna in his early childhood as a transforming experience. While not entirely enraptured by the reality of war, Nitsch inadvertently echoes the sentiments of the Italian Futurists in the sense that "war can assume an aesthetic appearance" and that "the compulsion to live life intensely, albeit in a world of suffering, is also undeniable."[5]

Hinting that the work of the Aktionists is far from over (and mildly criticizing select unnamed members of the movement for their 'addiction to method'), Aktionist admirer Genesis P. Orridge closes his personal encomium on the subject as follows: "The wordless scream of fervent rage against a national (and international) system of authority, mediated as an institutionalised obscenity of violence and oppression, seems unnervingly appropriate and relevant once more."[6]

With this conclusion, though, come the inevitable follow-up questions- how, and why, to scream with more 'fervent rage' than the Aktionists? Obviously P. Orridge himself tried with similar explorations in COUM Transmissions, Throbbing Gristle and eventually with Psychic TV's 'modern primitive' program of piercing, body modification, ecstatic dancing etc.- but at some point the model of Viennese Aktionism could go no further without crossing over into a form of perverse entertainment for the benighted masses. This was already evident when Günter Brus, upon returning to 'normal' painting and de-emphasizing his, was vilified as a 'sellout' by audiences just beginning to warm up to his former modes of activity.

Overall, sound and music was less of a contribution to the Aktionist oeuvre than it was for previous manifestations of the European avant-garde. For the set pieces of Otto Mühl and Hermann Nitsch, though, sound did occasionally become an integral part of their sense-overwhelming presentations- beginning in 1966, Nitsch had a ten-piece 'scream choir' on hand to accompany the religious ecstasy and spiritual purging of his choreographed bloodbaths, as well as a noise orchestra whose only scored instructions for performance were what level of intensity at which to play (there were three noise 'phases' in all.) Scores for Nitsch *aktions* also include instructions to play recordings of 'beat music' (whose music, exactly, is not made clear in the scores) at speaker shredding volume. In 1964 Otto Mühl held a whimsical 'balloon concert' and later, in 1972, recorded the *Ein Schreckliche Gedanke* [A Terrible Idea] LP, the penultimate statement of Mühl 's 'cesspool aesthetics' as a strategy against conformity. The ...*Gedanke* LP is largely composed of Mühl lovingly languishing over German-language vulgarities and gleefully erupting into shock tantrums. Elsewhere, a record of James Brown's greatest hits was a puzzling partial soundtrack (not including the screams and laughing fits of the participants) to a spastic 'total aktion' of Mühl's entitled *Führt Direkte Kunst in den Wahnsinn* [Does Direct Art Lead to Madness?].

Having already been the locus of one of the most demanding forms of 'body art' in the 20th century, it would make sense that one of the next artistic upheavals to come out of Vienna would be a non-corporeal one- and, in this case, one localized almost completely within computers. It was one that seemed to have no physical form at all, being incubated within hard drives, raised by software applications and sent out to the world through loudspeakers. And even though Viennese Aktionism of the late 1960s still remains a watershed movement, thorough examinations of the body would eventually move far beyond the Austrian borders, becoming *de rigeur* throughout the 1960s and 1970s. Players like Chris Burden, Marina Abramovic and Vito Acconci continued to raise questions about what constituted a transformative or abreactive act, and what was just sheer terror or torture (for themselves as well as their public.)

Several decades before meditations on institutional torture entered the mass consciousness via revelations about government agencies' brutal interrogative techniques in prosecuting the 'war on terror', the 1970s crop of body performerswere dragging themselves through glass, or forcing themselves to sit on an upright chair atop a sculpture pedestal until falling off from exhaustion. Even typically pleasurable acts like masturbating were, in pieces like Acconci's *Seedbed*, brought into the realm of confrontation and criminal threat- in this 1971 performance piece, Acconci committed said act underneath a gallery-wide ramp, fantasizing out loud about gallery patrons as they walked on top of him. Although there may still be some room for provoking the atypical reactions that can be provoked when, like in Acconci's piece, the private body becomes a social body, it seems difficult now to build on the work of these artists without eventually contorting the creative process into an insincere game of "one-upmanship".

Like the above artists, the new computer music in question would never show things purely in a positive light. Although there was the sepia-toned, daydreaming serenity of select pieces by artists like Christian Fennesz, and a separate clique of artists who swore by Brian Eno's brand of Zen ambience, there were also outlandish synthetic symphonies of choking, sputtering and shrieking. A new lexicon of abrasive, yet richly textured and meticulously mixed noises conjured nothing so much as modern history being redefined by its accidents; the unreliability of mechanical processes being the rule rather than the exception. Like Jean Tinguely's 'meta-mechanic' sculptures, which destroyed themselves after mimicking the utopian production line aesthetic of industrial cultures, a new kind of art was emerging that suggested the sound of the digital world collapsing upon itself. As the composer Nicholas Collins suggested, though, this was not reason for despair- such sound could be the sound of a "benevolent catastrophe."[7]

Computer Welt

Before discussing the merits of this new genus of computer musicians, it would be useful to reflect on the development of 'traditional' computer music, in order to ascertain the significant differences between then and now. The ubiquity of personal computers, along with the introduction of newer "walled garden" digital devices that are essentially computers yet not advertised as such, has made it too easy to forget a simple fact: until very recently, it was radical to use them as sound performance tools, or as devices for sound *production* in addition to sound *reproduction*. With their current ability to do so, computerized or "laptop" music is heir to the avant-garde gramophone experiments of Laszlo Moholy-Nagy (by means of scratching vinyl record surfaces at certain intervals, Moholy-Nagy accomplished the same combination of production and reproduction with the record player.) Of course, this state of affairs was preceded by a good deal of pop-cultural speculation and fantasy.

If we keep this story focused on the German-speaking cultural sphere of which Vienna is a part, then its relation to the world of personal computing has been a long and storied one; fueled in no small part by foreign audiences' pre-conceptions of Teutonic peoples as cold, calculating, technologically precise automatons. Well before the advent of personal computers, the machines were relegated to the subject matter of pop song whimsy, such as teenybopper queen France Gall's "Der Computer Nummer Drei," a peppy frolic about a computer programmed to seek for her *den richtigen Boy* ['the perfect boy.']

Kraftwerk, of course, took the above pre-conceptions and ran with them to previously unimagined heights of popular acceptance. The band applied a slick, reductionist technique to both their music and their stylized, uniform appearance, replacing girl-meets-boy romance with a romance of electronics and circuitry (going so far as appearing like gender-neutral robots), inhabiting a strangely asexual world in between rock 'n roll's preening masculinity and bubblegum pop's sighing femininity. This was done in addition to romanticizing, in songs like *Autobahn* and *Trans-Europe Express,* public institutions more associated with the European continent than with the Anglo-American sphere of affairs, with the ironic result of this being the enthusiastic absorption of the Kraftwerk aesthetic by that same Anglo-American culture industry. English synth-pop and American hip-hop, in particular, acknowledged Kraftwerk's influence (if only tacitly in some cases.)

However, by the time Kraftwerk had recorded *Computer Welt*, their unequivocal paean to the information age, there was still not anything resembling a personal computer in the group's sound studio. Their most acclaimed music was composed on analog, voltage-controlled synthesizers, and even their most convincingly 'computerized' sounds, like their deadpan vocoder incantations, were achieved using analog systems. Credit should be given the band, though, for sparking an argument about the human role in live performance of electronic sound: long before the first musician appeared on stage with only a laptop - calling into question who the true "performer" was - the band had performed concerts using automated dummies bearing the band members' likenesses.

The *Neue Deutsche Welle*, a German-speaking punk and new wave movement active during the late 70s and early 80s, also embraced computers while criticizing certain aspects of the rising inorganic and administered culture. In the case of the group Der Plan, they pointed out attributes of Germans' collective behavior that were more computer-like than computers themselves. This tendency can be seen in their single *Da Vorne Steht 'ne Ampel,* an incisive little number which ridiculed Germans' obsessive need to follow rules regarding traffic lights and crosswalks, even if there was no traffic in sight. NDW hits such as Abwärts' "Computerstaat" were jittering and spiky blasts of paranoia emanating from fears of an Orwellian surveillance state, of which the computer would be a prime enabler- this was already being evinced by contemporaneous events such as , the computer-enabled, counter-terrorist *negativen Rasterfahndung* [negative dragnet] set up in Germany and overseen by the so-called "Kommissar Computer"[8] Horst Herold.

In most cases, though, a widespread interest in musician interface with computers would have to wait until the 1990s, whether in Germany, Austria or elsewhere. One of the main reasons for this was the now unimaginable amount of latency (noticeable lag between any kind of user input and any audible result) present in computers. This was to say nothing of the flaws that computers exhibited even before fingers took to the keypad: 'clunky' awkwardness or weightiness, impersonal command-line interfaces instead of the more customizable graphic user interfaces, and an unattractive design that did not lend itself well to an individualistic class of beings like musicians (although this may be a purely subjective judgment- it is possible that many still prefer the beige and chocolate hues of a mid-80s Apple IIe to the clean, android silver of a 21st century PowerBook or MacBook.)

Out of all the above, though, the latency problem was perhaps the most pressing issue- one could still perform music on an ugly computer or one in which commands were carried out by typing lines of code rather than manipulating pictorial representations of instrument controls. Max V. Mathews, one of the founding fathers of the computer as a performance instrument (his 'Music I' program on the IBM 704 computer is credited with the first computerized micro-performance in 1957), touched on this issue when explaining the dilemma of using electronic instruments prior to the current digital age:

> Until recently, general-purpose music programs all had one major restriction- they could not be utilized for performance because computers were not fast enough to synthesize interesting music in real-time, that is to say it took more than one second to synthesize a second of sound. Special purpose computers called digital synthesizers overcame this limitation. But real-time synthesizers brought with them a new major problem- rapid obsolescence. The commercial lifetime of a new synthesizer is only a few years, and therefore music written by such machines cannot be expected to be playable in a decade.[9]

Matthews' predictions have so far turned out to be true, as evidenced by at least one software performance application - Miller Puckette's MAX/MSP - which has been utilized by sonic voyagers from Autechre to Merzbow. MAX/MSP and other applications like it - PureData, C Sound, SuperCollider - were practically unlimited in terms of what sounds they could synthesize, yet unlike keyboard synthesizers, they contained no preset instruments, relying on a musician's proficiency with coding skill in order to come up with the necessary algorithms.

It is often touted that these programs annihilate the need to "pay your way" into musicianship, because of this emphasis on ingenuity and intellectual dedication over gear accumulation. So, in a way, such software encouraged a continuation of the do-it-yourself ethic built up over the previous few decades of revolt against the music business, and permitted a massive increase in audio fidelity and timbral or tonal variety. Instruments which exhibited this astonishing variation in tone / timbre could be built up by musicians from scratch, with no equipment needed other than a conventional PC. The only real limitation, other than the processing speed and hard drive storage capacity of one's computer, was the amount of effort that the individual musician wanted to put into designing a patch. This may have still been too much of a "left brain" activity for those whose education was purely in the arts and humanities- but on the other hand, it was a validation for those innovative music producers who, nevertheless, didn't have the dexterity or innate sense of rhythm to master "real" instruments- it must have been gratifying to, with a patronizing smirk, finally counter the nagging, dubious presumption "*anyone* can play guitar" with another one- "*anyone* can program a MAX patch."

Opponents of live computer music performance could, of course, fire back that this was a lazy capitulation to the 'law of least action,' e.g. if there is a choice between an escalator and a staircase, people will take the escalator every time. But is there really anything *wrong* with 'taking the escalator', provided that it doesn't leave a more effort-intensive option available, and doesn't deny others the choice of 'taking the stairs' if they so desire? This fear of being supplanted or is somewhat irrational when applied to music (rock bands are swelling in greater numbers than ever now, thanks to computer-based home recording environments like ProTools), and worse yet, it puts us in a position where the amount of physical exertion involved in a creative enterprise is the focal point of the art and *not* the end results. This, it would seem, takes us outside of the aims of music and into the realm of athletic competition.

Yet the prevalence of new computer music software has, according to Bob Ostertag in his 2001 paper *Why Computer Music Sucks,* also stirred the guardians of serious Computer Music (the capitals are Ostertag's own) to silence the more 'populist' musicians and exploratory amateurs[10], claiming exclusive rights to the methodology of computer-based sound. Ostertag comments acidly on this elitism, saying that the Computer Music of academia is mainly just the digital-era replacment for their previous plaything, serialist composition. According to Ostertag, "...it is a phenomenon seen time and time again in academia: the more an area of knowledge becomes diffused in the public, the louder become the claims of those within the tower to exclusive expertise in the field, and the narrower become the criteria become for determining who the 'experts' actually are."[11]

It is one thing to hear so-called Computer Music being denounced by the 'man on the street,' or by someone with clearly Luddite tendencies, but it is another thing entirely to hear incisive critiques from people like Ostertag, who have worked extensively with computers and are well aware of their technical specifications. Ostertag is especially well versed in the MAX/MSP language, having rigged up joysticks and computer drawing tablets as the real-time controllers of his patch designs. Speaking about his experience as a judge for the Prix Ars Electronica's coveted Digital Music prize in 1996, he admits that

> ...after listening to the 287 pieces submitted to Ars Electronica, I would venture to say that the pieces created with today's cutting edge technology (spectral re-synthesis, sophisticated phase vocoding schemes, and so on) have an even greater uniformity of sound among them than the pieces done on MIDI modules available in any music store serving the popular music market. This fact was highlighted during the jury session when it was discovered that a piece whose timbral novelty was noted by the jury as being exceptional was discovered to have been created largely with old Buchla analogue gear.[12]

While suggesting that ancient electronic relics are still capable of producing striking music, Ostertag also suggests that the results coming out of more high-end digital equipment hardly justify the hours of coding and computer maintenance involved in making a simple etude (which may be no different from a thousand others of its kind.) Still, there are those who will insist that concessions to this kind of formalism are a necessary precursor to artistic greatness (or acceptance by one's peers, at the very least.) Psycho-acoustic sound artist John Duncan, who shares some kinship with the more radical new breed of computer musicians (thanks to releases on the U.K. record label Touch and elsewhere), suggests the opposite- that refusal of these formalist rites of passage provides the true creative spark:

> From what I know of history, this has always been so: academics reinforce tradition and frustrate change. The exceptions to this -frustrated outsiders creating change - are exciting. That's where the real inspiration is, the energy that drives the creative process.[13]

From the comments of Ostertag and Duncan, we can surmise that resistance is steadily mounting against the type of Computer Music that will only be enjoyed by a select clique of individuals, whose appreciation of compositions comes from an expert knowledge of the "system building" process, and from an ability to accurately note what sounds and timbres are being created by what algorithm within a larger piece. This is quite a different thing than the enjoyment of pieces for their actual sonic qualities, and music as a whole will be in dire straits if these qualities are ever fully subordinated to formalist concerns. However, lest this essay seem like a rote exercise in academy-bashing, it still has to be conceded that - as Janne VanHanen suggests - "the *tools* of laptop music [...] are mainly derived from the academic community," though the "*methodology* of laptop music [...] takes its cue from the low-budget, do-it-yourself production values of the bedroom community."[14]

Sadly, being exiled by the academy does not always mean that an artist will be greeted with open arms by the public at large, either: there still exist market forces to deal with, imposing their own constraints on creativity and allowing only token expressions of true threshold experience. Rejection by both academic culture and leisure-oriented culture can, of course, be a deathblow to many aspiring artists. But then again, numerous art movements of the 20th and 21st centuries - the Vienna-based *Direkte Kunst* being only one among them - made their impact without seeking either formal accreditation or financial gain.

Rise of the Twisted Hard Disk

One of the more consistently impressive organizations involved in the shaping of early 21st century digital music was Austria's Mego label. Other splinter groups doubtless arose around the same time (thanks to the technological advancements listed earlier in this chapter), and therefore giving Mego pride of place here may raise the hackles of some. But if they did not merely kickstart this scene, their collective aesthetic sensibility, more than the sum of its parts, has been instrumental in drawing attention towards the peculiar methods and maneuvers of a larger network of electronic artists.

The Mego label was originally an offshoot of the Austrian techno label Mainframe, the brainchild of Ramon Bauer and Andreas Peiper. The Mainframe label, while not reaching the same dizzy heights of un-compromise that came to define Mego, did deviate from the standard techno / rave template in some vibrant ways. The label's flagship act Ilsa Gold, for one, was known for fish-out-of-water experiments like combining distortion-fueled 'hardcore' techno elements with the sampled (and decidedly unfashionable) sounds of German-language folk relics like Karel Gott, or perhaps with the plaintive wailing of some 'alternative' coffeehouse rock leftover from the early 1990s. The pounding aggressiveness of Ilsa Gold's more anthemic numbers, combined with a sampling method that placed exuberant irreverence at center stage, would also be a harbinger of things to come.

The nucleus of the Mego label would eventually be formed when Peter 'Pita' Rehberg joined forces with Bauer and Peiper upon the dissolution of Mainframe. Rehberg, the most visibly active of the original trio today, keeps the archive of older Mego releases in print under the newer Editions Mego label (which, in spite of the name change, does not differ significantly in content or approach from its predecessor.) Rehberg transferred from London to Vienna in the late 80s, a musical omnivore previously busying himself with numerous rock-oriented groups, DJing, and fanzine writing- also taking time out from the scene for an extended visit to Minneapolis at the dawn of the 1990s (he now operates most frequently in Vienna, London and Paris.) Having previously subsisted on an eclectic musical diet of post-punk, industrial noise and the dub offerings from the On-U Sound label, Rehberg was somewhat skeptical of the new 'electronic dance music revolution' spreading through warehouse raves and a deluge of white-label vinyl releases. That is to say, it appeared to him as just another development in electronic music, rather than the clean wiping of the slate that - in their usual hysteric tones - culture observers and scene-makers were making it out to be.

Still, the 'electronic dance music revolution' provided some of the necessary cover for Mego to engage in its more intense and unmoored sonic experiments: with a thriving local techno scene to draw upon (proximity to hubs like Munich also helped in this respect), and the credibility that came from playing an intimate role in that scene's growth, some deviation from the norm was permitted them. Simultaneously, the nascent Mego label had support from the more hazily defined post-Industrial and noise subculture in Vienna; local alliances with organizations like the Syntactic label (known for its collectible 7" single releases of the genre's leaders) gave the Mego team a rare opportunity to 'play both sides of the field', as it were- local connections even helped to secure gigs at unlikely venues like the hip youth hangout Chelsea (whose website boasts of it being "simply the best of indie, pop, and beats"), where Rehberg recalls blowing out the house speakers in a live collaboration with psycho-acoustic stalwart Zbigniew Karkowski.[15]

The up-front, blasting energy of such performances was, to say the least, unexpected in environments where electronic music had previously taken on a subservient "support role," a function much like that of mood lighting. Electronic dance music, in all its endless variations, had previously added color and exotic flourishes to the ongoing Continental European social drama, plugging the awkward silences that occurred in between flirting with strangers, or perhaps seeking out local varieties of pharmaceutical recreation. Now, here was an electronic music which manifested itself in unbelievably loud sheets of sound as techno did, yet forced passive bystanders not to divert their attention elsewhere (unless they just chose to flee from the performance venue altogther.) Though some may disagree, the physicality or immersiveness of this breed of computer music initially made for live events defying Tad Turner's claim in *Contemporary Music Review*, i.e. that "the laptop computer's business symbology is not transcended in the act of musical performance."[16] Reviewer Mark Harwood, reporting on Rehberg & Bauer's performances at the "What Is Music?" festival in Australia, accurately describes both poles of audience reaction when suddenly being sucked into this whirling vortex of disorientation:

> Pita thrilled the Melbourne crowd (one male witness reported to have shed tears, while other folk moved about in what can loosely be described as 'dancing') and diced the Sydney audience, shredding one of his tracks by cutting out every few seconds. At a safe distance, you could see numerous people exit, fingers firmly in ears.[17]

Reviews such as this one do much to contradict the otherwise well-considered opinions of critics like Turner. While he correctly identifies how "the metaphors of business computing and the performer's attention on an unknown screen location are no less a restructuring of the audience's expectations than the safety pins, torn shirts and swastikas of the Punks in 1976," there may be some reason to argue his conclusion that "post-digital music" is "not delivered with the same frontal assault" as punk (or any highly energetic musical subculture, for that matter.)[18] Moreover, many performers seem content to achieve a selfish ecstasy from full-volume live immersion in their own works, regardless of whether audiences are moved by it or not. This rejection of certain performance-based anxieties is evident in the wolfish, screen-illuminated grin of Karkowski as his live music reaches a satisfying plateau of intensity, and in his own apparent suggestions that one can exude live energy in spite of one's humble live setup: "live performance is mainly about attitude and presence- it can even be more important than what is created...I am convinced that the performer's attitude and energy on stage is more important than the sound coming from the speakers."[19]

Andrew McKenzie of The Hafler Trio - who was not directly allied with Mego, but whose work maps a similar psychic terrain - also summarizes the performer-audience disconnect that could come about when listeners are forced to decode an incoming rush of mutated sound signals, often in the form of genuinely painful frequencies or tonalities, without any form of 'visual aid' to assist them:

> Focusing on output requires attention, practice, and a

degree of consciousness. None of these come for free, and none of these can be assumed to be existing qualities of an audience. The best that can be done is to attempt to attract those qualities by means of developing them in oneself. What follows from that is feedback on the state of things as they are, not as we might like them to be.[20]

McKenzie has already dealt with the dilemma of being perceived as the "non-performing performer," having lived through earlier periods in which live appearances might be by powered by ADAT machines or arcane assemblages of table-mounted electronics (as employed by post-industrial groups like P.16.D4.) In fact, the prevalence of digital samplers in post-industrial performances also makes the "laptop concert" seem less like something that has its provenance in the 21st century: samplers, too, were "meta-instruments" that contained within them an infinitude of sounds, yet offered few options for performers to connect with audiences on a gestural level.

Confronted with these dilemmas, at least some of the "glitch"-oriented artists hanging around the Vienna scene decided to take advantage of the incongruity of these laptop-based live performances, rather than to be cowed by it. If the effect of this sound was jarring within a venue whose express purpose was to showcase music, then hearing it broadcast from more unorthodox locations took things to a whole other level of bewilderment. One such unorthodox location was the *Riesenrad* ferris wheel at the Prater amusement park in Vienna, which movie buffs will recognize as the site of a now-infamous Orson Welles monologue in *The Third Man*. Originally built to commemorate the golden jubilee of Franz Josef I in 1897, it was one of the first Ferris wheels ever built, and became a universally recognized landmark of the city. So, what better place to stage the defiantly outré sound of the local Mego-affiliated computer music group Farmers Manual than in one of the city's most beloved tourist attractions! In the summer of 1997, Farmers Manual prepared a novel live set that would last the duration of one ferris wheel ride (about 15 minutes), conflating sentimentality and nationalistic pride with 'the shock of the new' and with the decidedly more alien.

Such high-concept performances (albeit 'high-concept' infused with playful mischievousness) may not have approached the spectacular overkill of Karlheinz Stockhausen's composition for a quartet of helicopters, but they did speak to the elasticity of this new music: its lack of lyrical dictation, its tendency to not be pinned into place by a metronomically perfect beat, and its use of portable electronic devices for both recording and playback meant that it could be performed in all variety of public places while generating the same polarized reactions of curiosity and hostility. In a nod to the clandestine punk rock concerts staged on riverboats during the period when certain Central European countries were Soviet satellites, Farmers Manual and several others have taken this approach to the waters on the 'Mego Love Boat.' The tongue-in-cheek whimsy of such actions extended even to the formation of a Mego go-kart racing team, with Mego catalog number 052 being assigned to a 2-stroke racing vehicle.

Farmers Manual in particular have been fanatical about documenting the live aspect of this music- one web archive features gigabytes worth of live material from themselves and allied Mego acts, while their *RLA* DVD catalogs every surviving live recording made of the group from 1995-2002. It is a brutally effective comment on just how much the music subculture has changed since the days of, say, The Grateful Dead: where once fans devoted years of their lives to tracking down and swapping bootlegged, "no-two-are-alike" cassettes of live performances by the torch-bearers of the psychedelic flame, now fans of such a computer music 'jam band' could have their every single performance delivered for a comparatively meager investment: only the cost of a commercial DVD, or the time and energy it would require to download all the shows from the Net.

All innovations in live performance aside, Mego is a label mostly judged on the merit of its recorded output. Mego's initial foray into the world of conceptual music, and away from techno as we now know it, was the *Fridge Trax* collaborative effort between Peter Rehberg and General Magic, itself an alias for the Bauer / Peiper creative duo. The latter duo is also responsible for the mind-bending 1997 computerized song cycle *Rechenkönig,* a surprisingly cohesive collection of shimmering and strobing audio debris. This particular album epitomizes the 'Mego style's' emphasis on the primacy of the abstract sound assemblage rather than linear narrative, yet with the same good-natured irreverence that informed the earlier Mainframe releases (note the familiar cloying patter of Barney the purple dinosaur on the album's opening track.) In a description that reminds us Farmers Manual's mischievous appropriation of the Riesenrad, reviewer Alois Bitterdorf states that "...much of this sounds like the amusement park rides were left to run, and run around, on their own a little too long, and in the meantime some of them have gotten into the medicine cabinet again, oh no, heavens!" [21]

In many ways *Rechenkönig* is a culmination of the work begun earlier on *Fridge Trax,* itself an intriguing study in the sampling and manipulation of household appliances' hidden sound world. The album ranks with Frieder Butzmann's mid-80s curio *Waschsalon Berlin* (a recording of the unique, churning rhythmic activity of Berlin laundromats) as a slickly listenable attempt at humanizing the apparently inert and voiceless. At once an alluring piece of music and a possible joke directed at those who complain of electronic music's "frigidity", *Fridge Trax* capably threw down the gauntlet, which would be picked up in turn by the lush, uncannily organic computer compositions of guitarist and laptop manipulator Christian Fennesz, and by a whole supporting cast of other wild brains, whose work will be reviewed here soon enough.

Meanwhile, the aforementioned problem of presenting this music live was partially solved as the 'bar modern' Rhiz opened for business beneath the overhead train tracks of the city's U6 *U-Bahn* line. Specializing in presentation of 'new media,' and partially immune to noise complaints by virtue of being situated along a major traffic thoroughfare, Rhiz became the default venue for much of the Mego label's live presentation. The rumble of the overhead trains and chatter of passerby (who are free to peer in at the live proceedings, thanks to floor-to-ceiling glass windows on either side of the venue) might occasionally intrude upon the more contemplative moments of live performances, but all in all the venue has done a fine job of allowing this music to be itself.

However, support from other quarters - namely, the Austrian arts funding organizations - has been somewhat more tepid, As Peter Rehberg recalls:

> I'm one of the few Austrian / Viennese labels that doesn't get any support or funding from the funding bodies here, whatever they call themselves...which, on one hand, is a bit of a bummer because it's all got to be financed by myself, but on the other hand it gives you the independence to act on your own- you don't have to be obliged to be nice to anyone [laughs]. And I kind of like that kind of independence. It would be nice to get funding, but they obviously don't recognize my label as a worthy cause. It's a bit of a joke because every other scratchy label here gets funded, but I don't care, because I actually sell records- so I can get the money back. [22]

Acquiescing a little, though, Rehberg also admits that he is "...not anti-funding, as places like the Rhiz couldn't exist without. Although I do get annoyed with labels getting money for a release, and then they package it in the cheapest way possible..... ah, don't get me started.."[23]

Endless Summer, Get Out: A Tale of Two Sound Cards

It is tempting, in retrospect, to see Mego's progress as eventually coalescing around the prolific efforts of Peter Rehberg and Christian Fennesz. Consequently, it is also tempting for some to pit these two against each other in an adversarial struggle between aesthetic polarities: one reviewer, in a scathing review of Pita's 2004 release *Get Off*, even likens the two to being the "Lennon and McCartney of electronica", implying an absolute stylistic and ideological divergence between Rehberg's caustic, unfeeling experimentalism and Fennesz' aspirations towards melodic pop and pastoral simplicity. This rivalry exists more in the minds of such reviewers than it does in reality, though, as can be surmised by the number of live collaborations between the two (they have reunited in 2010, with Jim O'Rourke, as two thirds of the Fenn O'Berg trio) and by other shared traits: neither claim exclusive allegiance to the Mego label, and both are capable, when necessary, of making occasional breaks from their 'signature' style.

Although Christian Fennesz' contributions to this music are well deserving of their landmark status (his *Endless Summer* tops both the sales charts and critics' lists for the Mego label), it is Peter Rehberg's work which has most caught this author's attention. Fennesz' most noted works, with their blissful and asynchronous clouds of sound, are rife with references to idealistic worlds come and gone (see the sunny, utopian Beach Boys quotations of theaforementioned album), and as such it is difficult to divorce them from being either a critique of, or tribute to, past music. Stripped of the nostalgic aspect, or really of any human quality whatsoever, Rehberg's solo work as Pita has no easily identifiable cultural precedent with which to connect it, and thus makes this sentimentality nearly impossible- yet, in spite of this, some Pita works are striking in the emotional depths that they can plumb while maintaining their uncanny post-human edge (Pita compositions in particular are mostly based on patches and virtual instrumentation localized within the computer, with a minimum of sampled or environmental sounds.)

The 1999 release *Get Out* is one of the first and best examples of this approach: an unforgivingly stark and jolting montage of sonic atmospheres which, crossing the threshold into near-total unfamiliarity, serves as a nice extended fanfare for the death of the previous millennium. Without even track titles to base it in the world of consensus reality, it is a demanding listening experience for all but those who would intentionally seek it out, and one so highly subjective that even this author's assessment of it should not be understood as definitive.

Perhaps the linchpin moment of *Get Out* (and consequentially, one of the more canonical moments of computer music of the past decade) proceeds as follows: a ghostly inaudible murmur of filtered melody on the 2nd untitled track, seductive by way of its elusiveness and obscured by steely pinpricks of clipped, high-register sound, becomes resurrected on the 3rd track as a backwards orchestral loop of uncertain origin (playing the LP release of *Get Out* backwards helps somewhat, though the sourced music will still not be familiar to most.) The listener is lured into a false sense of calm contentedness, perhaps expecting that this track will play out as a balmy piece of oceanic ambience. This is clearly not the case, as the orchestration is abruptly overtaken by an exceptionally bracing form of digital decimation. For those who survive this unexpected ambush, the rewards are great, as the distortion causes all kinds of harmonics and auditory hallucinations to emerge from the simple looped phrase- which, at this point, is so laden with overdrive effects that you can no longer tell easily if the original sound source is being looped, or if gradual modifications are being made to the time axis. The track's technique of 'constant crescendo' seems borrowed from earlier forms of techno dance music, but, transposed to different instrumentation, could just as easily be a blast of white light from Swans, one of Rehberg's many influences in the post-industrial landscape of the 80s. A mish-mash of genre leaders like Merzbow and Terry Riley would be another way to describe this, although this scathing 11-minute beast seems less concerned with paying homage than with spawning new mutations of itself.

The remainder of the *Get Out* album plays out as a less epic, but still absorbing, set of viscera-tickling noise episodes and alluring disturbances, the kinds of things that are referred to as a 'mindfuck' in music fanzine parlance: maybe a lowbrow summation of a very complex compositional style, but an apt one nonetheless. After wandering through a sonic terrain so twisting and non-linear that it would put a smile on the face of even a hippie mystic like Friedrich Hundertwasser, we come at last to another lengthy track looping a single gliding bass tone alongside the restless rhythmic sputtering of a Geiger counter (a comparison which has been made perhaps too many times now when attempting to describe Mego-variety music, but, again, an apt one.) The un-emotive artlessness of this send-off is exquisite, and reminds us of how far society has 'progressed' since Industrial music first began to make its critique of mass media's indoctrination methods. It conjures images of blank sedation under brand-name soporifics and / or row upon row of modern, uniform office cubicles cooled by the pallid glow of computer screens, with only the alternation in the rate of the screens' flickering offering any hope of differentiation from one cubicle to the next. The dystopian sci-fi promise heralded by Throbbing Gristle's 1980 track 'IBM' - that of the computer's 'voice' dictating coded orders to spellbound and pliant humans - has been fulfilled here in a most unequivocal way.

And while this new form of computer music could have satisfactorily ended with the disembodied pastiche that was *Get Out*, it was really just getting started, and was growing too rhoizomatically for one to accurately chart its progress in linear terms of "who did what when": to see Peter Rehberg, Farmers Manual's occasional spokesman Matthias Gmachl, or any other individual affiliate of Mego and its companion labels as an ideological "center" or key "signifier" would be erroneous. An international scene of sorts was nevertheless born, which culture scribes - with their penchant for easily digested, monosyllabic tags like 'punk' and 'grunge' - were quick to catch in their butterfly nets and designate as glitch'. Musical taxonomy still refers to this music as such, perhaps giving too much credit to the generative computer music of Oval (a.k.a. Markus Popp) as the 'scene leader' within this milieu, and also assuming that the accidental composition inferred by the name is the *only* means utilized in making this music. More important than the unstable sounds known as glitches (which, again, could be deliberately sculpted and not "unintentional" excrescences) were the music's philosophical vagueness, and its refusal as a 'movement' to uniformly romanticize or condemn digital virtual culture. This was, and is, a refreshing departure in an age of insubstantial yet dangerous territorial claims.

Digital Chiseling

The Lettrist movement of poetry, initiated in Paris shortly after the second World War by Romanian expatriate Isidore Isou and Gabriel Pomerand (and with a notable early supporter in the Situationist Guy DeBord), proposed that every art form goes through a tidal ebb and flow of technique known as the *amplique* [amplic] phase and the *ciselante* [chiseling] phase. In the *phase amplique*, the form is refined and made more ornamental until, at last, the day finally comes when nothing more can be done to enhance that form- it is filled to bursting with ornamental flourishes, with grandeur and opulence, and it adequately encapsulates the spirit of its particular era.

Once this saturation point is reached, the 'chiseling' point begins, in which a critical summary is made of all the form's most distinctive characteristics, and afterwards the entire structure is 'chiseled' away at and destroyed. Or, as Andrew Uroskie suggests, "an advanced art practice ceases to employ the medium as a means to represent external subject and themes, taking up instead the very conventions and vocabularies of the medium itself as its subject"[24] - an interesting point to consider in light of how "glitch" either explicitly or implicitly critiques the digital age. It may be equally interesting to note, in the midst of this very computer-centric discussion, the etymological similarities between "chisel" and "hack," the latter being a devious means of manipulating computer code (and now a colloquial term for merely accomplishing any kind of complex 'work-around' within a computer's software, operating system, etc.)

That digression aside, those who most vigorously take part in the 'chiseling' also have the distinction of laying the foundations for the next amplic period. In his Lettrist manifesto of 1947 (*"Introduction a une Nouvelle*

Poesie et a une Nouvelle Musique"), Isidore Isou comically insisted, despite little public renown, that he was one of the key 'chiselers' of his day, and that he was already respected as part of a grand tradition- see chapter titles like "From Charles Baudelaire to Isidore Isou" for a giggle-inducing idea of Isou's exaggerated self-appraisal. While seeing oneself as a legend in one's own time is more than a little preposterous, Isou and his compatriots did indeed contribute to a post-war trend of 'breaking down the word,' which would see multi-disciplinary icons like Brion Gysin carrying the torch directly to the current generation of artists. In Isou's estimation, letters were the atomic particles of poetry- since the Dadaists and Futurists had already obliterated 'the word' through their experiments, all that remained was for the sounds and symbols associated with letters to be examined.

Along these lines, it is tempting to see the computer music of the Mego label and its fellow travelers as an aggressive but knowingly transitional "chiseling" phase of electronic music, simultaneously abrading away at the venerated technical accomplishments of previous styles and offering clues about how to proceed with the next artistic undertaking (even the emphasis on 'atomic particles' of creative material is carried over here, given much of the composition that is done using 'granular' synthesis techniques.) At the very least, this music consolidates the gains made by the more visceral forms of electronic sound coming at the waning of the last millennium: it often outdoes the Industrial music of Throbbing Gristle or Whitehouse for sheer intensity and (ironically, given the state-of-the-art technology being used) succeeds in connecting with the listener on a more primordial or pre-rational "animal" level. The 'Mego generation' also streamlined or helped to contextualize the formative works that were created long before the proclamation of a subcultural genre known as "glitch," such as Yasunao Tone's "wounded CD" compositions from the mid-1980s and Nicholas Collins' CD player surgeries[25], (neither artist relied on the personal computers considered as the driving engine of this genre, but on the clever customization of compact disc software and hardware.) Meanwhile, at the other end of the pole from Industrial harshness, the sound can be reduced to tiny pixelated flakes floating about the listener's headspace- inviting listeners to hear the world in a grain of sand, as it were.

The act of 'tearing down', though, is not something that can hold the attention of the general listening public for long, and eventually needs to be supplemented by something other than the demonstration of clearing away dead cultural waste. While a handful of 'chiselers' have a definite plan in mind for how to improve on the cultural landscape once they have reached a new 'zero point,' many are are assuredly along only for the chance to be "big fish" in the "small pond" of a sparsely populated subculture, or are just caught up in the admittedly intoxicating thrill of destroying P.A. systems and frying unsuspecting minds. Kenneth Goldsmith, in his editorial *"It Was a Bug, Dave: The Dawn of Glitchwerks,"* warned against the deceitful instant gratification that can come from the simple act of plugging in and tearing down:

> ...as is generally the case with new technologies, most artists are simply exploring what sounds the computer is capable of when it's programmed to go apeshit. As a result, there've been scads of discs released recently that make for worthless listening experiences; most seem to be little more than musicians flexing their muscles, trying to establish the parameters of a vocabulary. In hindsight, it took an awful lot of aimless experimentation before the vision of a Stockhausen or a Pierre Henry emerged to give shape to the then-new forms of electronic music or music concrete.[26]

Goldsmith is correct in suggesting that this kind of thing does take time to refine- the "less is more" maxim of architect Mies Van Der Rohe is something too often ignored by novices in any field, who are so delighted with the new functions a new device or technology has to offer, that they use them indiscriminately and to the detriment of other equally useful tools.

Composer Kim Cascone, known for innovations his with programming tools such as CSound, also proposes that the 'failure as evolutionary mechanism' ethic of the newer computer music is nothing new, although he does add one crucial distinction between then and now:

> Much work had previously been done in this area, such as the optical soundtrack work of Laszlo Moholy-Nagy and Oskar Fischinger, as well as the vinyl record manipulations of John Cage and Christian Marclay, to name a few. What is new is that ideas now travel at the speed of light, and can spawn entire musical genres in a relatively short period of time.[27]

Further downplaying the need to play by any one set of rules, Cascone continues:

> The technical requirements for being a musician in the information age may be more rigorous than ever before, but - compared to the depth of university computer music

studies - it is still rather light. Most of the tools being used today have a layer of abstraction that enables artists to explore without demanding excessive technical knowledge...more often than not, with little care or regard for the technical details of DSP [digital signal processing] theory, and more as an aesthetic wandering through the sounds that these modern tools can create.[28]

Inviting suggestions like Cascone's have encouraged a slew of young experimenters to begin wielding chiseling tools of their own- and the elder statesmen of this new intensity haven't completely discouraged them from doing so. Lettrism itself made direct appeals to the youth of the day, especially the so-called 'externs' who felt that the social system of the time presented them with no clear function or political voice. In the same respect, computer music innovators have had encouraging things to say, such as this from Zbigniew Karkowski:

...I think that today all the art and music schools are absolutely obsolete, they are not necessary. There is no need for people to go to art school anymore. You can find access to all the necessary tools you need on the Internet. If you want to use digital technology, you can download the applications you need and learn how to use them in a rather short time [...] Young creative people don't go to schools, they buy a computer, a small, portable home studio, they travel, make some records and become millionaires after six months [laughs]! [29]

To hear this kind of encouragement from a self-educated D.I.Y. artist is one thing, but it is more interesting coming from the lips of someone who, according to the *curriculum vitae* laid out in *Computer Music Journal*, "studied composition at the State College of Music in Gothenburg, Sweden, aesthetics of modern music at the University of Gothenburg's Department of Musicology, and computer music at the Chalmers University of Technology" (Karkowski is also credited as "studying with Iannis Xenakis, Olivier Messiaen, Pierre Boulez, and Georges Aperghis, among others.")[30] And while many will undoubtedly read this as an example of *"do as I say...not as I do"* that conceals some ulterior motive, these comments are in keeping with a larger trend in which Karkowski sees personal discipline and cultural enrichment as an extra-institutional affair.

Peter Rehberg, at least, has made good on Karkowski's advice: although not a university graduate, he still claims he has been into music "since I was about 12"[31] and was one of the many beneficiaries of gradually more affordable electronic music equipment in the 1980s (evidence of this is available on the Spanish Alku label's *82-84 Early Works*.) One of the successes of digital music constellations like Mego is their simultaneous appeal to a younger, more anxious (and, as per Karkowski's quote, non-academic) audience of digital age 'externs', as well as the more established and studied avant-garde. Take for example Mego ally and Tokyo improviser Otomo Yoshihide, who likened the Austrian label's 'computers on auto-destruct' abrasion of to an amalgam of electro-acoustic music and punk rock.

While the total noise wash of a Mego disc like Kevin Drumm's *Sheer Hellish Miasma* might appeal to the 'externs', the 'wounded CD' experiments of Yasunao Tone (who shares a Mego disc in collaboration with Florian Hecker) might resonate with those students of earlier avant-garde lineages- Kenneth Goldsmith, for one, is an admitted fan of the aesthetic that Tone fraternally co-developed with the intermedia artists of Japanese Fluxus. Since the music is not bound to a corresponding visual (read: fashion) culture, as earlier music-based subcultures have been, the audiences for the above artists could change with relative ease, and with a minimum of squabbling as to who 'represents' or even 'deserves' the culture more. And so, an interesting paradox arises from all this: a music that has so much of the perceptibly 'human' element vacuumed out of it, yet refuses to make its 'target demographic' known and thus ends up addressing a broader section of humanity than many other genres you could name.

The wide-ranging audience for Mego likely would not have happened, though, without a cast of music producers who themselves came from divergent backgrounds and creative perspectives. For every street-level Peter Rehberg, there is a mathematically-minded *wunderkind* like Florian Hecker, trained in the stochastic technique of modernist mastermind Xenakis and offering CD liner notes that will make the technical layman's head explode with their references to pulsars, particle synthesis and spatio-temporal confusion (with this in mind, EVOL's Roc Jiménez de Cisneros deviates a little from Cascone's statement above, i.e. "the relative popularisation [of computer music] has little to do with ease of use.")[32] Hecker is also noticeable for using the Pulsar Generator software of Curtis Roads, editor of the *Computer Music Journal* and author of the very left-brain oriented (though not aesthetically uninspiring) audio manual *Microsound*.

Both Hecker and Rehberg, regardless of how their training and methodology may diverge or overlap, often come to the same conclusions with their sounds themselves: they are equally capable of wringing intense shrapnel storms and more delicate, sparkling sound artifacts out of their computers. It is also telling that both have a habit of using the word 'acid' in the titles of their pieces (see 'Acid Udon' from Pita's *Get Down*, or

'Stocha Acid Vlook' from Hecker's bracing *Sun Pandaemonium*)- although it is not clear if this is a mutual nod to the disorienting, dissolving properties of LSD (and the similar effects delivered by the music), a self-referential nod to the overdriven 'acid sound' of Roland's TB-303 bassline generator, or some other devious in joke cooked up between the two.

Dig deeper into the Mego back catalog, and you can find episodes of teeth-shaking, elemental noise from Russell Haswell alongside the bittersweet digital cloud gazing of Tujiko Noriko. Still more faces of the label emerge in the multi-media synergy of Farmers Manual, the alternatingly cruel and hilarious stage dramas of Fuckhead, and Merzbow, who puts in at least one appearance on the label (the inclusion of Merzbow invites an interesting parallel between Masami Akita's reassessment of urban detritus and the other Mego artists' willful embrace of the computer error.)

Finally, no overview of Mego is complete without considering the visual design and layouts of house artist Tina Frank, who did much to validate Mego's claim of being a platform for all electronically-conveyed information (not "only" music.) Her special oversized CD folders helped the label's releases to stand out amidst the standard CD jewel cases on store shelves- a shrewd move that often forced retailers to place Mego music in a privileged position before having even heard it. Frank's designs are also notable for their playful use of patchwork assemblages and toxic colors, certainly a deviation from the geometric puzzles and sterile schematics which graced the covers of the first generation of 'computer music' LPs. Her work, though claimed as a collaborative endeavor between recording artists and herself (i.e. "never 100% Tina Frank"[33]), would come to be utilized by the first Austrian Internet provider (EUnet.) While much of her design would be modulated by the needs of corporate clients, she would retain a purer form of expressivity working in the video field- a 2006 video collaboration with General Magic, *Chronomops*, is a dizzying but energizing race through a forest of light columns.

This colorful cast of characters that made up the original Mego roster is not uniquely a product of the aforementioned geographical particularities of Vienna, nor the social invention of a single charismatic personality, nor even the creation of taste-making journalists (Peter Rehberg routinely denies that there is even "a genre of 'laptop music.'"[34]) If it seems otherwise, it is maybe because our communications media has a predilection for suggesting sensational 'Big Bang' cultural events, in which new paradigms are created *ex nihilo* with one brave *fiat* declaration or happy accident, either of which is oblivious to past historical developments. The truth is usually a comparitively more mundane, long-term, and invisible accretion of separate cultural micro-events. Disillusionment with the academic music circuit, the "access principle" of new recording and duplicating technologies, the "horizontal" method of forging bonds with peers in distant locations instead of proving one's usefulness to higher-ranked entities in one's local environment: all of these societal trends were bound to converge with a little luck and patience. That the Mego aesthetic appeared completely "new" in the late 1990s was just a testament to how naturally and imperceptibly these factors converged. And, in that moment of convergence, it seemed to validate even the most romantic assumptions of tech-utopians like *Wired* magazine investor Nicholas Negroponte: "Like a force of nature, the digital age cannot be denied or stopped. It has four very powerful qualities that will result in its ultimate triumph: de-centralizing, globalizing, harmonizing, and empowering"[35]

There is much to refute in Negroponte's overly sunny reckoning, but if we play along with that for now, it is worth noting that these techno-utopian conditions have enabled numerous other organizations similar in scope to Mego.

Electric Friends

The open-minded ethos of "available to anyone who understands it" is not, by any means, an exclusive Mego property: several other record labels and organizations have such an overlap with the artists represented by the Mego label, that it is counter-productive to use that label as a metonym for the stylistic innovations that it represents. The OR label, for example, which was organized around Russell Haswell and erstwhile Touch boss Mike Harding in London, features releases by Karkowski, Hecker, and Farmers Manual (whose *Explorers_We* sits alongside Pita's *Get Out* as a *pièce de résistance* of the genre) alongside the more free-form, noisy, and non-computerized entries from Daniel Menche and Incapacitants. One 2003 omnibus release - *OR MD Comp* - offers some trenchant humor in the form of a surreptitioulsy recorded Farmers Manual audience member in Sheffield, who offers a dissenting view on the new computer music phenomenon (e.g. vulgarly expressing his bewilderment that the trio can manufacture neither bassline nor backbeat with multiple computers on stage.)

Like Mego releases, OR releases distinguished themselves from the outset by dint of their unique packaging. OR CDs came packed in jewel cases without corresponding booklets, the printed graphics on the CD surface substituting for 'covers' in a skeletal form of graphic presentation that was rife with interpretations, any of which could be correct: were the CDs released in this manner as an ecological consideration (saving paper), an economical necessity (printing costs would be severely reduced), or as a revolt against commodity fetishists who demanded that all their consumer products come in pointlessly ornate packages? Whatever the case, it was a shrewdly simple move in which the CDs' exceptionality was multiplied through the subtraction of a very 'standard' component.

Other OR compilations, designed by Haswell, would feature the inverse of this design: a clear CD jewel case with an austere graphic-stripped booklet (text and UPC code only), but with the CD laid bare by a missing tray card. The audio of select OR CDs was likewise 'subtractive' in its method: the *Datastream* release by Edwin van der Heide and Zbigniew Karkowski simply converted digital data from the Microsoft Word program into audio signals, with no real attempt to 'play' or edit the results. This subtractive aesthetic was taken to one logical endpoint when GESCOM (a portmanteau of 'Gestalt Communications'[36] featuring members of Autechre, Russell Haswell, and a rotating cast of other players) released the first non-Sony album in the *world* to be commercially available on that company's Mini Disc format. The only problem? A very small segment of music consumers outside of Japan had the equipment to play it on, although the Mini Disc format had existed since 1992. It was one thing to pare down graphics and audio content to the bone, it was another entirely to consciously cut the art off from its target audience. Although there is some humor involved in the way this release confused and inverted typical patterns of consumption: fans would be forced to buy a new piece of playback equipment to play a single album, instead of stocking up on albums to feed the hungry home stereo equipment which they already owned.

The Falsch label was another unique outpost for all the above-mentioned digital quirks and disruptions: this time Florian Hecker and Oswald Berthold were the sound curators, with "hyper-music on purpose" being their apt slogan. Running from 2000-2005, Falsch offered music in a much more minimally packaged format than even OR: that is to say, hardly any physical objects at all. Falsch was basically an outlet for 'releasing' downloadable sound files of the now-familiar artists in this chapter, along with unclassifiable mavericks like Voice Crack and CoH. Compilations eventually appeared in CD form (such as *FB25,* a 3" MP3 CD that celebrated the disk space-maximizing potential of said audio algorithm.) This was only done, however, after a good deal of material had been relayed across the fiber-optic pathways of the Internet.

Spain's Alku features a familiar cast of characters: Messrs. Hecker, Rehberg and Tone all feature in their catalog, along with the often scathingly loud combo EVOL, consisting of Anna Ramos and Roc Jiménez de Cisneros. What the label also offers in spades is fun at the expense of orthodox technology: Alku's commentaries on the fragility and frustration of our relationship with technology having taken the form of numerous prank-infused conceptual releases. One Alku CD-R release, *El Formato is The Challenge* (a wry poke at a McLuhan-ism which still haunts us), features only a couple tracks in 'conventional' music formats, while the rest of the release is given over to computer files with file extensions varying in degrees of usability and obscurity. Most amusing of the contributions on this disc may be V/VM's track, *Scanner, Wire Magazine August 1999*. This is a play on words using both the name of the British sound artist Scanner, and the method used to make the track- according to one net review, "V/Vm have scanned music-mag *The Wire*'s front cover image of Scanner to see if the music sounds as pretentious as Mr. Scanner does."[37]

Another Alku release, *Imbecil*, contains no music at all, but a series of ridiculous computer programs which range from the amusing to the simply useless. It is a kind of micro-rebellion in itself against the unquestioning adoration of computers' "smooth functionality"- via *Imbecil* you can make a 'kernel panic' (a sudden unexpected shutdown exclusive to Macintosh computers) happen on your expensive machine at any time you like; and if that isn't enough of a tip of the hat to Tinguely's 'auto-destructing' art, you also have an option to have a special Microsoft Word script write a suicide note for you. Yet another *Imbecil* side project, a curious Macintosh UNIX script called 'foofoofoo,' is not useless at all, and is actually quite convenient for those wanting to make 'automatic' compositions which can later be edited. Foofoofoo will raid a user's hard drive for sound files, taking miniscule clips from each one and reassembling them into one unpredictable juggernaut of a non-linear digital composition (the more soundfiles one has, the more epic the effect, obviously.)

Meanwhile, the titles of essays by Alku flagship act EVOL reveal a more serious and ponderous approach that mines chaos theory and fractal geometry, and questions the perceived use of computers as randomizing machines- in one short yet revealing essay from the computer art exhibition *e +*, the Alku team answers the question "can a computer come up with a random number?" as such:

> Technically, NO. Practically, there are hundreds of computer programs and computer-driven algorithms out there that -at least- claim to do it. But when it comes to the philosophical part of it, things get trickier: if a computer is a deterministic machine (that is, all it does is completely determined by its current state), it certainly cannot do something "by chance". You can do it, your friends can do it, but not a computer.[38]

It is an interesting conclusion for those who compose 'computer music' while quoting from John Cage on indeterminacy, yet is also a much-needed rebuke of what Nick Collins and A.R. Brown refer to as "algorithmically uneducated critics," who have "often derided much digital art as exhibiting 'randomness', though this view is essentially naive, showing an ignorance of probability theory."[39]

The Alku team seems very eager to show us, as do so many other 'glitch' musicians, that computers are still somewhat imperfect even in areas where we deem them to be already superior to humans. In fact, we are still far from being overtaken by artificial intelligence, for those who take comfort in this fact. Consider the 'Turing Test': in this famous test, a human judge monitors a conversation between a human and machine, with both attempting to have a typically 'human' conversation (marked such 'exclusively' human traits as irony and a sense of humor.) If the judge cannot tell human from machine over the course of the conversation, the machine is said to have passed the test. No computer system has done this as of this writing, and many are often prone to hilarious (or at least tragicomic) communication breakdowns. It is not this ongoing irreconcilability between man and machine that frustrates Cisneros, but rather the attempt to give a human face to phenomena that may be more aesthetically inspiring without one: "It's amazing how academia is still trying really hard to make computers play music like human beings. I thought the whole point of using computers to make music was to do things you cannot do without them...not [to] pass musical Turing tests."[40]

It is also an interesting fact for those who think music of the kind represented on Mego, Fals.ch, Alku etc. is a form of brazen computer idolatry (for what it's worth, the latter of the three has released records using primarily the sounds of air horns or small balloons, both of which manage to have sonic signatures oddly similar to those of computer-generated "timbral novelties.") The work of the so-called 'glitch' squad shows us that we often give computers more power as omniscient devices than they really deserve, and so maybe Otomo Yoshihide was not that far off in calling this music a kind of computerized 'punk': it, too, is a musical form celebrating the fact that the power structure - and the technology enabling it- cannot function perfectly all of the time; occasionally things just happen to slip through the cracks.

Even as this has been said, though, another of the Alku label's releases from 2007, *Less-Lethal Vol. 1*, abruptly dispenses with the humor and compiles tracks meant to be used as 'sonic weapons,' giving a musical voice to the dark suspicions swirling around the clandestine activity of the military-industrial complex. Hannah Arendt's famous proclamation of the "banality of evil" does not apply to the mean, bracing tracks on this CD, with the artists intent on portraying the very non-banal, spectacular destructive capabilities of the global military machine. As the mass media discusses brainwashing and torture (re-branded for the squeamish as "enhanced interrogation technique") in a manner as detached and methodical as the pain dealers whose resumés are padded with these activities, it is up to artists to once again provide a more convincing running commentary. Lasse Marhaug and Zbigniew Karkowski contribute some of their noisiest, direct work here, while Dave Phillips' steadily rising and claustrophobically multiplying spoken mantra of *"there is no right or wrong"* need only be played under the influence of the right psychoactive pharmaceuticals in order to turn the listener into an impressionable zombie / berserker hybrid. It is a release which leaves a distinctly unpleasant aftertaste, warning us that, even as we make Negroponte-like claims of technology empowering us as citizens, a vast network of military, security, and 'intelligence community' officials earn their pay by fashioning that same technology into a digital straitjacket. The unique performative violence of this music, in fact, raises some questions about how it might really be used by coercive authorities if they were aware of it. Perhaps the fact that this music has always has some degree of "untranslatability" built into it - a fact that we will turn to now - has kept it out of the hands of those who would use it for the worst.

Embracing The Alien

> For years one of my main activities was making music with computers. I remember when the first music software for personal computers became available in the 1980s. The music created with this technology played with an electronically precise meter (the time between beats), making it sound radically different from the rhythm of music made by humans. Most musicians working with computers at the time had the same response I did: 'Well, this is sort of cool, but it sounds so *machine-like,* no one will ever listen to it. To be really interesting, this technology is going to have to evolve to sound more human.' And software engineers busied themselves trying to make computer music sound human. But before they could solve the problem, a new generation of kids had come up who *preferred* the machine-like quality of computer music. Music with an electronically precise, not-humanly-possible meter has now flooded the world.[41]

-Bob Ostertag

In the essay from which the above excerpt is taken –Bob Ostertag's

"*Are Two Dimensions Enough? The Networked Screen and the Human Imagination*"- the author puts forth the argument that supposedly 'second best' virtual experiences, like playing a game of video football rather than watching it live, are actually more appealing to many people than the "real life" equivalent, owing to a greater degree of control placed in the user's hands (as the argument goes, why would one want to watch a TV football broadcast cut through with advertisements and other diversions, when they can command a virtual copy of their favorite team and have some direct effect on steering the game's results?) Internet pornography is also an obvious and prevalent example of this, what with its possible use as a 'testing ground' for certain fantasies, and its low risk factor when compared with interpersonal contact and intimacy: Ostertag proposes that "pornography was previously something that one looked at while fantasizing about being with another person...pornography has moved from being the substitute to being the ideal."[42]

John Cage once noted, of the theremin, that though it was "an instrument with genuinely new possibilities," its first players nonetheless "did their utmost to make the instrument sound like some old instrument, giving it a sickeningly sweet vibrato, and performing upon it, with difficulty, masterpieces from the past."[43] Along similar lines, it is interesting to consider how much the developers of computer-based instrumentation once fretted over its inability to reproduce the unique timbres of naturally occurring sounds. Kim Ryrie, who co-founded the company responsible for the groundbreaking Fairlight CMI [Computer Music Instrument], eventually decided to try building a microprocessor-based synthesizer after some disappointments in the 1970s. "My frustration set in because of my ability to produce more natural sounds,"[44] Ryrie sighs. Elsewhere, the promotional material for the E-mu Emulator sampler, released in 1981, asked "how would you like to play a turkey?" proudly mentioning the ability to accurately reproduce a plethora of other natural sounds (dogs, violins, etc.)[45]

Nowadays, the presets on digital synthesizers and the sample banks included with music software tend to do the opposite of what Ryrie and the E-mu staff hoped to accomplish: to make synthetic sounds distinctly at odds with the realm of the natural, sounds which intrigue through their distance from reality and not their closeness to it. Moreover, in a culture where sampling technology can now easily imitate organic sounds, the real hallmark of sophistication has become sounds that are 'neither here nor there'- sounds whose sources cannot be easily discerned as a sampling of "real life" or as a computer-created chimera. The curiosity surrounding these novel sounds bypasses the realm of the sentimental and directly stimulates the imagination of the listener.

The generation gap indubitably plays some role in computer music of the day: the older generation often seeks a reinforcement of tradition and a vindication of their past culture-shaping victories, and most young people are invigorated by a 'cool noise' whose brightness and novelty can be attributed to *their* era and none other, while convincing them that their generation is helping to dismantle the orthodoxy of previous generations. But this argument is somewhat flawed when we consider that the generation of Peter Rehberg, Ramon Bauer, Zbigniew Karkowski, Russell Haswell et. Al. is in its 40s already (to say nothing of the nearly octogenarian Yasunao Tone.) Although there are a slew of younger counterparts to these musicians, their creations are, so far, not much more radical than the works of their seniors. The middle-aged segment of the new digital music milieu came of age just in time to see the failures of the hippie counter-culture, with its reliance on absolutist exhortations like "never trust anyone over 30!!!" Nor were these musicians ever an ideal representation of the *zeitgeist* of their own generation, functioning mostly as intellectual outsiders whose dual immersion into artistic and scientific concerns did not always mean appreciation by the specialists of either sphere. The present speed and omnipresence of electronic communications once again plays a role in bringing together and extracting the common motives from the myriad of differences between the post-1960s generation, Generation 'X', and Generation 'Y'.

If imbibing alien sounds is a demanding experience for the traditionally minded music consumer, continually eluding attempts to connect them with familiar events and memories, then *talking about* these sounds is even more of a challenge. A certain amount of "shut up and listen" attitude, or a certain degree of refusal to explain that which remains partially unkown to the artists themselves, does permeate this scene, clearly separating this artistic subculture from the text-based experiments of much Conceptual art. Nevertheless, a linguistic component does exist within it that is not merely an exigency of music releasing (e.g. the requirement for albums and individual tracks to be titled for ease of location and indexing.) Some lexical analysis of the texts connected with the music shows them to be an integral part of the music's adventure in disorientation, and to also be informed by much of the historical avant-garde.

For example, the idiosyncratic project names and track names of these computer musicians have more in common with F.T. Marinetti's Futurist poetry (or, again, with the atomized creations of the Lettrists) than they do with any kind of instrumental conversational exchange. Impossible-to-pronounce project names like GCTTCATT are like onomatapeia for the incomprehensible speed of computer processes, or at least bring to mind the explosive neologisms used in comic books to give readers an idea of the sound accompanying a sudden action. Likewise, Florian Hecker's habit of using those very processes as track titles borders on the infuriating: tracks / albums like 'Femtoje Helical', 'Ciz-Glemp 2' or *[OT] Xackpy*

Breakpoint are so unlike the phonemes normally heard in human languages, that one can only compare them to instructions fed into a machine- or, stranger still, as the undecipherable, time-distorted, and polyglot communications which take place in one's dreams.

Even the Futurists, in their mania for smashing traditions, still had conventional titles for their sound and poetry works. However, Russian Futurist poet Alexei Kruchenykh may have been a century ahead of his time when he formulated *zaum* poetry in 1911- built from the phonemes *za* (beyond) and *um* (mind), Mel Gordon describes this phenomenon as follows, offering some clues as to the possibilities of the strange new digital-age neologisms:

> According to Kruchenykh, the Futurist poet has at his disposal this other form of vocalization, one rich with private associations and new sound ideas: *zaum*. The secret of primordial creation, that is, the trans-rational language, could lead the artist far beyond the restraints of socially sanctioned patterns and the vise of national vocabularies.[46]

As the linguist Roman Jakobson observed, Kruchenykh also viewed his laundry list as alphabet as a great work of poetry, putting him in the company of those who "admired the poetic quality of a wine list (Vjazemskij), an inventory of the tzar's clothes (Gogol), [and] a timetable (Pasternak)."[47] Seen in this way, the Heckers and GCTTCATTS of the world - who are developing their own "poetry of processes" - are simply involved in a positive enterprise of finding aesthetic pleasure within the stuff of formulae and algorithms, and swapping out their utility for a sense of real mystery.

Having said this, it is worth returning for a while to the audio techniques that figure into this program of "inspiration through de-familiarization." Heavy distortion, bit degradation, and convolution (a technique in which the 'acoustic signature' of one sound is mapped onto another sound, resulting in strange new hybrids), all work in concert with other forms of digital signal processing to create music which is enticingly *unlike* one's immediate surroundings. As words like 'degradation' might imply, the axiom 'cleanliness is next to godliness' has little value here: clean, hi-fidelity sound samples are often ignored in favor of wading through the digital murk. The music appearing on Mego-style recordings often features sounds that could be likened to the jagged-edged or lossy 'raster' versions of graphics, rather than smooth vector images that maintain their resolution no matter how much they are expanded (a point not lost on the German label Raster / Noton.) There is a high preponderance of low-resolution sound within new computer music, and in one instance - the Rehberg & Bauer CD *Faßt* - the final mix of the album was inexplicably reduced to an inferior 8-bit resolution instead of the 16-bit resolution common for commercial CDs. Much as the "glitch" has become a celebrated part of computerized music's toolkit, so too has the aliased "digital artifact" or the sound that represents a compression algorithm's failure to make a perfect facsimile of uncompressed sound.

The creation of deliberately junky, "lo-bit" sound artifacts using state-of-the-art equipment and complex coding was a novel move that has since spawned its own sub-sub-genre[48]: and this, once again, confirms Otomo Yoshihide's claim that Mego music is a computer-based upgrade of at least some punk rock ideals. Out-of-control punk musicians destroyed their own equipment as the apotheosis of their stylized "I don't care" nihilism, hinting that such gear was ultimately mass-produced and expendable, without the spiritual value conferred on it by the previous generation of 'dinosaur' musicians (of course, there was also the underlying hint that the musicians themselves were seen as expendable in the urban landscape.) Computer musicians, using their laptops for a number of functions beyond music production and performance, were not so quick to smash their equipment (I have still not seen such a gesture at even the most violent concerts of laptop-generated noise), but they could still resort to smashing the bits themselves, taking streams of 'clean' audio and trashing it with ingenuous software plug-ins. This, then, fulfills the dual purpose of criticizing the utopian elements of digital culture in a unique, non-verbal way, and also of providing the Mego niche audience with something enjoyably alien. Whether it is a biting critique, or just a 'cool noise,' depends only on the listener's personal inclinations towards technology.

+

It remains uncertain whether the music generated in the wake of the 21st century computer music 'boom' will ever reach a mainstream audience. Certainly music styles that were once thought too sonically extreme, socially confrontational for public consumption - punk, thrash metal, hip hop - are now fused to the grid of commercial culture. One thing is certain, though, and that is that the critics of computer-based performance and composition will have even more contentious developments to face with music interfaces becoming even more compact and farther removed from the realms of technical skill exhibition: patches for open-source programs like Pure Data have already been ported to tiny devices like the iPod, making real-time performances possible from within the most squalid of personal spaces and making composition something which can be done on commutes by train (a practice which Christian Fennesz has already admitted to.)

More radical, far-flung developments, like the implementation of wireless, antenna-transmitted electricity, would even overcome the battery power constraints faced by these portable devices, if the studies of researches like MIT's Marin Soljačíč bear fruit (apparently Soljačíč has already sold a conference populated by 18 Nobel Prize winners on the subject.)[49]   More importantly, time that would otherwise be spent transitioning from one activity to another could be spent on at least some rudimentary form of creative work. For better or worse, the shrinkage of electronic musical interfaces may also lead to more unprecedented occurrences: another step in the direction of an eventual 'first-level cyborg' symbiosis between flesh and synthetic material- music generated by a direct brain-computer interface, or by means of special sub-dermal implants hooked up to amplification.

Before any of this speculative activity comes to pass, though, there is still the issue mentioned above- whether this music will be accepted by the general public as a stimulating distillation of the increasingly complex human experience, or whether it will be rejected as just more willful obscurantism and aesthetic nihilism from increasingly disliked 'contemporary artists'. If we chart the progress of previous forms of extreme electronic music, though, the most likely result is that elements of it will be assimilated by and used as the ornamentation for more standard musical fare- maybe a "glitchy" introduction to add exoticism, or a looped sample of static electricity buried underneath a lovelorn, pining vocal. And, of course, thanks to the voracious and mutable nature of advertising and marketing culture, and its propensity to censor itself far less than the music business proper, there are always plentiful opportunities to sneak these materials in through a back door.

VanHanen suggests that the dilution and commercialization of the "glitch" aesthetic is already upon us, in fact, as evinced by "...car adverts, MTV inserts and music videos [...] now decorated with glitchy filigree, in the domain of graphic design as well as in the audio sphere...it seems that glitch has lost all its 'power of the false' and become another stylistic choice."[50] Terre Thaemlitz, in a fairly dour accounting of 'electronica' politics at the millenium's dawn, goes further still, disapprovingly noting "Calvin Klein's use of Markus Popp" and making the sweeping statement that "electronica liberated digital synthesis from the tedium of academia...[only] to fill our lives with video game and movie soundtrack filler, product tie-ins and football anthems."[51] While I imagine Thaemlitz would attribute this to capitalism's insidious need to subsume any and all potentially radicalizing cultural forces, there is a simpler, more banal explanation for the advertising world's capture of this music. This kind of assimilation has already occurred with the electronic dance music from which artists like Peter Rehberg and EVOL have claimed some influence: the mostly non-verbal, atmospheric nature of that music (along with the relative ease of crafting a passable facsimile of its signature sounds) made it an attractive proposition for advertising departments, and the same would seem to hold true for a more domesticated, subdued or carefully abridged version of the music discussed in this chapter.

Yet time will tell whether this state of affairs is a triumph or a tragedy, and whether or not a state of widespread dilution will prevent individuals from seeking out the "purer" forms of this music, unsullied by the motives of its appropriators. In the meantime, it would be wise to ditch the romantic fiction that of radical computer music being "brainwashed" or hoodwinked into commercial distillations and abridgements of their sound. Besides, it may be worth simply enjoying the humorous incongruity of such a situation. That is to say, it would be worth re-imagining situations in which it appears that these appropriators are laughing at the artists that they have supposedly subdued: seen from another angle, it could be these "domesticated" artists who are indeed laughing at their hosts. It was not too long ago that one Austrian bank perfectly exemplified the possibility for almost anything to be re-assimilated into the daily functions of commerce. Their reward to new bank account holders upon signing up? Bank books and ATM cards adorned with aesthetic representations of spilt blood, courtesy of Viennese Aktionist Hermann Nitsch.

To Kick A King[1]:
The Kingdoms of Elgaland / Vargaland

Prologue: the globalization of what?

In a report on the 1st Congress of the micro-nation known as the NSK State, its authors note a salient fact: "a decade ago the defeat of the nation-state seemed all but absolute. It was widely argued both on the political left and on the right that the state had exhausted its historical role in the age of globalization and that its power, derived from now-antiquated modernist social formations, had been eroded by meta-national forces."[2] In fact, it would be difficult to say, with any degree of conviction, that the 21st century push towards a 'global village,' or the 'new world order' once proclaimed by George H.W. Bush, are now a plausible reality. The formation of new continental super-states like the European Union (which has collectively received a Nobel Peace Prize as of this writing) may have temporarily eroded away at the concept of national sovereignty and geographical borders, yet a new spate of geographical fragmentations and proclamations of tribal identity or autonomy makes one wonder how long this arrangement will last.

China, Taiwan, and Japan have all staked claims upon an uninhabited set of islands, leading to speculation of Japanese re-armament or full-scale regional war (China of course has its hands full with the ethnic replacement by Han Chinese of Uighur and Tibetan peoples.) The Russian government, which has engaged in a similar dispute with Japan over the Kuril islands, has also shown indications that it sees ethno-nationalism as the 'new world order' of the future, mobilizing youth groups such as *Nashi*[3] to intimidate the insufficiently patriotic and to aid in cyber-warfare against perceived Western (that is to say, globalist) proxies. The examples here are far from exceptions to the rule, with localized identity movements surfacing in nearly every habitable land mass on the planet and arraying themselves against the extra-territoriality enjoyed by both multinational corporations and super-states.

In the present climate it is fashionable to blame this state of affairs on economic concerns alone, e.g. the failure of neoliberalism. However, as John Gray noted well in advance of the 2008 market crash that made this failure a perennial front-page topic, the new demand for sovereign nation-states did not originally come "on the back of hyperinflation and mass unemployment" as it did in the 1930s: the rise of far-right nationalist parties in Austria and the Netherlands occurred in countries then boasting some of the lowest unemployment rates in Europe[4] (though the same cannot be said of newer neo-fascist organizations like Greece's Golden Dawn.) By not understanding that forces resistant to globalization are more ultimately concerned with the preservation of indigenous or unique cultures than they are with unfettered economic growth or technical progress, the flag-bearers of global progress dismiss them too carelessly, accusing them of being pointlessly atavistic and unrealistic. This dismissal is foolhardy, firstly because it ignores the original fascist movements' own grounding in techno-scientific thinking (as Gray puts it, their "faith that progress demands the use of science and technology to transform the human condition, without regard to the moralities of the past."[5]) A secondary assumption, that right-extremists or fascists are the driving engine of anti-globalization, ignores the many left-aligned independence or "Euroskeptic" movements still operative in the Basque Country, Catalonia, Ireland and elsewhere- all of whom make cultural self-determination at least as strong a priority as economic self-determination, if not moreso. Aslo ignored is the curious situation - personified by the radical *Rote Armee Fraktion* lawyer turned far-right agitator Horst Mahler - in which certain critiques of anti-globalization can survive the ideological leap from one extreme to the other, or even dissolve these extremes.[6]

Thinkers like Paul Virilio, who are inclined towards musings on techno-eschatology, see globalized activity as a bizarre inverted state of being in which acting at a distance seems more natural than taking action locally. Thus "globalization is turning the world inside out like a glove...from now on, the near is foreign, and the exotic close at hand."[7] Virilio's mistrust of globalization also extends to the fact that it "*provides the 'state of emergency'*, that foreclosure which transforms, or will soon transform, every state into a *police state*, every army into a *police force* and every city into a *ghetto*... [italics from the original text]."[8]

Virilio's histrionics aside, though, the question remains whether a de-centralized supra-nation can be more or less humane than a sovereign nation-state. Fluxus practicioner Ken Friedman, given his personal involvement in art projects of the 'networked' variety, argues in favor of separating the globalist de-centralization that is, paradoxically, centrally planned from those global tendencies that develop organically and without coercion from a militarized foreign power. Friedman notes, for example, that "the first great movement to end the slave trade in America came from the nineteenth-century forces of 'globalization,'" and that "many who engage in slavery still resist efforts to end the slave trade, in the name of local sovereignty against globalization."[9]

As Friedman's comments might suggest, the figures put forward as the very antithesis of globalization are not averse to globalizing or networking their own projects of liberation- just as the defenders of the nation-state come from either side of the Left / Right divide, so do defenders of globalization come from opposing poles of, say, mercantilism or anarchism. Take the celebrated Subcomandante Marcos of the EZLN: his declaration of *"through me speaks the will of..."* is applied by him to an implied network of subjugated groups throughout the world, causing the oft contrarian philosopher Slavoj Žižek to note the similarities between this speech and "the standard cliché of totalitarian leaders [...] the dark implication being, "so anyone who attacks me personally is effectively attacking you all, the entire people, your love for freedom and justice!"[10] The only difference, for Žižek, lies in the fact that totalitarian regimes made such statements from the seat of power while the EZLN does not (e.g. " The greater the poetic potential of Marcos in opposition, as a critical voice of *virtual* protest, the greater would be the terror of Marcos as an *actual* leader."[11]) One could also see where the manufactured "attack on all of us" is very similar to Virilio's permanent police state made possible by a globally distributed governing body.

So perhaps one question to be asked, in light of all this, is how much of a "trade-off" we can really expect from the new "inside out" form of state authority: how much and what kind of freedom must be sacrificed to an all-pervasive security state, and what kind of liberation will be allowed in exchange. To some, this is already the wrong question to be asking, and there is no liberation that does not also contain within it the seed for future restrictions. According to a historical example provided by Håkan Nilsson, a spokesperson for the enigmatic KREV [Kingdoms of Elgaland and Vargaland]

> The state, of course, will never admit that any of its actions are carried out to preserve its power and/or the existing order. It will always pretend that everything is done with the utmost care for the benefit of the citizens. The fact that this is not the case is amply demonstrated by several examples of state actions. In the late 19th century, Baron Haussman created the boulevard system we now find emblematic for the city of Paris. The question is, as is well known, was this an action of a philanthropic government, which tried to open up a closed city, bringing daylight into a maze-like infrastructure? Or was it rather something that allowed the same government to easily transport troops from one area to another? Given the history of the Paris community, and given the fact that city planners from ancient history to the present have been in military service, the most common and obvious conclusion is the latter one.[12]

The example of Haussman is a pertinent one for this discussion, since it is a case of, as Nilsson points out, making the city of Paris more appealing to tourists and apparently more 'free'- in reality "this was the first application of the idea of opening a space as a means to fortify it".[13] The same tactic has arguably occurred with the globalized communication networks of cyberspace: the creation of a superficial autonomy which causes citizens to 'let down their guard' and act a little too freely while under observation. However, more recent signs have shown that, if this was originally intended as a masterstroke of Haussman-style control agreed upon by the governing bodies of soon-to-be-dissolved nation-states, it has become too unwieldy and prone to subversion. After all, the primary target of many post '9/11' anti-terrorism bills was the Internet. There is of course no 'headquarters' for the Internet, it is a network composed of countless micro-networks, none of which are expected to report back to a single higher authority. Seen as such, the true surprise is that state authorities had not begun talk of censoring / regulating the Internet *sooner*- given its ability to provide convincing counterpoints to 'official versions' of reportage on the state of the nation (which are usually brought to you by news networks sponsored by major defense contractors.)

With the situation as such, it was perhaps inevitable that some of the more innovative actors within the arts community would choose to critique much of the above - Virilio's "inversion" caused by instantaneous de-centralized global communication, and the panic arising from those who feel this convenience is one more weapon in the arsenal arrayed against self-determined cultures and independent thinkers. The KREV project was one novel means for people to declare their independence without also falling back on ethno-nationalism for their identity: an independence achieved not solely through the means of independent record labels, or concerts and other events held in autonomous spaces, but through the founding of an entire de-centralized 'state' of their own. As announced by one of this project's principal planners, Leif Elggren, "everyone knows that artists rule the world,"[14] hinting at the fact that this would not be any conventional nation-state in terms of its social organization. While it would be another face of the globalization already mentioned, its boundaries would be demarcated in an unorthodox way that will soon be discussed.

Leif Elggren and Carl Michael von Hausswolff, the two individuals at the heart of the KREV undertaking, have been in collaboration since 1979-1980. By von Hausswolff's admission, they had been working with concepts such as hierarchy and symbology from that point up until the formation of KREV in the 1990s. Von Hausswolff claims that KREV was the logical conclusion to a lengthy flirtation with these ideas, saying "we realized that it would be interesting to move these concepts into a practical function – we decided to use the concept of the State."[15] The twin kings have a long history of de-centralized artwork building up to this conclusive act- and at least some of this is worthy of summarizing before going into detail about their invisible empire itself.

Claiming the Thrones

The official motto of Linköping, Sweden is *"Där idéer blir verklighet* [where ideas become reality]"- whether they had people like Carl Michael von Hausswolff in mind when offering up this simple prayer to ingenuity, it is hard to tell. Von Hausswolff was born in Linköping (he now lives in Stockholm), after a long stint in the 2nd city of Göteborg) and he has certainly taken the concept of "ideas becoming reality" to heart. Where raw sound is concerned, he has (like many other artists in this book) re-claimed its physicality and / or substantiality without sacrificing its elusivity- or, as colleague Randy Yau has put it, has pointed to its existence as "a force of nature both ephemeral and permanent."[16] The *curriculum vitae* on his personal website proudly proclaims his music's "polyfrequential ability", which has the power to alternately lull audiences to sleep and to provide a "'feeling that the flesh came off the bones,' due to the vibrations of the low frequencies used."[17] The von Hausswolff *oeuvre* can involve a number of things from unprocessed field recordings, at its most static, single electronic tones melting away at a listener's psychic defenses. Asked about the whys and wherefores of this sound, he replies:

> I think it's my lack of concentration and focus that makes me want to go deeper into a specific sound. A stripped and persisting sound forces me into it - there's no escape! The reason why I started to work with recorded material was that from a certain point of view there were not many references and I could go about doing what I wanted to do without being interrupted by negative criticism. I was too lazy to learn an instrument and just wanted to go on doing something new... so I created my own world and continued from there. Now, of course, I see references everywhere because I have moved into a certain kind of community of composers and artists - but at that time (1979/1980) we were not many around.[18]

The approach that von Hausswolff mentions might be likened to the 'minimalism' of trans-media pioneers like Tony Conrad, though not necessarily as applie to volume of sonic output or the sensory impressions received from it. It does, however, share one effect that Conrad biographer Branden Joseph associates with "returning to the point of origin". Namely, it "does not seek to correct or to complete an 'incorrect' or 'incomplete' historical understanding" so much as it "seeks to rebegin the discourse...to initiate it anew so that its structure develops differently."[19]

Regardless of where this approach has taken him personally, Carl Michael von Hausswolff is practically synonymous with the advancement of sonic art in Sweden, working as the bonding cement for a polyphonous but fairly cohesive 'scene.' Among other accomplishments, he has curated the 2nd Göteborg Biennale (2003), launched the mixed-media event *Against All Evens* (the antagonism suggested by the title was also directed, as per its official statement, against "the insipid") and curated the *Freq Out* collaborative sound exhibition, which consisted of prominent sound artists being invited to an electronic tone composition within a specified limited segment of the audible frequency spectrum. The basic concept behind *Freq_Out* has also featured in the 2003 project "Sound As Space Creator," held at the Charlottenborg Exhibition Hall in Copenhagen. As Brandon LaBelle recalls, "each participant was assigned a "zone" within the Exhibition Hall, roughly 7 meters square, and a range of frequency, between 0 and 11,000Hz, with which to produce a sound piece...as a final presentation each zone was equipped with its own sound system and CD player from which the individual participants' works would be amplified."[20] LaBelle's praise for the concept highlights its elegant functionality, i.e. "any 'interference' between works would only function to heighten the acoustical experience...that is to say, the sound installation functioned *through* interference by creating overlaps, overtones, intersections and deflections across the frequencies."[21]

Von Hausswolff has also had a hand in the formation of the Radium 226.05 and Anckarström record labels (the former being the logical extension of the short-lived magazine.) Radium 226.05 was recognized as the leading support network for sound art in Sweden, while the discography of the latter documents a slightly more specialized movement based around highly concentrated sound with a bare minimum of ornamental flourishes or crossover with transitory popular culture. While on the board of the Swedish art organization Fylkingen (which was formed in 1933 and has remained active ever since), von Hausswolff was also instrumental in the reformation of the Fylkingen Records label, which archives the past and present electronic music compositions from a country that boasts more pioneers in this field than any of the other Scandinavian nations. On this subject, he states that

> Fylkingen and Moderna Museet [The Modern Museum] played a large role in the history of Swedish experimental music and performance art, and artists like

Sten Hanson, Bengt af Klintberg, Öyvind Fahlström and Lars-Gunnar Bodin have not only been creating a large portion of works - they have also promoted younger artists in order to build up a strong tradition. The Swedish artists have also been well connected to the outside world of electronic music, sound poetry and performance, and this has created a flux of art coming into the country and going out. In Finland, the electronic music scene has always been to connected to an underground type of movement...and in Denmark and Norway this scene has basically been dead. Only recently have a bunch of great musicians, composers and artists been emerging in these countries. A good example is the case of Else Marie Pade from Denmark. She composed her first electronic music pieces in the mid 1950s - a pioneer!! - but no one in Denmark (and in the rest of the world) knew anything about her music until 2001, when two CDs were released by her...a perfect case of total ignorance from the musicologists, critics and cultural spheres.[22]

Although the respective destinies of von Hausswolff and the Fylkingen organization are not totally inseparable from each other, Fylkingen does deserve some further acknowledgement for nurturing the creative climate that would culminate in artists like von Hausswolff and Elggren, and the Kingdoms of Elgaland and Vargaland by extension. The history of Fylkingen, in particular, parallels the history of the avant-garde and of the non-conformist urge in Swedish art. Early LPs released by the organization focus on indeterminacy in electronic music and 'text-sound compositons' by Sten Hanson and others, with an impressive variety in the results. Arguably there would be no forum in Sweden for electro-acoustic music without Fylkingen, much less documentation of the more radical activities that took place in Sweden in the 1960s.

That intense anti-authoritarian spirit was embodied in adventurous souls like Åke Hodell, the former fighter pilot whose disillusionment with military regimentation led to concrete poetry works like the *Verbal Hjärntvätt* [Verbal Brainwashing] LP. The maddening verbal repetition on the LP tracks, such as 'General Bussig,' begins to hint at how easily mental resistance can be abraded away at in situations of focused indoctrination (military or otherwise.) More interestingly for students of electronic music's development, though, is another military-inspired piece from 1967 entitled *Strukturer III* [Structures III]. For Sweden, this was a kind of breakthrough in 'noise as music,' or at the very least a vindication of the Italian Futurist program (with regards to sound presentation, if not politics.) At a time when academic (read: mainly serialist) electronic music and tape music was just starting to court wider attention, Hodell dared to use the medium in a decidedly less ponderous and comforting way. According to Torsten Ekborn's notes for the Fylkingen reissue of *Verbal Hjärntvätt*:

> I assume that the audience, reading the title in the programme, envisioned a calm electronic glass pearl display of serially trimmed sinus tones. When the piece started, a hellish noise came from the loudspeakers, strategically placed in a ring around the audience. [...] *Strukturer III* turned out to be a sound collage which authentically and chronologically demonstrated the acoustic happenings of both world wars. Perhaps the most frightening part of the piece was that no one ever heard any human voices, neither commands nor moans from the wounded. It was the death machines themselves which got to perform, the infernal concert presented by humanity when it tries to murder itself.[23]

The piece in question, if nothing else, was a harbinger of the current era, wherein people readily consume such soundscapes as entertainment in movie theaters rigged with Dolby surround systems blasting at 120 decibels. However, Hodell's piece would still be quite a challenge to these same moviegoers if it were only the raw sound presented without an accompanying heroic narrative. The military phase of Hodell (which Ekborn cautions us was not "radically pacifistic," given Hodell's position as one of just a few fighter pilots preparing to defend Sweden against invasion by the Nazis) was just one phase in a diverse, but cohesive, program of avant-garde innovation. Hodell's next phase would concentrate on sound pieces which were a striking mélange of narrated / spoken text, dramatized text, purely electronic atmospheres, taped sound events and even interludes of 'traditional' music. These "text-sound compositions," as they came to be called, were a distinctive art form building on the 1960s' intercontinental explosion of sonic art re-assessing and atomizing "The Word" (as personified by Brion Gysin, John Giorno, William Burroughs, Francois Dufrene, Henri Chopin, and others.) Within these sound experiments are the germ for later creative work by von Hausswolff and Elggren - the former had befriended Brion Gysin in Basel in the early 1980s, and featured work by Burroughs and Gysin in issues of his *Radium 226.05* magazine. The possibilities of the "text-sound composition" also provided an incitement for Hodell's contemporaries, like Lars-Gunnar Bodin, to see what they could achieve with this medium. Sadly, the 'total ignorance' that von Hausswolff applies above to Else Marie Pade also seems to have extended to Hodell, Bodin and others, as documentation on their activities outside of Sweden was quite limited.

Like Hodell's compositions, Carl Michael von Hausswolff's sound art, whether 'comfortable' or not, suggests the human organism's inextricable bond to forces of decomposition and decay- yet it also documents mankind's attempts at defying this inevitability with the architectural triumphs that serve as concretizations of the human spirit. As to the former, he has released a trio of mini CDs on the Viennese Laton label dealing with rats, maggots and insect pests, even including with the CDs such dubious prizes as packets of rat poison and real insect larvae from Thailand. Another title - the 2006 release *Leech* on Carsten Nicolai's Raster / Noton label - references such organic processes by naming itself, and the composition process involved in recording the CD, after a creature which feeds off of decomposing bodies and open wounds (von Hausswolff's digital "leeching" here involves sucking sonic elements from original sound pieces, the remixed versions bringing to mind the depopulated space of buildings condemned for demolition or, perhaps, waiting to be occupied as well.) The effect of all this is to highlight a striking similarity between how 'transitional' states of existence - both of 'coming into being' and crumbling apart - can be perceived.

This abiding interest in the interplay between emptiness and saturation, decay and vitality, and the intersection of "pure affect" with fixed meaning runs through von Hausswolff's visual experiments as well, such as his ongoing series of *"Red"* art actions (e.g. *Red Pool, Red Night, Red Code, Red Empty* and *Red Mersey*, conducted over a time period from 1999-2004.) For each of these events, von Hausswolff explores a city at night, looking for select locations to be illuminated with blaring red floodlights, photographed in this reddened state, and then returned to normal. This act has been carried out in locations from Liverpool (where the Mersey river was reddened) to Santa Fe (where an abandoned cemetery was given the same treatment in *Red Night.*) Photo documentation of these 'reddenings' reveals how easily a human habitation can have purposefulness either stripped from it or re-invested in it: in some cases, the red flood lighting feeds life into the sleeping structures, in others it parasitizes them *a la* von Hausswolff's digital "leeches," casting a pall of death or fear onto landscapes that would otherwise be quaint and idyllic (as for the choice of color, the artist admits to a sort of quasi-synesthetic association of red with low audible frequencies.) This 'reddening' process reveals how the malleability of human nature can be applied to virtually anything that mankind builds, that our extensions and 'second skins' may shelter us from the elements, but not from being prone to an unpredictable mutability.

+

Contrasted with the surgical intellect that marks much of von Hausswolff's work, KREV's co-ruler Leif Elggren (another son of Linköping, born there in 1950) can seem positively impish, a comic foil in a sense. This is not to say that the multi-disciplinary Elggren lacks a capacity for serious and severe introspective work, playing on universal fears of mortality- his semi-autobiographical book *Genealogy* is partially dedicated to the concept of "death as a lifelong friendship." Elsewhere, his striking line drawings of faceless and polymorphous humanoid figures permeate one with a discomfiting sense of fragility (for examples of such, see the John Duncan retrospective catalog on Errant Bodies Press, or the cover of the Anla Courtis / Lasse Marhaug release *North and South Neutrino,* on Antifrost Records.)

The two kings also share past artistic undertakings which, though often done independently of each other, practically mirror each other in their intent. The von Hausswolff LP *Operations of Spirit Communication* used electronic devices such as sonar and oscilloscope to detect ghostly presences hiding within the electric grid, while a later installation entitled *Establishing Communcation With the Fallen Angel* (2002) attempted to communicate with Lucifer himself by the quotidian means of midwave radio receiver, P.A. system and a pitch shifter applied to the audio data received. Von Hausswolff is in fact the trustee to the personal archives of Friedrich Jürgenson[24], who in the 1960s claimed to be receiving polyglot messages when he recorded the various non-broadcasting radio frequencies onto a reel-to-reel tape recorder (an experiment that began after he claimed to have inadvertently recorded the voice of his deceased father when attempting to record bird songs instead.) Elggren has shared this long-standing fascination for communicating with the dead using almost alchemical methods. He narrates a compilation CD entitled *The Ghost Orchid,* which serves as a primer for the research of EVP [electronic voice phenomena] researcher Konstantin Raudive (a Latvian psychologist who was Jürgenson's assistant in Uppsala) and his successors- EVP study being the hunt for possible spirit voices or inter-dimensional voices contacting the Earth-bound through unexpected "breakthroughs" onto radio signals.

One of Elggren's most idiosyncratic sound installation pieces, *Talking To a Dead Queen,* was inspired by a recurring vision of Napoleon's, in which the great conqueror saw vibrating copper staves hovering in midair, and heard them assuming the voices of influential figures from his past which gave him – much like in the case of Joan d'Arc - strategic tips on when and where to strike his enemy. Elggren inserted a copper wire or 'antenna' into five scale replicas of the coffin of Sweden's Queen Christina (who took the oath as king rather than queen, to satisfy her father's wishes), and also placed a television within each coffin, all of them playing footage of Greta Garbo playing the Queen in Rouben Mamoulian's 1934 film *Queen Christina*. Using copper materials as a kind of 'medium' in both the spiritual *and* technical sense of the word, Elggren amplified them with contact microphones and recorded the resultant electronic feedback for a CD release.

This sort of activity is sure to invite a chorus of groans from those skeptics within the art world that have long since disavowed paranormal activity (often pointing to the tendency towards pareidolia as a more rational explanation for EVP) and the possibility of post-mortem survival of consciousness. However, it is clear that - unlike the work of many self-styled "paranormal professionals" - there is little attempt to steer any of this material in the direction of one particular truthful interpretation. Daniella Cascella has defended this body of work for this precise puprose, claiming that it does not engage with truth but "rather with uncertainty and a perpetual state of flow…[it does] not aim at 'revealing' but rather at hinting, suggesting, evoking in a state of tension rather than release, of potentiality rather than actuality."[25]

More relevant to future projects (both KREV and others) is another aspect of this work that Cascella infers here: it "reaches out to what's limitless."[26] In doing so, the value of the artwork resides not within whatever "success" is attained with the spartan communications apparatus employed, but in its suggestion that present and future technological advancements will fulfill many of the same functions that are assumed to be the antithesis of technological development, such as the cultivation of the mysterious or uncanny. The artist Mike Kelley has also defended the practice's ability to be appreciated as a broader interrogation of our relations to our communicative apparatus, sharply differentiating between it and the activity of trance-channeling mediums (whose impressions of celebrity personae suggest that " the same social hierarchies that exist in this world extend into the next.")[27] By contrast, the "multitudinous poetry of discourse attendant to these tapes"[28] allows them to be approached from angles other than that of paranormal research.

Besides the fascination with spirit world and ether, both Elggren and von Hausswolff have experimented with techniques of lengthy, voluntary isolation and/or deprivation, which invites speculation as to whether their high tolerance for 'stripped-down' sound seems to come from a mastery over the chaotic vicissitudes and manifold needs of their minds and bodies, steadily burned out of them through these self-willed ordeals. Von Hausswolff once inhabited a gallery for a week with only three chickens as his constant companions (they were named after the sounds of their clucking: 'Pboc', 'Pbac', and 'Bpuc'.) This act that brings to mind Joseph Beuys' notorious 1974 performance piece *I Like America and America Likes Me*, in which he co-inhabited a gallery space with a wild coyote for three days' worth of eight-hours shifts, risking definite physical harm (though the shredding of Beuys' blanket seems to have been the worst he suffered.)

Elsewhere, Elggren spent ten days in an even more self-obliterating fashion: for his 1981 piece *10 Days: An Expedition*, Elggren fasted and deprived himself of both sleep and communication for a 10-day duration, allowing people to view him through small holes in the wall of the exhibition space. A diary was kept of this event (which has not been read by Elggren since the original performance.) Such willful excursions into absolute pain and near-insanity would, in many principalities, earn you a long period of time under lock and key and constant observation.

Another commonality between von Hausswolff and Elggren is their capability for balancing rigorous avant-garde inclinations with a joyously anarchic sense of humor. Of the former, reviewer Thibaut de Ruyter says "[he] perpetuates an experience that is too poetic not to be artistic, while having fun with modern technologies,"[29] and it would not be dishonest to apply this to Elggren as well. He has to his credit a growing archive of works which, on one hand, have very clearly defined artistic aims and exhibit a keen knowledge of the 20th century avant-garde's conceptual and critical inclinations. Many of these same works, however, are infused with the knowingly mischievous humor of schoolchildren outwitting their dull, stentorian teachers.

One such example of this method, already something of a classic among aficionados of concrete poetry and so-called 'outsider art', is the book *Experiment With Dreams* that Elggren co-authored with regular collaborator Thomas Liljenberg (Liljenberg has more recently joined Elggren for an absurd CD purporting to contain the final unpublished poems of the hard-living Charles Bukowski.) Among the most roaringly funny items in this tome, whose comparitively solemn purpose is to shine light on "the frighteningly unjust distribution of human opportunities that continues to occur on earth"[30], is a series of letters written from fictional aliases to a host of inaccessible celebrities, world leaders and captains of industry. The aliases themselves are all deserving of a hearty chuckle or two: see 'Pinnochio Fish' and 'Stromboli Oil Ltd.', for starters. More humorous still is the sincere and optimistic tone of the missives as they try to convince these cultural elites to (among other things) buy the sperm of famous people from them, provide Camille Paglia's nose for kissing, or elevate German ex-chancellor Helmut Kohl to the position of Pope. There are also, of course, multiple entreaties to *"send money on [sic] Swedish postal number 15 99 80-2"*, directed at everyone from John Lee Hooker to Santa Claus. The pair's May 1995 dispatch to French pop chanteuse, animal rights activist, and controversial "hate speech" provocateur Brigitte Bardot is worth reprinting in full, simply to illustrate the delirious extremes to which this particular project goes:

"Dear Miss Bardot!

We are planning to start a fish factory in Lofoten, Norway. Our plans is [sic] codfishing, but we are not interested in the fish, but what's in the stomach of the codfish. So we will have a lot of fish refuse that we now will offer you. We know that you are a great friend of animals, and perhaps this could serve as catfood?

Looking forward to your answer.

Sincerely,

-Leif Elggren / Thomas Liljenberg"[31]

What seems to be, at first, a series of prank letters being sent into the wilderness with little hope of reply from the actual addressees, blossoms into a much more potent piece of cultural criticism on closer examination. Like children's letters to God or, more recently, the ubiquitous "spam" messages from non-existent West African royalty promising to deposit large sums of money into recipients' bank accounts in exchange for temporary access to these same accounts, the letters in *Experiment With Dreams* ooze charming naiveté, and the reader can be be more or less certain that no replies to these requests are forthcoming. In reality, though, many replies to the letters *did* arrive (Elggren maintains that these were "personal and indignant"[32]), although the two dreamers chose not to publish the replies in the book. The point of the project, in sending out letters to characters whose public lives had leaked into the sleepers' nightly visions, was "merely to give our dreams 'full access' in the play of values that characterise human activities."[33]

Few artists, in any discipline, seem to have the determination to critique power relationships as concisely as Elggren does, and to do this in a way that does not reek of either sanctimonious posturing or the unreflective *ressentiment* that Nietzsche presented as his diagnosis to life's perpetual underdogs. Elggren's works have surveyed not only the power relationships existing within human social structures (the rule of royalty over commoners, governments over civilians, etc.), but also the disproportionate distributions of power that exist between humans and other living organisms. To this end, even power struggle on a microbiological level has been considered by Elggren, in his CD-length sound study of viral behavior, *Virulent Images / Virulent Sound*. In the liner notes of this particular project, Elggren tries to build a case for the possibility of viral contagion not spreading various modes of human contact but through *visual* means (looking at photographs, films etc.) In this project, the quirky advertising concept of "viral media" - i.e. audio-visual artifacts that gain a presumably unplanned, undirected spike in popularity - takes on a different and markedly more sinister meaning. In a brief but startling statement of caution, Elggren makes cunning use of the fear-implanting techniques that have kept so many otherwise marginal political figures in power. Elggren urges us to contemplate the following nightmare scenario:

> Imagine: a poster campaign of photographs of the Ebola virus, massively enlarged, posted on the walls of the world's cities during the night, fully feasible with today's world-spanning subversive networks. One look at these posters on the way to work in the morning and an Ebola epidemic would ensue...[34]

Whether Elggren sincerely loses sleep over this possibility or not is difficult to ascertain, although the fact remains that he hasn't followed up on this thread in more recent public exhibits and recordings- perhaps suggesting that this was a one-off hoax meant to parody the prevailing power structure's method of keeping its citizens continually pre-occupied by fear of an unseen yet omnipotent bogeyman (and thus less capable of noticing the erosion of other daily living standards.)

Elggren's alarming text could be seen as merely transposing the current discussion of terrorism onto the realm of microbiology. The *Daily News* of New York at least thought the same of Elggren's warning, publishing it on the 1st anniversary of the Sept. 11 terror attacks. Two other newspapers - a Slovenian paper and an Austrian one, respectively - refused publication of the same piece. As if removing the mask of the paranoia-stoking authority figure to reveal the artist beneath, Elggren concludes this text with a claim that "being excluded from the vision of Paradise has always created an opposite reaction and nourished grand dreams of the highest form of revenge".[35] At *this* point we can more or less tell that Elggren is speaking 'as himself' rather than as a trouble-stirring *agent provocateur,* since most governing bodies would never admit to something like economic unfairness being the wellspring of societal discontent (and, indeed, vicious eruptions of terrorism.) It is much easier for them to hand down a Manichean myth that pure good and pure evil simply spring fully-formed from the womb, without any socio-economic factors at all contributing to the spread of 'evil' acts. In a single cogent observation, Elggren hints at the truth of the matter: that grandeur and opulence, being held within tantalizing reach of the economically and spiritually impoverished, will often lead to equally grandiose and opulent acts of destruction, or at the very least, violent fantasies of the same.

Death, Be Not Proud…KREV Banishes Mortality

Virulent Images… is but one passing example of how Elggren engages the myriad of power relationships in the present world, and throughout history. Elggren's frequently hilarious, occasionally devastating critique of authority highlights nature's parsimonious distribution of happiness to the unfortunate masses born without silver spoons in their mouths. This in itself would be enough subject matter to adequately pad an artistic career from start to finish, but Elggren widens his attack to deal with even more insurmountable problems: namely, the tyranny of mortality itself. Indeed, an irregular newsletter published by Elggren is titled *The New Immortality* (taking its name from a similarly titled 1939 book by John William Dunne), and its very limited printable space is sometimes saturated with observations on the vulnerability of the human organism, especially the internal bodily functions not immediately visible to the naked eye (one issue of *New Immortality* also offers a surprisingly cogent argument on why we should fill toilets with Coca-Cola instead of potable water.)

One full-page spread in the 2nd issue reprints a 1689 autopsy report of the Queen Christina, which, in the broader context of Elggren's work, can be read as a suggestion that class struggles are ultimately irrelevant in the face of mortality's tyranny. No discussion of mortality can proceed, though, without some thought given to the irreversible forward thrust of time, and it is Elggren's consideration of time's limitations that has made for some of his most unique sound work. Take, for example, another two of his CD-length audio collaborations with Thomas Liljenberg, entitled *9.11- Desperation Is The Mother Of Laughter* and *Zzz*, The audio information on these discs is little more than an hour's worth of laughing and snoring, respectively. However, in both scenarios, the action is forced or simulated rather than spontaneously generated and recorded in real situations of deep sleep or giddiness. The *'ha, ha, has'* running the length of "Desperation…" sound stilted and alien, carrying with them too much of a metronomic or mechanical rhythm and too much of a 'flat affect' to really be construed as an irrepressible response to something funny. Sound art archivist and poet Kenneth Goldsmith, in a twin review of *Desperation…* and *Zzz*, makes a fairly accurate analysis of these records' contents when he writes:

> Elggren and Liljenberg are not *really* sleeping and laughing–they are only pretending to. As such, its fiction is more akin to hysterical Artaud-inspired theatre than to

documentary. Both discs start off straight enough: At the beginning of *Zzz...it* simply sounds like two people sleeping, a snore here, a cough there. But as the disc progresses, the snoring gets more theatrical and obnoxious until, about half way through, it turns into a snoring opera, with the two protagonists taking turns belting out twisted arias of snorts, yawns and honks. Same goes for *9.11 (desperation is the mother of laughter)*: The first few minutes are just two guys sitting around laughing. 30 minutes into it, it's obvious that the exercise is verging on the absurd and the laughter becomes forced and sinister. By the end of an hour, it's positively painful to think that two men have been laughing as hard as they could for such an extended period of time.[36]

Goldsmith, who has actually given "Zzz" airplay on his weekly WFMU radio show, also notes the similarity between these recordings and the endurance trying, epic-length films of Andy Warhol (see *Sleep, Empire* etc.) It's an apt comparison, one which Goldsmith builds upon in a manifesto of sorts called 'Being Boring':

Nothing happened in the early Warhol films: a static image of the Empire State Building for eight hours, a man sleeping for six. It is nearly impossible to watch them straight through. Warhol often claimed that his films were better thought about than seen. He also said that the films were catalysts for other types of actions: conversation that took place in the theatre during the screening, the audience walking in and out, and thoughts that happened in the heads of the moviegoers. Warhol conceived of his films as a staging for a performance, in which the audience were the Superstars, not the actors or objects on the screen.[37]

So could it be, then, that through such apparently monotonous and tortuous exercises, Elggren and Liljenberg are actually trying to empower their listeners, to 'level the playing field' by giving them an authority equal to or even surpassing that of the artist? With such aims in mind, the Kingdoms of Elgaland and Vargaland were formed.

Both Warhol and the Swedish duo of Elggren / von Hausswolff have made a continual project of bestowing 'divinity' upon 'mortals' (for Warhol, whose points of reference were more primarily American, this applied to those without celebrity status.) However, while Warhol was content to do this through the aforementioned films, through silk-screen portraits of ordinary people (patterned after his original silkscreens of bona fide screen immortals Liz Taylor and Marilyn Monroe), and through other visual means, Elggren and von Hausswolff upped the ante by conferring actual governmental authority upon themselves- authority which they would, in turn, make freely available for anyone else who wanted it. While such a regal self-appointment seems like a comical novelty, Leif Elggren reminds us that

> All power is self-appointed, it is only a matter of who stipulated the rules. If you are a highly ranked person in the present society, you can manipulate the rules for your own good and create the social structure around you. For instance, Napoleon Bonaparte crowned himself. Adolf Hitler manipulated himself to the highest position via threats and violence. George W. Bush bought himself this position. Christ was the most powerful as all because he was intelligent (or smart) enough both to claim or refer to a power that was beyond our worldly life, an almighty spiritual power that was the only basic power in this universe that appointed him to his position and gave him his task.[38]

The Kingdoms of Elgaland and Vargaland are now over 15 years into their existence. Elgaland is a portmanteau of 'Elggren' and 'Land', while 'Vargaland' is likely a similar play on words with von Hausswolff's name ('varg' being a Scandinavian word for 'wolf'.) Formed in 1992, Elggren describes KREV as

> a youthful union and nation that spreads over the whole of our planet, bordering all existing nations...a wholly unique position in which, for the first time in the history of the world, we have a real opportunity of developing a worldwide, boundless society, in which we every individual as King or Queen over their own lives.[39]

While KREV was in the germination stages, Elggren also attempted to form a political party, Partiet [simply "The Party"] with Liljenberg, and said party was allowed to take part in the official Swedish election campaign. One major plank in their party platform was that the world itself should be renamed "Me", an act which presaged the consummate power which KREV would accord to each and every individual being. Partiet, though a novel form of political theater for Sweden, was not quite as attractive and radical as the joint project with von Hausswolff, which soon came to take precedence and to absorb many of the ideas of the

Partiet consitution.

The official Constitution of KREV, ratified in October 14 of 1992, makes audacious claims on authority, nullifying the privileges accorded to those born into prestigious bloodlines, or those who use wealth as their sole signifier of worldly status. Although the authority of the King is listed in the Constitution's third article as "dictatorial and unrestricted", and again in the fourth article as "superior to all religions, past and future," this authority is actually that of the citizen, since they may enter into KREV at any position they choose. This is made more clear by scanning further into the Constitution; the eighth article makes it clear that "every citizen owns unrestricted power over his / her / its own life in harmony with his / her / its personal model and idea".

This melding of unprecedented authority is made clearer still by a 'hierarchical diagram' included in the Constitution, which shows no clear hierarchy at all, but an intertwining of royalty and commonality via an 8-pointed star-symbol (at other points on the star there are a 'monad' symbol, a 'recycling' symbol suggesting infinity, and arrows marking both ascent and descent.) Furthermore, the adoption of the title 'King' by Elggren and von Hausswolff (and consequently, by all their subjects) seems to be a purely semantic gesture: a 'king' is simply the highest, most well-known and most romanticized form of earthly authority that some can conceive of, especially in the Northern Europe of the two KREV protagonists. The usage of the 'king' title, in their case, does not betray an actual desire to replicate all the nomenclature and symbology of royalty, though personalized variants on these concepts have figured into the project. Take for example Elggren's 'crown', as proudly displayed on the cover of the book *Flown Over By An Old King*, which is merely a battered old engine filter for a SAAB automobile.

Elggren's partial inspiration for this self-coronation, that of the "madmen" who fashion paper crowns for themselves and shout grand proclamations from public squares, sees him at once adopting a practice of so-called "Outsider Art" and suggesting the degree to which "outsider" and "artist" are interchangable terms in a society completely geared towards instrumental rationality, or a society whose organizations are too massive in size to be concerned with or to trust those who attempt to cultivate individual lives. The distrust of artists' willed individuality, and their subsequent "outsider" status, comes from its paranoiac confusion with "individual*ism*"- which Melvin Rader describes as "the system of every man for himself, and the devil take the hindmost...true individuality is violated by such a system."[40]

If anything, the fallibility associated with royalty has long been a recurring theme in the works of Elggren and von Hausswolff: Elggren has used King Carolus XII (1682-1718) as the principal figure to illustrate this point, noting how Carolus' overly ambitious militarism caused his humiliation at the hands of Peter The Great, stripping Sweden immediately of its status as a 'world power'. On the subject, Elggren says:

> The King and his 30,000 soldiers were defeated outside Poltava in Russia, and the great Swedish dream of total power over the world was destroyed. Carolus XII died in Norway in 1718, shot in the head by God knows who. Sweden was totally devastated and bankrupt because of all the war projects out in Europe. [...] The Swedish people were totally exhausted and on their knees with misery and poverty. They hated the war, and the assassination of the King at last stopped the endless fighting. The country needed to be rebuilt.[41]

An interest in regicide also lends itself to the name of the Anckarström record label, formed in 1991 and named after Jacob Johan Anckarström, the assassin of King Gustav III of Sweden. The label, which includes Elggren, Phauss, John Duncan, Zbigniew Karkowski, If,Bwana and Dror Feiler, is notable for bringing the notorious assassin's name into public usage for the first time since a 200-year ban on uttering the name "Anckarström" was lifted. Even the official motto of KREV –"for every king, there is a ball"- warns of the mortal limits on the reign of those who would put forth a public image of immortality and divine descent. While this phrase may sound perfectly innocuous to non-residents of Sweden, the underlying message becomes clearer when we learn that Gustav III was killed by Anckarström at a masquerade ball at Stockholm's Royal Opera.

KREV and NSK: A Comparison

Among Leif Elggren's many personal statements, his call for a reconsideration of the artist's societal position is particularly impassioned. To this end, he claims that artists are the only profession permitted to work with all the materials of life (e.g. "in art everything is allowed [...] that gives you the right as an artist to move wherever you want, to be an intruder wherever necessary and to do whatever there is to be done."[42] By this reckoning, Elggren might argue, we should wonder why artists maintain the barely tolerated "outsider" status that they do in modern states and societies. Defenders of this state of affairs could, of course, make the counter-argument that "progress" in those areas that art speaks to (morality, beauty etc.) is far less quantifiable than progress in techno-science, and this is one reason why artists remain at the societal fringes of modernity in spite of their many exclusive insights about humans' inner lives. Rader suggests that "to end the alienation of the artist" is a task equal to "bring[ing] art back to the center of life's text, [achieving] an artistic culture high in its thrust and wide in its spread, [uniting] vivid individualities against the background of community." He then prescribes that "small, intimate circles... become the focus of rich and immediate cultural activities."[43] Seemingly not content with this prescription alone, Elggren's virtual state allows for the intimate and small-scale to become a new type of authority.

Nonetheless, the Kingdoms of Elgaland-Vargaland are not the only virtual state founded by culturally critical artists. The concept of the Utopian island – or, at the very least, an isolated and fortified space where one can concentrate on creative work rather than contributing to the external world's historical narratives - has surfaced a few other times within recent history. Among this largely unwritten history of artists' colonies, squats and the like, the example of Fela Kuti's Kalakuta Republic (established in 1970s Nigeria) is a particularly audacious one. Although the Kalakuta Republic was little more than a multi-purpose compound squatted by hundreds of young, loyal Fela devotees (wherein the infamous Afro-beat maestro engaged in polygamy with dozens of wives, enjoyed a steady flow of marijuana smoke, and often held court wearing little more than a pair of bikini briefs), it was a crucial respite for those who sought it out. It was a parallel universe where intoxicated musical frenzy drowned out the brassy, insubstantial rhetoric of Nigeria's failed "militicians" (a local expression for military men becoming civilian rulers) and where tribal divisions were diffused in the midst of all-night jam sessions. Of course, this challenge to authority did not go unheeded, and the almost inevitable military raids on Kalakuta would deal a blow to Kuti's faith in the power of indigenous *juju* magic to resist evil. As a cruel post-script to the Kalakuta siege, Kuti's mother was even thrown from a second-floor window of the compound, resulting in injuries that would hasten her death.

With such terror tactics at the disposal of the world's more dysfunctional and paranoid governments, the example of Kalakuta shows how difficult it is to create any truly secessionist state without violent interference. As such, the creation of a simultaneously unified and fragmented entity like KREV – a virtual or 'imaginary' state - points to one way in which people can use a kind of mass projection like this as a critical stop-gap on the way to more concrete forms of resistance. Leif Elggren is noted for his aforementioned alchemical audio experiments, "proto-science" at the best: but just as alchemy has ended up being the spark for actual, verifiable advances in chemistry, perhaps this "proto-territory" can lay the theoretical groundwork for an actually existing state which is recognized as "real" by more people than just its voluntary citizens. It is easy or some to dismiss the proclamations of von Hausswolff and Elggren as charlatanism, as calculated in-jokes and reckless eccentricity: but, as it was once written about the hopelessly Utopian Charles Fourier and his contemporaries, "it is true that they were all dreamers...but, as Anatole France said, without dreamers, mankind would still be living in caves."[44]

Closely paralleling KREV's own push for an artist-founded 'virtual State', the Slovenian arts collective Neue Slowenische Kunst [New Slovenian Art] upgraded the NSK from an "organization to a State" in 1991 and after over a decade of playing with the imagery and aesthetics of state control (there is no rivalry or enmity between NSK and KREV, in fact NSK is listed as a 'diplomatic relation' of Elgaland-Vargaland.) The 1992 collapse of Yugoslavia, followed by Slovenia's declaration as an independent state, also provided NSK with a status as an independent state within another, and gave it much room to critically reflect the historical developments in the Balkan region. The NSK was a multi-media collective sub-divided into groups or 'departments' specializing in certain artistic disciplines: the industrialized music group Laibach provided the bombastic soundtrack, IRWIN functioned as a painting and design group, Scipion Našice Sisters[45] focused on theatrical productions, while the Department of Pure and Applied Philosophy under Peter Mlakar (heralded by the NSK website as the "De Sade of Slovenian literature") managed the NSK's theoretical apparatus. For those who were curious about exactly who did what within NSK, the group published an infuriatingly obtuse organizational diagram, in which "immanent, consistent spirit" informed all stages of the NSK undertaking, with things getting far more vague from there on in (and also mischievously "creating the impression that more people were involved than really were.")[46].

Like KREV, the NSK State issues passports to its citizens (along with bank notes and postal stamps for the former), a practice that has led to numerous comical misunderstandings of these objects' legitimacy.[47] The NSK's passports are enticingly advertised as having "...a unique nature and a subversive value," the latter of which is confirmed by the announcement on the Slovenian government's website that these passports are not "official." NSK and KREV also share the habit of setting up 'embassies' or 'consulates' in any geographical territory where their respective cultural output is exhibited. In the case of both virtual territories, these makeshift embassies can often be situated in humble, private spaces like apartments and personal kitchens: the graffiti-encrusted walls of the Nanba Bears music club in Osaka represent one such KREV consulate visited by the author. In other cases, such annexations of territory have coincided with gallery-based exhibitions or concerts: in return for KREV's participation in the 2007 "Slash Fiction" exhibition at London's Gasworks venue, visitors had to apply for a visa as a precondition to gaining entry to the show. Initially, such spaces make the 'embassy' project seem like a mischievous nose thumbing at the assumed grandeur of official diplomatic bases, or an extension of the "Intermedia" artists' environmental approach that ignored limitations set on what is permissible as a 'cultural space'. These actions, in effect, merge the extra-territorial nature of diplomatic bases with the intimacy of one's most immediate surroundings. It can be debated whether KREV is 'elevating' personal and cultural space to the level of administrative / governmental space, or reversing this strategy- an ambiguity with the eternally transitory nature of a nation composed of frontier zones.

As NSK archivist Alexei Monroe implies, this re-investment of administrative power into intimate or domestic spaces has historical precedents in other cultural undergrounds- it is "a serious reference to present and past realities." Namely, he recognizes that "the [NSK] Moscow project directly refers back to the 'Apt-Art' tradition of staging art events in private residences to avoid official censorship in the former USSR."[48] The Apt-Art concept that Monroe references, the early 1980s brainchild of artist Nikita Alexeyev, was indeed a radical (and, for the political climate of the time, necessary) solution to the question of how to get one's art recognized in an environment where cultural production relied exclusively on state approval- it was a 'temporary autonomous zone' long before the term came to be associated with rave parties and other subcultural social gatherings within the Western democracies-in-decline. Alexeyev's effort involved the total sacrifice of private space to the artistic endeavor: all available wall and ceiling space was given over to the hanging of artworks, and whatever floor space remained might often be occupied by underground acoustic music combos. It is also said that Alexeyev had no space for a bed, and had to sleep in an inflatable boat in the middle of his living room. The risk of being discovered by State officials was still omnipresent, as well: indeed, Alexeyev eventually had his apartment trashed by KGB agents in 1983. Nevertheless, various Apt-Art cells sprung up in the Soviet Union, with varying degrees of success, until Mikhail Gorbachev introduced the *glasnost* period and its focus on the transparency of information.

NSK was – although not without its own serious experiences with State monitoring and censorship - lucky enough to survive up until the present day. During the Soviet era of the '80s, the NSK operated in a Yugoslavia which was considerably 'freer' than the numerous other republics absorbed by the USSR: Yugoslavia had open borders to the West, and the political concept of "self-management" (inaugurated by Tito and Edvard Kardelj) attempted to distance itself from the Stalinist model followed by other Eastern states. However, "self-management", despite its attractive resonance along the lines of concepts such as "independence" and "autonomy", unsuccessfully tried to create the illusion that the State was taking a completely 'hands-off' approach to Yugoslavian cultural development.

Yet, in spite of that, NSK refused to merely pander to Western paranoia about a monolithic Eastern empire (and, later on, about the Balkan states descending into a morass of brutal ethnic and religious war.) One of the defining features of NSK was its ability to make equally damning critiques of both Western hegemonic tendencies and the more distinctly 'Eastern' modes of totalitarianism, not presupposing that either had a monopoly on the mechanisms of censorship and repression. The unflinching ambiguity of NSK's works made it all the easier to shift the weight of their criticism to one side or the other, as happened when Western hegemonic power and 'market censorship' became more of an issue following the Soviet collapse in the 1990s. This is especially evident in the Laibach records of the time, such as 'Wirtschaft ist Tot' [The Economy is Dead] and the subversive disco of their *NATO* album. Ironically, for a large-scale art project which sought to ultimately carve out its own identity independent of geographic boundaries, NSK and Laibach ended up becoming synonymous with Eastern European culture. Having done this, NSK reversed a situation which Alexei Monroe mentions: "...like the 'Third World', 'Eastern Europe' is still largely seen not as a source of cultural product but as a passive market for it."[49]

There are a few other key differences between the two virtual states. For one, the social, economic and political circumstances during their respective formations: the Balkan region, which was traumatized by the time of KREV's formation in 1992, was hardly comparable to an affluent Sweden which had been either at peace or officially neutral since 1814 (a state of simultaneous tranquility and *ennui* which is encapsulated in Elggren's biting spoken word piece "The North Is Protected".) The NSK project, in claiming "politics is the highest form of art,"[50] also seems less concerned with Elggren's proposal for raising the marginalized artist to the status of political power- in the NSK State, politicians and artists are already seen as identical in their abilities and aims.

Official KREV passports go beyond even the NSK concept of the "State in Time": the first page of the author's Elgaland/Vargaland passport proudly and curtly proclaims that "the bearer of this passport is immortal" and that the passport is "valid in every time and space- past, present, and future, existing or non existing." In an age of increasingly ridiculous and unfulfilled political promises, this one seems to trump them all: and in doing so, it handily parodizes the charismatic politician's claims to almost godlike power: the ability to completely transform human nature within a 4-year election cycle or '5 year plan'. By conferring such infinite access to its passport-bearers, the founders of KREV perhaps hope that no one will ever again be, in Elggren's words, "excluded from the vision of Paradise." In an interesting twist on the government legislation of mortality itself, the granting of immortality by KREV now contradicts official state policy in the People's Republic of China, where (in an effort to deflate the charisma of the Tibetan Dalai Lama, monks were banned from reincarnating in 2007.

A Democracy of Sounds

The NSK State has the popular band Laibach as its musical ambassadors, and a Department of Pure and Applied Philosophy to produce a formidable brand of theoretical text outlining the State's evolution and goals. By comparison, KREV has just a few brief explanatory texts and manifestoes to its name, and while its list of citizens is impressive in the breadth of its cultural contributions outside of KREV, few of those contributions have been explicitly 'dedicated' to furthering the idea of KREV. Or have they? It could be argued that 'living by example,' and allowing individual 'extra-curricular' contributions to speak for the integrity of the whole project, is a potent form of ambassadorship in its own right. Some, like KREV's "minister of lamination" 'Gen' Ken Montgomery, have contributed their talents to the cause by naming KREV ministries after them (Montgomery's special talent is the use of a laminating machine as a surprisingly versatile music composition tool.) Others have lent a hand in composing one of the increasing number of KREV national anthems, released in a series of 7" singles by the Ash International label. There now exists a version performed by an Afro-beat ensemble, a klezmer group, a mariachi band, one by organist Marcus Davidson and of course the requisite versions by Elggren and von Hausswolff.

Unlike the NSK State, though, there is no regular KREV musical agit-prop department, even though one can be the 'minister' of any personal interest at all that they might have, from Roquefort cheese to snorkeling (for those who are interested, the ministries of digital food, toxins, cartography and ambiguity are already taken.) This is interesting, since a disproportionate amount of KREV citizens are shared with the Scandinavian sound art scene, or with the more exacting modes of noise and electronic music. That individuals such as Daniel Menche and John Duncan can claim ministries or kingdoms as a "side" concern along with their artistic practices is intriguing, not for the simple 'quirkiness' of the situation but because it rejects the "artist-as-outsider" stigma mentioned earlier. Symbolic though the gesture may be, it does force us to consider what a kind of inverted civilization would look like in which the creative class plays a greater role as civic decision-makers than the technocrats and managers currently at the top of the pyramid (and, of course, may also make us wonder if this greater responsibility would cause artists to eventually take on the image of the technocratic class they have replaced in this fantastic scenario.)

The Swedish composer Dror Feiler is part of the aforementioned Scandinavian scene, and not an official KREV citizen, but some of his thoughts do clarify the correlations between anarchic music and a "state" that is in eternal flux. Certainly, much of the music already discussed in this book is simply doing with sound what KREV does with the nation-state: the micro-genres of "glitch," "cut-up," "noise," "*onkyo*" etc. all "set up residence" within a virtual frontier of communication, and these respective forms can be understood as the raw material from which to design new forms rather than as a pure "end product." Just as KREV's citizens seek to provide a new plasticity to territorial boundaries, musicians of Feiler's 'new avant-garde' are

> ...crossing the borders of categories, exposing and even creating unexpected relations , like composers do in their computer, sampler and synthesizer-based music, and DJs do in the mix. Such is the praxis of the NEW AVANT-GARDE [capitals in the original]: a democracy of sounds breaking through predictable hierarchies of instruments [...] and of narrative structures (the familiar dominance of plot and character in art.)[51]

Feiler warns us also that we "become deaf when and musically unconscious when we hear nothing but perfect melodies and perfect chords in popular music, [and] perfect structure, instrumentation and electro-acoustic sounds in the 'new music' scene [...] this is the potential fascism in music."[52] Feiler's anti-fascist angle is something to take into consideration, given the recent criticisms of electronic noise as a "fascistic" tool to obliterate contrary voices with its insurmountable display of deafening and physiology-altering power (and also if we take fascism to be a kind of generic "life-denying view... of renunciation, of the sacrificial subordination to Higher Goals.")[53] The argument over the political implications of supremely loud and physical music is far from over, but the very existence of this argument, and the diversity in opposing viewpoints, seem to confirm its freedom from the anti-individualist tendencies of all totalitarian systems. The 'fuzzy' nature of this variety of avant-electronic music, rife as it is with distortion, time-stretching and digital convolution techniques, lends itself nicely to the 'fuzzy logic' of systems far removed from the inflexible polarities demanded by such systems.

Taking Feiler's statements on music as a cue, the similarities between radical music and a radical anti-State like KREV, then, have to do with the 'borderlines' in their respective situations. Elggren says of KREV that "our physical territory is not very big...just the border areas around the planet, a bunch of very thin lines."[54] The focus on using the interstitial points as the basis for creation, rather than the established and clearly demarcated 'territory', seems to be what Feiler is proposing as the way forward for music, as well.

The sonic arts remain just one form of expressive ability, though, and it should already be obvious that many of the KREV citizenry, beginning with its kings, do not limit themselves to this mode: often they have the designation 'music' placed on their diverse activities simply by virtue of having them documented on an audio recording, which are often erroneously seen as vehicles for "music" regardless of their actual content. In the final reckoning, KREV is more art than "micro-politics", a project that does not merely mock or criticize mankind's collective yearning for some divinely conferred nationhood or collective power, but a project which embodies art's purpose as the 'ultimate discipline'- as Elggren says, it involves "working in a totally open field with all the unimaginable and imaginable parameters of life." [55] And here it seems appropriate to merge the two meanings of "field" as both a plot of land and as one's chosen area of interest and productivity- a fully open approach to creative life seems to demand an equally open space, be it actual or virtual, in which to act.

Coda: A Government in Exile?

The Kingdoms of Elgaland and Vargaland were happily gaining ground as of this original writing: the most recent acquisition of the Kingdoms to date has been the annexation of the Bodensee, the body of water situated between Germany, Switzerland and Austria. This was met with much fanfare, including the opening of the famed Cabaret Voltaire in Zurich as a KREV embassy. At the same time, however, KREV's application for membership in the United Nations, sent out in 1994, has remained unanswered. None of the 'real' countries of the world have officially recognized KREV either (even though Portland-based artist and KREV citizen Daniel Menche, in declaring himself the King of Italy, may try to use his clout in that area.) Elggren states that the citizens of KREV are living in a 'diaspora' as a result of such situations, placing them in the unprecedented situation of having citizenship in all of the world's states *and* in none of them.

However, writing off the actions of KREV's citizens as useless dilettantes and jokers may be premature. Leif Elggren is fond of, when describing this project and many others, invoking the image of the aforementioned street-corner lunatic with a paper crown who declares himself King. He also reminds us, though, that merely appropriating the 'virtual' symbols of power can convince others of power's actual possession by a certain individual or group. In this sense, the Kingdoms of Elgaland and Vargaland are hardly a joke- one needs look no further than the ceaseless procession of self-proclaimed Messiahs, only some of whom are universally dismissed, that led Cioran to call society "an inferno of saviors." A legal basis for the existence of KREV may not in place now, but when we consider the "rule" for against which this "exception" contends - that legal or formal recognitions of nationhood have historically been granted to those nations formed as a result of mass murder and forcible dispossession - KREV's claim to statehood seems more humane than outrageous. It is based on a spiritual unity of citizens that does not preclude the annihilation of others in order to secure an identity and a 'territory' of sorts. Hakim Bey once wrote that "all 'states' are impossible, all orders illusory, except those of desire,"[56] also claiming that there is "no *being*, only *becoming*- hence the only viable government is that of love, or 'attraction.'"[57] By these criteria, the Kingdoms of Elgaland and Vargaland - built purely on a foundation of wishes and dreams rather than on warfare and economics - have more of a claim to legitimacy than most.

Francisco López: The Big Blur Theory

As we stumble deeper into the dense forest of uncertainty that is the 21st century, something becomes painfully clear about our relationship to recorded sound: the overwhelming majority of it is now inextricably linked to an image of some kind. The art of the record album cover has, by now, been immortalized and anthologized in countless coffee table books and museum exhibitions, while the physical appearance and photogenic quality of the musician has become every bit as essential to marketing the "musical" experience as instrumental virtuosity. Consumption of recorded sound as a lifestyle accessory, or as a metaphor for some fixed set of experiences, has lessened its value by lessening sound's essential ambiguity in turn - suggesting, for example, that the sound of a distorted guitar must always be a 'soundmark' of youthful rebellion, or that the sound of harp strings must be a prelude to ascension into a stereotypical image of heaven, complete with angels frolicking on clouds. Our perceptual evolution along these lines has created new challenges for our creative enterprises: the sound artist Brandon Labelle, in discussing the challenges of perception involved in making site-specific sound, suggests an asynchronous relationship between the time it takes to comprehend audio information *vis-à-vis* visual information:

> I find that vision and sound differ radically in terms of duration: to enter a space and listen to sound is much different than entering to look at something. Often, sound just takes a great deal longer to comprehend and appreciate. Vision in a way is much more stable- well, maybe in the way I am using it- so, it somehow rivets attention; like a photo album, a viewer flips through during which time sound may enter the 'picture', as a kind of backdrop that suddenly comes forward on a corporeal level. Maybe that is presuming that sound 'interferes' with vision, straddles it, undoes it, etc. In this regard, often the visual operates almost as a 'musical' instrument from which the acoustical originates- that is to say, we look toward the instrument to understand the sound.[1]

As an artist who specializes in sound installation pieces, LaBelle likely knows all too well the frustration that can come from trying to communicate a sonic idea in spaces whose visitors consider themselves 'viewers' first and foremost (Latin students will have a head start on the rest of us here, noting that the root *vīsitō* implies *going* with the intent of *seeing* something.) Though it is foolish to paint all gallery / museum patrons (or even urban tourists) with a broad brush, many do come to view sound as an intrusive or parasitic influence on their complete digestion of visual data. However, the mediation of sound has existed long before the intervention of, or intersection with, the visual artifact- prior to this, it was language that intervened and imposed itself onto sounds and made them either complementary to, or subservient to, vocal and narrative elements. If sounds were "left alone", they might not be able to tell a *specific* story, but this would not mean that they didn't have some form of narrative quality to them, once organized in an evocative enough way. Humanity has had a long history of distrusting or fearing unmediated sound, giving it a support role in Bardic lore, theatrical productions, films, and other forms which enlarge and celebrate the human experience. This should not be taken as a dismissal of all sound experiments that involved stimulation of the other senses: there is a strong tradition of music, especially in the electronic field, of working with synaesthetic experience (to be touched upon in more detail next chapter) and with the way that pre-set behaviors and beliefs can be dramatically altered when a synchronicity of sound with sight, smell, taste or touch opens up hitherto obscured pathways.

Maybe the real problem, then, is not the 'visualization' of sound, but the attempt to present sound in an anthropomorphic way, or in a way that supports a grand teleological view of human history (i.e. that all we do as a species has some ultimate 'meaning,' that every miniscule word and gesture must signify something infinitely greater than itself.) I would argue that the most intense and successful synaesthetic experiences have been inspired when a sight, smell, etc. collided with a sound that was *not* being overlaid by unequivocally 'human' elements, and indeed this seems to have been the inspiration for the early synesthetic short film *Espectro Siete* by Javier Aguirre, who rejected the "banal and subjectivist correspondence between color and sound, without any kind of rigorous approach other than the purely technical"[2] while boasting of the "almost scientific severity" of his own work. It would indeed be disappointing if the freedo of non-signifying sound were phased out in order to make way for a world in which all the sound we heard was nothing but *symbolism*. This could apply to any number of other artistic disciplines, as Marcel Duchamp once spoke out against the preponderance of "retinal" painting for the same purposes, suggesting that mastery of formal (representative) composition was not always enough to stimulate the imagination.

Resisting a teleological appropriation of sound - and indeed any artistically arranged form of sensory information - can be difficult. It's not particularly easy to argue that the great musical works of the past, dealing with such teleological principles and themes as the Promethean spirit within humanity, have not had the ability to provoke and inspire. Even those whose method was destructive leaned towards a possible Utopian or apocalyptic premise for their work, as theorist Raymond Williams suggests the Italian Futurists did: "The Futurist call to destroy 'tradition' overlaps with socialist calls to destroy the whole existing order."[3] Williams attenuates this statement somewhat, though, also admitting to some ambiguity in the terminology of F.T. Marinetti's Futurist Manifesto: Marinetti's pronouncement that "we will sing of great crowds excited by work, pleasure and riot...the polyphonous, multicoloured tides of revolution"[4] was one that, per Williams, "carried with it all the ambiguities between revolution and carnival."[5] At any rate, this kind of thinking is extremely resilient and is hardly confined to the creative classes, having been bounced back and forth between both sides of the Left / Right political divide and having been adopted by evolutionary theorists and clergymen alike. Meanwhile, the blazing speed in technological development and the acceleration of human conflict seems to confirm the belief that "something is coming" on the horizon, although what that "something" is will likely remain hotly debated for the foreseeable future. If the various socio-political inclinations are united in any way whatsoever, they are united by a stark fear of insignificance, by an increasingly urgent need to expose secrets and to endlessly catalog minutiae into lists ordered by relevance.

La Bahia Inútil

In the middle of his book-length essay *Impossible Exchange*, philosopher Jean Baudrillard takes a brief detour to offer us an intriguing image of a curiously named geographical area within the South American land mass:

> When you travel from Punta Arenas to Rio Grande in the south of Patagonia, for a hundred kilometers you skirt La Bahia Inútil -Useless Bay - where the sky is low, purple, and immense, and the sheep have an air of night owls about them. It is all so vast and empty, so definitively empty, that it does not even merit a name; as though God had by some oversight cast this superfluous landscape down here- a landscape all the stranger for being part of an entire landmass, Patagonia, where all is useless and senseless.[6]

As Baudrillard's observations might suggest, purposelessness does not always have to equal bleakness or a terrifying void: if anything, his rich description of this 'superfluous landscape' inspires further investigation. Meanwhile, the world of recorded sound may have its own 'Bahia Inútil' in the works of the bio-acoustic researcher and composer Francisco López (formerly based in Madrid, with recent residencies in Montreal and Amsterdam.) López is certainly no stranger to the sweeping 'useless' steppes of Patagonia, and on the subject of 'uselessness' in general he has made a number of eyebrow-raising statements like "I have no interest in changing the world...actually, so little that I have interest in *not* changing it", "I work hard really hard to create useless things- and I'm proud of it", and finally "purposelessness...that's what we really need". It would seem, on the basis of these statements, that he is the anti-teleological artist *par excellence*. He seems fairly uninterested in what will eventually come of human endeavor, of adopting a kind of Taoist reluctance to impose design upon natural workings. López could also be seen as a sonic disciple of Romanian philosopher E.M. Cioran (an admitted influence on the composer), who acidly wrote that "we are not failures until we believe life has a meaning." Sound, for López, may still have valuable functions relating to the spirit, such as 'creating soul' (a proposal courtesy of Greek composer Jani Christou.) However, he rejects attempts to make even a spiritualized sound a shaper of the grand historical narrative, as the endlessly cited Jacques Attali did when suggesting that sound has a 'heraldic' or prophetic function. "To tell you the truth, this sounds like bullshit to me," is his retort: "I see no ability in music for 'prediction'. If anything, with regards to historical time, most music seems to have an ability to mark the present and, even more clearly, the past. Think of any example, from Elvis Presley to Inuit music."[7]

Restlessly criss-crossing the globe with just a selection of portable recording equipment, López' sound experiments bring to mind the characters in the Tarkovsky film *Stalker* (another admitted favorite of the composer): treading through the fluid and vast "Zone" where emerald foliage melts into rusted-out machinery and abandoned weapons, and where a curious, palpable irrationality and fluid sense of time is always in full bloom. Though this activity does not always inform his compositions, López is easily one of the most prolific agents of the art of field or location recording: an art which concerns itself with the seemingly neutral activities of documenting and cataloging the sonic phenomena of the biosphere, and its man-made extensions, without attempting to act as an arbiter - a 'narrator' - of any of these processes. It should be clarified that field recording is not merely, as the name would suggest, something which must take place in a pasture, savannah or other environment left relatively unmolested by humanity: the practice, as it stands now, extends to the most electrified, concretized, and developed sectors of the hyper-modern metropolis as well, thanks in part to the efforts of artists like López himself. The hum of generators, the strangely lulling drone of dissipated highway activity, and bubbling polyglot marketplace voices are all authentic field recordings on par with the ones more likely to be utilized as the backdrop to a *National Geographic* TV special.

While some of the more acclaimed works of field recording still deal exclusively with of the 'secret life' of the animal kingdom (Chris Watson's acclaimed 1998 Touch release *Outside The Circle of Fire,* for example, features astonishing recordings of African 'big cats' napping under trees), the other face presented by automated and electronic society can produce a documentary effect similar to that of raw nature recordings. Just as birds recorded in the wild sing different song phrases than when in captivity, humans and their activities sound different than when they are dragged into a recording studio or, other environments that make them aware of their being the center of attention: a desire to create an unvarnished 'sonic image' that presents things "as they really are" - i.e. the *image sonore* of *musique concrète* luminary Pierre Schaeffer - permeates the culture of field recording; and if this goal is not attained, then at least the adventure involved in traveling to and immersing oneself in certain locations can provide personal edification for the recorder. It is perhaps the latter action that is more important to Francisco López, since he remains skeptical about the ability of field recordings to truly substitute for any given environment. He has likened this process of perfect audio reproduction to "building a zoo", an activity which offers, at best, a limited synopsis of a total natural environment. Expanding on this idea, he states that

> I was specifically referring to the idea of field recordings making you 'feel transported to the place', so common in New-Agey interpretations of environmental recordings. Sitting comfortably in our favourite armchair - without the heat, the cold, the thirst, the flies, etc. - might indeed be an engaging experience, but certainly of a very different nature than that of 'being there'.[8]

As suggested above, the process of field recording, despite such 'New Age' methods of marketing it, does not end with furtive attempts at zoo building and taxonomy. Many sound artists have also applied the basic techniques of field recording to uncovering another kind of 'secret life': that of stationary objects, occasionally massive in scale, that are normally (incorrectly) perceived as static monoliths not making any kind of 'sound' whatsoever. For those who swear by the Goetheian maxim "architecture is frozen music," though, the urban center has always been perceptible as a continually unfolding "symphony" of natural elements and materials, or an environment aspiring to the freedom and malleability of sound. This is to say nothing of those instances in which daring new structural achievements were literally accompanied by bold new innovations in sound, like the usage of Iannis Xenakis' work *Concret PH* to complement his own elegantly curving, 'hyperbolic paraboloid' design for the Philips Pavilion in Brussels (1958).

Urban structures often seem to be giant abstractions of human bodies, hierarchically arranged in quadrants or formations that also seem like abstractions of our own social groups. Sonic information, throughout the history of urban spaces, has increasingly been difficult to connect to discrete processes, let alone to humanize. A Radio Leningrad experiment conducted in the late 1920s was perhaps a harbinger of the current state of things; wherein the radio station recorded and played back on air "noises of railroad stations, streets, harbors [...] and various other noise producers [...], [but] it was unclear to the listeners whether they were hearing thunder or trains or breakers."[9] This latent organicism within the built environment has been touched upon by sonic researcher and López collaborator Michael Gendreau, is another individual who has attempted to reverse the perceptual trend of seeing built environments as "dead", claiming that "every building speaks a unique language," while refering to buildings as *haut-parleurs* [loudspeakers]. Gendreau also urges us "to consider the building as a body, listen to the sounds of its structure as if it were alive: we will identify the sounds of breathing, digestion, blood flow."[10] López' own fascination with "industrialization" of the field / location recording practice is informed by realizations similar to Gendreau's, seeing built environments as

> sophisticated hyper-bodies we build around ourselves. Their physiology is controlled by metabolites and fluids such as electricity, air, water and gas. Wires, cables, gears, pipes, air ducts, boilers, clocks, LEDs, thermostats, computers, video cameras... work inter-connectedly to make up sensory, muscular, digestive, nervous systems that we set in motion, with a high degree of autonomy and self-regulation, in the service of our hyper-physiology [...] Their physiology is controlled by metabolites and fluids such as electricity, air, water, gas. [They are] a community of machines that breathe, roar, hum, rattle, beep, crackle...[11]

So, in this sense, this practice is not about going "beyond nature" as an inspiration for audio recording, but is in fact closely tied to nature, as it attempts to organicize the types of processes that Gendreau and López mention above. This approach is enacted also in the works of Stephen Vitiello, in - for example - the mic'ing of suspension bridges or the World Trade Center's 91st floor (Vitiello was a resident artist of the WTC complex two years prior to its destruction.) In Vitiello's case, the simple use of home-built contact microphones, applied to various pressure points of the structure, revealed a deep and ghostly rumble which is difficult now to see as anything but an ominous harbinger of the towers' ultimate role in the great game of ideological power struggle (this piece's inclusion in group exhibitions, like a war-themed show at Vienna's MOMUK in 2003, did little to minimize the historical overlay onto an otherwise open-ended sound piece.) Had the events of September 11 not occurred, this would have been just another in a series of Vitiello's similar experiments with contact microphones acting as stethoscopes, gauging the breath and pulse of the seemingly inanimate. This is unfortunate, as Vitiello's similar experiments with more mundane or less emotionally "loaded" materials - e.g. his *Contact Microphones on Steel Plate*, utilizing a rusted sheet of metal within the tiny desert principality of Marfa, Texas - are no less relevant to this practice as a whole.

Though all the aforementioned field recording techniques usually seek to re-integrate listeners into a world that is not tyrannized by retinal information, some amount of metaphorical comparison with visual culture is inevitable: there is Schaeffer's *image sonore* as noted above, and many allusions within the sound recording culture to theater, or a "cinema of the ear". The French acousmatic artist Lionel Marchetti is particularly enthusiastic about this expression; in one essay he invites prospective recorders to go on a "sonic [film] shooting", and also likens the acoustic space around a recorder to "...the poet's page, the painter's canvas, the calligrapher's roll...television, or the computer."[12] Yet, even while employing these visual metaphors, Marchetti does not ignore the dynamic potential of sound recording- in his reckoning, a kind of catalyst for the evolution of hearing itself:

> The purpose of painting is its ability to give us fixed visual images, framed- while at the same time very far from shifting reality- yet which can lead us to another version. Is it not the purpose of the recorded sound - we could say 'fixed sound' - to give us sonic images devoid of visual associations, which would thus powerfully stimulate another kind of hearing than that of one's interior imagination?[13]

On this point, at least - 'sonic images devoid of visual associations' - Francisco López would likely agree. The possibility of attaining 'another kind of hearing' that overrides the tumultuous noise of one's own inner dialogue seems like a monumental challenge, and in fact the discipline of listening in new ways has been proposed as the true innovation of *musique concrète* (rather than solely "[renewing] music through new methods of technique and composing.")[14] Being a discipline, it is not an easy task, and few have made the adequate preparations necessary to confront this challenge on the level that López has.

Invoking the Absolute

Whatever you do, don't call Francisco López "minimalist". While you could be forgiven for applying this overused designator to the man's packaging aesthetic (López usually releases CDs in plain jewel cases with no booklets, and with unassuming non-titles); it hardly applies to the man's actual output: with only a minimum of filtering, EQ adjustment and studio finesse, López records and presents sonic scenarios either too overwhelming or intimate in their character to be confused with cerebral, academic minimalism. From narcosis induced by the unaccompanied sound of a vinyl record's crackle, to buried memories unearthed by different shades of rain forest ambience, this sound's capacity to evoke or invoke sets it apart from the minimalist music typically performed in concert halls- in the end, lack of scored notation and an increased emphasis on extended duration of 'pieces' are the only aspects in common between the two forms.

Distance from minimalism also applies to the composer's breadth of lived experience. To remind his listeners from time to time of the sense of adventure that has been distilled into his voluminous body of recordings, López will tease the imagination with an unabashedly romantic tale: perhaps a scuba dive off the Cuban coast followed by a puff on a 'Montecristo A' cigar, or lying on the floor of the Costa Rican rain forest in total darkness with leafcutter ants as his gracious hosts. For most, this would be a vacation story to be recycled as a piece of pining nostalgia over and over again, during brief cigarette breaks outside of the office workspace. For Francisco López, it's merely what he did on that particular day- a footnote in an expansive diary of sensations and interactions that have accompanied a definitely above-average amount of global travel.

López is a cutting critic of formalist, academic minimalism, instead entranced by what he calls 'blank phenomelogical substance.' Not even the looming influence of a composer like John Cage is given a free pass by López, who attacks the 'proceduralism' of his work: López is particularly incensed by Cage's statement that "a sound is a sound" although only *certain* sounds are 'music'. If Cage himself comes under critical scrutiny, then his followers -'Cageans'- are held in even lower esteem by López. He writes:

> I believe that the Cage 'revolution', instead of 'freeing music from taste and traditions', re-restricted it again to

the fences of the same old Western paradigm of formalism and proceduralism. It's no use to fight the traditions just [by] running away from them within their land, and staying in a hideout offered by them and, therefore, illusory as such hideout. This is puerile and futile. Let's cope with the traditions face to face instead of exaggerating what we want to change from them in a convulsory movement of negation. I don't think it's possible for music to be freed from taste and memory (and Cageans themselves are a proof of this) but, what is more important and relevant, I don't think it should; even in the more extreme position of anti-traditionalism.[15]

As a reaction against all the aforementioned schools of thought, López suggests 'absolute music' as a more fitting signifier for his work. López cautions, though, against possible misperceptions of the term 'absolutist', a term often used in the West to criticize some obstinate individual mired in their own way of doing things, regardless of its efficacy. López is himself a champion of flux and continual metamorphosis, steadfastly denying that 'absolute' is a synonym for some kind of creative or conceptual metastasis:

> It has nothing to do with 'inflexibility' or non-change. The term 'absolute music' was created, during Romanticism, by poets defending the idea of music being the most sublime of all arts by its detachment from text and specific meaning. This was a reaction to previous epochs of intense dependence of music from text in opera, and heartily defended the notion of music attaining its full, real, essential potential and strength when devoid of descriptive or narrative elements alien to the music itself. This is a remarkable oddity in the universal history of music, and I personally find this idea completely akin to my natural perception of the essence of music and sound.[16]

López also explains that, according to Carl Dahlhaus and his opus *The Idea of Absolute Music*, 'absolute music' is a phenomenon "...whose contemplation alone allows one to escape the bounds of mortality in moments of self-forgetting." To this end, Dahlhaus' work posits Beethoven as a model of absolute music or the music of "essences." It thus stands opposite the 'program music' that, prior to the early 19th century rise of Romanticism that López alludes to, relied on some extra-musical concept or prefatory material to help one make sense of it (in this sense, López' resistance to album titling is merely a successor to the practice of 'titling' symphonies numerically.) Despite Roland Barthes' argument that "these two musics are two totally different arts [...] each with its own history, it own sociology, its own aesthetics, its own erotic,"[17] this attempt at reconciliation has not completely kept the 'absolute' and 'applied' forms of music from remaining in competition today.

López has earned his notoriety in the sound art world not just for offering a constant flow of new releases, but also for an adamant refusal to let textual references, visuals, and any non-sonic element sully the purity of the aural experience. To this end, López blindfolds his audience members (complimentary blindfolds have also been included with select CD releases of his), performs from a mixing desk in the center of the audience rather than on a proper sound stage, and veers away from any conversation relating to the 'tools of the trade': anything which will serve as a distraction from the listener being able to accurately form a sonic universe as unique to them as possible. Without a doubt, this tendency may startle or alienate concert audiences used to paying money for spectacular visual extras like laser light shows, film projections and the pyrotechnic eruptions cued to coincide with the more triumphal portions of the musical program, but no amount of complaint has yet convinced López to change course. It follows that he is also highly disinterested in linking his compositional output with personal experiences or epiphanies- a naïve attempt on my part to make the composer disclose some of this information was met with characteristic intensity: "I can't recall a single instance in my life in which 'understanding' the reason of any creative actions...has changed anything essential in my work. I find that kind of analysis completely useless and uninteresting."[18]

+

Confucius once said that *"when a finger points at the moon, the idiot looks at the finger,"* an axiom which might be applied towards the ongoing obsession with technologically up-to-date sound "gear" and other ephemera of the modern sound stage. Though it may be harsh to assume "idiocy" on the part of audiences, the persistent problem of audiences' displeasure with the retinally unstimulating "laptop concert" (and the desperate attempts by artists of "post-digital" live performers to offer some kind of a compromise in this area), have led to the answering of a question that - as López might suggest - never needed to be posed in the first place.

López is perhaps one of the most outspoken opponents of this stage - and hence, the innovations mentioned above - seeing it as a needless intermediary between an artist's vision and the audience's perception of the music. He proposes that "music should be liberated from theater," and also reminds us that "Pythagoras had such a great idea... all the concert halls should have a curtain to hide the orchestra; for the dignity of music."[19] The term 'acousmatic' does derive, after all, from the *akusmatikoi*, the group of Pythagoras' acolytes who would only listen to their teacher speaking from behind a veil. In modern acousmatic music, the veil of Pythagoras has been replaced by loudspeakers or sound amplification equipment, which project audio information but offer no hints as to the source material comprising the original recordings. In submitting to the acousmatic discipline called "reduced listening" by Schaeffer, the cultivation of one's own personal world of interpretations is one possible effect, but in the process of asking what one is hearing, another result of this process is the increased understanding of one's perception mechanisms themselves. This is perhaps why Schaeffer perceives music as a tool "that tends as much to set the grounds for knowledge than to create works of art."[20]

So, with this methodology in mind, López does not see the new trend towards reduced on-stage skill exhibition (e.g., 'performing' by blankly staring at a computer) as anything sincerely radical or contrarian. In fact, he believes that on-stage presence in and of itself is causes even the most radical new music to share common goals with pop music's development of a personality cult- whether dazzling virtuosity is exhibited on that stage or not. It is a sensitive issue, especially considering that most of the artists surveyed in this book, including some of López' own past collaborators, still rely on a conventional stage set-up for live exhibitions of their sound (although the exact reasons for doing this vary from one performer to the next, as do the degrees of willingness or reluctance to appear in such an environment.) In response to *Sound Projector* interviewer Gregory Gangemi's suggestion that appearing onstage with a laptop still reduces the performer to a kind of 'idol', López responds:

> ...well, it's an idol anyway, no matter what you do: if you're dancing like the Spice Girls or you have a laptop on stage you're an idol for a different kind of people. Or you're an artist or a star or whatever. It's like....what is the reason for someone with a laptop to be on stage? Originally, the reason for musicians to be on stage was for people to be able to hear the music and see them of course. But now I think those reasons are not operating anymore. Or a DJ on stage, for example....a DJ on stage, I don't see the point of that. It's sort of following the traditional rock 'n roll show aesthetic, translating that directly into something that could have more potential.[21]

The presence of onstage DJs has always stoked a debate about the degree to which audiences really desire total freedom: for each faction that wishes merely to dance uninhibitedly, there is another that enjoys being led around by the nose and following a clear set of cues that cement their role as a participant in a loosely-scripted, popular drama. It seems the 'idol' factor will remain with us as long as there exist those who enjoy the security of a hierarchical "performer vs.observer" or "'shaman' vs. initiate" relationship.

However, the idolization of the artist is not, according to López, the sole problem arising from the staging of live electronic music- there also exists a kind of technophilia among audience members, or a desire to know the precise technical specifics of the sound being produced: what hand movements and knob twists correspond to what noises, what plug-in or clever coding technique is causing 'x' effect. As Nick Prior reports, "many are responding to the ambiguity by giving the audience a peek at their craft, projecting live relays of their desktops onto large screens, displaying the frequency bands of their music in real time or placing miniature cameras on the equipment to show the work in close-up detail."[22] This proposed remedy has been both suggested and enacted by the performance group austraLYSIS, i.e. "what are needed for this purpose are still images of the performance interface: frozen images of digital ice rather than of frenetic manipulative performance 'incoherence'."[23]

Owing to the relative newness of electronic music tools compared with the traditional string, woodwind, percussion and brass instruments, the desire to decode the relationship between the artist's movements and particular musical functions becomes a game that, although it gives audiences something other to do besides lapsing back into conversation, can interfere with the actual direct experience of the sound output. As per López:

> If somebody is looking at me during the live show, they will be looking at what I am doing with the equipment, trying to figure out how I am doing that, what is happening...I'm concerned with this because it's a problem, and I don't want people to look at that. I want people to focus on what's going on in the space.[24]

López' objections should certainly raise a host of questions for the aspiring sound *artiste*. Yet it seems unlikely that musicians, armed with either the most bare-bones sound equipment or the most complex and unwieldy setups, will be able to tear themselves from the performance stage. The need for validation by an audience, deriving from humans' biological need for recognition, is something that only the bravest souls seem able to truly distance themselves from- and most would likely treasure the increased social contact that comes from having befriended audience members on the strength of a successful concert. Even the most confrontational noise artists seem to enjoy a bit of 'networking'; a good round of chatting or a post-show meal shared with enthusiastic audience members as the evening winds down after the performance. Human social nature almost invariably trumps the will to let art stand on its own merits, or to let it be enjoyed without regard foer its 'authentication' by any kind of critique or peer review. For López, though, who confesses to being a 'loner' and seems quite content when working as a solitary cell, the social element attached to even the most experimental of music is yet another corrupting influence:

> I'm one of those who believe more in the idea of creators having -for good or bad - their personal path, rather than one that is molded and defined in response to the degree of acceptance. The latter is a very dangerous path, and I naturally don't have any inclination to that.[25]

One release of López' – a cassette anomaly entitled *Paris Hiss*- perhaps sums up, better than any of the above writing, his attitude towards the role of personal identity in the final presentation of his work. This release, part of a similarly packaged series on the Banned Production label, comes with two sticker labels affixed to either side of a cassette, bearing the artist's name and the album title. Since these labels cover the two tape reels in the center of the cassette, it cannot be played without first destroying or rupturing the sticker labels. For each of the releases in this series, this act of preliminary destruction can be seen as having a different meaning, but for *Paris Hiss* it is tempting to view it as an act which, like López' cover-less CDs, discards the importance of the creator's persona in favor of actual content.

The Morality of Sound? Schaeffer vs. Schafer

Francisco López, in spite of his background in biology and entomology, and his strong emphasis on bioacoustics, has criticized the traditional 'acoustic ecology' blueprint as laid out by composer R. Murray Schafer in the 1960s (Schafer is author of the seminal *The Tuning in The World* and founder of the World Soundscape Project.) Although López is not anthropocentric by any stretch of the imagination, he is a vociferous opponent of Schafer's own reluctance to engage with to man-made technology, and is not necessarily alone in this: in a questionnaire forwarded by the *Soundscape* newsletter, Atau Tanaka speaks for a number of other composers assumed to have a connection to the mission of 'acoustic ecology,' saying that "the biggest statement I can hope to get across is how amazing everyday sound is,"[26] and thus leaving himself open to any number of technical and technological possibilties for doing this. John Hudak, while admitting that he would "love to be more affected by country / nature sounds,"[27] nonetheless realizes that "the man-made city sounds are too present for me to ignore," and thus chooses to work with them rather than against them (and it is well worth noting here that Hudak collaborated with López on the aforementioned *Buildings [New York]* disc, where he is credited for "allowing access to those odd places inside the buildings.")[28]

Associating Schafer with the practice of acoustic ecology as it currently exists is somewhat disingenuous, occasioning numerous defenses of the practice along the lines of Sabine Breitsameter's:

> It is a widespread thought, a prejudice mainly, that [Acoustic Ecology] is a nostalgic movement, considered not only weird because it is dealing with sound - a topic which is rather intangible for many - but also, so at least is the saying, celebrating ancient times without cars, machines, electric or electronic technology. I sometimes hear that Acoustic Ecology creates art which aims for "ecological correctness", and therefore, some say, judges and restricts the compositional material, dividing it between being "natural" and therefore ecologically correct, and being technical / artificial and therefore not feasible.[29]

Breitsameter is confident that these assumptions "cannot have been derived from the written or composed discourse of Acoustic Ecology, but may have other reasons and sources."[30] Yet it is Schafer who, in the same issue that this defense originates from, does much to contradict it focusing on the tyrannical or controlling aspect of technology to the detriment of all else. Elsewhere, Schafer recoils in horror at the artifice of urban environments, derisively calling them 'sonic sewers', and calling for anti-noise legislation in booklets such as *The Book of Noise*. Schafer has, in the past, composed sound pieces based on Vancouver traffic noise, although his forte has been elaborate performance pieces set in the wilderness, featuring an eclectic mingling of Asian, Egyptian and North American spiritual themes. Several of his attitudes to technology, e.g. his aversion to cellular phones[31], are easy enough to sympathize with, athough his prescription for rehabilitating the natural world through simply "putting names to its voices"[32] does not seem sufficient enough to give the natural world a greater say in human affairs.

Schafer is seemingly taking us down the same road of domestication that caused these problems in the first place. This, in spite of the fact that there is only so much of this domestication that is possible given the limited amount of audible frequency spectrum that humans can take in relative to other life forms: Dorion Sagan reminds us of bats' sonar emissions that, vibrating at some 100 kHz, are five times the upmost auditory limit of the human ear.[33] And even for those communications that are audible, developing an understanding beyond merely "putting a name to a voice" could require intense specialist concentration over time periods that many humans would not be willing to endure (see, for example, the "humpback whales [that] sing to each other in songs that completely change over a five-year period, using some of the same rules human composers [use]."[34]

Lodged within Schafer's attitude towards mechanical processes' noisy destructiveness, it seems as if there is a dismissal the ability of nature and humanity to co-evolve in anything but mutually destructive ways. The assumption that organic life cannot offer any other response to human agency than to succumb to it is harmful in itself: it is part of a larger assumption that nature has an "identity" which is not dynamic or continually emergent, and that nature is waiting for culture to locate its "voice" for it. Biologists such as Kevin Kelly have regularly refuted such thinking, citing nature's ability to "break any rule it comes up with," rather than its fixity, as the wellspring for much human innovation.[35] Of course, separations of nature and culture are themselves problematic, lending themselves to false dichotomies of good and evil so rigid that they overlook the similarities existing in organic life and human artifice. López reminds us that noise (in its simple cultural meaning as loud or disruptive sound) is just as much a component of nature as it is of the urban environment; that the rain forest is as saturated with audio information as vital intersections in major cities. Speaking at a lecture in Kita-Kyushu, Japan, López says this on his disconnect with Schafer:

> I have no intention of telling anyone how the world should be, especially like Hildegard Westerkamp and Murray Schafer. Where I deeply disagree with these people is that they feel that they have to tell the rest of the world how the world should be. The main concern of the World Forum for Acoustic Ecology, which is based on the ideas of Schafer, is to tell people that the world today is very noisy. And indeed it is, but isn't that the way it should be? Is nature better when it's quieter? Are machines evil because they make a lot of noise? Is that noise boring because it's always the same?[36]

The innate 'evil' of machines, computers etc. is, as López' comments hint at, a concept very much based in Western, Romanticist ideas of naturalism, with nature being a benevolent, protective matriarch, her silence being tantamount to tranquility of the spirit. However, an incident described in architect Jack Kerr's book *Dogs and Demons* (an intensely alarmist work chronicling the deterioration of traditional Japanese values) illustrates that some residents of urbanized areas in Japan can actually find *natural* noise to be an intolerable intrusion- one anecdote in Kerr's book recalls how, on the 'suggestion board' of a Japanese town's ward office, someone has writ large (and in total sincerity) KILL ALL THE FROGS in frustration at the sleep loss engendered by the amphibians' nightly performances in their residential area. At the same time, the Japanese Construction Ministry can mobilize cement mixers and other heavy equipment to these residential areas in the dead of night, with little public protest (although I *personally* didn't enjoy having a New Blockaders concert being re-enacted on the sidewalk outside my apartment, at 3 a.m. on a 'work night'.)

So, for one, Schafer's view of "destructive" machinery is not a cultural universal: many urban residents are either calmed or invigorated by the sureness of mechanical repetition, a welcome bit of certainty within an urban landscape otherwise clogged with sticky social dilemmas. Schafer's objection also seems to be based too exclusively on aesthetic grounds: rather than attacking, say, the long-term effects of constant mechanical noise on human sanity and functioning, he assails this noise-making apparatus from a mystical point of view. It begs the question: why is the swarming mass of trumpet calls and monks' voices in Tibetan liturgical music capable of lifting one to spiritual heights (even for someone with no knowledge of Tibetan language or religious custom), while meditation upon the dense, hypnotic sound qualities of a video arcade or factory isn't? Furthermore, what should be done about naturally occuring sound phenomena, massed insectoid noises for example, indistinguishable in rhythmic or timbral quality from a mechanical equivalent? Such things crop up in unexpected places: many who have ingested psilocybin mushrooms have reported an industrial-strength grinding and buzzing in environments far removed from any kind of industrialization.

López personally refuses to characterize any form of sound as 'evil', but then again, doesn't view it in any moral light whatsoever:

> I think creative work with sound should be allowed to have all possible levels of intensity for those who might want to go through them. In a way, this is nothing more than a reflection of what we find in reality, where things have very wide dynamics, in terms of loudness, frequency content, time / pace, etc. If by 'noise' we understand harsh, loud sounds (I'm not so sure this is the best way of defining it), a lot of people are already convinced of their interest in this. And, to be sure, I never had the intention of convincing anyone about any of this.[37]

López' reluctance to map a personal agenda onto nature separates him not only from the World Forum for Acoustic Ecology, but from much of the stigma surrounding 'ecology' in general: the term *ökologie* itself was first put into use by Ernst Haeckel in the 1860s, the Social Darwinist ideologue who used ecological concern as a front for providing a pseudo-scientific basis for the biological superiority of Teutonic peoples. The historian Daniel Gasman proposes that "racially inspired Social Darwinism in Germany...was almost completely indebted to Haeckel for its creation"[38] and that "his ideas served to unite into a full-bodied ideology the trends of racism, imperialism, romanticism, anti-Semitism and nationalism."[39] This ideology was the *carte blanche* that the Nazi regime needed to legitimize its quest for *Lebensraum:* since virtually all other peoples outside of the Aryan race had an inferior understanding of nature, it followed that their subjugation and eventual liquidation would be the salvation of all biological life on the planet.

While the pluralistic Schafer would undoubtedly bristle at being compared with such people, the belief in humans as liberators and saviors of nature is shared by both him and by the 'ecofascist' radicals who follow in Haeckel's footsteps. The urge to 'save' a supposedly inferior or helpless life form often warps into a brutish form of domestication or colonization, and for many this tendency to 'save' conceals a host of ulterior motives, or at least betrays a deep sense of remorse over past transgressions. Others have discerned a running theme within Schafer's theories that, if not 'fascist' in its implications, is at least authoritarian- this is the case with Jonathan Sterne's critique:

> [Schafer's] ideal sound culture is one limited to what he calls a *human scale:* the spatiality of the unamplified human voice. For Schafer, the human is the small. This definition of humanity reduces it to a scale of a single human being and confuses cacophony with social disorder or, worse, inhumanity. Schafer's definition of a "hi-fi" soundscape conceals a distinctly authoritarian preference for the voice of the one over the noise of the many.[40]

It is here where López' distinctly 'hands off' approach to acoustic ecology separates him from such tendencies- he refuses to set himself up as a 'chosen' emissary of mankind to the natural world, suggesting that "the more I like an object, the more I want it to be possessed by someone else...someone with the courage and skills I lack for keeping material things alive and healthy."[41]

The Wild Hunt for Beautiful Confusion

Undoubtedly, lengthy and sustained exposure to high-decibel output on either pole of the frequency range is going to have a damaging physical effect. While opponents of noise will certainly point to this as a key factor in the need for it to be regulated, this is not the only point of concern: there is also the psychological transformation that intense noise engenders; the possibility that it will turn otherwise meek souls into uncivilized, raging Berserkers. Those who fancy themselves as the defenders of a biosphere under attack from torrents of mechanized noise are put in a precarious position when also making this latter claim; because they must also admit the possibility of noise as an archaic, paganizing force- not the sole domain of Futurists and urban developers. One Austrian esoterica enthusiast, writing under the pseudonym of Adam Kadmon, reminds modern readers of the atavisitic use of noise in Teutonic rituals like the *Oskorei* or "wild hunt", which provided the antidote to monotheistic belief systems' divorce from the terror of nature:

> Noise played an essential role in the wild hunt, as it did in many pagan celebrations...magical noise as an archaic technique of ecstacy was a characteristic of many non-Christian cultic activities. Bonifatius, later canonized after cutting down the 'Thor Oak Tree' (for which he was killed by pagans for this outrage), cursed the noisy processions of the Germans in winter. The German language uses the term *Heidenlärm,* heathen noise. Deadly silence and murmuring apparently seemed to be the trademark of the Christian liturgy...[42]

Kadmon, drawing on a variety of sources, characterizes the *Oskorei* as a hellish and chaotic rite in which the goal of increased noise levels - the noise being generated by human cries, percussion, crashing of cymbals and so on - was to "awaken nature, which slept in the frozen earth"[43], not to distance technocratic mankind from earthly influence. Kadmon then proposes that this tendency has been, in the late 20th century, reinvested into the bloodthirsty werewolf subculture of extremist heavy metal: the cartoonishly-attired denizens of the Scandinavian Black Metal cult, in particular, bore some similarities to the *Oskorei* riders by masking their true personalities in grim face paint and demonic pseudonyms. The endless trance-like whirling of Black Metal instrumentation (queasy tremolo guitar riffing and strobing "blastbeats" played on multiple bass drums) causes Kadmon to ask "is Black Metal, with its hard, austere sound, the *Oskorei* of the Iron Age?"[44]

This brings us back to the relationship between noise and evil. This relationship is not wholly discouraged by countless musicians and noisemakers with definite pretensions to evil, who prefer their music as loud and distorted as possible in order to create a stimulus on par with that of cataclysmic events such as war or natural disaster. Black Metal, with its incessant, morbid miasma of guitar fuzz, and its cold, rasped and shrieked vocals, is widely noticed as one of the more evil manifestations of modern music. Queasy tritone intervals - one of the most dissonant intervals in the Western harmonic concept - are deliberately employed thanks to their accursed status as the *diabolus in musica* during the Middle Ages. Songs are intentionally under-produced or perversely stripped of mid-range sounds to make a kind of audio metaphor for lack of compromise (moderation and temperance being values which these Nietzschean ax-slingers find particularly abhorrent.) Black Metal musicians compliment their sonics with a hostile image, girding themselves with such misanthropic talismans as ammunition belts, homemade arm gauntlets bristling with nails, and invariably black clothing. Of course, a thorny mythology surrounding the scene- loaded with incidences of church burning, murder, racist agitation and ritualistic self-abuse (the bands Abruptum and Senthil have both claimed to torture themselves in order to produce more authentic recorded shrieks) irrevocably completes the 'evil' package, however sincere or insincere this imagery may be.

But without the harsh visual components, the severe blasphemies re-printed on the albums' lyric sheets, and the band members' own attempts to promote themselves as Vlad the Impaler reincarnate, could even Black Metal avoid being pegged as an ugly form of 'sonic sewage'? By Schafer's logic, no- since any attempt at liberating the sounds from their composers would be a deceitful task, a capitulation to 'schizophonia'. But, just as Brion Gysin claimed that 'poets don't own words,' López contends that musicians and composers do not own *sounds*, and therefore the entire concept of a 'connection,' and consequent 'separation,' between sound and source is false. Firing another shot across Schafer's bow, López states:

> Since sound is a vibration of air and then of our inner ear structures, it belongs to these as much as to the 'source'. To criticize sound recordings in [schizophonic] terms is simply not to understand the meaning of the Schaefferian concept of sound object as an independent and self-sufficient entity. The schizophonia of Schafer and the *objet sonore* of Schaeffer are antagonistic conceptions of the

same fact.[45]

Maybe it is no coincidence, then, that one of López' own better-known pieces, - *Untitled #104*, released on Montreal's Alien8 label - is a 40-minute hailstorm of extreme Metal samples, and that (despite the vague familiarity of one or two 'grooves' arising from the maelstrom) it sounds uncannily similar to his recordings of natural phenomena, while the vertiginous assault of drum sounds on the piece hearken back to López' distant past as a drummer for various punk bands. More to the point, though, one reviewer accurately summarizes the piece's ability to warp perception through a kind of stimulus flooding, noting "once you make it through the first 5 minutes, all that's left is a whistling rumble that mostly reminds of the sound of gas pipes."[46] This is an especially challenging piece for López to pull off, since the sounds are so hopelessly wrapped up in the willfully contrarian and harsh world of heavy metal. Or, maybe more accurately, it is a challenge to the listener to hear this bombardment and to decouple the sound from its 'metal' context; free from corresponding mental imagery of black leather, spilt beer and thrashing manes of hair. In recent years, plenty of musicians not aligned with the "metal" subculture have attempted such sound pieces, which tantalize the listener with something vaguely familiar, yet with systematically deleted key points of reference (e.g. the histrionic metal style of vocalizing), leaving them rudderless on a sea of indifferent noise and - when confronted with the music in such a puréed form - wondering how they came to embrace this music in the first place. *Untitled #104* can be counted among the better of these experiments, with a few others - Kevin Drumm's *Sheer Hellish Miasma*, selected works by Merzbow - offering the same sort of enlightenment through the total emptying out or exhaustion of a particular musical concept.

This feeling of intense dislocation is, to borrow from López' own lexicon of terms, a form of *belle confusion*- a voluptuous beauty that comes precisely from having no immediately discernible connection or relation to anything at all; having a vast sonic space all to one's own. This can be accomplished just as easily with the battering power of *Untitled #104* as it can with pieces so quiet and elusive that the ears would 'squint', if they could, to ferret out the carefully obscured, dustmite details. It should be noted that this skill for mining the depths of quietude has endeared López to other such representatives of this style (Bernhard Günter, Marc Behrens, et al.) just as his ability to transform sound from ethereal presence to physical force has placed him in a league with psycho-acoustic heavyweights Zbigniew Karkowski and John Duncan. It should not be assumed, though, that López' explorations of quiet have some more 'intellectual' basis than his into the visceral, flaring loudness of his recorded boiler rooms and war machines. Therefore he is careful to warn against "...a common misinterpretation of silence and quiet sonic events as having some kind of hidden 'conceptual' content"[47], stating that

> It is my belief that this has to do with the limited conception of narrow dynamics in most music standards. This applies to many sound creative frameworks such as the volume dynamics, the frequency range, the timbral palette and the pace of unfolding for sonic events. When music is a commodity for background 'ambience', for dance, for radio broadcast, for big live shows with crowds, and so on, the constraints (mostly unnoticed) keep holding a strong grip on us. When music is a world in itself, the territories are vast and thrilling. We can go from -60dB to 0 dB and feel all what is happening, we can endure deserts and oceans of 10 minutes of silence, we can flow in mountain and abyss crescendos of 40 minutes, we can walk on thin shreds of thin air or be smashed by dense waterfalls and things like that, which I do in my pieces. There's nothing conceptual about this, but rather an immense spiritual universe of open possibilities, or at least this is what I forcefully try to create.[48]

López also argues that silences and perception-testing murmurs within his work should not be seen as some kind of aberration when the visual equivalent of such has been accepted as a legitimate compositional technique. Arguments can in fact be made that the 'silences' in his work - namely those that are physically, yet not audibly perceptible - remain an integral compositional feature. For example, Eugene Thacker, in his review of the *Belle Confusion* CD, notes the "effects without sounds" that it produces, such as windows rattling and floorboards shaking despite nothing apparently coming out of the room's loudspeakers.[49] Nevertheless, a hostile response to low-volume information has always dogged the unwitting emissaries of so-called "extreme" electronic music.

The interest in capturing the full range of dynamics runs parallel with López' frequent invocations of the power of 'spirit' (although this should not be confused with religious questing, he has in fact called religion an unnecessary "side effect" of spirit.) López seems intent on creating something as amorphous and open to subjective definition as that which we refer to as 'soul', and it is hard not to draw parallels between his love of blurred boundaries / indistinct horizon lines and the spiritual goals of disciplines like Zen Buddhism (i.e. "what seems to be evolution for others is dissolution for me...a big *blur*...it's so beautiful.") What López strives for in his sonic transmissions could just as easily be the *satori* of Zen monks, that moment when all perceptible phenomena fuse into one, or the ecstacy in Rimbaud's *L'eternite* when he witnesses the sea mingling with the sun. Like such experiences, whose intensity can hardly be conveyed in human tongues (owing to the final dissolution that they cause between 'knower' and 'known'), the attainment of the 'big blur' is similarly an experience that defies the most sophisticated vocabularies: and López seemingly prefers it this way. It is his philosophical forereunner Cioran, after all, who referred to words as "silent daggers," also claiming that "we die in proportion to the words we fling around us." In López' appraisal, conversion of sound to language is no more likely to succeed than conversion of sound to visual information- and no more necessary.

When all is said and done, López' approach challenges more than just the conventions now associated with performed and recorded music, but questions the very nature of our human relations themselves (both our relations to one another, and to the biosphere we inhabit.) Whatever worth this approach may have for others, his unapologetically solitary method of exploration has revealed to him the sonic component of a universe that, while not becoming any more purposeful, becomes ever more lush and meticulous, if also exponentially more confusing with each would-be 'breakthrough' discovery, playfully evading our most carefully laid snares and our best attempts at dominance through rationality and pragmatism. López' ongoing, intuitive journey into total dissipation would be a painfully lonely one for most musicians, plenty of whom are fascinated with the process of metanoiac attempts to forge a novel worldview. Meanwhile, the Big Blur just seems to beckon more seductively with each failed attempt at novelty.

Vox Stimuli:
John Duncan's Unrestrained Communications

It is a perfect late spring day in 2006, alive and humming with warmth and light. I am hemmed in on all sides by old growth trees, which are in turn populated by innumerable small birds darting in and out of sight, their individual song phrases weaving together into an arabesque of whistles and chirps. If we were to go by stereotypical conceptions of "extreme" artists, this would be an unusual day on which to be conversing with John Duncan long distance, notorious as he is for his steely psychic discipline and voluntary interactions with the actually and potentially traumatic. Cautionary write-ups in the art press, if they are to be believed, can be very off-putting indeed: he has been called an "anti-everything coneptualist...a cruel American"[1] by the editor of a popular alternative music magazine, and has been described by the sympathetic American artist Mike Kelley as a man whose life "struck me as a living hell...his artwork...was completely caught up in self-loathing."[2]

However, John Duncan in conversation is almost complimentary to the surrounding idyll of springtime tranquility, hardly a dark and poisonous cloud creeping in on the idyllic scene. He speaks in a calm and metered tone that belies his decades of frontline experience - "mellowed out" would be an inappropriate term, although there is a certain sense of him being at peace with himself; content with the cumulative results of his past research. He also speaks with a noticeable absence of any kind of verbal filler, diving without hesitation or prevariction into lucid explanations of his work. As with so many other people populating the netherworld of so-called "extreme" music and sound art (an adjective inherited rather than forwarded by these artists themselves), raw sensationalism and "don't try this at home" cautionary nagging are all too often the elements that guide discussions on his work: artists like Duncan have also provided certain critics with an irresistible 'straw man' to set up in opposition to their alleged humanism and control of the moral high ground. But, if we equate morality with a sense of selfless sacrifice and commitment, as many do, John Duncan easily trumps the critics in this debate - at various points Duncan has sacrificed his physical safety, his national identity, and even his literal manhood onto the altar of creative research.

When Japanese music critic Takuya Sakaguchi refers to John Duncan as "never a conceptual [artist], but a stimulation artist,"[3] he strikes at the core of what makes this man's idiosyncratic body of work merit further discussion. John Duncan's sound works and installations largely eschew the theoretical and the metaphorical, and are especially untainted by any hint of the ironic - "lower-case" culture could not be farther removed from this repertoire of intense actions, which demand spontaneous and revealing reactions on the behalf of participants (as well as provoking a separate set of long-term, residual effects.) "Stimulation art" is, if nothing else, a more apt term than "conceptual" art, as attempts to situate Duncan within the history of that genre run up against problems, namely that his work is not as concerned with the "dematerializing" strategies so often associated with conceptual art, and does not prioritize linguistic communications as a raw material for projects in the way that many key conceptualists (e.g. Sol LeWitt, Joseph Kosuth) have, realizing that sensation is more universal than the of verbal communication and well capable of continuing in the absence of language.

Art aiming at the production of pure affect or sensation also arguably takes more risks as a communicative medium, as there is no guarantee that what Daniel Smith calls "primary, non-rational" sensations will ever become organized in more meaningful, reflective process of *perception*.[4] Much of Duncan's art rectifies the problem with conceptual art identified by Stephen Zepke - that it "has abandoned 'sensory-becoming' [...] for an experience-less art."[5] Zepke's laments that the situation in which "the desire to merge art with life simply evaporates art rather than transforms life" and notes that, therefore, "a new life requires a new art and both must be *constructed together*."[6]

What, then, are some of Duncan's attempts to incite 'sensory-becoming'? Concerts of shortwave radio noise performed in total darkness (or with thousands of watts of white light shining on the audience.) An event in which a voluntary audience enters naked and stranded into a darkened section of an Amsterdam cellar, with no clue as to when they would be eventually released. Direct confrontation of friends in their homes by the handgun-wielding artist, himself wearing a mask and later "unmasking" himself by calling up these friends and asking them their personal reactions to the confrontation.

Sensory information, in its polar extremes of saturation and deprivation, is at the heart of nearly all these actions: for every sense-flooding noise concert of Duncan's, there is an action which is literally imperceptible: pieces like *The Secret Film,* enacted in 1978, embody this latter ideal perfectly. This Super 8 film exists only in the memories of a scant few individuals whose identities themselves are secret, who agreed at a secret meeting to have the contents of the film burned, before the clandestine filming location itself caught fire and was destroyed. Even without any form of physical evidence, let alone much commentary by the artist on the piece's motivations, *The Secret Film* has the potential to encourage an endless variety of discussions about the nature of the creative act itself - what could an artist's end goals be in a piece that will, at best, only be remembered through an increasingly unreliable proliferation of rumor and conjecture? Is it an indictment of the cult of personality projected onto 'genius artists'? Is it a commentary on the way in which myths and legends still dog us in the age of mass media? Is it a gesture of unalloyed nihilism? Finally, can we consider something to be 'art' which exists only in the imagination, whose only acknowledgement as a previously existing cultural artifact is some terse posthumous documentation by its creator?

We can either allow ourselves to be liberated or enslaved by the truth that there is no clear answer, but what we come away with is ultimately something of our own formulation - not handed down from any higher, impersonal authority. So, both the techniques of saturation and deprivation are utilized, in actions like the above, to re-familiarize participants with concepts of selfhood. There is always a distinct possibility that the deployment of this information will go beyond any of the intended consequences, but this leap into unpredictability is the fair price to be paid for any art whose sensory impressions are strong enough to alter or awaken one's faculties for self-perception.

Duncan's role as a "stimulation artist" demands that he assess all kinds of sensory information - not only the most widely used forms of audio-visual data. With the possible exception of taste, he has indeed surveyed the entire territory of human sensory perception and reported back with discoveries ranging from the unbearable to the sublime. In my aforementioned conversation with the multi-disciplinary artist, he assures me that "the sort of fixed divisions between forms of creative expression, that I was taught as a kid, are breaking down really fast," adding "...and that's how it should be."[7] Duncan is, of course, partially responsible for this breakdown that he mentions: if any artist can be acknowledged for applying the now clichéd concept of "pushing boundaries" to his work, John Duncan is it. Currently based in Bologna, the American expatriate (born in Kansas in 1953) has made a career of pushing against - and occasionally dissolving - the complex arrangement of barriers we construct around our social selves. Duncan has gone through several distinct creative phases in Los Angeles, Tokyo, Amsterdam, and Italy, each phase bringing a new set of social relations into the picture to test the incorruptibility of Duncan's aesthetic- so far the purity of his approach has remained intact, although the challenges have been numerous.

Free Music, Black Rooms, Blind Dates: The L.A. Years

Had circumstances been different, this meager biographical sketch of Duncan might have veered closer to that of Kim Jones, an artist from whom he claims a flash of inspiration. Jones, a combat veteran of the Vietnam war, came to notoriety for his *Rat Piece*: while dressed in his full combat regalia, he set a live rat on fire in the performance space, explaining that this was one way in which deployed G.I.s dealt with the interludes of crushing boredom that linked together episodes of superlative fear and violence. Duncan himself escaped deployment to Vietnam through applying for Conscientious Objector status, but just barely. His application was, with some help from his school instructors, approved in 1971 by the draft board in Wichita, Kansas - a body that was not normally inclined to do so. Having dodged this particular bullet, Duncan relocated to Los Angeles and began his university-level artistic studies.

Originally trained as a painter, Duncan chose CalArts as the site for these studies, where he recalls becoming disillusioned with "the school's emphasis on career building at the expense of research"[8] and with the insistence of the school's administration that he "...crank out more and more big paintings, as I became obsessed with looking more deeply into the relationship between the maker and the viewer."[9] This obsession led Duncan to study and appreciate the work of playwright Jerzy Grotowsky, particularly his notion of a 'poor theater': that is to say, a theater in which the relationship between actor and audience was the guiding element of the presentation, rather than the spectacular visual elements which strove to raise theater to the level of mass media (TV and film) which were imparting a wholly different message. In a notable parallel to the aesthetic which Duncan would later develop, Grotowsky employed all-black stage sets and insisted that "by gradually eliminating whatever proved superfluous, we found that theatre can exist without make-up, without autonomic costume and scenography, without a separate performance area (stage), without lighting and sound effects, etc."[10] However, unlike television or film, it could not exist "without the spectator relationship of perceptual, direct, communion."[11]

Duncan's involvement in the arts did not, from the outset, involve sound- in a career which involved such startling levels of intimacy, though, it was inevitable that sound would become an integral component, given its need to emanate from a source existing 'here and now,' and its relationship to the listener always having something to do with present actuality. Eventually, the musically untrained artist would gravitate towards sound together with a circle of individuals – the Los Angeles Free Music Society - who cheerfully declared themselves "the lowest form of music" (a claim which would, incidentally, also be trumpeted across the Pacific by Masami Akita of Merzbow.)

The activities of the LAFMS ranged from Le Forte Four's comical breakdowns, electronically-enhanced sound poems and good-natured synthesizer abuse to Airway's overloaded, aggressive take on free improv (LAFMS founders Rick Potts, Joe Potts, Tom Potts and Chip Chapman participated in both groups.) Duncan also formed the cassette label AQM

[All Questions Music] during this period, whose first releases included recordings of his Reichian breathing exercises and an ambient recording taken inside a car being driven on a mountain road. The group CV Massage would also come into being in Los Angeles, its membership including Duncan as a drummer alongside Michael LeDonne-Bhennet, Dennis Duck, Paul McCarthy, Fredrik Nilsen and Tom Recchion - the group's sole live performance involved a 'solo' turn by Duncan performing on a jackhammer, which was sent careening dangerously throughout the performance space. The jubilant anarchy of the LAFMS was, by all accounts, a unique chapter in the city's musical history, although Duncan would come to embrace wholly different concepts of communicative or expressive sound.

One such petri dish for this activity was the *Close Radio* program broadcast on Los Angeles' KPFK from 1976-1979, an eclectic and interactive piece of episodal audio art coordinated by Duncan and Neil Goldstein, and featuring additional organizational efforts by Linda Frye Burnham, Paul McCarthy and Nancy Buchanan. In an unwitting echo of the type of intimate, confessional radio art made famous by Willem de Ridder in the Netherlands (who will be heard from again soon), *Close Radio* solicited unedited opinion from listeners calling in from public phones, as well as commentary upon the types of meditative or linguistic experiments that were occuring live in the studio. The program was abruptly curtailed after an edition in which Chris Burden, by asking listeners to send personal checks to his home address, clearly contravened FCC regulations governing individuals' use of the airwaves to solicit money. Before then, however, the program's tendency to give the phone-in audience a central role in the proceedings was (as columnist Annie Buckley notes) a clear precursor to the later confessional culture of YouTube and "reality TV"[12] - though a much more spirited and enthusiastic variant on this culture, given the greater sense of genuine novelty and risk involved in *Close Radio*.

✛

By Duncan's own admission, the formative experience of being raised in a strict Calvinist household - where rigidity of character and denial of emotional expression were the rule - informed at least some of this work, which boldly explores the emotional responses to human contact and the materiality of phenomena like sound, something which has been thought to have a solely 'ethereal' existence. Duncan magnifies the fundamental aspects of human communication to a point which can become, for the unprepared, genuinely terrifying- but unlike many of the current crop of derivative 'shock' artists, he has made a habit of not trying to reproduce terror for its own sake, instead suggesting that the projection and simulation of threshold situations are learning experiences for artist and audience alike. Duncan's one-time means of employment was one such set of experiences, which he describes as follows:

> ...the closest I've been to a war situation, in South Central Los Angeles. I was driving a city bus. All the other drivers who were driving that line or driving in that general area at the same time, which was midnight to six in the morning, had weapons of some kind. They carried guns, they carried knives, they carried meter-long chains that they could use as a whip. I didn't carry anything at all. They were always getting into trouble. The most extreme example was a driver on a line that was parallel to mine. He got cut in half by barbed wire. Someone came on the bus and sort of came up behind him, looped the barbed wire around him and used it like a saw. People were threatening me all the time, every 15-20 minutes, all night, every night, all through the year.[13]

Although Duncan never attempted to assail his audience in the same exact manner that his bus fares did to him, the general aura of confrontation and risk has pervaded much of his work. Experience with such a constant, elevated level of threat can be a crucible for those who survive it; Duncan himself relates how a strategy of 'absorption,' rather than retaliation, made this survival possible:

> I learned that if I ever carried something, I would attract someone who was more desperate than I was, and wanted me to test him. By not having anything, by not carrying a weapon, I managed... I carried psychology. I would listen to people, show them respect, and be ready to move out of the way as best I could if they lunged at me. It turned out that in just about every case, that was what they really needed most. This was the most effective tool for dealing with these situations.[14]

Not all the experiences on Duncan's bus route proved so easy to overcome - one such harrowing experience is alluded to on the 1981 *Creed* 7" release, one of Duncan's earliest recordings to be pressed to vinyl. A piece on the record's B-side, ironically entitled "Happy Homes", features Duncan in conversation with the L.A.-area radio therapist Toni Grant (an interesting role inversion considering his previous work on *Close Radio*.) Duncan discusses an incident when he witnessed two adult bus fares dragging a 6-month old baby in a pillowcase behind them, and recalls the initial shock that led him to call the police. If this is not disconcerting enough, there is a follow-up incident:

> I saw something similar to that about 3 weeks ago, and…did absolutely nothing about it. This time, the child was about 9 [years old], and her mother was blind, and…the child had open sores covering her arms and legs, every part of the body I could see that was exposed. This time I didn't call the police, I just drove, and didn't do anything about it. That is why I'm calling. I just feel completely numb, and that has me very worried.[15]

Immediately, the vulnerability and uncertainty expressed by Duncan on this recording sets itself apart from the would-be confrontational megalomania evinced on other "Industrial" recordings to have appeared since this time. Unlike artists whose work saw its potency diluted by a sort of historical and geographical distancing from personal experience - lyrical fixations on the Third Reich, for example - Duncan denies us the possibility of escaping into the myth that cruelty is the exclusive property of some possessed, yet spatio-temporally distant, historical anomaly. The "Happy Homes" dialogue reveals that such taboos as wanton abuse against the powerless are, unfortunately, universal - not confined to mythical conflicts that reach definite historical conclusions. During his Los Angeles period, Duncan would return to this theme at least once more, with an almost clandestine installation -*The Black Room* (alternately titled *If Only We Could Tell You*) - set in a fleabag motel. *The Black Room* conjured up the claustrophobia engendered by societal powerlessness: within the jet-black painted space, an electric sander was placed out of sight behind a closet door, which it violently rattled, at once simulating a child's convulsive fear of violence and the violent act itself. Across from this was a single typed page bearing countless repetitions of *"we hate you little boy"* and *"DIE DIE DIE"* complemented by such hallmarks of verbal abuse as *"We taught you everything you know…we always knew you'd be ungrateful"* and *"Look at all the horror…every bit of it is your fault."* It seems that creative acts of such stark potency are not done just as optional exercises in understanding the vicissitudes of human nature, but as compulsory means of abreactive therapy. And perhaps the "universalization" or "making intimate" of this horror may be seen as a necessary step towards a more serious attempt to diminish it.

Duncan's willingness to amplify the painful events localized within his own body and mind has earned him a reputation, somewhat unfairly, as a "masochist." But such a term would insist that Duncan receives an erotic charge from his self-willed endurance tests, and this is not always the case, even though he admits that "both ecstasy and suffering are two major components in my life."[16] If anything, his more frightening works are informed by an educational imperative more than they are guided by the pleasure principle: Duncan repeatedly stresses in interviews that he wishes for performances to be a transformative experience for both performer and audience, not merely a matter of generating catharsis through shock: "the whole idea of doing all this work is to set up a situation where at least *I* learned something. Hopefully the other participant learned something too, but I set these things up so that others can learn something from them."[17]

With these things in mind, it is necessary to touch on one of Duncan's most critically dissected works, *Blind Date*. Although the media's lust for sensationalism guarantees that *Blind Date* is often discussed to the detriment of understanding Duncan's numerous other works, its story does need to be recounted here for the unfamiliar. Duncan's period of American performance came to a dramatic close with this 1980 performance piece, and he states that the reactions to it "made it impossible for me to show art in public in the United States...that was one of several reasons why I left the United States in the first place."[18] Contemporaneous press reactions to *Blind Date* were limited to a couple of obscure magazine reviews, although the work has since taken on a near-mythical importance (which has not always gone hand-in-hand with an attempted understanding of the piece's motivation and implications.) Even requests to *initiate* the action in the first place resulted in physical violence (Duncan's being ejected from L.A.-area sex shops), since the centerpiece of the performance was to be sex performed on a cadaver. Duncan was eventually able to bribe a mortician's assistant in Tijuana to provide the cadaver, into which Duncan would spend his "last potent seed" before returning to the Los Angeles Center for Birth Control and having a vasectomy performed as the piece's *coup de grace*. Audio was recorded of the act, and some visual evidence of Duncan's vasectomy - as shot by Paul McCarthy- survives as well.

Duncan's caveat to a 1997 clarification of the piece's intentions -"*think of me as you will*"- acknowledges and accepts the, at best, mixed reaction to this work. In discussion with Takashi Asai, the editor of Tokyo's culture magazine *Dice Talk* and head of the Uplink publishing company, Duncan reiterates how *Blind Date* was a cleansing act of simultaneous destruction and rebirth, meant as the logical conclusion to an experience which was already having a deleterious effect on the artist:

> Asai: In your commentary you wrote that '*I want to inflict punishment on myself*', but are you masochistic?

> Duncan: No, I'm not masochistic. In order to discuss this action, it's necessary to discuss the fact that, at this time (1980), I lost a great love of mine. Even though I loved her immensely, in the end it was impossible to make her

happy. For this reason I wanted to inflict punishment on myself.

Asai: So punishing yourself was the intention of the work?

Duncan: In America at the time, the masculinity of white male society was completely defended through penis worship. However, I became aware of the superficiality of this kind of thinking, and my thought was totally altered by this experience with the loss of a loved one. Another factor like this: I've been living in Japan for several years. Japan was a completely unknown country- living in a country with an inflexible societal structure, where I did not know how to speak my mind or communicate through reading or writing, I became all too aware of the narrowness of my thinking and way of seeing things, and thought that I must create irreversible works in order to achieve a more universal viewpoint.[19]

So, in the end, *Blind Date* was meant to be only one in an ongoing series of radically re-configuring actions, rather than a stand-alone act of willful violence perpetrated on the self (or on the passive, deceased 'partner' in this case.) The involvement of the latter remains the problematic part of the whole presentation: not Duncan's voluntary vasectomy, nor even the suspicion that - given the non-conclusive nature of audio documentation - this transgressive act really happened. The latter is a fact that Duncan "[prefers] to leave [as] a question mark, [since] there are people who have trouble facing the possibility of that within themselves...the issue of people trusting whether or not it is true, is something I want people to bring to this work."[20] This is especially curious since the hue and cry over *Blind Date* came not from a religiously-inclined, socially conservative base, but from a largely secular and liberal humanist art world[21] that would not normally subscribe to concepts of an immortal soul, which we might imagine as the *sine qua non* for a situation in which a surviving ethereal intelligence is aware of its former mortal shell being violated. This attitude is evident in a recent TV interview on the occasion of the *Blind Date* audio recording's 2011 debut at Oslo's Rod Bianco gallery, wherein the concerned interviewer states "I can't help thinking about her...she couldn't choose for herself if it was something she wanted to be a part of."[22]

So, even in isolated incidents where the work was violently rejected, Duncan can still be said to have succeeded in teaching people about themselves - in this case, that a private belief in post-mortem consciousness lay buried beneath the publicly presented personae of certain secular, existential individuals. While critical rejection of *Blind Date* was damning in and of itself, just as bad is the misinterpretation by those who *accept* the work because of a misperceived ghoulish and inhumane quality: assorted misanthropes hoping to tie the work in with the world of 'snuff' films and sadistic strains of pornography, all the while conveniently ignoring any explanation by Duncan himself and relying largely on 2nd-hand accounts. Laboring under the delusion that any artwork offending the sheepish majority must be good, many failed to grasp that 'offending' with stark death imagery was never the *raison d'être* of *Blind Date*.

This is not to say, however, that Duncan shows no interest in human mortality and its widely varying complement of effects on those still living. Speaking on a fellow artist incorporating sound into her installations, Duncan shows that he is not the only one in his field to have used real human remains as a catalyst for some kind of psycho-spiritual transformation, and that others have carried the primordial ritual of re-invigorating the dead into the most modern of institutional art spaces:

> Right now, one of my favorite artists is someone who I don't know if she was really trained as an artist - her name is Teresa Margolles. She comes from Mexico City and...her art is based on her experiences working as a forensics technician at the Mexico City medical examiner's office. What she does is she prepares human bodies for autopsies- she performs autopsies as well, and her art is all about that- the human body and the spirit of the deceased. For example, making situations where you walk into a big room and it's filled with soap bubbles [*En el Aire / In the Air, 2003*]. And as you're moving through the room, these soap bubbles are sort of alighting on you and exploding. And then you find out that the fat used to make this soap is actually human fat. There was another [exhibit] where we met, actually - she had sound coming from these 4 speakers in this little white cube that she built. There was one open entrance, and the one thing you saw there besides the speakers was this framed A4 page, that you had to walk through this little cubicle to read. And when you got there and read it, you realized that the sound was of an autopsy being performed. Then you looked down and realized that you were walking through this white powder, which was human bone. And when you walked out, you noticed that there were these paths / footprints of white powder going away- the powder from these human bones was being traced all throughout this entire hall.[23]

This only begins to scrape the surface of Margolles' *ouevre* and its re-vitalization of the dead, who are often victims of the Mexico City drug wars (a major theme of Margolles' that has seen her painting with the blood of one such murder victim [e.g. *Pintura de Sangre*].) However, more recently she has "...gotten much more abstract- you see something and don't realize that it has some connection to human corporeal existence. You see a cement bench [with human bone fragments mixed into the cement] and it doesn't occur to you to think like that."[24]

It is easy to see here the kinship that Duncan feels with Margolles, not merely for the controversy both have generated through their aestheticization of the dead, but also because Margolles (as noted in a review of her *Operativo* exhibit) "[seduces] her viewers with the beauty of minimalist forms"[25] prior to the revelation of those forms' actual contents: a technique that Duncan has applied to sound work and other media. The question that reviewer Pascal Beausse asks of Margolles' exhibits ("where else can we hypermodem individuals, desensitized by the fantastic universe of technology, be put in a situation of co-presence with death without the company of religiosity?"[26]) is partially answered by directing audiences towards Duncan's own work. Both artists' work takes on another meaning as giving a "voice" or tangible presence to those who have been denied it. Consider: the dead bodies that often figure as Margolles' raw materials have, on many occasions, been given a more dignified and elegant parting ritual than they would have achieved otherwise, given that proper burials are regularly beyond the means of Mexico City's most destitute inhabitants, and also that many drug war casualties are prone to becoming grotesque roadside "exhibits" in order to terrorize potential informants or traitors. In the same way, much of Duncan's work from *The Black Room* to *The Keening Tower* (to be touched on later) operates by this same principle of ritual transmutation.

Nonetheless, the impossibility of placing a work like *Blind Date* into any convenient subdivision of the performing arts has led to a number of inapt crtical comparisons with other artists, in order to either validate or make sense of it: Paul McCarthy and Chris Burden are occasionally name-checked, with these two artists at least having shared the same geographical confines and creative environments as Duncan. Comparisons between the work of Duncan and the New York-based artist Vito Acconci, who has also worked heavily with sound in his installations - most often the unprocessed sound of his distinctive gravelly voice - occasionally arise as well. In some instances, similar territory is in fact being explored. In their 'performance' phases in the 1970s, both Acconci and Duncan conducted experiments attempting to discover what it must be like to be of an opposite gender, and both allowed audiences opportunities to possess, harass, or abuse the artist: one piece of Acconci's involved a standing long jump contest in which any participant defeating him could win a date with one of two female acquaintances, while Duncan's *For Women Only* involved a screening of collaged pornographic films, with a banal sound component of television snippets, to an exclusively female audience (this audience was invited after the screening to abuse him sexually.)

However, the choice of performance arena is one of the greatest differences between the two, and one which has perhaps vindicated Acconci while leading to heated arguments over whether or not Duncan is simply a petty criminal or provocateur. With the exception of his famous 1969 *Follow* piece (in which Acconci stalked total strangers through the city until they entered an enclosed space, and then mailed notes about his targets to other members of the arts community) most of Acconci's more confrontational performance work took place within the confines of a gallery atmosphere.

By comparison, Duncan repeatedly carried out actions on the streets of Los Angeles, and in public spaces that were unlikely to attract only people with a knowledge of performance and body art (or, in fact, to attract any people who were cognizant of being an "audience.") his 1976 *Bus Ride* saw him, on two separate occasions, pouring fish extract into the ventilation system of a city bus with locked windows, attempting to see if the resulting odor's olfactory similarity to sexual excretions would effect passengers. It did: in both cases, riotous and astonishing acts of violence resulted from the bus fares. Elsewhere, Duncan's 1978 piece *Every Woman* saw him returning to a street that he had surveyed the previous night "as himself", returning the next night dressed as a woman in order to experience the fear of possible assault.

Then there was *Scare*, a piece tangentially linked by art critics to Chris Burden's works, thanks to common iconography (in this case, a fired handgun is shared between *Scare* and Burden's *Shoot* - although it should be noted that the gunman firing on Burden in the latter piece did not intend for the bullet to find its mark.) Of course, André Breton had written in the *Second Manifesto of Surrealism* (1929) that the "simplest Surrealist act" was the firing of a loaded pistol into a crowd, a statement that essentially aimed to bind the revolutionary destruction of this act together with the revolutionary creative techniques of Surrealist painting, writing and the like. Rather than incorrectly positing *Scare* as a kind of Surrealist homage, though, Duncan's comrade Carl Michael von Hausswolff has deftly noted that it should be considered in the history of 'sound art,' since the firing of blanks from a pistol at point blank range provided an unequivocally sonic dimension to the piece, and was likely to be the strongest of any sensory impressions received. *Blind Date*, as well, was staged as a 'sound' piece in which audio of Duncan's infamous coital act was played before a Los Angeles gallery audience. Lest it seem like the hostility towards Duncan following this event has been exaggerated, it is important to give him the final word on this:

Several of my closest friends tried to arrange for me to be extradited to Mexico and arrested on necrophilia charges. When that effort proved to be legally formidable, they decided to threaten anyone publishing or showing my work with boycotts, which effectively banned my work in the US for several years. With other friends, it created a sense of separation, a wall that in some cases still remains. I felt, and was, abandoned by every one of the people I felt closest to. Some claimed that the cadaver had been raped, that the fact that the body was apparently Mexican meant that my action was racist, the fact that the body was female meant that the action was sexist, etc., etc., to the point of surreal comedy. This was an important lesson. It taught me that each of us has a psychic limit. When something puts sudden stress on that limit and has no apparent context we can use to 'frame' it, we instinctively resist. Because our resistance isn't based on reason, any attempt we make to try to explain our resistance logically, or morally, will sound absurd, just as these claims of rape, racism or sexism were and are absurd. At the same time, it's as real as anything else, so it's just as absurd to criticize anyone with such a limit as being personally or socially 'weak.'[27]

Underground, Rooftop and Ether: Ascending in Tokyo

Duncan's prior interaction with the particularly vast, American strains of fear, violence and sexual anxiety was soon to come to a close, as an invite to Japan initiated a number of shifts in the locus of the artist's activity. As suggested in the previous dialogue with Takashi Asai, Duncan's relocation to Japan was fraught with revelatory experiences and, as is often the case, numerous misunderstandings as well. A man by the name of Takuya Sakaguchi was the initial contact for Duncan in Japan, a biologist studying, as Duncan recalls, "higher nervous energy, which is how the Japanese title translates ...the connections between the locus sirius neuron and the visual cortex."[28] This research was carried out with the eventual goal of increasing human memory through the growth of brain cells. Sakaguchi's day job, with its emphasis on fostering some form of biological growth, conveniently merged into his interest in self-produced sound art. After first hearing Duncan on the 1979 *Organic* LP released through AQM, Sakaguchi began a letter-writing campaign that would provide the germ for Duncan's eventual arrival in Japan in 1982 - a timely turn of events, since the fallout from *Blind Date* had made further Stateside developments increasingly difficult.

The expatriate artist's local influence would expand significantly throughout the 1980s - this is evidenced by a number of friendships, collaborative concerts or record releasing efforts with groups like Merzbow, Hijokaidan, Toshiji Mikawa (of Incapacitants and Hijokaidan as well), Chie Mukai and O'Nancy In French. All of these individuals were, and still are, firmly planted in the underground, but - if high online auction prices of their original recordings are anything to go by - are now venerated as the brave, lonely souls whose diligence made broader developments in visceral expression possible. Like Sakaguchi, most of these individuals were tied to day jobs apparently dreary in comparison with their anarchic, colorful musical output. Unlike the generation of artists that had been formed by the anti-*Anpo* protests of 1960-1970, the performers in the post-Punk, post-Industrial underground had begun creating in a kind of "post-ideological" atmosphere where both the momentum of the extreme Left and Right were put on hiatus following the collapse of the *Rengou Sekigun* [United Red Army] and the patriotic suicide of Yukio Mishima. The lack of general societal revolt did not precluse (as per Tarou Amano) "a critique of the rampant materialism in contemporary Japanese society,"[29] but it did often require a more atomized, introspective approach, or (in the case of the infamous performances by Hanatarash) a purely cathartic violence.[30] Toshiji Mikawa remains, as of this writing, a section chief in a Tokyo bank, while other members of Hijokaidan were described by Duncan as "...a housewife, a secretary and an office worker." However, he advises not to make any assumptions based on this alone:

> Hijokaidan is known for their performances, where one of the women who does vocals will also do actions like pissing on stage, or shitting on stage, and the rest of the members will sort of move around on the stage after this...[or] in this...and play homemade electronics, and in the process destroy these homemade electronics. And, as I said before, when I introduce Hijokaidan, people who are not familiar with their gigs when they first see them are rather skeptical that these people are office workers that they're looking at on the stage. But then when they start playing, they shut up, and listen, and, well...change their minds, I hope."[31]

During the 1980s, few Japanese artists would equal this propensity for aggressive showmanship, which simultaneously showered audiences in humor and terror. However, Duncan would respond in kind with performances of his own - performance pieces like *Move Forward* (1984) featured about twenty minutes of massive, tangible sound output in the darkened, concrete-walled 'Plan B' space in Tokyo, accompanied with film collage - of war atrocities, S+M ritual etc. - being projected onto a paper screen that covered the entire visual space of the forward-facing audience (the projection screen stretched from ceiling to floor and from the left wall to the right.) In an unmistakably climactic moment, this screen would be set ablaze by Duncan at the end of the film portion, its fire-consumed remnants then sprayed into the audience with a fire extinguisher. Like the earlier *Secret Film*, here was another piece that ended in immolation, continuing Duncan's interest in the elemental - the final destruction of the projection surface, after being used for such an overload of provocative imagery, could on one hand suggest a return to a *tabula rasa* in sorts, an 'unlearning' or transcending of aggressive impulses. Then again, blasting the audience with the remnants of the projection surface could be seen as another none-too-subtle hint that some residue of these primal destructive urges would always be with them, flying back into their faces when least expected.

Actions like the above, which featured a level of un-compromise at least on par with the actions Duncan carried out in the U.S., need to be put in some sort of geographical and historical framework. If they do not seem particularly jarring to jaded veterans of 21st century information overload and post-'9/11' nihilism, we must remember that the mid-1980s were an unparalleled period of economic prosperity and optimism for Japan. The era of the *endama* - 'powerful yen', or yen appreciation - was about to begin, and according to one retrospective article on Japan's 80s prosperity, "Japan's per capita income hit $17,500 a year- second highest in the world. Land values soared. A square foot of Tokyo real estate sold for the equivalent of $2,000; a simple wood frame home for 1.5 million dollars. Japan's Economic Planning Agency calculated that the market value of the nation itself, a California-sized archipelago, was four times greater than that of the U.S."[32]

Just like the rise of Beat poetry in 1950s America, oppositional aesthetics in such a culture of easy convenience and economic dominance (Japan was also the world's #1 creditor nation at the time) would have seemed ridiculous to the rank-and-file 'salaryman' or 'OL [office lady]'. This is to say nothing of their elders, who, even if they may have found this culture rampantly materialistic, found it vastly preferable to the privation and horror of the war years. Defenders of Japan's mainstream culture could even argue that its market power was what allowed any contrarian activities in the first place: since everything else was so readily provided for her citizens, the existence of some fringe elements displaying a kind of *Nippon Aktionismus* proved, by exception, the rule that the dominant culture was robust and healthy.

But increased spending power and unprecedented diversity in consumer choices was only one side of the story, and at any rate, simple *availability* of radical culture and media did not equal broad-based *acceptance* of its content. At best, the ongoing saga of groups like Hijokaidan was carried out in tiny capsule reviews at the rear pages of magazines like *Fool's Mate* and *Rock Magazine,* who would cover the *noizu-kei* [noise movement] phenomenon less in the 1990s and 2000s than in the 1980s, even as concert performance and releasing activity in that corner of the underground multiplied exponentially. Having a safe existence as a contributor to a massively affluent society was not enough to satisfy all people all the time: this often brought with it intense levels of fatigue (as evidenced from the epidemic of slumbering businessmen on home-bound subway trains), and unsustainable levels of micro-managed hyper-competition frequently terminating in *karoshi* or 'death from overwork'.

There was also the accelerated alienation from the forces of nature, an appreciation of which was so vital to earlier manifestations of Japanese culture. Meanwhile, Japan's status of relative cultural isolation and insularity, even during its economic miracle, made the various escape routes into other cultures - such as learning second languages - more difficult than usual, and too time-consuming to commit to while already spending one's days at the office and nights at the *karaoke* bar in moments of compulsory camaraderie. While it was actually cheaper in the 1980s to spend one's slim allotment of vacation time abroad in Australia than within Japan proper, long-term involvements in other nations were not as common, which often made the appearance in Japan of a figure like John Zorn or John Duncan a welcome and necessary 'fly in the ointment' catalyst for new cultural developments.

Pockets of resistance - or at least pockets of people who acknowledged and attempted to examine their own 'outsider' status - sprung up not only in the culture of free noise and Industrial music, but also in the experimental theater scene arising from Shuji Terayama's colorful phantasmagoria, and also the 'alternative' comics scene rotating around weekly magazines like *Garo* and the willfully crude (but not inarticulate) comic artist / essayist Takeshi Nemoto. Direct collaboration between the various scenes seems to have been rare, but all persistently attempted to confront base instincts with the intent of reaching higher eloquence and awareness beyond the glossy but insubstantial artifice of consumer lifestyles. Nemoto's description of his comics as "propagating like the graffiti you find on a toilet stall" was interesting, especially considering men's toilet stalls were the precise 'exhibition space' of Duncan's 1985 collection of A1-size collage posters.

Like the alternately discomfiting and arousing materials used for the *Move Forward* performance, Duncan's collages of war imagery and distorted pornography were probably not what anyone had expected to greet them in an immaculately well-tended Japanese public restroom, where grooming rituals and maintenance of professional appearance were carried out in proximity to the less noble expulsions of bodily waste. The posters were placed in Tokyo's epicenters of fashion (Shibuya), finance (Hibiya), government (KokkaiGijidomae), and entertainment (Shinjunku)- with this strategic placement, Duncan's simple act hinted that, if the present technological and materialistic utopia was not alchemically developed from primal lusts and aggressive impulses, these things were certainly not absent from it. It should also be mentioned that Duncan's restroom exhibitions were inspired by, and an expansion upon, a kind of local genre of well-considered toilet stall artwork that transcended the murk of its immediate surroundings (and which Duncan claims would involve "guys staying in [the stalls] for hours and [doing] these really elaborate and wonderful drawings"),[33] thus being some of the only graffiti art in the country then. Duncan's actions also, perhaps unwittingly, figured into another local tradition - that of using the toilet stall as a "propaganda board" or "site of exchange for subversive information," particularly anti-imperial sentiment during the 1930s (prospective readers of toilet graffiti were often addressed on the walls as "toilet comrades.")[34]

Actions like the above were, however, anomalous compared to Duncan's period musical performances, done both solo and in collaboration. Takuya Sakaguchi claims that "the number of shows that John did during that short stay in Japan were not small",[35] and whatever this exact number may have been, doing just a monthly concert would have been an ambitious undertaking without the proper connections: the so-called *noruma* ['pay to play'] policies in Japanese clubs have traditionally priced regular performance schedules outside the range of all but the most dedicated or established musicians, which in turn has forced the usage of alternate performance spaces like record shops and cafes.

A 'no bullshit', 'get down to business' attitude was not confined to the Japanese underground musicians' unadorned physical appearance during live performances, but also manifested in their choice of sound creation devices, themselves a world away from the dazzling new array of electronic instruments being churned out in Yamaha and Roland workshops. Incapacitants and Hijokaidan had their short-lived, homemade "black box" electronics, while O'Nancy In French created and manipulated feedback from amplified oil barrels. For Duncan, shortwave radio was the instrument of choice: a highly portable tool which resisted a user's manipulative movements as much as it accepted them. It was also capable of an extensive dynamic range of sound, for those who were willing to hear the musical qualities and rhythmic structures arising from a panoply of hums, crackles, static blasts, and plaintive coded signals. Although he had already been using shortwave during his with the Los Angeles Free Music Society, its use really 'came into its own' (in the author's humble opinion) during the Japan years.

The shortwave radio was an interesting choice merely for its historical resonance: in the same way that the tiny cell structure of underground music rendered the support of giant media conglomerates unnecessary in order to participate in the shaping of culture, Guglielmo Marconi's brainchild made it unnecessary to have the princely sums of money necessary for longwave transmitters and giant antennae. In its way, it opened the communicative floodgates much like the Internet would, some 70 years in advance. The difficulty of censoring shortwave broadcasts and monitoring listeners' access to these broadcasts also gives it some distinct advantages over the latter medium. Duncan claims that, during his stay in Japan, he was staying awake until almost sunrise drinking coffee and making shortwave compositions, fascinated by the fact that

> ...it's always different, shortwave is never the same twice when you turn it on from night to night, you don't hear the same things ever. And I'm not talking about the regular stations, I'm talking about the events between the stations- that was where shortwave really got interesting- it was always unique, always different, and the human voice is [also] like that.[36]

Even though Duncan adopted shortwave for such aleatory qualities, it has uncannily adapted itself to his personality and his own artistic intentions: the results that he achieves with the shortwave radio cannot be easily compared to, say, the work of AMM's Keith Rowe with the same device. Rowe's subtle and almost cautious approach to this tool parallels the aesthetic he developed with tabletop guitar, while Duncan uses the instrument in a way that, like much of his other work, rewards concentrated, high-volume listening of the recorded results. Rowe also became a recognized 'virtuoso' of shortwave by his ability to maximize the serendipitous power of the instrument (suddenly finding broadcast voices which seemed to comment on AMM's improvisations as they were happening.) Duncan was, as he has stated above, more concerned with the interstices: in his hands the shortwave radio was not so much a medium for transmitting human communications as it was for transmitting the sound of atmospheric disturbances and galactic forces greater than what normally fell into our immediate field of comprehension. The sound artist / composer Michael Prime, who performs using a 'bioactivity translator' (a device which amplifies the fluctuating voltage potentials or bioelectric signals inherent in all natural life) has written simply, but eloquently, on the larger implications of harnessing shortwave transmissions as an expressive tool:

> Shortwave signals interpenetrate our bodies at all times, and provide a vast musical resource. The signals may originate from cosmic sources, such as the sun, pulsars, and quasars, or from human sources. However, they are all modified and inter-modulated by the earth's own nervous system, the magnetic particles that surround the planet like layers of onion. These layers expand and contract under the influence of weather systems [...] to produce complex patterns of manipulation.[37]

More fascinating than any of this, though, is the way in which these forces have combined to produce signature sonic elements whose source is largely taken for granted. Prime continues:

> Many of the characteristic effects of electronic music (such as ring modulation, filtering, phase-shifting and electronic drone textures) were first heard in the interaction of radio broadcasts with the earth's magnetic layers. Perhaps Gaia was the first composer of electronic music.[38]

Such sentiments have inspired a whole micro-movement within the music detailed in this book, populated by artists like Swiss 'cracked electronics' duo Voice Crack and the exacting Bay Area sound artist Scott Arford, whose hyper-real compositions tend to straddle the divide between 'concrete' and 'abstract.' It also has to be admitted that, as far as instruments go, the shortwave is an incredibly versatile producer of sound textures for the price - like most sound generators that are incapable of producing melodic music, it relies on variation in other audible phenomena: the thickness in the distortion of its signal, the velocity of its crackling and chirping noises, and the randomness in the attenuation of otherwise constant electrical hum. The shortwave functions both as a tool for personal enlightenment and amusement, as well as being a metaphor for the challenges we face in making meaningful communication, beset on all sides by countless forms of natural and human interference: at least this is the feeling one gets when listening to Duncan's shortwave-based pieces like *Riot* and *Trinity*; dense and occasionally opaque manifestations of elemental sound.

Radio waves would continue to be a productive tool in Duncan's hands in more ways than one, though, as he also set out to make pirate broadcasts of events that would likely never make it onto commercial Japanese radio stations (and, to this day, still haven't.) His pirate radio program *Radio Code* was the kind of thing which, given its superior ability to investigate and document street-level reality when compared to the mass media, calls into question the concept of "amateurism" that is attached to such practices. Although *Radio Code* was broadcast using no more than a Sony Walkman, a transmitter with a seven kilometer range, and a stereo microphone with earphones taped to it (this allowed for music to be played from the Walkman while "talking over" it as a typical radio DJ might), the sheer eclecticism of the sonic art it presented was well beyond the scope of other media outlets in the area. A radical fusion of preciously unheard music, social commentary and fairly innocent playfulness was employed: highlights included on-location broadcasts of O'Nancy In French and Chie Mukai's band Che Shizu, an audio portrait of an attempted suicide (recorded live from her home after hospitalization), and an episode of the show given over to some enthusiastic high-schoolers. The title of a Hafler Trio cassette culled from a broadcast on *Radio Code* (*Hotondo Kiki Torenai* [something you haven't heard before]) accurately summed up the refreshing nature of the technically simple yet journalistically sophisticated approach.

+

Infiltrating the world of radio, holding deafening live sound performances, serving as a core member in an expanding circle of dissatisfied urban primitives: these accomplishments could have been enough on their own, but Duncan did not limit himself even to these things, branching out into film and television production as well. His *John See* series of erotic films may be some of the only films from the era (1986-1987) to involve a non-Japanese director at the helm. Duncan became involved in this medium with the assistance of Nobuyuki Nakagawa (a protégé of Shuji Terayama's.) Needless to say, the results were an unorthodox style based on collaged images (similar to the kind previously used in *Move Forward*) rather than the awkward, superfluous varieties of 'acting' and 'narrative' that most porn films attempted.

The *John See* soundtracks, likewise, were a world removed from the silly synthesizer percolations and ersatz funk typically scored for mild pornographic fare. Looped orgasmic noises, treated with electronics, gave the impression of being adrift and weightless in some limbo of carnal desire (see the piece *Breath Choir Mix*), while other soundtrack segments heightened erotic tension through ambient rumble and vaguely familiar, low-pitched rustlings and murmurings (*Inka, Aida Yuki Passion.*) Duncan's experiences within this corner of Japanese society featured human interactions significantly different than the ones portrayed in modern-day cautionary fables: rather than descending into a slimy netherworld of the type scripted into Hollywood docu-dramas, which would have been populated by Yakuza bosses, drug-addicted runaways and emotionally stunted nymphomaniacs, Duncan's colleagues on the filming set were reportedly very pleasant, and diversified in their reasons for working in adult films [for the sake of not repeating myself, readers should refer to the 'Pornoise' section of the chapter on Merzbow for further details on these encounters.]

Meanwhile, Duncan's pirate TVC 1 station - broadcast on the frequency of the state-operated NHK after their 'signing off' time - was a small victory for guerrilla media in an environment which increasingly accorded advertising as much importance as regular 'entertainment' programming. TVC 1 also functioned as a sort of companion piece to *Radio Code*. Fans of the media hijacking made so popular by the 'cyberpunk' genre (not least because Tokyo was the staging ground for the seminal writing in that genre) would find Duncan's actions positively romantic: a lone insurrectionary broadcasting from Tokyo rooftops with equipment that could fit securely into a single briefcase (antenna, transmitter and all), melting into the darkness of night and slinking into the nearest subway train before his location could be triangulated by the authorities. Yet, for all this cool anti-hero romanticism, TVC 1 was less concerned with any kind of agitational "fucking up the system" as it was with merely filling the gaps in what people were able to perceive through local broadcast media: to wit, the station never interfered with any official NHK programming, and as such could project itself as an alluring alternative rather than as a disturbance made for its own sake. The intent was to be an additive rather than subtractive form of communication- and among the additions made to Japanese culture were things that likely had never been seen in the whole of modern Asia, e.g. footage of Viennese Aktionist artist Rudolf Schwarzkogler. Shaky production values merely contributed to the images' sense of otherness, as did the broadcasting of material whose originators had probably intended for it to remain private: careless play with a videocamera by a couple enjoying themselves after sex, or an 'accidental' set of artful visuals filmed by an electrical engineer in a small apartment.

Dutch Courage

The next major port of call for Duncan was Amsterdam, a locale buzzing with possibility for artistic cross-pollination, and also a place far removed from the workaholic confines of Tokyo, whose full spectrum audio-visual overload nonetheless concealed a fairly deep-seated social conservatism. The Amsterdam of the mid 80s-mid 90s was home to the adventurous Staalplaat / Staaltape record label, and a plethora of pirate radio stations, squats, and other unpredictable flare-ups of cultural autonomy. Scene historian Rinus van Alebeek pinpoints the "creative and political peak" of the autonomous movement as 1982, while also noting the more violent challenges to authority that came in the form of riots and tram burning.[39] Staalplaat member Erik Hobijn is also in accordance here, suggesting that the more "acceptable" range of creative activities spun off from the hectic atmosphere at the dawn of the 1980s, when the squatters' movement regularly engaged police forces in street combat. Hobijn also reports that

> The squatters did some pretty heavy actions. They broke into security places, stole computer files and published them, broke into police files and published them - they had their own magazines to expose all kinds of hot news [...] The squatters are generally horrible - very dogmatic. But in another way it was unbelievable, we had two years of riots just for *fun*, starting around the day the new Queen appeared.[40]

The smoke from these skirmishes had more or less cleared by the time of Duncan's arrival, but the heady underground violence of the early 1980s had helped to lay the foundations for one of Europe's most consistently rewarding creative environments. Claiming to end up in Amsterdam "by chance...as far as that concept goes," Duncan soon found himself part of another unique constellation of sound artists: one which has not been exactly duplicated to this day, and seems unlikely to be duplicated anytime in the near future. Since Duncan's departure from the U.S. owed itself to friction between himself and the arts community there, his exit from Japan tempts one to imagine fantastic scenarios of a daring escape from arresting authorities or shady underworld elements with a definite ax to grind. The real sequence of events surrounding his next major move, though, is less theatrical than this: with his Japanese wife of the time transferring to Amsterdam to work for the European branch of a Tokyo-based company, Duncan had the chance to follow along, did so, and that is that.

Relocation to the Netherlands was perhaps not as much of a dive into stark unfamiliarity as the Japan relocation, and it had the effect of solidifying a number of relations that had already begun in Japan, while steadily forging new connections. Z'ev (a.k.a Stefan Weisser), the esoterically inclined metal percussionist and text-sound artist was possibly the first link in the expatriate sound art community living in Amsterdam (like Duncan, Z'ev also attended CalArts.) If true, this would be another in Z'ev's penchant for "firsts": his *Shake, Rattle and Roll* was the first full-length music video to be commercially released on VHS format, and he was also among the first within the Industrial sub-culture to infuse tribal or 'primitive' motifs into his presentation, emblazoning intricate sigil designs onto his drum heads and swinging sheets of metal about him in a cyclonic, often hazardous dance. Like Duncan, Z'ev settled in the Dutch capital partially due to romantic involvements, in his case with University of Amsterdam professor Dorothea Franck. The sudden accident-related death of a roommate in Z'ev's previous New York loft residence also contributed to his eventual relocation.

Some credit for the cohesion in Amsterdam's myriad scenes should be given to the enigmatic, tireless activity of artist Willem de Ridder, the self-proclaimed "master story-teller" of the Netherlands (this boast is in itself tempered with a little self-deflation, as de Ridder has previously contended "throughout the centuries [...] the audiences didn't come for [the storyteller, but for the story.")[41] De Ridder was named the Fluxus chairman for Northern Europe by Georges Maciunas, and hosted a prodigious number of collaborative organizations whose whimsical titles keep one guessing as to the precise functions they carried out: among these were the "Association for Scientific Research in New Methods of Creation", the "Society for Party Organizing", the "Witch Identification Project", and the "Mood Engineering Society" (actually an absurdist semi-musical collaboration involving Louis Andriessen, Misha Mengelberg and others.) The Amsterdam club Paradiso, a vital hub for the continental European tours of independent musicians, was formed in part with de Ridder's assistance, while he labored away on several magazine and broadcast projects concurrently. As with Duncan's *Close Radio*, these generally aimed at denying radio listening its usual role as a "passive" activity - a fact that was made particularly clear when de Ridder invited some 30,000 listeners to follow his spoken instructions, as follows:

> "Please get up from your chair, yes, don't turn off the radio yet, but go find yourself a plant - you probably have a plant in your house somewhere - and then find a white piece of paper and some adhesive tape. Now take these and go to your car. If you don't have a car, just wait. And if you do, get into the car and turn on the radio. Now wait for instructions. Glue the white piece of paper to the window and put the plant on the seat next to you. Yes, just do it. And start driving. And if you don't have a car, go outside to hitchhike, and as soon as you see a car with a white piece of paper on the window, hail it and it will pick you up." About thirty thousand people did this - at 1 in the morning. There were traffic jams throughout the country![42]

With these sorts of activities, we can see clear parallels between Duncan and de Ridder - if not exactly in the mood of their respective pieces, then certainly in their attempts at increasing intimacy through the neutralizing of audience passivity. Allies of Duncan have been cognizant of this fact also: if nothing else, de Ridder's influence on the Northern European underground of non-specialist artists has earned him a place on Carl Michael von Hausswolff's *The Wonderful World of Male Intuition* album, whose track listing reads like an abbreviated 'who's-who' of maverick explorers of the scientific and spiritual (de Ridder's name and recorded voice is featured here alongside perception-benders like Albert Hoffman, Alvin Lucier, John C. Lilly, and Gregory Bateson.)

Certain of de Ridder's activities also overlapped with Duncan's desire to draw out the latent forms of pure expression within individuals not normally perceived as 'artists,' showing how expressivity could often be more intense and memorable when coming from those who did not have the social pressure to perform according to professional expectations. De Ridder's radio show *Radiola Salon* guaranteed airtime to virtually anyone who sent in a tape of themselves, not a far cry from Duncan's *Radio Code* experiments.

Personal affiliations overlapped to a notable degree, as well - de Ridder's affair with 'post-porn modernist' and highly sexualized performance artist Annie Sprinkle, and their concurrent desire to transmute their sexual desires into transmittable energy, brought Sprinkle into the orbit of the Hafler Trio's Andrew McKenzie, who himself was involved with Duncan on and off throughout his tenure in Amsterdam (McKenzie also shared a residence with de Ridder at one point.) A frank dialogue between McKenzie and de Ridder exists on tape under the title *This Glass is a Bicycle,* and some of de Ridder's personal thoughts on the nature of human suffering are worth re-printing here for the purpose of contrasting them with Duncan's own:

> There's not one single item in the universe which is out to destroy us. It doesn't exist. We can *think* it like that, and it starts to seem like that, but it's only an illusion. So all our suffering is only because we're volunteers there - it's really what we love to do [...] We don't know anything else. In fact we're so used to it, it feels so much like home, that a lot of people get very *angry* when you tell them they don't have to suffer. [They say] 'oh YEAH? Well I'm gonna suffer! It's my RIGHT to suffer!' You know what I mean? [...] And, great, if you want to do it, you should do it. But all of this feels very uncomfortable, because you're actively resisting the laws of nature.[43]

It would seem that, with positive-minded statements such as these, the ebullient de Ridder would be the perfect foil to Duncan - an artist who, if he has not directly welcomed suffering into his life, has not attempted to diminish its value as a kind of evolutionary mechanism. Whatever their differences may be on this issue, the two artists seem to be in agreement about the usefulness of spontaneity, or of ceding control to variables not given pre-set values by the artist. Continuing from his statements above, de Ridder notes the following:

> You see, our training in struggle, and absorbing discomfort on the path to success, encourages us to really plan in advance. We think we have to plan everything. But…we don't know. We really don't know what's going to happen, all the possibilities, we only make stupid decisions […] So *don't*. You limit yourself tremendously by planning. If you can trust that the universe is a support system, and that all the details are perfectly organized for you better than you could ever organize them yourself, then you [will] lead a fantastic life. […] All you have to know is *what you want*.[44]

With spritely, good-natured characters like de Ridder presiding over the counter-cultural development of Amsterdam (arguably taking on sort of 'elder statesman' role that would also be assigned in the U.S. to Allen Ginsberg or William Burroughs), artistic work done there was bound to have a different flavor to it than that the works accomplished in the blighted low-intensity warzones of Los Angeles or the insomniac mega-sprawl of Tokyo. Or was it? Amsterdam may have offered a stereotypically 'laid-back' atmosphere in comparison to Duncan's other places of residence, but one side effect of this was ample time for reflection and the conclusion of unfinished business, and for refining earlier ideas within the confines of more professional environments (including recording sessions at Sweelink Academy Electronic Music Studio and the STEIM [Studio for Electro-Instrumental Music] Laboratories, home of the LiSA real-time audio manipulation and sampling software.)

Notably, *Radio Code* broadcasts continued on a weekly basis, occasionally offering exclusive recordings of the Japanese underground to Dutch audiences. In Amsterdam Duncan also composed the epic electronic pieces *River in Flames* and *Klaar*, which in a way are his signature recorded works: most of the sonic elements associated with Duncan are painstakingly interwoven into these lengthy, exhaustive audio exegeses: a melting down of previous materials which have run their course, ready to be forged yet again into something new. Von Hausswolff describes *River in Flames* in more vivid terms than my own; as "a cleansing piece where nothing was hidden, nothing was obscure, and nothing was veiled. A naked John Duncan puking his past away like an overdosed Lacan on peyote."[45]

It is a *pièce de résistance* of its form, no matter how we choose to describe it: nerve-tingling computerized warning signals, unbearably intimate Janovian primal screaming and time-reversed moaning, indistinct grey ambience heard through solid walls, ecstatic electrical discharge, and the resurgence of Duncan's shortwave radio...all of these combine to make the penultimate portrait of a world which seems indifferent to our elaborately constructed fictions and histories. The giant coronal mass ejections from the sun, humbling our best attempts to communicate with each other across the radio spectrum, provide just one example.

Another key recording during this period was *The Crackling*, done in collaboration with Max Springer and using the linear particle accelerator at Stanford University as the original sound source. Although this particle accelerator's size now pales in comparison to the mammoth (seventeen miles in circumference) Large Hadron Collider beneath the French-Swiss border, it is still claimed to be the world's longest straight-line object: an amusing side note when considering the very 'non-linear' way in which Duncan's art usually proceeds. Also interesting is the fundamental concept behind these gargantuan atom smashers: making larger and more complex structures in order to seek out the infinitesimally small, the particles which would reveal the very secret of the universe's functioning. The purpose of these vast constructions -probing of dark matter and seeking the universe's early origins- is neatly analogous to Duncan's research with the human organism, seeing as it unashamedly seeks out the sources of our inter-personal friction and neuroses, and our own internal *terra incognita* or psychological and emotional 'dark matter'.

Any hope that Duncan's work, while being based in Amsterdam, would be attenuated in a haze of legalized marijuana smoke and general *laissez faire* ideals was further dashed by installation pieces like *Stress Chamber*, first enacted in 1993 at the "Absolute Threshold Machine Festival" in Amsterdam (the first major Dutch exhibit of 'machine art'.) Consisting of a metal shipping container large enough to accommodate humans inside, and with running motors mounted on three of the four container walls, participants in *Stress Chamber* were told to enter the darkened container completely naked, encountering intense sustained vibrations of a palpable character. Duncan's catalog description of this piece informs us that each motor, equipped with an eccentric flywheel, would cause vibrations at the container's resonant frequency - these fluctuations in vibration then created the sensation of sound as a kinetic object, another 'body' as it were- no longer just a ghostly presence whose place in the hierarchy of human senses was not as elevated or authentic as the sense of touch.

And by this point in Duncan's career, 'touch' is becoming the operative word for nearly all his exhibited and recorded works: and not merely because of his affiliations with a record label of that same name.

Sakaguchi's description of Duncan as a 'stimulation artist' begins to really ring true during this time, as both the touching caused by surface / skin contact and the figurative meaning of 'being touched' - having one's emotions stirred and beliefs interrogated - become recognizable as the sutures holding together this complex body of work. Of special interest is the fact that pieces like *Stress Chamber*, involving a solitary individual subjected to the elements, can arouse as diverse a set of physiological and emotional reactions as pieces involving a direct interface between two humans. The latter category would be best exemplified by *Maze*, another Amsterdam-based piece in which participants voluntarily went nude into a basement room, unaware of when they would be released (some flash photos of this exist as documentation, later projected with a shortwave soundtrack accompanying them.)

When all of Duncan's pieces to this point are surveyed and interpreted as a single ongoing project, several categories of 'touched' individuals emerge: the 'touched from a distance' voyeur (as in the *John See* series of films), the direct participant in a corporeal ritual or ordeal, and the artist himself (who is, after all, hoping to learn from these events, whether a satisfactory audience response is generated or not.) What all these myriad forms of contact achieve is to question whether one 'touch' is truly more 'real' and valuable than the other: obviously one could respond to physical touch with blank indifference and yet be wildly stimulated by erotic simulacra, and vice versa. To his credit, Duncan does not interject himself into the audience's assessment process by saying things must be otherwise, or that certain unguided reactions are contrary to his work's 'intent.'

Love In All Forms: Scrutto di San Leonardo and Beyond

Around 1987 or so, I was very interested in the musical area dealing with noise (more or less 'composed', or at least somehow regulated) and what's commonly intended as 'post-industrial'. It was right then that I met John Duncan's music for the first time, instantly remaining fascinated by that sound. It was clearly evident that his pieces communicated to my whole being through something much different than sheer 'noise'. John's sonic propagations – even the harshest ones – must be placed in the context of that big vibe upon which life itself is based. There's an underlying harmony at work, an awareness of phenomena that no word can explain, but upon which we can rely for the betterment of our persona. About ten years later, I was writing for an Italian new music quarterly so I contacted Mike Harding at Touch to see if Duncan was available for an interview. I thought of him as someone who didn't want to know about stupid things like explaining his art. Imagine my surprise when, fast-forward less than a week, I received a very nice letter from John, who agreed, with an Italian address! The man whose work I admired so much, who I believed to be hidden in some remote arsehole of the world, lived instead near Udine, Italy. When in the interview I asked him why, the reply was 'Love. In all forms'. That should say everything about the man. Needless to say, he's one of the nicest, humblest persons that I ever met."

-Massimo Ricci[46]

At least one form of love, shared between Duncan and the Italian multi-media artist Giuliana Stefani, prompted yet another relocation, from Amsterdam to the village of Scrutto di San Leonardo along the Italian / Slovenian border. This is not too far (at least by this author's hopelessly American interpretation of geographic distance) from where the flamboyant warrior-poet Gabriele D'annunzio once stormed the city Fiume (now Rijeka, in Croatia) and declared it an autonomous state.

The pair of Stefani and Duncan shared a studio in the small hamlet for nearly a decade, a period over which collaborative efforts between the duo expanded to become, in Duncan's own reckoning, "by far the most numerous and formative for my art.")[47] Though working with a host of other sound artists beginning in this period, and cementing his reputation as an innovator in this medium, Duncan does not assume full credit for this sequence of events: "through [Stefani], my work took on a repeatedly positive aspect for the first time...in a deeply intuitive way, she understood the search that drives my work and for a decade did an enormous amount to bring it out into the world, in ways I couldn't have imagined."[48] The duo engaged in a number of live audio performances, including two for *Palace of Mind* (one of which ended exactly as the rollover into the year 2000 occured.) Stefani also coordinated the digital releases of the All Questions label with Duncan, putting into place a label-wide design aesthetic based on her evansecent and landscape-oriented photography.

A stream of CD releases gradually appeared in which Duncan shared lead billing with Elliot Sharp, Asmus Tietchens, Francisco López, and Edvard Graham Lewis (of Wire.) Duncan's aesthetic increasingly lent itself to collaborations with those who were not afraid to use drones, noise, barely perceptible sonic nuances and unorthodox location recordings or experimental processes to activate all possible regions of the human sensorium. Although not directly connected with John Duncan, the ecologically focused Michael Prime again provides some insight into the efforts of this small but potent circle of sound researchers:

> In my music, I try to bring together sounds from a variety of environmental sources into a performance space-particularly sounds which would ordinarily not be audible. I also use live electronic processing to give these sounds new characters, and to enable them to interact in new ways. For instance, traffic sound may be filtered so that it resembles the sound of surf, while actual sea sounds may be transformed to conjure up images of an interstellar dust storm. Electronic processing allows microscopic and macroscopic sounds to interact on an equal basis.[49]

Prime's emphasis on microscopic and macroscopic - bypassing the more easily or readily perceptible aspects of our consensus reality - is something which animated much of the music being composed by Duncan and his colleagues during the late 1990s and the dawning of the 21st century. As such, the kinds of scientific instrumentation used to observe subatomic or cosmic processes were re-envisioned as devices for documenting these processes as a species of communication. Pieces like *The Crackling,* by virtue of their subject matter and source material, had already managed to tackle life at both the micro and macro level.

Meanwhile, affiliates like Mike Harding's Ash International record label, an offshoot of the slightly more "accessible" Touch, gradually became repositories of audio exploration into phenomena of the kind described by Prime. In the Ash International catalog, CD-length examinations of EVP [electronic voice phenomena, or the occurrence of unknown voices, attributed alternately to spirits or alien intelligence, breaking through radio signals] nestle alongside LPs of hypnotizing tones inspired by Anton Mesmer's experiments in animal magnetism, intended to induce hypnagogic states. Duncan's releases on other labels, such as the piece "Change" contributed to the *Mind of a Missile* compilation on the Heel Stone label, succeed on their ability to amplify the sounds of an non-sentient technology (in this case, a missile's guidance system) which nonetheless had a distinct "voice" and limited communicative range. Ambiguity of technology and malleability of perception came to the fore in pieces like this, where the electronic tones produced were ironically quite gentle and languid - even something to be meditated upon - when considering the sounds originated from a device of lethal power.

It is interesting to note that, despite working with such inhuman elements in his sound compositions, Duncan did not fully abandon the corporeal as raw material, a fact which points to his career-long oscillation between themes and materials, and - more interestingly - his refusal to dispose of any particular affective technique once a higher degree of creative technology could be put into play. His 1998 piece *Distraction*, in which strips of acetate were smeared with the artist's blood and set between glass sheets, shows this to be the case, in the most literal sense. The 1998 piece *Specchietto per le Allodole* ['mirror for larks'] also involved Duncan's blood smeared over a rotating cylinder (as seen with a small hole in a gallery wall), and the *Plasma Missives* series from 2009 onward takes inspiration from a Japanese Buddhist monk who copied the text of the sutras in his own blood.

Duncan's interactive installation works, meanwhile, required the audience themselves to submit to a higher-than-usual degree of physical intimacy and volunteered vulnerability within a public space. Duncan's *Voice Contact* piece, enacted in several locations in Stockholm, Tokyo, and Canada from 1998-2000, was one such example of intensified corporeality: this was accomplished by requiring viewers of the piece to strip completely naked and then enter a darkened hotel suite, where a heavy audible drone caused further disorientation and a quiet, beckoning voice would be heard offering instructions to move forward (note the echoes of the earlier *Maze* piece.) More recently (March of 2008) the theme of orientation within the unfamiliar was utilized for *The Gauntlet*, in which visitors to the exhibition space were not required to be naked, but were supposed to navigate their way through the space using small penlights. The uncertainty and fragility of this journey into darkness is occasionally amplified by blaring anti-theft alarms triggered by infrared sensors, once again forcing an unmediated, immediate and honest reaction along the lines of *Scare*.

The same can be said for his *Keening Towers*, an installation set up outside the Gothenburg Art Museum in 2003. Utilizing the recordings of Duncan conducting a children's choir in Italy, which were then projected from 24-meter tall, galvanized steel towers lording over the museum's entrance (making the piece a sort of 'gauntlet' to be run by museum patrons), the eerie piece is difficult to sever from the realm of emotional resonance; from nearly universal conceptions of purity and the sanctity of childhood. It should be noted that the recording of *Keening Towers* was one instance of Duncan taking on the new role of conductor- another from this period would be his concert appearance conducting the noise-friendly Zeitkratzer orchestra, an event for which the artist was veiled in darkness with the exception of his spotlit conductor's hands.

Duncan states that *Keening Towers* was done with the purpose of giving his personal 'ghosts' a voice, and indeed this points to a larger attraction to vocal phenomena - be they 'merely' expressive, or aimed at other communicative functions - as a whole. As Duncan says:

> All of the traditional instruments have their basis in the
> human voice - either imitating the human voice or
> accompanying the human voice. The human voice is so
> complex, it can be manipulated by even the most
> sophisticated instruments that we have available to us
> right now - state of the art, whatever - and at the same
> time, it's still possible to recognize the source as a human
> voice. That is fascinating- I really find that fascinating, and
> that's why I'm working with the human voice so much
> now.[50]

Perhaps the human voice gains this fascinating distinctiveness from its
ability to produce nonlinear effects - owing to the construction of vocal
folds from a tripartite material - whose properties cannot be duplicated by
the vibrating strings on manmade instruments. While these same
instruments would normally have an advantage, by virtue of having larger
resonators compared with that of the human voice, the voice compensates
by using an idiosyncratic energy feedback process: the vocal tract stores
energy during one part of the vibration cycle, and feeds it back to its
source at a more opportune time. The vocal tract can assume a variety of
shapes as well, "mimicking" both a trumpet (minus its valves and coiling
tube) and something like an inverted megaphone. Coupled with this
physiological basis for its unique audial features, the power and versatility
to be found in the small or invisible synchronizes perfectly with the themes
infused in the rest of Duncan's *oeuvre*.

In Every Dream House...

When an artist survives long enough to accumulate an *oeuvre*, this
siutation often demands that there will be an eventual effort by the artist to
take account of past progress, and to synthesize all that has been learned
into a single 'unitary object' or self-referential work. At first hearing,
Duncan's ongoing *Dream House* design project sounded as if it would fall
under this category - Duncan had described it as follows:

> A 7-story building in the shape of a human brain,
> composed of interconnecting 6 x 4 x 4 meter modules or
> rooms, mounted together and held in suspension by cables
> extending from a central mast. Each room, such as RAGE
> ROOM, is designed to embody or evoke a particular state

of consciousness, set in an area of the building that corresponds to its known or suspected location in the brain.[51]

However, Duncan is quick to note that this project is not intended as a "'John Duncan museum'...though the building would probably be large enough to include one."[52] The proposed modular nature of the design, in which "modules [make] it feasible to add many rooms, quickly leading to ones based entirely on fantasy" - with some fantastic exterior attractions including "a bungee jump, with an attendant who fixes a harness and blindfold on you on the way up to the maximum height, then pulls off the blindfold and gives you a kiss before pushing you out backwards," and "a transparent tank full of breathable 'water', where the participant can drown without dying."[53] This modular nature of the *Dream House* also brings Duncan's speculative design closer to radical arhcitectural works like Kisho Kurokawa's Nakagin Capsule Tower, which were intended to inaugurate a kind of non-finalized urban landscape that would 'grow' and decompose in cycles perhaps closer to those followed by organic life. So, with Duncan's cautions against "museum-ification" in mind, this project could be seen in the same way - not as the final statement on an accumulated body of work, but as a re-integration of these past concerns and fantasies into a new environment that has yet to unfold.

Whether we find John Duncan's cultural contributions enervating or invigorating, it is difficult to deny that they encapsulate the best aspects of modern autonomous artwork: they cut 'middlemen' and all other varieties of 'middle ground' out of the picture entirely, they steer clear of pedantry (the camouflaging of half-formed ideas with ornamentation) they champion immersion in the flux of the creative process rather than striving for a specific pre-determined result, and they value mutual exchanges of energy between artist and audience (yet do not always require an audience for the art to proceed in the first place.) The constant motif of purging the unnecessary, and reducing oneself to a compressed core of essential ideas and energy, is another key to both Duncan's process and end product.

The great paradox of an artist like John Duncan is this: the more he reveals himself, going well beyond the accepted boundaries of "confessional" artwork in the process, the more mysterious or enigmatic he seems to appear to the uninitiated. But this is not any fault of the artist himself: if he appears to be a suspect figure, it is a result of the prevailing warped perception of our common era, in which flagrant honesty (and not the faux-honesty of edited "reality" programming) courts suspicion, and ironic distancing is the preferred mode of "communication" for millions. There is no easy cure for a modern culture so heavily steeped in easy distraction, mixed signals or psychological double-binds, and simple self-deception. For those who are ready to accept it, though, the "stimulation art" of Duncan capably shows what is waiting beyond the heavy veil of distraction and deceit.

Uncommon Sense(s):
Synesthesia and Electronic Music

> "...that any affinity at all is possible between a musical composition and a visual representation rests, as we have said, upon the fact that both are simply different expressions of the same inner nature of the world. "[1]

> -Arthur Schopenhauer

Convergence Mania

As any techno-cultural pundit will enthusiastically tell you, the 21st century is the century of "convergence", in which communications technology is increasingly unveiling its own equivalents of the Swiss Army knife: pocket-sized, hand-held, wireless devices which function simultaneously as movie and music players, mobile phones, gaming engines, internet connectivity devices, still image and video cameras, musical instruments, calculators...who knows what other functions will be piled on top of these before this text sees the light of day. With so many functions now capable of being handled by so little equipment and energy expenditure, both utopian and dystopian visions of the future have flown off the shelves at a hitherto unprecedented rate. Prophesies abound that this synthesis of communicative modes and cross-pollination of technological functionality is a stepping stone towards realizing some kind of fully-integrated *Übermensch*; eventually our ability to communicate with and comprehend each other will accelerate to the point where humans morph into sophisticated telepaths. More grandiose yet, there will be some ultimate "awakening" along the lines of what Erik Davis describes in his dizzying techno-mythological primer *TechGnosis*:

> With matter and mind narrowing to a single point of what technology gurus call 'convergence', we will find ourselves sliding down a cosmic wormhole that [Pierre] Teilhard [de Chardin] dubbed the 'Omega Point'. At that node of ultimate synthesis, the internal spark of consciousness that evolution has slowly baked into a roaring fire will finally consume the universe itself.[2]

In other words, the present convergence of technologies - communicative or otherwise - will be just one further step towards the exponentially more awe-inspiring cataclysm that Davis mentions above. On face value this vision is hardly utopian, sharing more in common with the grim eschatology of Norse myths like Ragnarok (in which the earth is consumed by fire and the stars are extinguished from the sky.) Still other prognosticators, like the unabashedly hallucinogen-fueled author Daniel Pinchbeck (his book *2012: The Return of Quetzlcoatl* makes Davis' writings look genteel and unambitious in comparison), welcome such a fate, as it can only bring about a Golden Age, a reversal of the Tao, or some other such species-wide epiphany that will have made surviving the Kali Yuga Dark Age of Ignorance worthwhile. Technological 'convergence' or 'singularity' has become the plaything of starry-eyed eschatologists, whose hope for such may be somewhat more stylish within "alternative" circles than the more popular Christian eschatology. However, one gets the creping feeling that the yearning for salvation still remains among tech-convergence afficionadoes.

While technological synthesis is being put forward as the harbinger of unbelievable revelations to come, other forms of actually-existing synthesis have been somewhat ignored: fascinating fusions much closer to home than the apocalyptic mergers and comic book catastrophes suggested by overwhelmed "tech-Gnostics" and Silicon Valley shamans. Much has been said and printed about the ongoing fusion or dissolution of cultures, of gender, of technological functionality, and plenty more besides– but what about taking this obsession with convergence to a neural and perceptual level, and investigating the fusion of the senses themselves?

Such cross-modal investigations have been with us since antiquity: in China of the Confucian era, cross-sensory speculation occurred when the five tones of the musical scale were seen as harmonizing with the classic Eastern elemental properties of water, fire, wood, metal, and earth. In ancient Greece, the *sensus communis* of Aristotlean thought - a sort of translating faculty that was deemed as separate from the individual senses themselves - was carried over into the Middle Ages, where Thomas Aquinas posited it as one of three 'chambers' in the brain (wherein the *sensus communis* constituted the foremost brain chamber, ratiocination occurred in the middle chamber, and memory was relegated to the 3rd and final chamber.) Aquinas' proposal then survived into the Renaissance, where da Vinci made the slight adjustment of making the *sensus communis* the central brain chamber.

Later, within the intellectual climate of post-Enlightenment Europe, all of these efforts were resuscitated to some degree or another, with the involvement of Johann Wolfgang von Goethe being one of the great catalysts: as a major cultural producer and a theoretical physicist, Goethe's

1810 publication of *Zur Farbenlehre* ['Theory of Colors'] threw down a gauntlet only the most intrepid intellectual adventurers would be able to pick up, and made a daunting implication that anyone dealing with this special subject should be a highly skillful polymath. *Zur Farbenlehre*, a challenge to concepts laid down in Sir Isaac Newton's *Opticks* from the previous century (another work that attempted to match sonic vibrations with wavelengths of light), arguably gave a modern legitimacy to cultural interpretations that followed. Though not even Goethe's studies led to a precise algorithm for the translation of sound into sight, the combined efforts mentioned above had a significant impact on cultural, and particularly sonic, life of the exploratory artist- in the process expanding the disciplinary boundaries that the artist inhabited.

This fertile area of study is only beginning to take shape, as are the provisional alliances being formed between the handful of neurological researchers and multi-disciplinary artists that have found deeper meaning within it.

The Frequency Painters

Among the many famous and / or outrageous proclamations by the artist Marcel Duchamp, one deserves special attention within this discussion: his encouragement for other prospective artists to "make a painting of frequency." At the time, such a suggestion must have seemed like just another eccentric aphorism meant to further confound the guardians of the art establishment. In the present age, though, making a "painting of frequency" has never been easier: if we use the acoustical definition of frequency - the number of cycles per second (cps), now more commonly noted as hertz (Hz) - it would be simple to do this in a very literal sense. One would merely have to choose a frequency and paint a waveform, with the appropriate number of peaks and troughs, along a timeline: peaks and troughs massed more closely together for a higher frequency, and placed further apart for a lower one. However, painting a frequency, in the traditional sense of the word, has not been necessary since the advent of the oscilloscope: an electrical device that basically, on its display screen, makes a "painting" of a frequency every time it is operated. Its value as a tool that can provide visuals, however minimal, in a 1:1 ratio with a corresponding sound, is not lost on the group Pan Sonic. The Finnish duo have used oscilloscope readings in sound installations and concerts to further enhance the physical presence and precision of their rolling, faultlessly rhythmic sub-bass tides. Coming full circle, it was Duchamp himself who ended up following his own advice, during one of his many chess matches (Duchamp actually preferred chess to art, calling it "much purer than art in its social position".) In a now-legendary chess match with the composer John Cage, the chessboard was miked and attached to an oscilloscope which would 'interpret' the sounds of the chess pieces gently thumping on the field of play.

Synesthesia is the neurological term used for fusing of the senses, in which one type of sensory information leads to involuntary responses from another sensory modality. Within modern culture, this still seems to be a bizarre and novel thing, since we are acclimated to distinct compartmentalization and occasional hierarchical ordering of the senses. Synesthesia, although it has often been a topic of consideration by the post-Enlightenment scientific community, is still brushed aside by many as an unreliable pseudo-science, or as the whimsy of 'loose cannon' mystics who have the most tangential connections to the larger social universe. It is arguable that it has only gained any real traction in a peer-based research community only over the last quarter-century or so (papers looked over for material to supplement this chapter almost all dated from the past fifteen years.) If criticisms against researchers of synesthesia are harsh, though, then harsher still are the shots fired in the direction of actual people claiming to be synesthetes themselves. Many are assumed to be just attention-hungry, poetic eccentrics with an above-average skill for wordplay, or outcasts desperately trying to put a sexy gloss on their alienation by convincing the world at large that they possess a mutant sensory awareness. Still others are portrayed as the casualties of hallucinogen overkill, having fried their brains on dissociative drugs, now caught in a state where their senses have been permanently cross-wired.

The latter group of people are still some of the most maligned in pop culture: the stereotype of the "way-out hippie" who can barely maintain an ambulatory state while *"hearing colors, man"* has proven to be comic gold in a ruthlessly pragmatic era divorced from the psychedelic daydreams of yore. Their spiritual forebears among the Romanticists and Symbolists did, it must be admitted, do much to forge the link between synesthesia and voluntarily 'altered states' of consciousness, what with Charles Baudelaire's legacy of quasi-synesthetic "correspondence art" probably informed by his hashish-induced trances in the *Club des Haschishins*.

Of course, drug users would still be distinguishable from synesthetes even if they were in the quite impossible state of permanent 'tripping', since the sense impressions received by the former would have a much higher degree of variance than that of the latter: for true synesthetes, there is a striking and often life-long consistency among their responses in which, for example, the ringing of a telephone would not be perceptible as anything *but* "green." Neurologist and synesthesia expert Richard Cytowic notes that these connections are so deeply ingrained within synesthetes' percpetual faculties as the "logical" working of the world, that "to lose [synesthesia] would be a catastrophe, an odious state akin to going blind or not being alive at all...synesthetes have a well-developed innate memory that is amplified by use of the parallel sense as a mnemonic device."3

Curiously, not all drug users even experience synesthetic effects while 'tripping', either, thanks to a wide variety of variables in brain chemistry (and equally important to note is that drugs such as LSD often do not induce synesthesia within those already diagnosed with the condition.)4 If synesthetes are not mistaken for psychedelic drug users, the belief still persists that the various means of communicating the synesthetic experience, (especially verbally) are no more than particularly apt metaphorical expressions. This is what we might call instead *hyperesthesia*, or an increased ability to receive a stimulus in a single sensory modality, which then 'spills over' into other sensory impressions after this fact-something rather different from the synchronous triggering of sensory modalities that is synesthesia. Sorting out these *voluntary* metaphorical expressions from *involuntary* experiences with synesthesia can be a difficult undertaking indeed.

Having considered what synesthetes are *not*, some simple facts about the distribution of synesthetes among the general population is in order here. Statistically, the vast majority of synesthetes appear to be women, with multiple studies placing the occurrence of synesthesia at a ratio of 6 females for every 1 male. This is particularly interesting in light of the synesthetes acknowledged by recent pop culture who are skewed more in the direction of maleness. The synesthete's urge to creatively express their perceptive anomalies may also come from the predominance of synesthetes who are dominantly 'right-brained' (this in turn leads to a disproportionate amount of left-handed synesthetes.) It's also interesting to note the hereditary nature of synesthesia, which affected the family of author and acknowledged synesthete Vladimir Nabokov (and of which he writes in both "Portrait of My Mother" [1949] and his autobiography *Speak, Memory* [1966]). This hereditary aspect of the condition, in fact, has been used as a defense by one of synesthesia's leading legitimizers, Dr. Vilayanur S. Ramachandran. Responding to the common argument that many so-called 'synesthetes' are just adults who associate numbers and colors due to certain memory-enhancing games played during their childhood development, he dismisses the skeptics' claim that

> "...*synesthetes 'played with numerical magnets' when they were children.* Five was red, six was blue, seven was purple, and it just stuck in their minds. This never made much sense to me. If there's a relationship between playing with magnets and childhood memories and synesthesia, why don't we all have synesthesia? Why does synesthesia only run in

certain families?"[5]

Ramachandran is referring here to what is reported as the most common form of synesthesia: 'grapheme-color' synesthesia, a form which, when authentic cases of it are discovered, tends to be a congenital form of the condition passed down along the x-chromosome. In grapheme-color synesthesia, written or audible numbers, letters or other snatches of text are associated with a color that does not change from one instance to the next. A verifiable synesthete, although he or she might see a number written in black ink in front of them, may still ascribe a different color to that number in their mind's eye: without the black-inked number 7 placed in front of them, they will invariably "see" that 7 as "yellow." One prominent example of this grapheme-color coordination is, according to researcher Patrick Martin, "the almost universal agreement, amongst those who bear this ability, that 'O' has a brown texture and 'I' has a whitish hue."[6] There is a definite neural basis for this phenomenon, since the part of the brain's temporal lobe dealing with number recognition –the fusiform gyrus- is situated right next to the part normally associated with processing color information.

Having said all this, the type of synesthesia most often employed or simulated by electronic multi-media artists of the day -synthesis of sight and sound- is adventitious as opposed to inherited, raising the amount of skepticism that musicians may be true synesthetes rather than just creators of convincing yet scientifically ungrounded experiments in sensory flux. Obviously, in English a 'tone' can refer both to a grade of visible light and of sound, and in German the word for 'timbre' –klangfarbe- translates directly to 'sound color.' With the total number of practicing artists far outpacing the number of acknowledged synesthetes, the amount of art meant to *evoke* synesthetic experience is naturally far more common than art driven by the experience itself. Still, musicians as diversified in approach as jazz bandleader Duke Ellington and György Ligeti have confessed to some form of synesthetic experience. The latter stated that, for him,

> ...major chords are red or pink, minor chords are somewhere between green and brown. I do not have perfect pitch, so when I say that C minor has a rusty red-brown colour and D minor is brown this does not come from the pitch but from the letters C and D.[7]

Ellington's synesthetic confessions are more eyebrow-raising, however, considering the new variables he injects into the experience: the 'colors' of sounds can change depending on the *person* they are associated with, and the image of these sounds is broadened to include not just color, but texture:

> I hear a note by one of the fellows in the band and it's one color. I hear the same note played by someone else and it's a different color. When I hear sustained musical tones, I see just about the same colors that you do, but I see them in textures. If Harry Carney is playing, D is dark blue burlap. If Johnny Hodges is playing, G becomes light blue satin.[8]

The Russian composer Aleksandr Scriabin was aligned with Helena Blavatsky's Theosophical Society, also a considerable influence on the painter Wassily Kandinsky and his manifesto *Über das Geistige in der Kunst* ['Concerning The Spiritual In Art'], notable for its claim that "the actual expression of color can be achieved simultaneously by several forms of art."[9] A small but intriguing book from the Theosophist elite, *Thought-Forms*, was essentially an esoteric manual for determining corresponding values of sound, color, and emotion.[10] Scriabin - like Blavatsky, or any other Theosophist for that matter - was never proven to be a synesthete, but did develop one of the earliest 'synesthesia simulators' in his 'light organ', a feat for which he usually gets top billing among artists both genuinely synesthetic and 'pseudo-synesthetic.' As can be guessed by the frequent references within his work to divinity, ecstacy and all things Promethean, the composer was on a sacred quest to renew the world through art, and one way to do this was to merge audible and visual information. Blavatsky insisted, for one, that five "sacred colors" needed to be arranged in a specific way in order to properly conduct magical rituals.

Scriabin's theory of color was also influenced by Isaac Newton and his pioneering work *Opticks* (Newton assigned a different color to each interval in the musical circle of 5ths.) Scriabin then streamlined this theory by associating spiritual qualities to the tone-colors: blue and violet lent themselves better to spiritual flight, while reddish tones were more earthy or associated with the material realm. By this logic, one might instinctively expect a higher frequency to correspond to the a higher end of the spectrum of visual light, when mapped onto a keyboard. This is not the case with Scriabin's system, where F-sharp is the "blue" note while the lower D-flat is violet. Many contemporaries were understandably skeptical of these associations, although Scriabin did have an ally in 'colored sound' convert Rimsky-Korsakov. It was he who attempted to convince the wary Sergei Rachmaninoff about his theory, using one scene in Rachmaninoff's opera *The Miserly Knight* as an illustrative example that Rachmaninoff was unconsciously promoting a synesthetic compositional method. The scene involved the opening of some gold-filled treasure chests and was scored in D-major, the key that Scriabin associated with yellow or 'gold.'

As much as epiphanies like this one gave Scriabin reason to boast, posthumous discoveries point to the fact that he built up his theory of color gradually, rather than having known these correspondences from early childhood development, as a *bona fide* synesthete would. In the Scriabin museum, there exist notebooks containing several different hand-written versions of his correspondences between musical and visual tones- even without exact dates ascribed to them, it becomes obvious that the composer was gradually refining a system rather than always being possessed of a unique color-sound translation ability.

In The Simulation Arcade: DIMI, UPIC, and Beyond

It is precisely the association of synesthetic research with Blavatsky's impassioned, yet not always defensible program of enlightenment that has led neurological researchers such as Richard Cytowic to fret over the accusations of their peers, i.e. that such research is "too weird...too New Age." Yet modern musicians and composers seem to have, for the most part, gotten beyond the ideological 'Scriabin syndrome'- the belief that one's highly subjective theory of light and sound has universal resonance. As per Peter Christopherson of Coil:

> The generation of patterns of light triggered by sound is a tricky business. Mechanically one is quite limited to interference patterns etc. Automatic devices such as the I-tunes Visualizer do an amazing job given the limitations of the technology, but still tend to produce 'moving wallpaper' that lacks some element of humanity [...] Generally I know that the mind is able to assume or feel connections between all kinds of images and sounds, in all sorts of ways that are far more complex than the simple generation of pattern (interesting though that is), and it is these connections that I find more interesting at this point. For example the way the music of THBC [Threshold House Boys' Choir] effects one's perception of the images on the dvd [accompanying their *Form Grows Rampant* CD].[11]

Others from the post-Industrial milieu, like text-sound performer and percussionist Z'ev, seem similarly unconcerned with making a 'perfect' 1:1 correspondence between sound and any other sense, acknowledging that there will be a multitude of sensory reactions to any given sound stimuli, and that a universal reaction will be very difficult to attain. Yet some still believe they can instill aspects of the synesthetic experience in an audience by means of sonic overload, or by the removal of sensory elements that would normally be present in a concert environment. The habit of performing in the dark - a practice increasingly common among electronic musicians, from Francisco López to Andrew Liles[12]- is one way to bring this about. Z'ev suggests that, in a situation where there is paradoxically much more sonic information than visual information, some kind of synesthesia can arise through entoptic phenomena (light being *visualized* without light actually penetrating the eye):

> After about 1985 […] I started to perform primarily in the dark , and in that context the music triggers a synesthetic experience. That is, it triggers the naturally occurring phosphene activity, like what will happen if you close your eyes right now… you will be seeing some sort of *something* there. When you are in the a place that is so dark that when you open your eyes there is no light, the phosphene activity is enhanced and begins to respond to the sound stimuli which is occurring as I play. People have a variety of experiences, ranging from abstract imagery to geometric imagery to cartoony type things to visuals which are as very representational, as if it were a dream.[13]

One manifestation of the phosphene activity that Z'ev mentions is the habit of 'seeing stars': amorphous blotches of deep color appearing before the eyes when there has been some form of bodily impact - a blow to the head - or occasionally from an explosive bout of sneezing. Given the sheer volume and bodily impact that can be generated by Z'ev's chthonic play with metallic percussion, this sort of thing is far from impossible. Francisco López also bears witness to this fact, suggesting complex eidetic imagery can result from a forced hyper-concentration upon audio output exclusively:

> I have extensive direct experience of this from audience feedback in my concerts with blindfolds for the audience, which I've been regularly carrying out since the mid-90s. The forceful and voluntary acceptance of the blindfolded listening (more emphatic than having a dark space, as most spaces in these situations are not really dark) dramatically promotes synesthetic "visions" in most people, from the abstract / emotional to the weirdly narrative (in the long list of imagined narratives I've heard things like "I felt like on a trip from hell to heaven",

"flying inside gigantic moving machines", "dinosaurs eating soup", or "shreds of laminar light going through my body.")[14]

As maligned as the stereotypical "way-out hippie" of the 1960s may be, with his catalog of unrealized dreams, the sensual creatures of this era at least provided the enthusiastic atmosphere in which some impressive innovations could occur, among them some prototype sense-fusing machines. The Finnish composer Erkki Kurenniemi is one such character, who, surprisingly, considering the work he has accomplished, did not graduate from university, claiming that he "...found the theoretical physics of the time faulty and wrong."[15] Elaborating on this, he states that "perhaps my rebellion also involved the question whether the world is definite or indefinite, continuous or discrete. I made a somewhat loud exit in the early 1970s."[16]

Kurenniemi tapped into the '60s' spiritually-inclined and sensual 'flower child' *zeitgeist* with a variety of novel electronic devices, one of the most whimsical being the DIMI-S or "sexophon", an instrument to be played by 2-4 players, whose tactile interactions with each other's bodies would cause wild sonic fluctuations (with practice, functions like tempo and pitch can be tamed by careful users, but unbridled randomness may also be part of the fun.) A recent DVD overview of Kurenniemi's work features footage of the composer teamed up with CM von Hausswolff and countrymen Pan Sonic, in a rare moment of physical humor, mischievously tagging each other on the forehead and clasping each other's hands as the machine converts their movements into sound. It's amusing to observe the DIMI-S' electronic warbles uncannily corresponding to the musicians' bodily interchanges: evasive little musical phrases with metallic timbres zip in and out of one's perception like a ball being kicked through midair. Although these movement-sound syntheses could eventually be developed into a communicative system, the lure of pure play seems to be stronger.

Other tools developed by Kurenniemi included the "andromatic sequencer", the DICO [digitally-controlled oscillator], the DIMI-A 2-channel digital synthesizer, and the DIMI-O video-controlled organ. The latter instrument was a keyboard with a 4-octave range and an attached video camera and video monitor. Images captured by the camera and visualized on the attached monitor could by 'played' once the image was stored into memory. A horizontally moving vertical bar, appearing on the monitor screen, represented a time axis during playback of pre-drawn images. In a promotional image for the DIMI-O, circuit designer Hannu Viitasalo is shown sitting in front of the keyboard and cheerfully 'playing' a frozen image of his own face. For machines built in the tail end of the 1960s and the early 1970s, Kurenniemi's devices appear amazingly versatile in terms of their interfaces. Kurenniemi, no slouch when it came to tonal theory or computer science, also realized early on the ability of 3D computer graphics to represent musical notation: rather than merely porting the old system of staff-based sheet music over to the computer, Kurenniemi felt that "geometrical objects in the tonal space, like divisor lattices and cylinders...offer a natural way to classify musical chords and scales."[17]

Maybe it is the misfortune of Finland's non-central position in world culture (and the difficulty of translating the Finnish language, with its complex streams of harmonic vowels and its baffling morphology) that keeps Kurenniemi's work somewhat obscure while the synesthetic developments of a composer like Iannis Xenakis continue to gain traction and generate discussion in intellectual forums. Whatever the reason, it is a shame that Kurenniemi does not receive larger exposure, but at the same time it does not diminish the great value of Xenakis' own discoveries. Principal among these is the development of the UPIC[18] musical composition tool (completed in 1977), a freehand drawing interface for musical composition powered by 64 oscillators, and championed by, among others synthesis wizard Jean-Claude Risset. Having been trained as an architect in addition to his training in musical composition, Xenakis had always had a connection to using graphic representations as a starting point for a final work, although the composer warns that the genesis of the UPIC system was more a matter of "music itself", and the accessibility thereof. Xenakis had, since the composition of his work *Metastasis* in 1953-1954, utilized graphic notation as a means of drawing out complex musical effects that could not be achieved with traditional stave notation. As he recalls,

> ...when I wrote for orchestras, some of the things were too complicated to be specified in stave notation. So I had to introduce a graphic notation which, by the way, is also more universal. Everybody can understand a line, whereas you have to do specific studies in order to understand what the symbols of traditional writing in music mean.[19]

UPIC's functioning is not all that different from Kurenniemi's DIMI-O equipment, or the waveform-shaping tool used in the seminal Fairlight CMI [Computer Music Instrument]: patterns are drawn with an electromagnetic stylus on a tabletop screen containing an x-axis (for a composition's duration) and a y-axis (pitch.) Like Kurenniemi's DIMI-O, a horizontal line moves across the screen containing the graphic score during playback. The UPIC system interprets this playback in real-time, allowing the composer / performer to make further manipulations and envelope changes to a score as the score's information is being processed by the computer. Yet it can still not be emphasized enough that Xenakis, despite his own academic pedigree, clearly intended the UPIC system not to be used exclusively by professional musicians: to advertise the fact, a charming picture exists of the seasoned composer smiling as three small children hover around the machine, one standing on tip-toes to reach its control panel. This realization would take some time, as the first "real-time" operation of UPIC would only be achieved in 1987, and the only PC or commercial version made available in 1991. Yet like much in this book, the concept's survival into the 21st century has spawned some of its most interesting and meaningful output to date.

During a residency at CCMIX Paris, the computer-savvy artists Russell Haswell & Florian Hecker used music composed on the UPIC device to initiate what they called 'diffusion sessions,' concerts in which massive volume, extended frequency range and the coordinated activity of sweeping light beams all came together in a sense-fusing spectacle. It was a demonstration of adventitious synesthesia on two levels, since it involved both converting graphics into sound on the UPIC machine, and then loosely syncing that sound output to the house lighting. Although fancy laser light shows have long been a mainstay of big-budget concerts, and a useful distraction from sub-par music, some observation of these diffusion sessions shows that the lighting is not behaving in a completely arbitrary manner. For example, as the UPIC tones glide from low rumble to keening highs, a column of blue light beams will rise from the floor to the ceiling, or fan-shaped swathes of green light will move with a dizzying speed that accompanies the complicated morphing of the UPIC sound signals. In many circumstances, the artists forego the typical stage setup and situate themselves in the center of a performance space for the diffusion sessions, letting the audience mill around them and try to find their bearings. Ironically, considering the colorful way in which these UPIC sessions proceed, a 2007 recording of Haswell and Hecker's UPIC-based compositions is called *Blackest Ever Black,* inspired by a special laboratory-engineered black paint that is used on optical devices to swallow up any light that strikes them. Also notable is the graphic information which the artists fed into the UPIC machine to be interpreted: photo documentation of the 2004 Madrid train bombings, nuclear test sites, and so on- the uncomfortable shudders of atonality and spastic violence on *Blackest Ever Black* are all that we, as listeners, have to go by, but they would seem to sync all too well with visual information of this kind.

While artists such as Haswell & Hecker captivate audiences with their exhibitions of UPIC-based diffusion synthesis, others have been hard at work developing synesthetic software for home PC use. If nothing else, this progression grants Xeankis' wish, i.e. "I hope that this development will continue also with the help of manufacturers; their task is to forge ahead in implementation technology and to make it better, faster, and cheaper!"[20] Digital-age tools for producing synesthetic experience are indeed becoming more and more accessible, with many of them available as shareware or freeware programs (though determining whether or not these tools are "better" than their predecessors is a hopelessly subjective matter.) It can be argued that their proliferation owes itself to the long-standing tendency of electro-acoustic composers to begin work on new pieces by graphic means rather than sonic ones: in a notable survey, the research team of Jean-Baptiste Thiebaut and Patrick G. T. Healey noted that, among these composers,

> the most commonly reported initial representation of a [musical] piece was a drawing (50%)...in most cases these concepts are rendered in a visual representation. In contrast to this, only 5 people in the sample develop the first stages of composition using specific sound parameters.[21]

Given that Xenakis' UPIC machine was developed long before currently popular music software suites such as ProTools, its main strength lay in the creation of convincingly original timbres rather than in its use as an editing tool. Perhaps hoping to correct this, Adrien Lefevre and the La Kitchen studio began work in 2001 on the Iannix program, the output of which can be mapped to applications such as Max / MSP. The irony of focusing on such integrations was that the user interface of Iannix was nothing like the 'sketch tablet' of UPIC, instead offering the user a set of manipulable, pre-built objects as controllers. However, this has been far from the last word on synesthetically inspired composition software. With a notable increase in the number of tools capable of "transcoding", i.e. initializing the state in which "a given dataset or signal is simultaneously visualized or sonified,"[22] the claims made in 2009 by a *Contemporary Music Review* research team (regarding the lack of "computer musicians'" interest in algorithmic synesthesia) are being increasingly refuted.[23]

Although they are both dated by several years now, the Metasynth program, IRCAM's AudioSculpt, Hyperscore and the Coagula 'light organ' (a nod to Scriabin's innovation of the same name) still have the potential to surprise those who are new to ideas of sensory fusion: both programs allow an user to have an audio engine interpret on-screen brushstrokes or color gradients, resulting in sounds that would be described as glassy and luminous at best, hollow and anemic at worst. Slow firing of laser beams, monochromatic bursts of white noise and muted, peripatetic warbling are recurring motifs. The results rarely, if ever, are recognizable to the conditioned ear as melodic or harmonic, but careful looping and editing of the results can add the desired level of musicality while still retaining the alien timbres unique to the software. Some of the light-sound correspondences in a now-dated program like Metasynth are dead simple: a plain black patch signals an interlude of silence, while alternating strips of black and white color will create a crude rhythm using the aforementioned white noise bursts. The tempo increases or decreases depending on how far apart the bars of color are spaced. When it comes to interpreting more complex visual information, though, we are left wondering what things would really sound like if a more sophisticated method of interpretation existed. Surely the glassy and static-laden sound output coming from these programs is too limited in comparison to the variety of visual input that can be fed into the software.

Then there is Argeiphontes' Lyre, a synthesis program developed by the magical realist and romanticist Akira Rabelais- this freely downloadable toolkit comprises many of the functions normally contained in academically-based synthesis software, such as the randomizing and convolution of sound files, and it also visibly sets itself apart from the vast majority of software applications by employing a translucent, cloud-like graphic user interface. No documentation or 'help' file exists to tell you what controller corresponds to what function; one tool named "The Lobster Quadrille" (which overrides the computer's buffering in order to make violently chopped and stuttering sound streams) can only be learned by regular practice since its control buttons are labeled with lines from a Lewis Carroll poem.

While one manipulates the program's various parameters, random phrases and clusters of symbols appear across the bottom of the Lyre's screen, which in turn become the name of the user's saved output file. The Lyre is a distinctive meld of soft-edged Surrealism and cold, hard coding. It is something that would best be appreciated by those who are as enthralled by automatic writing as they are by, say, Fibonacci chains and "floating point" arithmetic. It certainly points at one direction computer-based art may be heading as interfaces become much more 'organic', 'squishy' and ductile (Bruce Sterling refers to this trend as the rise of the "blobject.") And, naturally, it contains a synesthetic audio-to-video converting function. The user selects a sound file and then manipulates the size, resolution and playback speed of the video output file, also choosing a background color and dominant foreground color (subject to some deviation) for the resulting visuals. What one gets varies from flickering and fading flames of to an approximation of the chaotic whorls and scribbles in Harry Smith's hand-painted films. Like Metasynth or Coagula, the anticipation of the result is half the fun, and points to the ever-expanding possibilities of using computers as improvisational tool. Like the above programs, though, the parameters to be manipulated do not really contain enough variables to make a perfect 'translation' of a sound, even though startling synchronicities do crop up from time to time. Just as Metasynth produces an increasingly predictable palette of sounds from an infinite number of visuals, the reverse occurs with the visualizer in Argeiphontes' Lyre.

While the aforementioned software applications seem tailored towards use on home or studio computers, other interfaces have been developed with an eye towards the performance arena. Early developments such as Kuriennemi's DIMI-S seem almost quaint in comparison to the tools used by the Sensorband trio, which again brings the influence of Xenakis (as well as of legitimate synesthete Olivier Messiaen),[24] into the picture (Sensorband member Zbigniew Karkowski studied under both individuals). Each individual in this group (Karkowski, Atau Tanaka and Edwin van der Heide) performs on a novel instrument functioning as a 'bio-musical signal interface.' Karkowski's instrument, the 'strings' of which are infrared beams cutting through a scaffold enclosure or 'cage', produces percussive sounds that vary in accordance with his physical movements, e.g. the strength of his hand slashes or duration of a hand being placed directly in a beam's path.

The Soundnet is a tool built along the same principles, meant to be played by all three members at once. Bert Bongers notes that its "technology aspect is modest compared to the physical aspect...the rope, the metal, and the humans climbing on it require intense physicality, and focus attention on the human side of the human-machine interaction, not on mechanistic aspects such as interrupts, mouse clicks, and screen redraws."[25] This 11 x 11m net-like structure, strung together with 16mm-thick shipping ropes that are fitted with movement sensors on their endpoints, appears like some sort of military training implement meant to develop recruits' climbing skills. The physical challenge that Bongers hints at above is a key to the unpredictability of its sonic output, and also to the need for its players to be completely reliant upon each other in order to pull off a passably musical performance (the digital sound samples triggered by the sensors are recordings of natural phenomena, which heightens the already strong feeling of "natural, organic elements...in direct confrontation with technology.")[26]

For reasons that will have to remain speculative (but may have something to do with a high learning curve[27] and production costs), nothing exactly like Sensorband's instrumental innovations has yet appeared on the consumer electronics market. This is unfortunate, since these tools answer a question about electronic music performance previously posed by Bob Ostertag:

> I think most musicians working with electronics are probably not very satisfied with the state of electronic music today, and the crucial missing element is the body. Many of us have been trying to solve this problem for years, but we have been notoriously unsuccessful at it.

> How to get your body into art that is as technologically mediated as electronic music, or anything with so much technology between your physical body and the final outcome, is a thorny problem.[28]

Despite the fact that we are always responding 'bodily' to sound, since it is a physical phenomenon that - especially when experience at high volumes and extreme frequencies - can cause noticeable metabolic effects like nausea, it seems that we still expect some proof of this via the exagerrated or dramatized movements of a sound performer. Writing on Atau Tanaka's work with the BioMuse, Louise Provencher lauds his theatrical production of an "immersive situation" and the "seductive" nature of this performance, which is "not one of subjection... [it] opens up the possibility of a free play between control and relinquishment...it is the contrary of domesticated sound."[29] So one obvious use for these types of performances is their reintroduction of a component of challenge, or even struggle, into an arena that audiences are increasingly perceiving as being automated and pre-programmed to minimize any form of uncertainty (even if said uncertainty could be an illuminating part of the total experience.) Karkowski himself has criticized the risk-free performances of Ryoji Ikeda and Carsten Nicolai (to be introduced in short order) for their habit of "just playing sound files" unmodified from what would appear on their commercially available CDs.[30]

So while the performances of Sensorband arguably have more to do with dramatizing our proprioceptive awareness and environmental orientation than they have to do with synesthesia, both their work and that of 'live' displays of algorithmic synesthesia seem like attempts at addressing similar ontological concerns.

On The Crest of a Wave

In reviewing a performance of Alvin Lucier's 1972 piece *Queen of the South,* Morag Josephine Grant uncovers an intriguing visual phenomenon, described as follows:

> [the piece] is written for a number of instruments connected via amplification to raised, responsive surfaces on which granulated material is strewn; the surfaces are arranged in such a way that they are excited by the sounds created by the performers (for example, through amplification placed directly underneath). In a

performance which took place in Berlin in 1999, each performer played a single, elongated tone. As they played, the vibrations created caused the material on the surfaces to move. As they continued to play, the material formed into wave patterns, slightly different for each instrument. Few pieces could better demonstrate that music, far from being the stuff of angels, is the stuff of the world, depending as much on physics as metaphysics for its existence. And Lucier's sonogram in the sand is perhaps the most blatant and yet effective demonstration possible of that form of signification which distinguishes experimental composition.[31]

While this spectacle was, without a doubt, executed well by Lucier, its signature element of "sonograms in the sand" is not Lucier's own- proper credit for this aesthetic device belongs instead to one Dr. Hans Jenny. It is somewhat interesting to note that, despite the admirable efforts of software and hardware designers to create new means of simulating the synesthetic experience, one quite successful method was discovered over a half-century ago by Jenny, *without* the aid of any computerized equipment. His particular school of synesthetic study would be called *cymatics* (from the Greek word for wave, "kyma".) Jenny's studies in wave phenomena, their kinetics, and their dynamics are sadly overlooked or unknown by most practitioners of electronic music -only two volumes of Jenny's studies are currently in print- but the conclusions drawn by his research into phenomenology would be well worth looking at again, as we collectively lurch towards the discovery of more accurate and effective light and sound machines.

Dr. Jenny's method seems almost laughably simple compared to the complex algorithmic instructions necessary to realize some of the software already mentioned; a decidedly more "low-budget" form of scientific rigour. For his cymatic experiments, Jenny would place substances such as sand or viscous fluids on a metal plate, which was in turn attached to an oscillator controlled by a frequency generator. The plate would amplify the vibrations of the oscillator, and, as the tones produced by the frequency generator were raised or lowered, different patterns would appear in the previously stationary materials: almost without fail, higher frequencies would produce more intricate and elegant patterns in the vibrating piles of sand, gelatin, or whatever other material Jenny was using at the time. As was the case with Lucier's *Queen of the South*, these transformations depend "not only on the aural presence of sound waves but their physical impact on inanimate as well as animate bodies…the waves in the sand do not merely represent the sound waves but are actually caused by them."[32]

The current publisher of Jenny's cymatic studies admits to his awe when seeing a small pool of glycerin reveal a "snake" while under the influence of sound waves and some strategic lighting. In these experiments, the tendency of the higher frequencies to 'sculpt' forms with spiritual connotations, such as complex *mandalas* or *yantras*, eerily approached Arthur Schopenhauer's personal philosophy of frequency: namely, that higher tones corresponded to a striving toward superhuman greatness while the lower, almost inaudible tones corresponded to the inorganic: the planet's lifeless and will-less forms and masses. It is interesting to note that Scriabin reached roughly the same conclusion with visible light, insisting that the colors we understand to be the highest on the electromagnetic spectrum also correspond with the "higher" qualities of man: violet was the color representing the transformation of matter into spirit, or the color of 'will to creativity.'

Schopenhauer quoted Aristotle on this matter as saying "how does it come about that rhythm and melodies, although only sounds, resemble states of the soul?" Answering this question, Schopenhauer wrote that "I recognize in the deepest tones of harmony, in the bass, the lowest grades of the will's objectification,"[33] and that "…in the high, singing, principal voice leading the whole and progressing with unrestrained freedom […] I recognize the highest grade of the will's objectification, man's conscious life and endeavour."[34] To Jenny's line of thinking, density or heaviness, manifested in bass tones, represented physicality, while flights of thought and emotion were manifest in 'lighter', more evanescent, higher tones. The only key difference here is that Schopenhauer wrote explicitly of his era's *music* – lavish symphonies and concertoes - while Jenny deals primarily with the simple, constant tones produced by standing waves.

At any rate, Jenny's own will was being crystallized by his cymatic experiments: his desire to display to others a 'unitary phenomenon,' a more holistic way of perceiving, bore more convincing results than his meager present-day fame lets on. His primary concern was with demonstrating nature as a "triadic phenomenon" of periodicity, shape and dynamics, not with simulating synesthetic experience- although the latter has seemingly come about as an unintended consequence of researching the former. Seeing that changes in the vibrational field were the fundamental cause of changes in natural phenomena, it was not difficult to at least try and detect some correlation between sound and visuals. Jenny was an enthusiastic polymath, both a musician who was "equally at ease improvising jazz as performing a piano sonata,"[35] and who was also a "tireless observer of the natural world."[36] Thanks to such universally applicable enthusiasm, he has had a few prominent acolytes within the fields of music and sound art: if nothing else, Jenny's work with standing waves was no small influence on Alvin Lucier's highly influential *Bird And Person Dyning* installation.

Younger proselytizers of Jenny-ism exist in the upper echelons of 21st century art, as well. One artist with both feet firmly planted in the cymatic - or at least synesthetic - mode of creativity is the ambitious Carsten Nicolai (Rob Young affirms his forays into algorithmic synesthesia by noting a now-familiar theme: "in Nicolai's work neither music nor visual art are by-products of one another - the one calls the other into being.")[37] The artist's most "Jenny-centric" work is probably *Milch* from 2000- true to its title, the piece involves pools of milk being subjected to imperceptible audio frequencies from 10 to 150 Hz, causing the liquid to reconstitute itself into a number of different irregular patterns: concentric circles at the lowest frequencies and densely-packed masses of quivering goose bumps at the slightly higher ones (some of the visual results have since been used as the cover artwork for one of Nicolai's CDs, *For*, recorded under his Alva Noto alias.) Cymatics are a motif that Nicolai has returned to time and time again in his work, including the 2001 piece *Wellenwanne* ['wave pool'] and the captivating phenomenological study *Snow Noise*. For the latter installation piece, gallery visitors approach a set of 3 glass cylinders aligned in a row and placed atop 3 identical white boxes containing cooling units. Almost instantaneously, snow crystals begin to form as random noise generators provide the soundtrack to this of transformation of matter. The congruence between the irregularities of the tiny crystals and the random attacks of audio "fuzz" is startling, even though we have been inundated with cultural references (white noise as "snow", etc.) pointing at this relationship before, and often took this relationship for granted.

In the East German town of Chemnitz in 1994, the trained landscaper Nicolai founded one of the more unique electronic music labels to date, in terms of a holistic or integrated approach to packaging and aural content: the Noton *Arkhiv für Ton und Nichtton* [archive for sound and 'non-sound'], later consolidated as Raster / Noton in 1999 with partners Frank Bretschneider and Olaf Bender (also his partners in the electronic trio "Signal.") Nicolai's abiding fascination with mathematics leaks into the design scheme of his releases: the characteristic static-proof bags and translucent clam-shell cases which house Raster / Noton CDs, overlaid with their unassuming and unobtrusive fonts, can seem at times like "crystallized mathematics," as can the deftly mastered music contained within. Ear-hugging stereo headphones are practically a must to experience the scalpel-sharp sounds of skittering static, depth-charge thump and needling ultra high frequencies encoded onto Raster / Noton discs. The label's name, coming as it does from the computer graphics term "raster imaging", has its own synesthetic connotations to it. As Nicolai explains:

> We were graphic designers…so we had a lot to do with
> raster points, which we were working with on the screen

every day, so for us it was a nice idea because the music we did also completely on the computer. And because you can divide the rhythm into rasters, you have units and you can measure.[38]

The Raster / Noton label attitude towards its roster of artists is, however, more flexible than the mathematical and digital façade would suggest- according to Ben Borthwick's 2003 exposé on the label,"...like Mego, it's an artist-run label without a fixed roster, rather, it has a fluctuating attendance around a core of artists who often release across a broad swath of likeminded labels."[39] Unlike Mego, however, the label's aforementioned design aesthetic demands that its contributing artists sacrifice some of their 'public image' in exchange for a more anonymous identity: at first sight, Raster / Noton's standardized packaging and textual communications seem to obliterate any traces of individual charisma. The great irony of this, though, is that the increased ratio of restraints to affordances - in both packaging and sonic content - leads to work of a more distinct "personality" than what many single artists or full label rosters are able to accomplish. The antiseptic, airtight products offered by Raster / Noton can be spotted by record store shoppers without them having to break a stride. Another paradox arises from the unshakable (and not always comfortable) intimacy that some of the individual sound works produce, in spite of their often binary towards signal / noise or imperceptibility / presence (these are not randomized "glitch" works.)

Carsten Nicolai's official press releases certainly paint him as being an emissary of synesthetic simulation: his *curriculum vitae* boasts that he is "part of an artist generation who works intensively in the transitional area between art and science,"[40] with numerous critical appraisals echoing these precise words.[41] Nicolai's C.V. adds the following:

> As a visual artist Nicolai seeks to overcome the separation of the sensual perceptions of man by making scientific phenomenons [sic] like sound and light frequencies perceivable for both eyes and ears. His installations have a minimalistic aesthetic that by its elegance and consistency is highly intriguing.[42]

Nicolai's host of professional accolades, among them a couple of 'Golden Nica' awards from the Prix Ars Electronica festival, attest to his above-average skill in synchronizing sensory information, and then sculpting it into forms whose clarity and sense of purpose are not overwhelmed by their "cold" artificiality (he has occasionally been referred to as a "plastician," a suitable designation given his liberal use of these synthetic materials as contextual framing devices.) Among his more talked-about works are the 1998 installation, a row of four Technics turntables each adorned by a translucent sperm-white slab of vinyl containing a number of locked grooves. *Bausatz Noto* succeeded on multiple levels: as a merely visual artwork and as a participatory experience, in which anything from one to four patrons could enact a concert on the turntables, no two being exactly alike. The piece contains rhythm both in a musical sense, generated by the interlocking selected by the players, and an architectural rhythm as well, with its even spacing and forceful symmetry. It is the kind of piece that could would turn off fans of rococo eccentricity in an instant, but it can't be that it isn't beautiful in a sense: by Le Corbusier's definition (*"when a thing responds to a need, it is beautiful"*[43]), *Bausatz Noto* succeeds. If we understand the desire for restraint and clear definition to be a pressing need in a time of perplexing clutter and clatter, then the beauty of a work like *Bausatz Noto* follows.

If Nicolai and the Raster / Noton crew are successful in their multi-media ventures, perhaps it is because they place such a high value on phenomenology untainted by polemical grandstanding and prosaic proclamation of intent. One of Nicolai's stated goals is, as hinted at above, to erase his "signature" from his creations- although the small number of people tilling this particular artistic field guarantees that certain pieces of his may still be recognized as "a Nicolai" for some time to come. Whatever the case, the graphics, sounds, and even the tactile nature of Raster / Noton releases do not lend themselves to moralizing or politicizing, as Nicolai himself confirms:

> Something that is really important for us, coming from the East, is that we do not inscribe political meaning into the label. Basically, while we were growing up, everything was inscribed with meaning. This is also where these minimalist ideas come from: to prevent it from delivering pre-existing information –in the worst case you would say propaganda- or delivering any kind of existing opinion about the thing and what it is.[44]

Nicolai's statement rings truer the further one dives into the Raster / Noton back catalog: upon listening to a baker's dozen of the label's releases, it is striking how rarely - if at all - human vocals are employed. A personal survey of this label's work has shored up very little in the way of recorded verbiage; with the main exception being a brief monologue from the late John Balance on a track by Ivan Pavlov's project CoH. One could easily say that this is just an extension of a trend already begun by earlier manifestations of electronic dance music, but even the most robotic forms of Techno rely, from time to time, on sampled vocal snippets or pat declarations to 'inscribe meaning': bites of film dialogue permeate all varieties of club-friendly music, their content ranging from simple territorial "shout-outs" or sung / spoken "watermarks", to mockery of the hysteria contained in vintage anti-drug documentaries, to amplification of low-budget kung-fu wisdom.

For Carsten Nicolai and his cohorts, though, raw electricity is the *lingua franca* of modern cultural development, and not vocal utterance, no matter how articulate. Although Nicolai is far more involved with computers than Jenny ever was, both Jenny and Nicolai rely on electricity to reach their conclusions about the unitary nature of perceptible phenomena: Jenny worked largely with piezo-electric amplifiers in his experiments, while Nicolai uses a full complement of electric equipment – from the voltage-controlled oscillators and filters on vintage analog instruments, to the now-omnipresent silver Powerbooks and MacBooks. Nicolai's use of electricity as an illuminator, in both the literal sense and a psycho-spiritual one, is evident in his appropriation of Thomas Edison's middle name for his alias, Alva Noto. Under the Noto banner (minus the Alva), one of Nicolai's most novel releases – and one most pertinent to synesthetic study - appeared under the name *Telefunken* in 2000.

Telefunken, a humble little tool for developing image-sound correspondence, embodies many of the more engrossing aspects of 21st century digital art: namely, the chance for a non-artist to complete the work on their own, the possibility for the perceived results to differ depending on variable factors like the quality of one's equipment (Nicolai personally recommends a Sony Black Trinitron TV for best results), and non-interference by the artist himself. The *Telefunken* CD is intended to be placed in a CD player which is hooked up to a television via its S-video and audio jacks; with the audible frequencies from the CD – sounding in a range from 50-8,000 Hz - determining the visual output on the television screen. Anyone who has experimented with video camera feedback by pointing it at its output monitor - creating undulating, vertiginous tunnels of white light and explosive bursts of white flak- will be intrigued by the results.

Like said phenomenon, the results also bear similarities to the reality-deforming nature of Op art pieces, striving to escape the confines of the two-dimensional with their insistent 'hyper-visuality.' The micro-sized tracks on *Telefunken* (only a few seconds in length, and thusly to be treated like the digital equivalent of 'locked grooves') have more in common with shortwave radio noises than with anything noticeable to the average individual as "music". To be sure, they are a world removed from the ecstatic and overflowing symphonies of Scriabin, but they do represent a fascinating step forward in the search for audio-visual congruence. As with Jenny's cymatic experiments, the audible frequencies on *Telefunken* create rippling and strobing patterns rather than mere solid colors, and the work as a whole points at the larger role that machines will eventually play in determining the vocabulary of this language. The concept has caught on well enough that it has undergone several permutations as an installation, finally appearing on LCD flat-screen monitors in 2004. Nicolai encourages us that "the standards of the new technology permit new visual interpretations with the same set-up, expanding the acoustic and visual spectrum of the installation substantially."[45]

An editorial written by Nicolai on an influential exhibition - the 1965 *Responsive Eye* exhibit curated by William Seitz - helps to bind together all of the aforementioned works in their intent. This highly representative and well-attended showing of Op artworks, made public in the year of the artist's birth, still resonates with him for the reason that it overcomes "the distance between production and presentation,"[46] That is to say, the artworks advanced from their traditional role as contemplative devices or atmosphere enhancers to become "productive" tools or templates for building new environments. The works in the exhibition, though not meant to be touched, nevertheless made "art more touchable than ever"[47]- as such, these works were not meant as stimuli that might produce quickly extinguished reactions, but as stimuli that initiated further acts of creation.

The Martian Solution: Kiki and Bouba

All of these tendencies of new electronic music to foster the synesthetic experience are thought provoking, but they beg the question- where is all of this leading? Will those on the receiving end of these sensory revelations have some distinct advantage over those who cannot train their senses to work in a relatively synchronous way? Would an ability to hear color or smell sound, distributed among a wider section of the general populace, precipitate a positive change in our daily dealings with each other, owing to a newfound hypersensitivity to our surroundings? It is nice to fantasize about a new humanity whose higher-evolved sensory apparatus contributes to a deeper awareness of, and interaction with, the phenomenal world. Yet, with the studies in this field just now gaining recognition as being something more than pseudo-scientific, there is clearly a long way to go. The gulf between inherited and adventitious synesthesia is one problem to deal with; and even among these 'adventitious synesthetes' there is such a formidable difference in social backgrounds, education and preferred artistic style, that developing a normative aesthetics is no mean task. On the other hand, all is not total randomness in this area either. If that were the case, then there would be no international standard for things like warning signs. We could expect, upon traveling to another country, to encounter traffic signals where we "stop" on a brownish light and "go" on a purple one. In situations like these, which require the most urgent attention, some very rudimentary color-sound connections are already in place- televised warnings for incoming storms almost invariably pair high-pitched beeps or whines with flashing red or yellow graphics and text. Such examples suggest that there are already some 'cultural universals' in place, at least as far as the more primal human behaviors (the 'fight or flight reflex,' in the case of audio-visual warnings) are concerned.

With this in mind, the study of synesthesia - through electronic music composition and other means - is of value not solely as a means of modeling possibilities for future connections, but as a means of communing with our past. This activity is not limited to mapping a sort of collective or ancestral unconsciousness, but to understanding the thought processes and sensory impressions of our selves in earlier developmental stages, and even (as Richard Cytowic puts it) ganing knowledge of our "ascend[ing] the phylogenetic scale."[48] Since, according to the popular theory, more phyletic development leads to a more decisive separation of neural 'building blocks' and sensory apparatus, some understanding of synesthesia gives us insight into the *Umwelten* or lived environments of other species that presumably have no such separations. It is then possible to shape the future (and not only that of art) by using the knowledge of this continuity.

Many developmental theorists' studies also point to human infants as being precorticate, or interfacing with the world as a "sensory primordial soup", with more clearly defined perceptions arising, as per Canadian researcher Daphne Maurer, when "idle neural connections between sensory domains are 'pruned' [...] most intermodal connections are eliminated in the first six months; the process becomes slower from the ages of one to eleven years."[49] More specifically, infants' lack of myelination / axon coating is proposed as a contributing factor here. Adult humans, legitimate synesthetes included, are cognizant of their sensory impressions' origins (i.e. that separate sense organs exist) whereas infants do not make these distinctions. Using his term for synesthetic mappings - 'biograms' - Brian Massumi claims that they "persist as a subsequent underpinning of all subsequent [adult] perception" and that "'normality' is when the biogram recedes to the background of vision...biograms are always in operation, it is just a question of whether or not their operations are remarked."[50] So, research into these sensory correspondences is simultaneously a matter of understanding the personal evolution of our relating to the world, and the species-wide understanding of the same.

Another justification for further synesthetic study is not that a proliferation of synesthetic experience would change our deeply ingrained belief systems or prejudices, but that our abilities to express ourselves across cultures would be increased dramatically. As we progress further into the digital age, new subculture tribes with their own distinct linguistic patterns are popping up with alarming frequency, often bending the syntax of their 'parent' languages as far as it can possibly go without breaking: just the Internet-based subcultures alone, like the snarky and disruptive denizens of the 4chan bulletin board / image board, are so steeped in obscure in-jokes, deliberate misspellings, incorrect conjugations and puzzling neologisms so as to be totally incomprehensible to fluent speakers of 'proper' English (or any language, for that matter.)

All of this seems concocted merely as a means of self-amusement for people with desperately short attention spans and with large reserves of disposable time, side-stepping the usual reasons for a subculture's creation of linguistic deviations (outwitting or confusing the dominant culture, inventing coded terminology for illicit acts in order to avoid punishment.) The existence of such tribes certainly challenges the theory that a networked world will be one of increased understanding between cultures. In the meantime, there still exist spiritually oriented and non-materialistic cultures like the Jamaican Rastafarians, who have comparatively little to do with computer networks. Although they speak a variant of English, they would no more understand a 4chan subscriber's frequent use of "lulz" to mean laughter than a 4chan subscriber would understand their habit of replacing disagreeable syllables with the letter "I" (e.g. removing the disagreeable 'ban' from 'banana' and transforming it into "I-nana.") New communicative quirks are constantly arising in order to serve the highly specialized needs of increasingly smaller, non-assimilated culture cliques, and separatism / specialization seems to be the name of the game rather than the finding of common ground. Having a steadily increasing number of planetary inhabitants who understand each other less and less seems like a surefire recipe for disaster.

When confronted with conundrums like these, we can always do worse than to get as close to the source as possible, mulling over the various theories of linguistic origins. Dr. Ramachandran is a proponent of what he calls the "synthetic bootstrapping theory of language," which is the notion that

> ...language evolved as a result of fortuitous synergistic interactions between mechanisms - called exaptations - that evolved originally for other, completely unrelated functions. It's a striking illustration of the principle that evolution often involves the opportunistic co-opting of pre-existing mechanisms.[51]

Basically, Ramachandran is insisting that synesthesia had a role in shaping language from its earliest origins. To illustrate this hypothesis, he refers back to the now-notorious "Kiki and Bouba" test conducted in 1927- in this scenario, subjects were shown pictures of a sharp-edged figure akin to a piece of broken glass, and a more soft-edged figure like a pool of spilled liquid. Test subjects were told that, in "Martian language," these two figures represented the words "kiki" and "bouba," and it was up to them to interpret which was which. There was an almost insignificant amount of deviance from the end result, with around 98% of all participants assigning the word "kiki" to the sharp figure and "bouba" to the rounded one. As the 'Kiki and Bouba' experiment suggests, shared perceptions of things lead inevitably to a shared descriptive vocabulary (e.g. a jagged piece of broken glass corresponding to a "ki-ki" sound.) If this theory is correct, then its implications are not hard to imagine: all of communication as we know it comes from making indisputable connections between visual and audible phenomena; of agreeing upon the fact that sharp spikes are equal to "k's" and formless pools of viscous fluid are equal to "b's". We may not all be synesthetes of the first order (until the cloning of genes is upon us in earnest), and not all of us will ever have a knack for Nabokov's inimitable fine-tuning of language. However, we have the tools now to make an astonishing array of art from with which we can re-assess and re-wire our communicative faculties, or just understand how we came to be in our present position. As far as *that* is concerned, it is, more often than not, an essential prerequisite to knowing where we are going.

Silence is Sexy:
The Other 'Extreme Music'

> "Burn flutes and lutes, and plug Blind Kuang's ears, and then they'll really be able to hear again."

> - Chuang Tzu

Parental Advisory: Explicit Quiet

In the summer of 2004, I found myself collaborating on a radio program with sound artist John Wanzel at Chicago's WLUW (on the University of Loyola campus.) I recall a discussion we had at the time about radio broadcasting laws, particularly how it was technically illegal to broadcast a small amount of silence, or dead air, during normal operating hours- less than 20 seconds, if I remember correctly. This bothered me, since, by that time, I had amassed a good number of sound recordings in which pieces contained stretches of silence longer than the FCC-allotted maximum amount. Could the intentional silences on these CD recordings an integral part of their compositional approach, really be classified 'dead air'? I figured that it would be difficult to make a case to an FCC agent if complaints were in fact lodged to the station, saying that the programmers were being negligent and were continually, mischievously dropping the volume levels down to zero. It seemed like it would be futile, and a little comical, to try and explain the difference between long, deliberate silences used as an aesthetic element within sound works, and the long silences which resulted from a programmer's personal failings- i.e. fumbling to cue up the correct tracks, or falling asleep on the job. To someone in charge of upholding broadcast standards and practices, what would be the difference between inaction on the behalf of a pre-recorded or in-studio artist, or inaction on behalf of a live disc jockey?

The more I thought about such things, the less I was able to come up with an answer that would satisfy someone unfamiliar with the phenomenon of extremely quiet music. At the same time, I realized how much antipathy there was, in our modern society at large, towards moments of quiet in general. It is too often taken as common knowledge that the quiet individual iscounter-productive, aloof, nihilistic, incompetent, or some nasty cocktail of all this and more. As the story goes, because it is "simple" to deploy silence as a compositional tool but "difficult" to actively listen to it, those who do the former are to be accused of charlatanism, and reminded in no uncertain terms that "I could write that as well as you." John Cage's reply to this question - "have I said anything that would lead you to think I thought you were stupid?"[1] - illustrates how the "anyone can do that" attitude tends to automatically assume bad intentions on the composer's part. In any society where silence is seen as tantamount to anti-communication, rather than as a shared moment of reflection between performer and audience (from which either or both can gain), it will be continually difficult to make proper use of it.

If silence could be viewed as a compositional element, then placing limitations on its use speak to some more insidious agenda that would, ironically, involve a bit of 'silencing' itself (for example, disallowing deep, reflective thought.) Yet even in a pop-cultural landscape where supposedly "anything goes" in music, getting people to view silence as a compositional element is no less of a challenge today than it was when Cage's landmark piece 4'33" dared to break the non-sound barrier. The caveat, of course, was that this piece revealed the impossibility of 'pure' silence in the sensory apparatus of the living (as an outgrowth of his rejection of pure silence, Cage also proclaimed that "there is no such thing as an empty space or empty time.")[2] In a way, it is more difficult since the number of sonic distractions in metropolitan and suburban life have become manifold in the 50+ years since Cage's breakthrough.

One thing about this particular subject seems certain: contemporary appreciation of silence is truly subjective, and those who do not appreciate it tend to absolutely, unequivocally abhor its presence, viewing it as an aggressive weapon or interrogative device when used in interpersonal or social situations. Tales abound of negotiations during the 1980s between Western business executives and their Japanese counterparts, the latter of which craftily used *Ma* (literally 'interval', meant here as an extended period of conversational silence) to fatigue their comparatively loquacious business partners. The latter, unfamiliar with anything but instantaneous response, would then be pressured into accepting proposals less beneficial to them, if this technique was deployed skillfully enough. The practice is apparently so ingrained in Japanese communications that sonic researcher Christophe Charles, on witnessing a 1992 performance of Merzbow's "magma of sound" notes how "one might say there is not much space for the *Ma* to be heard" within it.[3] The celebrated architect Arata Isozaki also assents to its centrality to all Japanese art forms, noting how it exists in both dimensions of time and space (though within Japan it is "perceived without distinction") and thus could be regarded as "the ultimate doctrine for artistic disciplines."[4]

Though I was not making any conscius attempts at cultivating *Ma*, I recall a handful of instances in which, during moments of protracted silence during telephone conversations, the speaker on the other end would become audibly uncomfortable and would begin dishing out intimate details about other people within our immediate social circle. All it took, in some cases, was a pause of fewer than 10 seconds to spur on the disclosure of confidential, 'off-the-record' information relating to mutual friends' romantic lives, financial track records, and embarrassing quirks obscured from public sight. This was never actively sought out- yet I found this information was disclosed with disturbing regularity in situations where I was, owing to work-weariness or just brain-dead incoherence, unable to hold up my end of a conversation, yet was not allowed to hang up for other reasons of communication etiquette. It was surprising, to say the least, how a raw fear of apparently blank audio space could drive certain individuals to desperation, and to fill this sonic void with whatever was immediately at their disposal. This phenomenon became much more evident to me when, a few years down the road, the explosion in the popularity of mobile phones annihilated moments of private contemplation or internalized dialogue while phone users were roaming in public.

The seemingly primordial fear of silence is easier to understand if we compare its compositional qualities to that of other sounds: by Cage's reckoning, silence is only measured in terms of *duration* whereas all other sonic material is measurable by timbre, frequency and amplitude as well. Placing a large magnifying glass on time's passing, particularly in music performance situations where one must passively and politely observe "non-events," brings many too close to an acute awareness of their own mortality. The number of comforting situations in which any external noise serves to pierce the silence are manifold: when being jolted awake from sinister and portentous nightmares, it is a relief to have some utterly banal sound pierce the darkness that we lie in, and to jar us out of the hypnagogic terror that would convince us we are alone with the phantasms of our minds (though this does not explain why we approach brightly illuminated and decently populated spaces with the same primal fear of silence associated with excursions into isolated, cavernous darkness.) When the AIDS awareness group ACT UP chose "silence = death" as their rallying cry in 1987, "silence" referred to the mute indifference of communications media and the political class to the existence of a rapidly spreading, mortal disease- yet, twenty years later, this same rallying cry seems to apply to consumer culture's attitude towards all forms of silence. It is equated with all social evils from un-productivity to insolence; seen as a void only willfully inhabited by the anti-human.

Silence in the Digital Age

Richard Chartier, when describing his own work as an investigation of "the relationship between silence, sound, and the act of listening"[5] speaks to the exploratory imperatives of an entire aesthetic: from the 1990s up to the present, there has been a gradual, curiosity-provoking influx of electronically aided sound artists who make regular use of quietness as a compositional tool. Such work has served to partially confirm an earlier statement of Douglas Kahn's, i.e. " ... the delectation of the underheard, whether they be small sounds or overtones, has been the stalwart tactic of experimental music in the second half of the century."[6] Like much of the other music discussed in this book, pockets of such expression arose simultaneously, within so many different lived environments, that drafting up a linear chronology of actions would be difficult (if not somewhat pointless.) The culture seeded by these musicians is, refreshingly, free of egotistical attempts to elbow one's way to the front of the 'public acceptance' line- and therefore no one is really brazen enough to claim they were "the first" to innovate or revolutionize any aspect of this music. Such claims would naturally be met with skepticism and would be viewed as bad form within a culture that de-emphasizes the need for celebrity. Besides, for every musician that we know of through recorded evidence, there may be another who came to the same conclusions years before, and yet was content to keep such discoveries private (or, though it seems an impossibility in the Facebook era, is equally content to see his or her ideas being adopted in other forums regardless of whether he or she receives proper attribution.)

The name of this sonic genre changes depending on where the form arises: in the metropolitan regions of Tokyo and Kansai it is referred to as *onkyou* [meaning loosely "sound reverberation" or just "sound"]: a term which was originally associated with a sort of *onkyou* "school"[7] and its tutelary performances at Tokyo's multi-purpose Off Site venue from 2000-2005 (Off Site functioned as a gallery and coffeehouse as well as a live space.) Though the essential elements of *onkyou* playing have been closely tied in with the aforementioned intricacies of the Japanese communicative style, one has to be careful of seeing Zen influence *everywhere* within this creative milieu. In Off Site and numerous other micro-spaces within urban Japan, the style's formation was modulated by modern societal restraints as much as it was inspired by an explication of philosophical 'roots': given that these live spaces were not situated within officially recognized entertainment districts, the players at *onkyou* nights had to craft a very restrained style in order to not disturb neighboring residents or businesses. Furthermore, other compatible styles exist in other countries: in Western Europe, a parallel set of sonic maneuvers was christened with the label of New Berlin Minimalism. Steven Roden, an American practicioner, has tried to foreground its tendency towards subtlety and near-imperceptibility by referring to it as 'lower case sound', going as far as to refuse the use of capital letters on the appropriately sparse artwork accompanying his recordings.

I myself would (for lack of anything more universally acceptable) use the term 'digital-age silence'. Unimaginative as it may be, it refers to a characteristic I find unique to this music: its genesis followed the rise of the CD as the dominant format for music storage, as well as all the formats like MiniDisc, MP3, and FLAC [Free Lossless Audio Codec] that followed on the CD's heels. In any of these formats, the introduction of silence or near-silence into the recording can be sharply distinguished from doing the same on a cassette or a vinyl LP: the amount of 'system noise', or the sound being generated by the sound playback equipment itself, is infinitesimally small on a digital format. No form of interference or system noise, like tape hiss or vinyl crackle, is readily detectable, in many cases you would have to place your ear next to the playback device simply to be reminded that moving parts are at work, to hear the restless whirring of the disc, the liquid squelching sound of the laser navigating its way through the tiny indentations on its playable surface, or perhaps the dyspeptic noises being made by one's hard drive as it processes a new playlist of audio files.

Despite the central role that silence takes within this music, an impressive variety of voicing and tonal color is to be found underneath whatever umbrella term we use for it. Some artists use the feedback from audio and video devices as the *prima materia* from which to compose, some use electronically manipulated or wordless vocals (the idiosyncratic and occasionally frightening output of Ami Yoshida is a standout in this regard, even when not electronically treated), some use output devices devoid of any conventionally 'playable' transducer (e.g. Toshimaru Nakamura's no-input mixer and Taku Sugimoto's manipulation of guitar amplifier hiss.) Still others play a form of computer-based acousmatic music that sounds like the scattering of sonic dust particles or (to use Bernhard Günter's apt metaphor, still relevant since its 1993 introduction) "*un peu de neige salie*" [" a bit of dirty snow."]

Flourishes of conceptual humor often surface to combat the misperceptions of po-faced seriousness within this culture. Before the coming of the digital age, there was a rich history of "anti-records" containing little or no sound on them, but acting as comical enlighteners in other regards: it's hard to stifle a laugh when being confronted with, say, The Haters' silent 7" vinyl platter entitled *Complete This Record By*

Scratching It, Before You Listen To It On Your Stereo, or another Haters contribution to participatory art, the *Wind Licked Dirt* LP. The latter features no grooves at all on the record's surface, but does compensate for this shortcoming by including a bag of dirt in the packaging, which the lucky owner can then use to recreate their very own Haters 'performance', rubbing the dirt across the vinyl. Seeing as how contemporaneous Haters performances involved band members watching mud dry and staring at blank TV screens, this activity may provide a decent substitute for their live appearances, for those whose hometowns are not included on the Haters' tour schedule. Another "anti"-album more relevant to the present era is the Argentinian band Reynols' *Blank Tapes:* a compact disc release assembled solely from the noise produced by, yes, unused cassette tapes. One proud owner of *Blank Tapes* sees it as a multi-purpose object, at once a 'joke,' an honestly intriguing listen, and also

> ...a subtle attack on the medium of excess, the CD. How many albums need to be trimmed of their fat because the artist felt compelled to fill every millimetre of silver? Now, we're moving into the age of the Deluxe Edition! Not this one, sir. This is a wonderful tribute to the many minutes of negative space that haven't yet been violated by forgettable b-sides and studio flotsam.[8]

When it comes to instrumentation, the incorporation of silence into the music can be accomplished in a number of ways, as well: it could either be done through literal inaction, such as not touching a hand to an instrument, or through an action which is borderline imperceptible, like playing constant electronic signals at such high frequencies that they teeter on the threshold of audibility and eventually vanish in the upper atmosphere...only to re-appear later in phantom form through the effects of mild tinnitus; a belated 'encore'. An artist like the Syndey-born guitarist and electronics manipulator Oren Ambarchi – also organizer of Australia's "What is Music" festival, host to many of this book's surveyed artists - reverses the polarity by using bass and sub-bass tones which can be felt but not always heard. Trente Oiseaux [lit. "Thirty Birds"] label boss Bernhard Günter shapes electro-acoustic sound clusters of satisfying variance, then mixes the results down so low that ferreting them out becomes more of a personal quest on the behalf of the listener than a mere receipt of audio information. Günter's more intriguing creations could also be an audio herald of nano-technology to come- the sound of impossibly tiny machines at work, as they float through the bloodstream.

To further complicate (or merely diversify) matters, some artists operating within this silence-enhanced realm will refer to their music as 'improvisation', while others consider it a form of 'composition'. Such partitions can be dismantled very easily, though. Taku Sugimoto, whose work since the dawn of the new millennium has relied more and more on intensified emptiness, suggests that it can be seen as both: "[music] *means neither 'theme and variations'...nor 'chained and dancing'...listen to the sound as it is...there is almost no distinction between improvisation and composition...to accept all the space.*" [9]

Returning to the World

Whatever we choose to call this variety of sound that relies on low volume / perceptibility, intense concentration, and reflective pauses on behalf of both performer and audience, it has to be admitted that it is followed by a loyal coterie as limited as that which enjoys other ill-defined pursuits like "noise". Those who oppose it often assume that its motives are purely intellectual ones, and perhaps they are relying a little too much on the trite image of the verbally nullified, introverted "bookworm" buried in library stacks. Like certain minimalist forms of visual artwork, it is assumed to be a cynical gesture of opposition from an incomprehensible, hermetic clique: a small cadre of people with such a distaste for the shared human experience that they deliberately cocoon themselves in alienating expressive forms. Others will insist that such sound should be reserved as the plaything of ascetic religious brotherhoods, or for those who live deeply internalized lives, wishing for no place in a vibrant social universe and preparing themselves for the ultimate silence of biological death by maintaining strict regimens of wordlessness. Some brave souls, like the Berlin-based guitarist Annette Krebs, have in fact submitted to severe ascetic routines as the inspiration for recording, but such cases are still the exception rather than the norm.

Within popular culture, silence has been used just as much in scenarios of seduction as in occasions where one intended to alienate, to repel, or to make others cower before a display of dominant intellect or spiritual awareness. Although Hollywood films, with their habit of cueing up swells of lush romantic music to heighten cinematic representations of love-making, have increased the appetite for having a musical backdrop to these moments of intimacy, silence still wields an incredible power as a seducer and consequently as an amplifier of emotions. Its ability to create an illusion of time's cessation for everyone but the perceiver makes for some of the most intoxicating, intimate moments in the romantic ritual, as does its ability to yank certain bodily processes (e.g. the beating of the heart, and the rhythm of exhalation and inhalation) to the forefront of consciousness. Even the titles of many hit pop songs - see "Don't Talk (Put Your Head On My Shoulder)," "Enjoy The Silence" and "Hush", for starters - seem to acknowledge the fact that silence carries as much of an erotic force with it as do poetic wordplay and baroque, gushing verbal confessions. You could always propose maudlin, introspective titles like Simon & Garfunkel's classic "The Sounds of Silence," written in the wake of America's grief over the Kennedy assassination, to rain on this particular parade- but even a song such as this confirms the role of silence in deeply stirring, communal experiences, rather than its role as a denier of such experiences.

Interestingly, silence does not begin or end with the *music* produced by these artists: a certain silence is also evident in the artists' self-promotion (or lack thereof), and in the advanced degree of self-restraint or inaction that accompanies CD releases, concerts, and other supplemental activities. Secondary literature and biographical information becomes an inessential adjunct to the act of recording and performing, especially when there is no stated goal beyond merely transmitting sound and observing as it assumes its place in the daily flux of energy and sensation. Photographs of artists are rarely used in promotional materials (when such materials even exist at all.) Magazine features on the artists and interviews with the artists, when they appear, tend to ignore quirky anecdotes, gossip, and "shop talk," instead going straight for the jugular: the ideas driving the music. There is, within this milieu, a greater-than-average desire to not see the performer as the center of the music, as Steve Roden illustrates with these comments:

> The whole thing is not about me as the artist, as the focus.
> It's about making these things that don't necessarily point
> back to me as being more important than the work. The art
> and sound culture right now is so much about the artist,
> the persona of the artist. I talked to someone recently who
> said he wanted to be 'the first superstar of noise', without
> thinking that Kenny G is the first superstar of jazz! I mean,
> it's not a good place to be![10]

With such limited attempts at promotion and outward projection of personae, music of this genre survives mainly thanks to a famished niche audience willing to discover it on their own, and to make old-fashioned, unadorned word-of- mouth or Internet bulletin board notification act as the most effective means of information dispersal. This situation is encouraged by some artists, such as the Tokyo duo Astro Twin (Ami Yoshida and Utah Kawasaki) who humbly and humorously describe their music as "…boring sounds / un-evolving sounds / unproductive sounds / lazy sounds / garbage-like sounds,"[11] adding the caveat "each sound is junk, but some may be important. They are for you to seek. We want you to find them…that is Astro Twin's request."[12] When they are found, the surprises are plentiful, and present plenty of challenges to those who expect relatively "quieter" music to be a serene shortcut into easy narcosis: Ami Yoshida's vocal repertoire is a pastiche of drawn-out wheezes, glottal aberrations, keening bird-of-prey shrieks, reptilian slurps and occasional sung notes, all of which are then combined with smooth washes of electronic tone (her other partners in electronic sound have included Christof Kurzmann, Günter Müller and Sachiko M.) for devastating effect. With many of these sonic elements regularly employed within the same short audio piece, the unique 'push-pull' effect of the music –a continuous alternating between erotic attraction and outright alienation- is achieved with a greater degree of success than in most other creative genres.

The more well known record labels dealing with digital-age silence and the musical micro-gesture, like Trente Oiseaux, rely on a simple design template that is applied to all of their releases: in the case of this label, each new release up until a point in the early 2000's featured no more than the artist's name and title on a textured paper background (the color of which changed with each successive release.) The CD *Warzsawa Restaurant* by Francisco López (who relies on a similarly reduced graphic design template for his releases on other labels), bears only minor dissimilarities when placed alongside Marc Behrens' *Advanced Environmental Control* or Hervé Castellani's *Flamme*. The end effect of this common design scheme effectively mirrors the aesthetics of the sound contained within. In a desperate panic to find some 'hidden' substance within this sparse packaging, the listener's tactile sense is instead engaged by the coarse paper of the CD booklets, an intriguing situation in which the impressions "found" are not necessarily the ones that were originally sought out. As is the case with the music, the lack of a familiar framing device, and the refusal on the artists' behalf to lead the listener by the nose into a world where all is explained, uncovers those phenomena and epiphenomena which were 'always there'. This extends to how a listener perceives the compact disc itself: in such a context, the bold spectra of color dancing about on the reflective surface of the aluminum-coated polycarbonate plastic disc become all the more vibrant, and even the transparent center hole by the larger ring of clear plastic seems to take on greater significance. These mundane little items become as close as they will get to being perceived as living organisms, rebelling against their status as mere static objects.

This brings us to the other half of the Chuang Tzu quote which opened this chapter: *destroy decorations, mix the Five Colors, paste Li Chu's eyes shut, and in All-Under-Heaven, they'll begin to see the light again.* My seemingly careless play with Taoist ideals here may upset some readers who wonder how a state-of-the-art, technological form of expression can mesh with this largely organic way of life, but closer inspection reveals that the use of digital-age expressive tools is not an automatic disqualification from such a lifestyle. On this subject, I can only defer to Taoist and Zen scholar Alan

Watts, who reminds us that

> ...the Taoist attitude is not opposed to technology per se. Indeed, the Chuang Tzu writings are full of references to crafts and skills perfected by this very principle of 'going with the grain.' The point is therefore that technology is only destructive in the hands of people who do not realize that they are one and the same process as the universe. Our over-specialization in conscious attention and linear thinking has led to neglect, or ignorance, of the basic principles and rhythms of this process, of which the foremost is polarity.[13]

Watts goes on to relate the concept of electricity itself - without which very little of the music mentioned herein could be reproduced - to the Tao, noting that neither force can be explained on their own; both are fundamentals only comprehensible in terms of the phenomena which manifest them.

The concept of 'emptiness' in Taoism also takes on a special meaning far from a concept of 'the void' as purgatory or hell, a fact that is worth considering when confronting the fear of silence. Chuang Tzu refers to the "Tao of Heaven" as "empty and formless," a sentiment Fritjof Capra expands upon in his book *The Tao of Physics:* "[Lao Tzu] often compares the Tao to a hollow valley, or to a vessel which is forever empty and thus has the potential of containing an infinity of things."[14] Put this way, we can see "emptiness" not as a terminus point into which all irretrievably sinks, but as a starting point: we can see silence not as a capitulation on the behalf of the artist, but as an invitation to go beyond sound itself and to experience all available aspects of the phenomenal world. "Empty audio space" has the potential to severely irritate those who expect sound to "explain" something, but for those who go beyond this, the apparent absurdity of making "music" from nothingness takes on the same role as a Zen riddle: illustrating that nature is a unitary phenomenon, a deeply intertwined organism in which every part contains every other part within itself.

Mutual Sacrifice

Like the more violent, droning, high-decibel creations that occupy another wing of the same sonic mansion, this form has not met with blanket critical acceptance. It has its obvious champions in music scribes like *Oceans of Sound / Haunted Weather* author David Toop, but it has also generated a host of skeptics who wonder how, if at all, this music differs from the kind of ersatz 'easy listening' experiences meant to be played in the bath by such stereotypical characters as the 'bored suburban housewife' or 'self-conscious yuppie'. Take, for example, this review by Stefan Jaworzyn (formerly of Skullflower, Whitehouse live, etc.) of Steve Roden's first 1993 outing as in be tween noise, *so delicate and strangely made:*

> ...hardcore Art it most definitely is -with all the trimmings- the title being a dead give-away, perfectly encapsulating Roden's prissy self-image and tedious *modus operandi*- fussy, neo-minimalist puffing, blowing, scraping, tweaking and tinkling...ugh...'experimental' pabulum for New Age sissies. In fact, the more I think about it and the more I listen to it, the more I hate it.[15]

Jaworzyn's impatience with Roden is indicative of a larger public view that digital-age silence is something created by, and for, meek souls: a pandering form of 'relaxation music' camouflaged in the Emperor's New Clothes of inscrutable, 'difficult' avant-garde experimentation. It is sometimes difficult to build a case against such naysayers, when positive reviews of this music make constant allegorical reference to the delicate, transient seasonal phenomena of nature, likening the character of the sounds to that of falling snowflakes, autumn leaves and wisps of summer breeze. Such reviews, unfortunately, do the makers of *onkyou*, 'Berlin Minimalism' et. Al. no favors when they fail to mention the intense *concentration* of energy necessary for making convincing exemplars of this music. This is something that easily equals the intense *release* of energy inherent in louder musical genres, and cannot be said, on a whole, to be the collective mewling of effete "pussies". It should also be mentioned that some performers' re-envisioning of silence as musical material has brought them to the brink of legitimate personal risk- as Paul Hood relates in an interview with David Novak,

> In Northern England during the "Japan-o-Rama" tour in 2002, for example, an audience reacted to the extended silences and high-pitched sounds of a performance by Sachiko M by shouting and throwing objects at the stage in what the London promoter described to me as a "near riot." During an Italian tour the same year, the vehicle transporting a group of *onkyou* musicians from a festival was reportedly surrounded by angry fans who blocked the passage of the car and beat their fists on the roof.[16]

It's amusing to consider an earlier set of events in which audiences were agitated to a similar degree - namely, the 'live aktions' of Whitehouse throughout the 1980s and 1990s - since they seem to confirm that audiences may have identical reactions to any given set of unfamiliar extreme phenomena, not solely those that are seen as having a violent or aggressive tincture to them. It is precisely this sense of risk that is proposed by the Basque "computer actor" Mattin as the redeeming feature of "going fragile," or improvising in the "ultra-quiet and sparse" mode of his collaborator Radu Malfatti (and Mattin is himself no stranger to audience confrontations, both self-initiated and uninvited.) Among Mattin's demands to sound improvisors: "you must engage in questioning your security, see it as a constriction. You are aware and scared, as if you were in a dark corridor. Now you are starting to realise that what you thought of as walls existed only in your imagination."[17]

Mattin's enthusiastic pep talk does come with disclaimers, e.g. "when one uses music, not as a tool for achieving something else (recognition, status) but in a more aggressively creative way, it is going to produce alienation."[18] Yet this is all to reinforce the idea that improvisation (again, implied here as the silence-enhanced form that Mattin has produced alongside Malfatti) requires a determined embrace of uncertainty and fear. When, to this end, Mattin quotes Walter Benjamin's essay *The Destructive Character* ("because [the destructive character] sees a way everywhere, he has to clear things from it everywhere"),[19] the similarity between his own attitudes and that of the noise-loving Italian Futurists is remarkable. As such, it is fascinating to see the far-Leftist Mattin agreeing on at least tactical matters with otherwise ideological foes.

Yet the important message implied within this statement is not that extreme ideologies can find common ground in methodology, but that 'voluntary vulnerability' and lack of self-censorship is an essential prerequisite of real 'experimental' music. Naturally, opposing viewpoints do arise from other artists working within the more cutting-edge areas of 21st century electronic sound- Terre Thaemlitz has suggested that this 'no backup' approach is a hindrance rather than a help, preferring "the documentational aspect of studio recordings to live performance" because "...in terms of discourse, I equate it with a person's deliberate writings versus their drunk ramblings (presuming, of course, they have anything interesting to say in the first place)."[20] Here the question has to be asked, though- is the drunkard's 'rambling,' by its unguarded / unscripted nature, the *true* personality of the inebriated person? If we step outside the bounds of music performance and survey human activity as a whole, it seems that greater societal value is placed upon those individuals who can withstand either self-inflicted bouts of unpredictability (like the 'drunkards' mentioned here) or sudden changes in external circumstances, and that the responses to these challenges indicate authentic personality. It would not be unfair, I submit, to attribute some considerable strength of character to those musicians who mine the silence with no guarantees that it will be perceived as anything but a contrarian annoyance.

With all this in mind, Jaworzyn's earlier dismissals also do little to explain away the fact that some of this book's noisiest players also have close ties with the ever-expanding constellation of 'quiet' artists. John Duncan, though much of his catalog comprises sound of the white-hot, speaker-destroying variety, can still find time to share a collaborative CD with Bernhard Günter. The oft -demonic Portland noise artist Daniel Menche can also boast of a kinship with Günter by way of a Trente Oiseaux release. The late Koji Tano, who recorded teeth-grinding tectonic noise under the name MSBR, helped to co-organize improvisational performances of an intensely quiet character, when not organizing noise concerts, and penned reviews of such artists for his encylopedic *Denshi Zatsuon* ['Electronic Noise'] magazine. Individuals like Sachiko M, Otomo Yoshihide (whom David Novak recognizes as the *de facto* leader of [the] group that put Off Site and *onkyou* on the map"), Annette Krebs, Ralf Wehowsky, Kevin Drumm and even Keiji Haino[21] easily bridge the gap between trumpeting loudness and apparent stillness, giving them a special status as sonic omnivores. Even Taku Sugimoto and Steve Roden began their respective musical journeys in punk rock bands, the latter after chancing upon a performance by notorious L.A. synth-punks The Screamers.

Like it or not, the number of such people is increasing in the 21st century in accordance with the expansion of the globe's overall population; and those who would criticize them as being 'confused' for playing in more than one mode are sounding increasingly reactionary when they mistake resilience for weakness. In discussion with the cellist and record store owner Mark Wastell, David Toop reveals a valid counterpoint to the 'silence is weak' argument:

> Wastell once favoured Reductionism as a way to describe [his music], although now rejects that. He also rejects terms such as sparse, barely audible, quiet, and fragile, all of which suggest a weakness belied by the powerful impact the music can have on those that hear it. [...] 'A musician is defenceless in this genre,' says Wastell. 'He or she has nowhere to hide. His / her material is delivered with such care and diligence that it cannot be destroyed in ill-conceived collaborations. As Morton Feldman said, 'now that things are so simple, there's so much to do.'[22]

Terms like 'reductionism' are still a thorn in the side of the new breed of musicians who dare to commune with quiet, since they imply the creators are cantankerous sorts with a hatred of 'busy' music rather than people who merely have a love of building something out of nothing: Taku Sugimoto faces this conundrum by stating that he is an "additionist" rather than a reductionist, starting with a white canvas every time he sits down to play. In his case, this music *is* being set up as an alternative to something - namely superficiality and 'cool' transience - but not for reasons of mere cynicism:

> The most important thing for me is to make something really vertical, something spiritual, like a tower. The whole of the culture is very horizontal, it's surface. We don't really need it, it's just for amusement. Art has become like TV, there's nothing to believe in. We need something spiritual, real culture.[23]

At any rate, you don't need to have achieved the Tao mindset to understand the veracity of Sugimoto's or Wastell's statements: all you have to do is attend a performance of such music to witness the strength this music possesses when done correctly. In Japan I was lucky enough to have access to venues like Off Site and the Uplink Factory, where international showcases of such music were irregularly held. Presentation of this music almost requires an unspoken compact between performer and audience, a mutual willingness to let the long periods of silence unfold and ring in the ears without losing nerve or patience- the audience's struggle to impose restraint on their mouths, bodies and portable electronic devices becomes an appendage to the 'main' performance, and in many cases the feeling of sacrifice is also reciprocated between performer and audience: both parties must give up some freedom of movement or communication in order to more effectively immerse themselves in the silences.

While the filling in of blank spaces by feisty audience disruption may have been the intended effect of the famous endurance-testing Warhol films, it does not seem to be the case with this music. Bodily processes that would be completely ignored while grooving to the 120-decibel sounds of a modern rock combo suddenly re-assert themselves in a most intrusive way: a full complement of coughs, sneezes, wheezes, sniffles and general shifting of body parts can arise from the audience and wreck the sonic construction process- and heaven help you if any involuntary digestive noises assert themselves in such a scenario. In such a setting, it is almost refreshing to see the 'extensions of man' being checked at the door as well, since the audacious nagging of a mobile phone ringtone will most certainly get you escorted from the performance venue and / or personally lambasted by the performers.

One such scenario is as follows: it is a hushed yet "full house" evening at Tokyo's Uplink Factory, where the Dutch label Staalplaat is hosting a characteristically eclectic evening of electronic music, split evenly between the visiting Netherlanders and locals like the young psychoacoustic maestro Kozo Inada. A wall-to-wall crowd of inquisitive listeners sits cross-legged on the floor of the space, which resembles a well-tended artist's loft: white track lighting shining down onto naked white walls and parquet floorboards. A couple of lanky Goths in leather accoutrements and bullet belts stand pinned against a far wall, looking on with healthy curiosity, and the one-time Staalplaat employee Frans de Waard (also part of the Freiband trio playing that night) is sunk into a leather armchair in the same far corner of the room, trying not to look incongruous as he puffs on a wooden pipe in this venue loaded to the gills with consumer electronic devices. Smoke from the more conventional cigarettes rises from the floor-sitters' lips and nostrils like a thick swamp fog.

For the current performance, Roel Meelkop's calm, lean presence graces one of the many tables strewn with electronic equipment, the now all-too-familiar silver laptop and portable mixing unit perched in front of him. Formerly of the electro-acoustic trio THU20 and also in the group GOEM, Meelkop has an above-average talent for warping naturally occurring sound phenomena into electronic particle streams of varying density and vibrance. Like most artists on the bill tonight, there's a dearth of literature available to explain his exact sound construction methods, and this is presumably intentional. The "schizophonic" feel of this material's obscured origins, and the apparent lack of any desire to clarify such things, make it all the more seductive. Meelkop's performance, while not nearly as challenging to the distraction-starved consumer as Taku Sugimoto's music, is loaded with indefinable and ephemeral sound events; distant breezes and clean hovering tones acting as the shaky bridges between those portions with a greater 'presence' to them.

Just as interesting as Meelkop's computer-generated sounds, though, are the choreographed and humorously self-conscious actions of the audience (which can be seen more easily than usual since the house lights remain only slightly dimmed.) People tiptoe across the room and maneuver with exaggerated caution around the patrons still sitting on the floor, while the Uplink bartender delivers drinks to his thirsty customers in hesitant, slow motions, wincing while placing glasses down on the countertop and hoping that this action does not disrupt the show by coinciding with another dive into the depths of silence. Sign language is improvised on the spot, with some people even going so far as to draw Chinese characters in the air with their fingertips in order to get a point across. Not every extraneous sound can be suppressed for the good of the performance, though: the air conditioning unit abruptly lurches and rattles to life, and even the recurring sound of cigarette smoke being exhaled through pursed lips is highly audible. Given the nature of the sounds Meelkop produces himself, though, these intrusions are actually complementary to the performance- this time, at least, the balance seems to be right.

Walking Into Midnight

If the audience for the Meelkop show seems appreciative – and they are, as their sincere, beaming faces attest - it is because this is the kind of thing that can be experienced very rarely in one of the world's commercial epicenters, whether as performance or as the mundane material of everyday, unconsciously enacted routines. Just a few blocks away from the hermetically sealed environment of the Uplink Factory,[24] the incessant burbling of voices rising from the 'Hachiko' exit of Shibuya Station melts into a cacophony of looped advertisements emanating from loudspeakers. The rhythmic growls and pukings of assorted motor vehicles add a kind of percussive undercurrent to the whole sonic drama. The noise itself is too blurred to be instantaneously irritating at a sensory level, unless we consider the unspoken message behind much of it: a fusillade of incoming commands and directives urging lockstep uniformity and punctuality, or at the very least a ceaseless transit from one point of consumption to the next. Tokyo and its Japanese metropolitan cousins, unlike those cities built upon the European model (i.e. an administrative center nested within a gradually less active series of inner and outer rings), is a de-centralized aggregate of "functional clusters" designed to each accommodate its own type of activity - rarely, even in the cities' impressive subterranean developments, are there "clusters" that exist for a kind of "constructive inaction." Even the larger parks or "green spaces" are colonized for coordinated dance routines, acoustic guitar sing-alongs and other leisure time activities- doubtlessly lots of fun for those involved, but intrusive upon those who wish for a space of reflection that is not a specifically monastic setting.

So, as with Francisco López and his "restless pursuit of nothingness," there is a sense among the Asian 'quiet music' audiences of searching after something that will function as a pause button for their hectic lives and give them more time to discover the multitudinous, exquisite details which normally glide right by them. With life screaming by at Shibuya speed, there really is no time to put it into context, to determine where one fits into the larger scheme of things (or even if 'fitting in to the larger scheme of things' is necessary at all.) It is a quest that expands beyond the world of the audible, as can be discovered in an offbeat travel guide entitled *Yami ni Aruku* [Walking in Darkness]. The author of this 2001 volume, "night hiker" Jun Nakano, dedicates chapters to listening for the 'voice of stones' while on his solitary mountain treks, as well as penning a chapter entitled "The Pleasure of Being Buried in Darkness", and even one dedicated to finding web pages which are no more than darkened screens. The last item is especially interesting in light of Noriyuki Tajima's assertion that the Internet represents the "emerging virtual agora" in those Japanese mega-cities where the physical public space serving similar functions is shrinking.[25]

A resurgence of archaic values is slowly, but surely, sneaking into the subculture of the hyper-modern citadels of Asia, and I can attest personally that Taku Sugimoto is not alone as he wearies of "horizontal" culture. Despite its being at, or near, the forefront of global commerce and having a pronounced desire for the transient and gimmicky, Japan still has the world's largest population of citizens aged 60 and over (it also has the world's highest median age), those who might be more inclined towards a less turbulent way of life. There are many others, and not just in the musical realm, who seek a reprieve from modern relentlessness: a reprieve from being nearly blinded by the banks of halogen lights installed in Japanese electronics stores and supermarkets, and from other staples of an "always on" society.

Quieting the mind has been the goal of Eastern mystical traditions for thousands of years, but only recently has 'congestion culture' –Asian or otherwise- provided the impetus for non-mystical rationalists to attempt this. While massage parlors and public baths provide adequate stress release for the average work-a-day businessman, other more radical forms of escape are part of the urban landscape, for those who look hard enough: hermetically sealed flotation tanks (or "isolation tanks") filled with warm water and Epsom salts can be found in Manhattan, Chicago, and elsewhere (a website named "Float Finder" lists a scattered number in the U.S. and along the Eastern coastline of Australia, but no Japanese entries as of yet.) Such methods, largely associated with the hallucinogen-based experimentation of John C. Lilly, have not exactly become popular after decades of public availability- but the time may yet come where congestion culture leads to a resurgence in demand for these and other extreme forms of willful noise-cancellation (one caveat here: Lilly himself saw sensory deprivation method of the flotation tank as a means of generating "white noise energy," a hitherto filtered-out data which he understood as allow[ing] quick and random access to memory and lower[ing] the threshold to unconscious memories [expansion of consciousness.])"[26]

As could be guessed for a musical culture which is so diversified in terms of its tools, approaches, and geographic bases, not everyone is "of one mind" about how to clear the mind of , or even if the aim of "playing" silence is to internalize that silence. Different treatments of time (which, again, is the only real compositional metric for silence) provide the most dramatic differences in the quest for some meaningful self-realization: like

Taku Sugimoto, one could choose to simply not play or act where an action is normally expected. On the other hand, you could fill the space around you with some simplistic, yet constant sound element, in order to prevent the mind from wandering off on its endless digressions. *Touching Extremes* editor Massimo Ricci has preferred the effects of the latter method, saying

> I used to play Klaus Wiese's Tibetan bowl loops day in, day out at high volume to fight the extreme noise that my neighbors made. It was like living in an aquarium, yet those external noises were somehow silenced and I managed to reach some moment of calmness amidst total mayhem. Now that my surroundings are definitely more tranquil, if I hear birds and wind, or my overall favorite sound – the distant moan of airplanes, which I often quote while writing about certain kinds of music – I can imagine walking a path that could hypothetically lead to a sort of inner quietness, but silence? No way.[27]

Ricci elaborates on his distinction between 'quiet' vs. 'silence' as follows, while explaining his fondness for the drone as an ideal vessel of the former concept:

> What I can say is that static music – the really deep one, not the shit coming from the 'dark ambient' market - is the best symbol of silence. It represents it better than music that includes 'silent' segments, as long as they could be. When I listen to Phill Niblock, god bless his soul, or to something like Mirror's *Front Row Centre* – dozen of tracks, a single majestic drone – that sounds like REAL silence to me. The silence of the mind. When the mind isn't wandering around looking for popcorn reflections about evolution, netherworld, big doors and presumed meditations, but is only blessed by the essential purity of sound, then you've reached what's the nearest thing to silence. All the rest is bullshit – including 4'33".[28]

Sensory Overload, Or Information Deprivation?

It might seem odd to be profiling this style of music in a book that also lauds the abrasive, engulfing, sensory overload of Industrial culture- but after scratching the surface, we can come to realize that one animating spark behind both sonic subcultures – a zeal for 'awakening' dormant perceptual faculties in the listener - is quite similar, although the production processes and ideological subtexts may differ wildly. Proper, concentrated use of both noise and silence takes music beyond the realm of mere sound, making it a total awakener of the senses: 'active' rather than 'passive' listening occasionally forces us to fill the moments of vague perceptibility with other kinds of information, be it visual, olfactory, or tactile. Naturally, 'vague' perceptibility could apply to high-volume showers of white noise in which – like white light - all audible frequencies are contained, but could apply as well as to the musical nano-technology of someone like Bernhard Günter; rhapsodies of tiny mechanical anomalies that require close attention to discover or, if one finds no excitement in the discovery process alone, to be invested with meaningfulness.

To illustrate this concept, consider an anecdote from Samuel R. DeLany's titanic "city book" *Dhalgren*. In this extended prose poem of oneiric strangeness, characters inhabit a city, Bellona, which seems to be a living entity owing to its mysterious spatial and temporal distortions: twin moons and other celestial anomalies appear in the sky, never to be seen again, or major landmarks shift location from day to day. Against this idiosyncratic backdrop, the story's main protagonist, Kid, encounters a former astronaut named Kamp, who relays to him the following about a 'sensory overload' experiment he once encountered:

> They had spherical rear-projection rooms, practically as big as this place here. They could cover it with colors and shapes and flashes. They put earphones on me and blasted in beeps and clicks and oscillating frequencies [...] After two hours of fillips and curlicues of light and noise, when I went outside into the real world, I was astounded at how...*rich* and complicated everything suddenly looked and sounded: the textures of concrete, tree bark, grass, the shadings from sky to cloud. But rich in comparison to the sensory overload chamber...*rich*...and I suddenly realized what the kids had been calling a sensory overload was really information deprivation.[29]

Within this story, those who have undergone the same experiment as Kamp are instructed to sift out specific pre-set patterns from the barrage of incoming sights and sounds, although there is a catch: the test group that Kamp belongs to is the 'control group' in the experiment, which did not receive any such patterns, even though they were told this would be the case. Any patterns that Kamp creates are the result of imposing his own will onto this heavily random mass of sensory information. In Kamp's case, it was over-saturation of noise and light that led him to once again see the external world in all its fullness, but this same 'experiment' could be carried out very easily with music of incredible quiet or austerity. Straining our minds to seek out information with which to 'fill the gap,' we are re-introduced to the textures and elements which had long been dismissed as extraneous or transitory information, or merely as tools to help with proprioceptive orientation. Kamp seems to confirm the possibility of this by using a visual example: "Take any view in front of you, and cut off the top and bottom till you've only got an inch-wide strip, and you'll still be amazed at all the information you can get from just running your eye along that."[30]

It is, in the end, just a matter of willfully deciding to do this "cutting" in the first place: we can rise to a newer and more exciting level of contact with the most quotidian occurrences and the most menial objects, but only as active participants, and not as people who expect all incoming information to be presented to us with the naked simplicity of an instruction manual. It will take definite work to overcome years of being inundated with of pop culture trivia, the loud-yet-insubstantial blather of talk show pundits, and other modern media detritus. Thankfully, though, there is music that makes this process seem not so much like 'work' at all. Once the hostile attitude towards silence is shed, it moves from being a yawning void to being a voluptuous substance. Silence, as employed by the artists mentioned here - and many more like them - is not death, but an essential component in the process of revitalization.

Technology Beyond Technology:
Electronic Audio and Post-Humanism

The past several years have seen a noticable uptick in the amount of publications dealing with the most experimental or radical forms of electronic audio. At one point not so long ago, a harvest this bountiful seemed impossible, and it seemed as if several manifestations of audio creativity would be forgotten and left behind for a yet newer "wave" before any lessons had been learned or any conclusions had been drawn. Many of us in this scene can still remember the mild shocks received when, as recently as 1999, a full-size monograph on Throbbing Gristle - still one of the more widely recognized artists associated with "all this stuff" - came on the market. Even as pre-millenial cultural re-assessment went into overdrive, it seemed surprising that a fairly resourceful publisher (of mainly architectural books) would give this subject the time of day. But the brief sense of surprise coming from incidents like these eventually gave way to a sense of vindication, or even relief. They signaled a growing understanding, within the sociological or 'cultural studies' circuits, of something that was already known to the people dirtying their hands with unorthodox electronic music: that the numerous 'electronic' subgenres were much further apart aesthetically than music enthusiasts were socially, and that the audience for Alvin Lucier or David Tudor could very well be the same audience for Coil or Merzbow.

The days of bewilderment over non-'dance' electronic music seem to be mostly behind us, with an exponential increase in the discussion (documented or otherwise) on this culture. New academic and critical volumes regularly appear on such previously unapproachable topics as "noise," supplemented by a worldwide distribution of conferences and workshops (many of which now follow a familiar pattern of explicating how "noise" or other such problematic "genres" elegantly confirm some other socio-cultural or phenomenological thesis - but this is not necessarily a bad thing.) Magazines and journals unaffiliated with music now deign to review albums of "extreme computer music" or near-silence, in thoughtful tones that are a far cry from the notes of exasperation or dismissal that might have been sounded in the past. It could also be said that the performance stages for this material have finally come to represent radical electronic music's own shared lineage with multi-media or intermedia art, and that the days of presenting this music before hostile audiences - who are expecting perhaps a "band" or a virtuoso DJ - are also mercifully numbered.

So, of course, the first question that has to be asked *en route* to this book's conclusion is - *why now*? Given that musing on electronics already has us thinking in a technological mode, the easy answer is the coming of the accelerated, broadband information age and its globalization of the "access principle" associated with pre-internet "d.i.y." cultures. Yet quasi-mystical narratives based on the rise of the internet too often make it seem like the internet itself was an independent, conscious being that persuaded billions of people over time to become absorbed in its energy - as if the global network of computers communicating with each other could be decoupled from the global network of humans relaying their own communications within this code, or as if the information system had always existed fully apart from the nervous system. Too many internet encomia do not seriously consider the types of people and types of activities that enabled and embraced this new connectivity. The steady rise in fiber-optically connected, cyberspace-savvy citizens occurred thanks to their interest in amplifying and refining their public images (via social networks, laboriously constructed avatars, etc.), or forming new and different bonds with other members of the species. Certainly much fetishization of the enabling technology took place during these processes, but this was largely distributed among the who saw the etherealization of technology as a necessary step towards a great evolutionary end. The majority of the "wired" populace, however, used these means with no regard for this larger picture.

I believe the increased interest in analyzing the new species of electronic art is related to a fatigue with such techno-centric narratives, which ignore a "push-pull" dynamic interaction between humans and technology in favor of a much more simplistic telling. This story is one wherein humans are ineluctably drawn into the nets of technology, which has been "playing dumb" all along and feigning passivity, but now reveals itself to be a possibly predatory force independent of its creators. Other versions of the same story may simply portray the technology as a benevolent, yet nonetheless independent, force. Given this state of affairs, Krzysztof Ziarek's thoughts on technology and art seem especially worth relating here: "With the rapid advances of informational technologies and the internet, even cultural and aesthetic changes and innovations seem to lie more in the domains of the informational and the virtual than the aesthetic."[1]

It is a point worth discussing- do the overloaded computer compositions on some of the 'classic' Mego releases represent a real, quantifiable aesthetic shift, or does their strength lie in a kind of non-aesthetic documentation of technological imperfection? Do "lo-bit" MP3 recordings, with their near-total distribution over the internet and their intentionally degraded sound, count for someone's idea of beautification, or are they, too, a counter-narrative to that of exponential techno progress? Do sample-laden "media jams" and mash-ups come to this same fork in the road? None of these questions seem to have a definitive answer at the moment, yet they do lead us back to a larger question of which these questions are variants- is technologically sophisticated audio work limited to only teaching us about our relationship to that technology? According to Nick Prior, it is dangerously close to becoming publicly perceived as only making reference to technology. As he suggests,

> ...so much more creative agency is being attributed to the machine than the musician that it becomes difficult to hold together the hegemonic idea of music as logocentric (i.e. having a human author) with an unambiguously positive relationship to the performance.[2]

In such a climate, the earlier comments of Roc Jiménez de Cisneros - about making computers pass "musical Turing tests" - come to mind. It can only be good news if we stop using these tools as a means of replicating what we already have before us, and, provided we still agree that computers are worth having, focus instead on their capabilities for bringing about some new sensation or experience. Yet in this process of trying to make some kind of evolutionary difference, it is interesting to note how much of the more successful or influential electronic audio is a kind of hybrid experience where neither a human nor 'post-human' element takes precedence: from the screamed glissandi of Whitehouse's William Bennett to the decomposed guitar of Christian Fennesz, there seems to be a much greater receptivity towards those forms that are not clearly "meta-technological," and which rely on electronic composition for a greater expressive or tonal range rather than for their ability to document our current phase of technological mediation. The increase in music intended as part of a synesthetic experience, and also that which allows one to "hear with the body," seems to appeal on the same level - it dramatizes or even eroticizes our pre-rational sensory connection to the entire world. This is an intense experience that is not appreciably heightened by knowing what technology is being used to that end, and, as Gareth Loy suggested even the surprise generated by discovering new interfaces means little if it is not "a surprise that reveals something."[3]

De-emphasizing the role of electronics in electronic audio may seem paradoxical, but, then again, the "electronic music" designation is just one in a long series of similarly needless terms. The tool-specific classiciation system that gives us "string music," "computer music," etc. has made it seem like audiences cared more about tools *qua* tools rather than about their many intended and unintended effects. This perception of things is, again, rather like the study of the internet as an entity that acts apart from human agency. From here, we are only one step away from a historicism that sees the triumph of technological automation as a - like it or not - our collective destiny. And with such of a vision of an "inevitable" future in place, subjugating or annihilating millions of sentient beings becomes a justifiable sacrifice in order to hasten its realization.

The desire to sacrifice all other needs to the advancement of the "mega-technic" civilization (as Lewis Mumford called it) has often been associated, not always incorrectly, with the reactionary modernism of fascistic, imperialistic regimes. Yet it has always been a more bi-partisan affair than this. While the idea of a technological salvation continues to have some traction in the "archeo-futurism" of New Right cultural critics like Guillaume Faye, the same totalitarian urge was rife within the Soviet Union during its quest for the so-called *novy byt* ['new living'.] The building of the utilitarian *Homo Sovieticus* even necessitated, in the eyes of the Constructivist avant-garde of the late 1920s, coercive eugenics programs, which were dramatized in at least one eyebrow-raising theatrical production (Sergei Tret'iakov's *I Want A Child!*)[4]

Meanwhile, one pernicious feature of global capitalism - its tendency towards ephemerality or pre-planned obsolescence of its products - was ironically the same feature that animated many of its ideological rivals: the marriage of ephemerality to a relentless march of techno-scientific progress also has its roots in the New Left of the 1960s and beyond. The Parisian think-tank *Utopie* was fond of noting, in early issues of their eponymous magazine, that the construction of houses lagged severely behind that of other modern products: this durability of construction was in fact a drawback since it made for lived environments that did not truly reflect human advancement in other areas (thus their half-serious, half-parodic proposals for *habitations gonflables* or inflatable / pneumatic architecture.) An echo of this came from architect Cedric Price's lament of the "constipated city" with its "legacy of redundant buildings," whose "resultant use patterns act as a straitjacket to total use and enjoyment."[5] An odd man out in the new utopian architectural movements of the 1960s may have been the Japanese Metabolist architects, who came from too many different ideological positions to be given any one political orientation, yet did provide some inspiration to utopian designers of the Left (*Utopie* included.)

The Metabolists called upon a host of different organic metaphors to envision an anthropomorphic urban landscape in continual flux. Metabolist godfather Kenzo Tange (along with his assistants Kisho Kurokawa, Sadao Watanabe and Arata Isozaki) used the imagery of biological circuitry to propose a new city of endlessly recombinant "cellular" dwelling units- the Metabolist affiliated architect Kiyonori Kikutake even conceptualized, as early as 1959, a set of built environments supplemented by a kind of inhabited "foliage," or rather "a 'move-net' in which fixed structures allow building units to 'grow and die and grow again'".)[6] In the 21st century, the microbiological inspiration for the development of cities, social processes and telecommunication has been scaled down even further. Or perhaps it would be more accurate to say that this process has been inverted - instead of, say, designing urban sectors in which housing units are "cells" blown up to greater proportions, numerous thinkers now consider shrinking technological artifice back down to invisible "nano" levels where it will be indistinguishable from the microbial. As the performance artist Stelarc suggests,

> We already have colonies of microbes and bacteria and viruses inside the body. To introduce nano-machines would mean to augment the bacterial environment and to construct surveillance systems for the body that at the moment it doesn't have.[7]

Stelarc's own predictions seem downright modest in comparison with that of the inventor Ray Kurzweil's great extropian hope, the "nanobots": tiny artificial intelligences that are seen as being the future hosts of human consciousness, or a kind of silicon-based vehicle for metempsychosis. Though no larger than a nanometer in scale, Kurzweil posits that these units will be able to configure themselves into intelligent, modular and polymorphic swarms comprised of "foglets," after which the fun will really begin - once the nanobots infiltrate the human brain, they can then act upon the brain's neurons and multiply the intelligence contained within until non-biological intelligence reigns.

So, whereas Stelarc envisions the future cyborg as "a biological body with all its machinery inside instead of outside"[8] - still a symbiosis of biology and technology - Kurzweil sees the nano-technology as a means to *transcend* biology (the actual subtitle of his 2005 book on the subject), immortalizing human consciousness within human artifice. Not content with this alone, Kurzweil proposes immortality itself as being a logical step *en route* to the colonization of the entire universe by human intelligence. The term "post-humanism" is often used when describing this process, yet it is more appropriate to call it a "pan-humanism" in which the entire explorable universe is now permeated with the products of our own intelligence.

So, the "musical Turing tests" mentioned by Cisneros come from very much the same place as the prognostications of Ray Kurzweil or certain self-contradicting pronouncements of Stelarc[9], and all of these lead to the same conclusion. Namely, their shared goal is a post-humanity that is in fact highly anthropocentric, not based in true speculation as to what may lie beyond us but rather in a questionable attempt at attaining species immortality through techno-scientific means. Kurzweil's vision of human consciousness being ported into nanobots with tiny human-like appendages seems, when we consider all else that may be possible, as silly and narcissistic as the alien species in vintage *Star Trek* shows (most of whom were humanoid creatures with no evolutionary distinctions greater than pointy ears, antennae, or the occasional menacing goatee.) Yet the chain of "anthropocentric but 'post-human'" forms of artificial intelligence to is not at all a shock, coming from a species that has historically designed thousands of gods in its own image. And now we strive to *become* those gods- a situation that John Gray synopsizes by remarking how God is now "seen as the end-point of evolution…in this version of theism it is not God that creates humans. Rather it is humans who are God in the making."[10]

✛

I contend that the most meaningful artwork is not that which acts as a reflective allegory or a "mirror" to the society in which it exists, but that which can be both the mirror and a portal into other unexplored territories. Of course, fashioning such portals and convincing audiences to go through them does imply a program aiming at constructive change or progress - but this does not have to be a change that can be quantified equally in each person who passes through, and the act of crossing this threshold may involve a personal evolution that is negative just as well as positive, or may have absolutely no teleological value. This is a fact too often ignored by techno-eschatological fantasies of an evolutionary end point. The "other side" of this portal may present something different for each person who passes through it, and the seductive or mysterious quality of the pre-passage state is what we might call the aesthetic value of such an experience. The transformation that can be undergone by such experiences does not need to have anything to do with further technical progress.

Returning briefly to Stelarc's vision of post-humanism from above, he suggests a teleology of constant self-intensification:

> We have never been biological bodies, really. What it means to be human is to construct tools, artifacts, to use language and so on. In a way then, we have always been cyborgs. We fear the involuntary, we fear the automatic but we fear what we have always been and what we have already become. We have always been zombies, and we have already become cyborgs.[11]

Much of what has happened in this book, however, is a partial refutation of this scenario. Existing technology has been used solely as a means of creating artwork that puts mystery back into the human world, and that sidesteps this ineluctable zombie-like pull towards the "singularity." From the 'schizophonic' sound work of artists like Francisco López to the alleged alien communications of ElPH, much work has been done to puncture human hubris about its centrality its own home planet (to say nothing of the universe), and even to de-accelerate those technological processes that are seen as moving inevitably forward. An aesthetic built around the quieting of electronic processes (Bernhard Günter), or upon their disruption (Yasunao Tone) may still be enabled by technology, yet no longer has anything to do with kinesis for the sake of further kinesis. The increasing lucidity, fidelity, and ease of transmitting this work can be attributed to technological refinement as well, but these qualities no longer have to be taken as this work's meaning.

This work represents a kind of technology against, in Ziarek's reckoning, "power-oriented modes of being,"[12] which we can certainly take to mean either Kurzweil's or Stelarc's self-intensification. Yet this does not mean powerlessness as a kind of suicidal act, carried out to spite a human species that recognizes no other value than its own propagation throughout the farthest reaches of the universe. For Ziarek, this is something quite different: "When attached to art, the 'less' in the adjective 'powerless' does not necessarily mean lack of power but, instead, indicates a trace of a release, an economy or constellation of forces that unfold otherwise than power."[13] To put it simply, it is art that seeks out the limitless regenerative possibilities of chaos.

Bibliography / works cited

Armitage, John w/ Virilio, Paul & Kittler, Friedrich. "The Information Bomb: A Conversation." *Angelaki: Journal of the Theoretical Humanities*, Vol. 4 No. 2, pp. 81-90.

Attali, Jacques. *Noise: The Political Economy of Music*, p. 12. University of Minnesota Press, Minneapolis, 2003.

Barber, Llorenç & Palacois, Montserrat (ed.) *La Mosca Tras La Oreja: de la Música Experimental al Arte Sonore en España* Ediciones Autor, Madrid, 2009.

Barthes, Roland. *Image-Music-Text*. Noonday, New York, 1977.

Bataille, Georges. *Eroticism*. Penguin Classics, London, 2001.

Baudrillard, Jean. *Impossible Exchange*. Verso, London / New York, 2001.

Beausse, Pascal. "Teresa Margolles: Primordial Substances." *Flash Art* #38 (January 2005), p. 108.

Behrens, M. "Merzbow." *SIAM Letter* Vol. 5. No. 1. (July 1992) pp 31-33.

Bell, Clive. Review of *Rectal Anarchy* by Merzbow and Gore Beyond Necropsy. *The Wire* #163, (September 1997), p.59.

Besant, Annie & Leadbetter, C.W. *Thought-Forms*. Theosophical Publishing Society, London / Benares, 1905.

Bey, Hakim. *Immediatism*. AK Press, San Francisco, 1994.

Biehl, Janet & Staudenmaier, Peter. *Ecofascism: Lessons from the German Experience.* AK Press, San Francisco, 1995.

Blau, Herbert. "From the Dreamwork of Secession to Orgies Mysteries Theatre." *Modern Drama*, Vol. 52 No. 3 (Fall 2009), pp. 263-282.

Bodroghkozy, Aniko. *Groove Tube: Sixties Television and the Youth Rebellion*. Duke

University Press, Durham / London, 2001.

Bongers, Bert. "Interview With Sensorband." *Computer Music Journal,* Vol. 22 No. 1, pp. 13-24 (p. 20.)

Borthwick, Ben. "The Perfect Strom" *The Wire* #283, December 2003, p. 40-45.

Boulanger, Richard (ed.) *The C-Sound Book.* MIT Press, Cambridge MA, 2000.

Boutoux, Thomas (ed.) *Hans Ulrich Obrist Interviews, Vol. 1.* Charta Books, Milan, 2003.

Breitsameter, Sabine. "Acoustic Ecology and the New Electroacoustic Space of Digital Networks." *Soundscape: The Journal of Acoustic Ecology,* Vol. 4 No. 2 (Winter 2003), pp. 24-30.

Buckley, Annie. "Viewpoint." *Artweek* Vol. 38 No. 9 (2007), p. 4.

Buckley, Joshua (ed.) & Moynihan, Michael (ed.) *Tyr* #2. Ultra Publishing, Atlanta, 2004.

Cage, John. *Silence.* Wesleyan University Press, Middleton CT, 1973.

van Campen, Cretien. *The Hidden Sense: Synesthesia in Art and Science.* MIT Press / Leonardo Books, Cambridge / London, 2010.

Capra, Fritjof. *The Tao of Physics.* Shambala Books, Boston, 1991.

Cascella, Daniella. "Carl Michael von Hausswolff." *Organised Sound,* Vol. 13 No. 1. (April 2008), pp. 21-29.

Cascone, Kim. "The Aesthetics of Failure: 'Post-Digital' Tendencies in Contemporary Computer Music." *Computer Music Journal,* Vol. 24, No. 4 (Winter, 2000), pp. 12-18.

Castelvechhi, Davide. "The Power of Induction: Cutting the Last Cord Could Resonate with Our Increasingly Gadget-Dependent Lives." *Science News,* Vol. 172 No. 3 (Jul. 21, 2007), pp. 40-41.

Chandler, Anne-Marie & Neumark, Norie (ed.) *At A Distance: Precursors To Art And Activism On The Internet.*MIT Press, Cambridge MA, 2005.

Charles, Christophe. "Megalopolis Aborigines: The Tokyo-Osaka Action Art Ensemble's 1992 Tour." *Leonardo Music Journal,* Vol. 4 (1994), pp. 99-102.

Collins, Karen. "Dead Channel Surfing: the Commonalities Between Cyberpunk Literature and Industrial Music." *Popular Music* Vol. 24. No. 2. (May 2005), pp. 165-178.

Collins, Nick & Brown, Andrew R. "Generative Music Editorial." *Contemporary Music Review,* Vol. 28 No. 1, pp. 1-4.

Cox, Christoph. "Case Sensitive." *The Wire,* # 229 March 2003, p. 28-33.

Critical Art Ensemble. *Electronic Civil Disobedience and Other Unpopular Ideas.* Autonomedia, New York, 1996.

Csicsery-Ronay, Jr., Istvan. "Pre2K Post2K Virtualities: *Television, Media Art, and Cyberculture* by Margaret Morse; *Digital Delirium* by Arthur Kroker; Marilouise Kroker; *Virtual Futures: Cyberotics, Technology and Post-Human Pragmatism* by Joan Broadhurst Dixon; Eric Cassidy - Review." *Science Fiction Studies,* Vol. 27 No. 3 (Nov. 2000), pp. 485-493.

Cytowic, Richard E. *Synesthesia: A Union Of The Senses.* MIT Press, Cambridge / London, 2002.

Davis, Erik. *TechGnosis: Myth, Magic and Mysticism in the Age of Information.* Three Rivers Press, New York, 1999.

Dean, Roger T. w/ Whitelaw, Mitchell, Smith, Hazel & Worrall, David. "The Mirage of Real-Time Algorithmic Synaesthesia: Some Compositional Mechanisms and Research, Agendas in Computer Music and Sonification." *Contemporary Music Review,* Vol. 25 No. 4, pp. 311-326.

DeLany, Samuel R. *Dhalgren.* Vintage Books, New York, 2001.

Deleuze, Gilles. *Cinema 2: The Time-Image.* University of Minnesota Press, Minneapolis, 1989.

_____. *Francis Bacon: The Logic of Sensation.* University of Minnesota Press, Minneapolis, 2005.

De Ruyter, Thibault. "CM von Hausswolff." *Art Press* No. 310 (March 2005), pp. 76-77.

Duchamp, Marcel & Cabanne, Pierre. *Dialogues with Marcel Duchamp.* Da Capo, London, 1971.

Dufour, Frank. "Pierre Schaeffer and the Invention of Musique Concrète." *Soundscape: The Journal of Acoustic Ecology,* Vol. 8 No. 1 (Fall / Winter 2008), pp. 17-19.

Duncan, John. *John Duncan: Works 1975-2005.* Errant Bodies Press, Copenhagen, 2006.

Dworkin, Andrea. *Pornography: Men Possessing Women.* The Women's Press, London, 1991.

Dwyer, Simon (ed.) *Rapid Eye Vol.3.* Creation Books, London, 1995.

Elggren, Leif. *Genealogy.* Firework Edition, Stockholm, 2005.

Eliade, Mircea. *Shamanism: Archaic Techniques of Ecstasy.* Princeton University Press, Princeton NJ, 1992.

Ford, Simon. *Wreckers of Civilisation.* Black Dog Publishing Ltd., London, 1999.

Friedman, Ken (ed.) *Fluxus Reader.* John Wiley & Sons, New York, 1998.

Gangemi, Gregory. "Francisco López: Belle Confusion." *The Sound Projector,* No. 11 (2003), p. 32.

Gendreau, Michael. *Parataxes: Fragments Pour Une Architecture Des Espaces Sonores.* Van Dieren Editeur, Lausanne, 2010.

George, Don. *Sweet Man: The Real Duke Ellington* by Don George. G.P. Putnam's Sons, New York, 1981.

Goodman, David. "New Japanese Theater." *The Drama Review: TDR,* Vol. 15, No. 2 (Spring 1971), pp. 154-168.

Grant, Morag Josephine. "Experimental Music Semiotics." *International Review of the Aesthetics and Sociology of Music,* Vol. 34, No. 2 (December 2003), pp. 173-191.

Gray, John. *Heresies: Against Progress and Other Illusions.* Granta, London, 2004.

_____. *Straw Dogs: Thoughts on Humans and Other Animals.* Granta Books, London, 2002.

_____. *The Immortalization Commission: Science and the Strange Quest to Cheat Death.* Farrar, Strauss & Giroux, New York, 2011.

Green, Karen. "De Sade, De Beauvoir, and Dworkin." *Australian Feminist Studies,* Vol. 15 No. 31, pp. 69-80.

Green, Malcolm (ed.) *Atlas Arkhive Documents of the Avant-Garde 7: Writings of the Viennese Aktionists.* Atlas Press, London, 1999.

Grof, Stanislav. *The Holotropic Mind.* Harper Collins, New York,1990.

Grotowsky, Jerzy. *Towards a Poor Theater.* Simon & Schuster, New York, 1969.

Gunderson, Philip A. "Danger Mouse's Grey Album, Mashups, and the Age of Composition." *Postmodern Culture* Vol. 15 No. 1 (2004).

Harris, Stephen L. & Platzner, Gloria. *Classical Mythology,* 2nd edition. Mayfield Publishing Co., London / Toronto, 1995.

Harwood, Mark. Review of "What is Music?" festival. *Wire* #194 (April 2000), p. 85.

Hegarty, Paul. "Noise Threshold: Merzbow and the End of Natural Sound."

Organised Sound, Vol.6. No. 3. (December 2001), pp 193-200.

Heinbroner, Robert L. *The Worldly Philosophers.* Touchstone, New York, 1992.

Heyler, Ruth. "Parodied To Death: The Postmodern Gothic of American Psycho." *MFS Modern Fiction Studies,* Vol. 46 No. 3 (Fall 2000), pp. 725-746 (p. 736.)

Hovagimyan, G.H. "Art in the Age of Spiritual Machines (With Apologies to Ray Kurzweil)." *Leonardo,* Vol. 34, No. 5 (2001), pp. 453-458.

Jenny, Hans. *Cymatics: A Study of Wave Phenomena and Vibration.* Macromedia Press, 2001.

Joseph, Brandon W. *Beyond The Dream Syndicate: Tony Conrad and the Arts after Cage.* Zone Books, New York, 2008.

Jung, Carl Gustav (ed.) *Man And His Symbols.* Aldus Books Ltd., London,1964.

Kahn, Douglas & Whitehead, Gregory (ed.) *Wireless Imagination: Sound, Radio, and the Avant Garde.* MIT Press, Cambridge MA., 1992.

Kandinsky, Wassily. *Concerning The Spiritual In Art.* Dover Publications, New York, 1977.

Keister, Jay & Smith, Jeremy L. "Musical Ambition, Cultural Accreditation, and the Nasty Side of Progressive Rock." *Popular Music,* Vol. 27 No. 3. (October 2008), pp 433-455.

Kelly, Kevin. *Out of Control: The Rise of the Neo-Biological Civilization,* Addison-Wesley, Reading MA, 1994.

Kinsella, Sharon. "Subculture in the 1990s: Otaku and the Amateur Manga Movement." *Journal of Japanese Studies,* Vol. 24, No. 2 (Summer 1998), pp. 289-316.

Kollectiv, Galia & Kollectiv, Pil. "Birth of a State: A Distant Report on the First Congress of the NSK State in Berlin." *Art Papers* Vol. 35 No. 2 (March/April 2011), pp. 30-9.

Kopf, Biba. Review of *Space Metalizer* by Merzbow. *The Wire* #163, (September 1997), p. 67.

Jakobson, Roman. *Language in Literature.* Harvard University / Belknap Press, Cambridge MA, 1990.

Jones, Keith. "Music in Factories: A Twentieth Century Technique for Control of the Productive Self." *Social & Cultural Geography,* Vol. 6 No. 5, pp. 723-744.

Juno, Andrea (ed.) and Vale, V. (ed.) *Pranks!* Re/Search, San Francisco, 1987.

_____ & _____. *Re/Search* #4/5. Re/Search, San Francisco, 1982.

_____ & _____. *Incredibly Strange Music Vol. II.* Re/Search, San Francisco, 1994.

Kaier, Christina. *Imagine No Possessions: The Socialist Objects Of Soviet Constructivism.* MIT Press, Cambridge / London, 2005.

Kelley, Mike. "An Academic Cut-Up, in Easily Digestible Paragraph-Size Chunks; Or, The New King of Pop: Dr. Konstantin Raudive." *Grey Room* #11 (Spring 2003), pp. 22-43.

Kromhout, Melle Jan. "Over the Ruined Factory There's a Funny Noise": Throbbing Gristle and the Mediatized Roots of Noise in/as Music." *Popular Music and Society,* Vol. 34 No. 01 (2011), pp. 23-34.

LaBelle, Brandon. "Sound as Space Creator: Frequency, Architecture, and Collaboration." *Soundscape: The Journal of Acoustic Ecology,* Vol 4 No. 2 (Fall / Winter 2003), pp. 48-49.

_____. *Site Specific Sound.* Errant Bodies Press, New York, 2004.

_____ & Breitsameter, Sabine. "Questionnaire." *Soundscape: The Journal of Acoustic Ecology,* Vol. 3 No. 1 (July 2002), pp. 11-14.

Lanza, Joseph, *Elevator Music.* University of Michigan Press, Ann Arbor, 2004.

LaTartara, John. "Laptop Composition at the Turn of the Millennium: Repetition and Noise in the Music of Oval, Merzbow, and Kid 606." *Twentieth Century Music,* Vol. 7 No. 1 (March 2010), pp 91-115.

Le Corbusier, *Towards a New Architecture.* Dover Publications, New York, 1986.

Ligeti, György. *Ligeti in Conversation.* Eulenburg Books, London, 1983.

Lilly, John C. *Programming and Metaprogramming in the Human Biocomputer.* The Julian Press, New York, 1972.

Lohner, Henning & Xenakis, Iannis. "Interview with Iannis Xenakis." *Computer Music Journal,* Vol. 10, No. 4 (Winter 1986), pp. 50-55.

Marchetti, Lionel. "The Microphone and the Hand." *Fo(a)rm* #5, p. 115.

Mattin & Iles, Anthony (ed.) *Noise And Capitalism.* Arteleku, Madrid, 2009.

Marcuse, Herbert. *Counterrevolution and Revolt.* Beacon Press, Boston, 1972.

Massumi, Brian. *Parable For The Virtual: Movement, Affect, Sensation.* Duke University Press, Durham NC, 2002.

McDonald, Scott. "Against False Distinctions." *Film Quarterly,* Vol. 35, No. 1 (Autumn, 1981), pp. 58-60.

Michael, George. "The Ideological Evolution of Horst Mahler: The Far Left–Extreme Right Synthesis." *Studies in Conflict & Terrorism,* Vol. 32 No. 4, pp. 346-366.

Miyake, Akiko (ed.) *Substantials #01.* CCA KitaKyushu, KitaKyushu, 2003.

Monroe, Alexei. *Interrogation Machine: Laibach and NSK.* MITPress, Cambridge MA., 2005.

Montgomery, Harper. "Teresa Margolles." *Art Nexus* Vol. 7. No. 71, pp. 139-140.

Moore, Nathan. "Nova Law: William S. Burroughs and the Logic of Control." *Law and Literature,* Vol. 19, No. 3 (Fall 2007), pp. 435-470.

Morell, Virginia. "Animal Minds." *National Geographic,* March 2008, p. 54.

Morgan, Ted. *Literary Outlaw.* Avon Books, New York, 1988.

Morse, Erik. "Music Box." *Modern Painters,* March 2010, pp. 30-31.

Motherwell, Robert. *Max Ernst: Beyond Painting And Other Writings by the Artist and His Friends.* Wittenborn & Schulz, New York, 1948.

Moynihan, Michael & Søderlind, Didrik. *Lords of Chaos: The Bloody Rise of the Satanic Metal Underground.* Feral House, Los Angeles, 1998.

Mumford, Lewis. *The City In History.* Harvest Books, San Diego / London / New York, 1989.

Munroe, Alexandra (ed.) *Scream Against The Sky: Japanese Art After 1945.* Harry N. Abrams, New York, 1994.

Neal, Charles (ed.) *Tape Delay.* SAF Publishing, Middlesex, 1987.

Nechvatal, Joseph. *Towards An Immersive Intelligence: Essays On The Work Of Art In The Age Of Computer Technology And Virtual Reality, 1993-2006.* Edgewise Press, New York, 2009.

Negroponte, Nicholas. *Being Digital.* Alfred A Knopf, New York, 1995.

Neill, Ben. "Pleasure Beats: Rhythm and the Aesthetics of Current Electronic Music." *Leonardo Music Journal,* Vol. 12 (2002), pp. 3-6.

Nicolai, Carsten. "The Responsive Eye: Beyond What We Call 'Art.'" *Flash Art,* March / April 2011, pp. 74-76.

Novak, David. "2.5 x 6 Metres of Space: Japanese Music Coffeehouses and Experimental Practices of Listening." *Popular Music* Vol. 7 No. 1 (January 2008), pp. 15-34.

Novak, David. "Playing Off Site: The Untranslation of Onkyo." *Asian Music,* Vol. 41

No. 1 (Winter/Spring 2010), pp. 36-59.

Odier, Daniel (w/ William S. Burroughs.) *The Job: Interviews with William S. Burroughs*. Penguin Books, New York, 1989.

O'Quinn, Jim. "Squat Theatre Underground, 1972-1976." *The Drama Review: TDR*, Vol. 23 No. 4 (December 1979), pp. 7-26.

Ostertag, Bob. *Creative Life*. University of Illinois Press, 2008.

Paglia, Camille. *Sexual Personae*. Vintage Books, New York, 1990.

Parikka, Jussi. *Digital Contagions: A Media Archaeology Of Computer Viruses*. Peter Lang, New York, 2007.

Payton, Rodney J. "The Music of Futurism: Concerts and Polemics." *The Musical Quarterly*, Vol. 62, No. 1 (Jan. 1976), pp. 25-45.

Pedersen, Michael. "Transgressive Sound Surrogacy." *Organised Sound* #16, pp. 27-35.

Penman, Ian. "England's Dreaming." *The Wire* #194, April 2000, p. 28-33.

Pinsent, Ed. Review of *Our Telluric Conversation* by John Duncan & CM von Hausswolff. *The Sound Projector* #15 (2007), p. 92.

Poggioli, Renato. *Theory Of The Avant-Garde*. Belknap/ Harvard, Cambridge / London, 1997.

Pomorska, Krystyna & Rudy, Stephen. *Roman Jakobson: Language In Literature*. Belknap Press / Harvard University Press, London / CambridgeMA, 1987.

Price, Cedric & Littlewood, Joan. "The Fun Palace." *The Drama Review: TDR*, Vol. 12, No. 3 (Spring, 1968), pp.127-134.

Prime, Michael. "Explorations in Bioelectronics." *Resonance* Vol. 9 No. 2 (2002), p. 17.

Prior, Nick. "OK COMPUTER: Mobility, Software and the Laptop Musician." *Information, Communication & Society,* Vol. 11 No. 7, pp. 912-932.

Provencher, Louise. "Atau Tanaka: Le Corps Sous Tension Ou De L'eloquence du Geste." *Parachute* No. 121 (Spring 2006), pp. 62-77.

Rader, Melvin. "The Artist As Outsider." *The Journal of Aesthetics and Art Criticism,* Vol. 16 No. 3 (March 1958), pp. 306-318 (p. 310.)

Rezaie, Shervin. "Play Your Part: Girl Talk's Indefinite Role in the Digital Sampling Saga." *Touro Law Review* No. 26 (2010), pp. 175-205.

de Ridder, Willem. "Willem de Ridder." *Contemporary Music Review,* Vol. 25, Nos. 5/6, (October/December 2006,) pp. 397 – 402.

Robbins, Ira (ed.) *Trouser Press Record Guide* (4th edition.) Collier Books, New York, 1991.

Roberts, Lucien. "Profile: To Be Frank." *Design Week,* May 1 2003, p. 15.

Rush, David. "A Noisy Silence." *PAJ: A Journal of Performance and Art,* Vol. 21, No. 1 (Jan., 1999), pp. 2-10.

Russolo, Luigi. *The Art Of Noise.* Ubu Classics, New York, 2004.

Ruthven, Malise. *A Fury for God: The Islamist Attack on America.* London / New York, Granta 2002.

von Sacher-Masoch, Leopold. *Venus in Furs.* Belmont Books, New York, 1965.

Sargeant, Jack (ed.) *Naked Lens- Beat Cinema.* Creation Books, London, 1997.

Schaeffer, Pierre. *Traité des Objets Musicaux.* Éditions du Seuil, Paris, 2002.

Schafer, R. Murray. "Open Ears." *Soundscape: The Journal of Acoustic Ecology,* Vol. 4. No. 2 (Winter 2003), pp. 14-18.

Schauwecker, Detlev. "Verbal Subversion and Satire in Japan, 1937-1945, as

Documented by the Special High Police." *Japan Review*, No. 15 (2003), pp. 127-151.

Schopenhauer, Arthur. *The World as Will and Idea*. Tuttle Publishing, North Clarendon, 1995.

Sherburne, Philip. "12K: Between Two Points." *Organized Sound*, Vol. 6 No. 3 (December 2001), pp 171 176.

Sherburne, Philip. "Donna Summer: He's a Rebel." *Wire*, April 2003, p. 14.

Singh, Abhilasa & Abraham, A. "Neuro Linguistic Programming: A Key To Business Excellence." *Total Quality Management & Business Excellence*, Vol. 19 No. 1-2, pp. 141-149.

Skinner, Heather & Stephens, Paula. "Speaking the Same Language: The Relevance of Neuro-Linguistic Programming To Effective Marketing Communications." *Journal of Marketing Communications*, Vol. 9 No. 3, pp. 177-192.

Sterne, Jonathan. *The Audible Past: Cultural Origins of Sound Reproduction*. Duke University Press, Durham / London, 2003.

Strauss, Neil (ed.) & Mandl, Dave (ed.) *Radiotext(e)*. Semiotext(e), New York, 1993.

Stuart, Caleb. "Glitching and Skipping Compact Discs in the Audio of Yasunao Tone, Nicolas Collins and Oval." *Leonardo Music Journal*, Vol. 13 (2003), pp. 47-52.

Sweezy, Stuart (ed.) *Amok Fifth Dispatch*. Amok Books, Los Angeles, 1999.

Szwed, John F. *Space Is The Place: The Lives And Times of Sun Ra*. Da Capo Press, Cambridge MA, 1998.

Tajima, Noriyuki. "Tokyo Catalyst: Shifting Situations of Urban Space." *Perspecta*, Vol. 38 (2006), pp. 79-90.

Thaemlitz, Terre. "Operating in Musical Economies of Compromise (Or . . . When do I Get Paid for Writing This?)" *Organised Sound*, Vol. 6 . No. 3 (December 2001), pp 177-184.

Tiepel, Jürgen. *Verschwende deine Jugend*. Suhrkamp Verlag, Frankfurt am Main, 2001.

Tomii, Reiko. "State v. (Anti-)Art: Model 1,000-Yen Note Incident by Akasegawa Genpei and Company." *Positions: East Asia Cultures Critique,* Vol. 10, No. 1, Spring 2002, pp. 141-172.

Toop, David. *Haunted Weather: Music, Silence and Memory*. Serpents' Tail, London, 2004.

Turner, Tad. "The Resonance of the Cubicle: Laptop Performance in Post-Digital Musics." *Contemporary Music Review,* Vol. 22 No. 4, pp. 81-92.

von Üexkull, Jakob. *A Foray into the Worlds of Human and Animals (With a Theory of Meaning)* p. 23. Trans. Joseph D. O'Neil. University of Minnesota Press, Minneapolis, 2010.

Urban, Hugh B. "The Beast with Two Backs: Aleister Crowley, Sex Magic and the Exhaustion of Modernity." *Nova Religio: The Journal of Alternative and Emergent Religions,* Vol. 7 No. 3 (March 2004), pp. 7-25.

Uroskie, Andrew V. "Beyond the Black Box: The Lettrist Cinema of Disjunction." *October* #135 (Winter 2011), pp. 21-48.

Vail, Mark (ed.) *Vintage Synthesizers*. Miller Freeman, San Francisco, 1993.

Vallee, Mickey. "The Media Contingencies of Generation Mashup: A Žižekian Critique." *Popular Music and Society* iFirst (June 2012), pp. 1-22 (p. 2.)

Van Hanen, Janne. "Virtual Sound: Examining Glitch and Production." *Contemporary Music Review,* Vol. 22 No. 4, pp. 45-52.

Virilio, Paul. *Unknown Quantity*. Thames & Hudson, New York, 2003.

de Waal, Frans. *Chimpanzee Politics*. Johns Hopkins Press, Baltimore, 2000.

Watts, Alan. *Tao: The Watercourse Way*. Pantheon Books, New York, 1975.

Wicke, Jennifer. "Through a Gaze Darkly: Pornography's Academic Market." *Transition*, No. 54 (1991), pp. 68-89.

Williams, Raymond. *The Politics of Modernism: Against the New Conformists.* Verso, London / New York, 2007.

Wishart, Trevor. "Connections." *Contemporary Music Review,* Vol. 15 No. 3-4, pp. 89-97.

Wu, Tim. *The Master Switch: The Rise And Fall Of Information Empires.* Alfred A. Knopf, New York, 2010.)

Wylie, Timothy & Parfrey, Adam (ed.) *Love Sex Fear Death: The Inside Story of the Process Church of the Final Judgment.* Feral House, Port Townsend WA, 2009.

Yamanouchi, Hisaaki. "Yukio Mishima and his Suicide." *Modern Asian Studies,* Vol. 6, No. 1 (1972), pp. 1-16.

Young, Rob. "A Glitch In The System." *Modern Painters* June 2006, pp. 90-93 .

Zepke, Stephen. "The Concept of Art When Art is Not a Concept." *Angelaki: Journal of the Theoretical Humanities,* Vol. 11 No. 1 (2006), pp. 157-167.

Ziarek, Krzysztof . "The Avant Garde and Power." *New Literary History* Vol. 33, No. 1 (Winter, 2002), pp. 89-107.

Žižek, Slavoj. "The Ongoing 'Soft Revolution.'" *Critical Inquiry,* Vol. 30, No. 2 (Winter 2004). pp. 292-323.

Recommended Listening

The following is a list of titles that figure into this text, in one way or another. Many of these are no longer available under the catalog numbers given; and may now be re-released on completely different record labels than the ones listed here. As a rule of thumb, the *original* labels and catalog numbers under which these releases appeared have been printed, for the sake of historicity. While hopelessly unavailable "collectors' items" do populate this list, have no fear: the vast majority of this music is digitized and available to those with the patience to seek it out.

Akita, Masami / Haswell, Russell, *Satanstornade*, Warp Records WARP CD666.

Alva Noto, *Prototypes*, Mille Plateaux MP 082 CD.

Ambarchi / Fennesz / Pimmon / Rehberg / Rowe, *Afternoon Tea*, Ritornell RIT014.

Ambarchi, Oren & Z'ev, *Spirit Transform Me*, Tzadik TZ8123.

Burroughs, William S., *Nothing Here Now but the Recordings*, Industrial IR 0016.

Burroughs, William S., *The Best of William Burroughs from Giorno Poetry Systems*, Mercury 314 536 701-2.

Cabaret Voltaire, *The Voice of America*, Rough Trade ROUGH 11.

Cascone, Kim, *Blue Cube [ ]*, Raster / Noton cdr014.

Cascone, Kim, *Cathode Flower*, Ritornell RIT 006 CD.

Cascone, Kim, *Dust Theories*, c74 c74-004.

Cazazza, Monte, *The Worst of Monte Cazazza*, The Grey Area MONTECD1.

Chopin, Henri, *Audiopoems*, Tangent Records TGS 106.

Chopin, Henri, *Poésie Sonore*, Igloo Records, IGL 013.

COH, *Iron,* Wavetrap WAV02.

COH, *0397 Post Pop,* Mego MEGO 076.

Coil, *ANS,* Eskaton ESKATON 034.

Coil, *Constant Shallowness Leads to Evil,* Eskaton ESKATON 024.

Coil, *Horse Rotorvator,* Force and Form ROTA 1.

Coil, *Love's Secret Domain,* WaxTrax! WAXCD 7143.

Coil, *Musick To Play in The Dark Vol. 2,* Chalice GRAAL 005CD.

Coil, *Scatology,* Force and Form FFK1.

Collins, Nicolas, *It Was a Dark and Stormy Night,* Trace Elements CD TE-1019.

Collins, Nicolas, *Sound without Picture,* Periplum CD P0060.

Cosmos, *Tears,* Erstwhile Records erstwhile 024.

Cyclo, *s/t,* Raster-Noton cdr041.

Cut Hands, *Black Mamba,* Very Friendly / Susan Lawly VFSL 012.

Duncan, John & Günter, Bernhard, *Home, Unspeakable,* Trente Oiseaux TOC 964.

Duncan, John, *Riot,* All Questions Music AQM204.

Duncan, John, *River in Flames,* Anckärstrom R9.

Duncan, John, *Send,* Touch TO:20.

Duncan, John, *Palace of Mind,* All Questions Music AQ-01.

Duncan, John & López, Francisco, *Nav,* .Absolute.[Osaka] / All Questions .a.[o] 004–01, AQ-02.

Duncan, John & von Hausswolff, Carl Michael, *Our Telluric Conversation,* 23five 008.

Duncan, John & Springer, Max, *The Crackling,* Trente Oiseaux TOC 961.

Elggren, Leif, *Flown Over By An Old King,* Radium 226.05 RAFE 044-61.

Elggren, Leif, *Talking To a Dead Queen,* Fylkingen FYCD 1008.

Elggren, Leif, *The Cobblestone is the Weapon of the Proleteriat,* Firework Edition FER 1051.

Elggren, Leif & Liljenberg, Thomas, *9.11,* Firework Edition FER 1015.

Elggren, Leif & Liljenberg, Thomas, *Cunt 69,* Firework Edition , FER 1063.

ELPH, *Worship The Glitch,* Eskaton ESKATON 007.

ELPH, *Zwölf / 20' To 2000.December,* Raster/Noton 20TO200012.

EVOL, *Punani Quatre,* Alku alku 61.

Farmers Manual, *Fsck,* Tray TRAY 2.

Farmers Manual, *Explorers_We,* OR SQUISH 4.

Farmers Manual, *RLA,* Mego MEGO 777.

Fennesz / Harding / Rehberg, *Dì-n,* Ash International ASH 4.8.

Fennesz, *Hotel Paral.lel,* Mego MEGO 016.

Fennesz, *Endless Summer,* Mego MEGO 035.

Fennesz, *Live in Japan,* Headz HEADZ 10.

Filament, *Filament 1,* Extreme XCD 045.

Furudate, Tetsuo / Karkowski, Zbigniew, *The World as Will II*, 23five 003.

GOEM, *Stud Stim*, Raster / Noton cdr 007.

Ground Zero, *Ground Zero Revolutionary Pekinese Opera (Ver 1.28)*, ReR Megacorp ReR GZ1.

Günter, Bernhard, *Un Peu de Neige Salie*, Selektion SCD 012.

Günter, Bernhard & Wehowsky, Ralf, *Un Ocean de Certitude*, V2 Archief V222.

Gysin, Brion, *Poem of Poems*, Alga Marghen 8vocson021.

Gysin, Brion, *Self-Portrait Jumping*, Made to Measure MTM 33 CD.

Haswell & Hecker, *Blackest Ever Black (Electroacoustic UPIC Recordings)*, Warner Classics & Jazz 2564 64321-2.

Haswell, Russell, *Live Salvage*, Mego MEGO 012.

Haswell, Russell, *Wild Tracks*, Editions Mego eMego 099.

von Hausswolff, Carl Michael, *Operations of Spirit Communications*, Die Stadt DS 31.

von Hausswolff, Carl Michael, *The Wonderful World of Male Intuition*, Oral CD10.

Von Hausswolff, Carl Michael, *Three Overpopulated Cities Built By Short-sighted Planners, An Unbalanced And Quite Dangerous Airport And An Abandoned Church*, Sub Rosa SR 217.

Hecker, *Speculative Solution*, Editions Mego eMego 118.

Hecker, *Sun Pandämonium*, Mego MEGO 044.

Hijokaidan, *King of Noise*, Alchemy Records ARLP-006.

Hijokaidan, *Modern*, Alchemy Records ARCD-004.

Hodell, Åke, *Verbal Brainwash and Other Works,* Fylkingen FYCD 1018.

In Be Tween Noise, *so delicate and strangely made,* New Plastic Music NPIB-1.

Incapacitants, *Repo,* Alchemy Records ARLP-027.

Incapacitants, *No Progress,* Alchemy Records ARCD-070.

Karkowski, Zbigniew, *Uexkull,* Anckärstrom K4.

Karkowski, Zbigniew / López, Francisco, *Whint,* Absolute.[London] .a.[l] 003-01.

Kurenniemi, Erkki, *Äänityksiä / Recordings 1963-1973,* Love Records LXCD 637.

Laibach, *Nova Akropola,* Cherry Red BRED 67.

Laibach, *Opus Dei,* Mute Records STUMM 44.

López, Francisco, *Belle Confusion 969,* Sonoris SON-05.

López, Francisco, *La Selva,* V2 Archief V228.

López, Francisco, *Paris Hiss,* Banned Production BP-81.

López, Francisco, *Warszawa Restaurant,* Trente Oiseaux TOC 951.

López, Francisco, *Untitled #104,* Alien8 ALIENCD 020.

López, Francisco, *Untitled (2010),* Alone at Last AAL[1].

López, Francisco & Arford, Scott, *Solid State Flesh / Solid State Sex,* Low Impedance Recordings LoZ 04.

Lucier, Alvin, *Bird and Person Dyning,* Cramps Records CRSLP 6111.

M., Sachiko, *Sine Wave Solo,* Amoebic AMO SAT 01.

MacLise, Angus, *Astral Collapse*, Locust Music LOCUST 17.

MacLise, Angus, *The Cloud Doctrine*, Sub Rosa SR 182.

Marchetti, Lionel, *Sirrus*, Auscultare Research Aus 014.

Marclay, Christian, *Record Without a Cover*, Recycled Records (no catalog number.)

Marclay, Christian, *More Encores*, ReR Megaccorp ReR CM1.

Mattin & Malfatti, Radu, *Going Fragile*, Formed Records Formed 103.

Meelkop, Roel, *9 (Holes In The Head)*, Trente Oiseaux TOC 962.

Merzbow, *Batzoutai with Material Gadgets*, RRRecords RRR005.

Merzbow, *Ecobondage*, ZSF Produkt, SH62-01.

Merzbow, *Great American Nude / Crash for Hi-Fi*, ARCD-035.

Merzbow, *Live in Khabarovsk CCCP 'I'm Proud By Rank of the Workers'*, ZSF Produkt SH63-01.

Merzbow, *Metalvelodrome*, Alchemy Records ARCD061-064.

Merzbow, *Music for Bondage Performance*, Extreme, XCD 008.

Merzbow, *Pornoise 1KG*, ZSF Produkt (no catalog number.)

Merzbow, *Pulse Demon*, Release Entertainment RR 6937-2.

Merzbow, *Rainbow Electronics*, Alchemy Records ARCD-017.

Merzbow, *Scumtron*, Blast First BFFP 138 CD.

Merzbow, *24 Hours- Day of Seals*, Dirter Promotions DPROMCD 50.

Merzbow, *Timehunter*, Ant-Zen act 146.

Mühl, Otto, *Ein Schreckliche Gedanke*, no label.

Mumma, Gordon, *Dresden / Venezia, Megaton*, Lovely Music Ltd. VR 1091.

Nakamura, Toshimaru, *No-Input Mixing Board*, Zero Gravity ZGV-026

Nakamura, Toshimaru, *Vehicle*, Cubic Music CUBIC MUSIC 08.

Nakamura, Toshimaru and M., Sachiko, *Do*, Erstwhile Records erstwhile 013.

Negativland, *Escape from Noise*, SST Records SST 133.

Negativland, *Helter Stupid*, SST Records SST 252.

Negativland, *U2*, SST Records SST 272.

Negativland, *Dispepsi*, SEELAND CD 017.

Neumann, Andrea / Krebs, Annette, *Rotophormen*, Charhizma cha009.

New Blockaders, *Symphonie in X Major*, Hypnagogia GOG01.

NON, *Pagan Muzak*, Graybeat Records GB 3301.

NON, *Physical Evidence*, Mute Records STUMM 10.

Noto, *Telefunken*, Raster / Noton cdr032.

Noto, Alva, *Transspray*, Raster / Noton R-N 63.

Noto, Alva, *Xerrox Vol. 1*, Raster / Noton R-N 78.

Okura, Masahiko / Müller, Günter / Yoshida, Ami, *Tanker*, For 4 Ears CD 1759.

Ostertag, Bob, *Sooner or Later*, ReR Megacorp ReR B01.

Ostertag, Bob, *Burns Like Fire*, RecRec Music, RecDec 53.

Ostertag, Bob, *DJ of the Month*, Seeland SEELAND 526 CD.

Oswald, John, *Discosphere*, ReR Megacorp ReR JO CD.

Oswald, John, *69 Plunderphonics 96*, Seeland / fony 515 CD / 69 96.

Oval, *94 Diskont*, Mille Plateaux MPCD13.

Oval, *OvalProcess*, Thrill Jockey thrill 081.

Pade, Else Marie, *Face It*, DaCapo Records 8.224233.

Pan Sonic, *Kulma*, Blast First BFFP 132 CD.

Pan Sonic, *A*, Mute Corporation Mute 9078-2.

Pita, *Seven Tons for Free*, Mego MEGO 009.

Pita, *Get Out*, Mego MEGO 029.

Pita, *Get Off*, Häpna H.19.

Prime, Michael, *L-Fields*, Sonoris SON-08.

Rabelais, Akira, *Spellewauerynsherde*, Samadhisound SOUND-CD ss003.

Reynols, *Blank Tapes*, Trente Oiseaux TOC 002.

Rice, Boyd, *self-titled*. No label.

Roads, Curtis, *Point Line Cloud*, Asphodel ASP 3000.

Roden, Steve, *Forms of Paper*, Line Line 007.

Roden, Steve, *Light Forms (Music For Light Bulbs and Churches)*, Semishigure semi 003.

Schwitters, Kurt, *Ursonate- Sonate in Urlauten*, Hat Hut Records, ART CD 6109.

SPK (as 'System Planning Korporation'), *Information Overload Unit*, Side Effects SER01.

SPK, *Auto-Da-Fé*, Walter Ulbricht Schallfolien, WULP002.

Sugimoto, Taku / Akiyama, Tetuzi / Wiget, Bo, *Periodic Drift*, Corpus Hermeticum Hermes 06.

Sugimoto, Taku & Krebs, Annette, *Eine Gitarre Ist Eine Gitarre Ist Keine Gitarre Ist Eine Gitarre...*, Rossbin RSS005.

Throbbing Gristle, *Second Annual Report*, Industrial IR 0002.

Throbbing Gristle, *D.o.A.- The Third and Final Report*, Industrial IR 0004.

Throbbing Gristle, *20 Jazz Funk Greats*, Industrial 0008.

Throbbing Gristle, *Heathen Earth*, Industrial IR 0009.

Tone, Yasunao, *Wounded Man'Yo #38-9/2001*, Alku hajime39.

Tone, Yasunao / Hecker, *Palimpsest*, Mego MEGO 060.

Tone, Yasunao, *s/t*. Asphodel ASP 2011.

Tujiko, Noriko, *Haado ni Sasete (Make Me Hard)*, Mego MEGO 062.

Van der Heide, Edwin / Karkowski, Zbigniew, *Datastream*, OR ORCDR001.

Various Artists, *Fals.ch*, FB25.

Various Artists, *OR MD Comp*, JUST 13.

V/VM, *Sick Love*, V/Vm Test Records OFFAL 003.

V/VM, *The Green Door*, V/Vm Test Records OFFAL 004.

Wehowsky, Ralf / Marchetti, Lionel, *Vier Vorspeile / L'Oeil Retourné*, Selektion SCD 026.

Wehowsky, Ralf, *Pullover*, Table of the Elements Ge 32.

Whitehouse, *Birthdeath Experience*, Come Organisation WDC 881004.

Whitehouse, *Cruise*, Susan Lawly SLCD024.

Whitehouse, *Erector*, Come Organisation WDC 881007.

Whitehouse, *Great White Death*, Come Organisation WDC 881069.

Whitehouse, *Halogen*, Susan Lawly SLCD007.

Whitehouse, *Racket*, Susan Lawly SLCD029.

Whitehouse, *Right to Kill*, Come Organisation WDC 881033.

Xenakis, Iannis, *Electronic Works 1 - La Légende D'Eer*, Mode mode 148.

Yoshida, Ami, *Tiger Thrush*, Improvised Music From Japan IMJ-504.

Yoshida, Ami / Kurzmann, Christof, *Aso*, Erstwhile Records erstwhile 047.

Yoshihide, Otomo, *The Night Before the Death of the Sampling Virus*, Extreme XCD 024.

Z'ev, *1968-1990: One Foot in the Grave*, Touch TO:13.

Z'ev, *My Favorite Things*, Subterranean Records SUB 33.

Index

H

Notes

Chapter 1

[1] Herbert Marcuse, *Counterrevolution and Revolt,* p. 133. Beacon Press, Boston, 1972.

[2] Genesis P. Orridge. "Re: AOL." email to Ashley Crawford, January 18, 2000.

[3] I refer to the trans-gendered Genesis P. Orridge using masculine pronouns throughout this text, for the sake of historical accuracy- P. Orridge was male during the time all the events in this chapter took place. For the sake of fairness to other quoted sources in this book, I have also replaced Orridge's characteristic misspellings (e.g. "ov" or "thee" rather than "of" and "the") with the more common English words from which they derive.

[4] Jim O'Quinn reports that "The most serious repressive measures came in 1973, after Squat Theatre attended the Open Theatre Festival in Wroclaw, Poland, as spectators, and gave a performance without an invitation or a license to perform. The contents of the play, made up on location, included 'half-nakedness lengthwise, vein-cutting, drinking milk with blood, men holding arrows, incarnation, pieta, baby handling and a dwarf. The official reaction was strong and immediate: passports for half the group were withdrawn for four years, and Squat was censured for behavior 'not appropriate as Hungarian citizens.'" See Jim O'Quinn, "Squat Theatre Underground, 1972-1976." *The Drama Review: TDR,* Vol. 23 No. 4, Private Performance Issue (December 1979), pp. 7-26 (p. 8.)

[5] Jussi Parikka, *Digital Contagions: A Media Archaeology Of Computer Viruses,* p. 47. Peter Lang, New York, 2007.

[6] With regards to synthesizers being used in the classic 'synth pop' sense by Kraftwerk, the late artist and admitted industrial music fan Mike Kelley seems to make a case for Throbbing Gristle's use of the same as more 'realist': " in the depressed seventies, when technological utopianism could hardly be conceivable given the economic downslide that left many industrial cities veritable wastelands, Kraftwerk's evocation of Modernist aesthetics could only be read as a cruel joke." See Mike Kelley, "An Academic Cut-Up, in Easily Digestible Paragraph-Size Chunks; Or, The New King of Pop: Dr. Konstantin Raudive." *Grey Room* #11 (Spring 2003), pp. 22-43 (p. 29.)

[7] Genesis P. Orridge quoted in *Wreckers of Civilisation* by Simon Ford, p. 9.6. Black Dog Publishing Ltd., London, 1999.

[8] One of the thinkers notable for recognizing how 'democratic' means of mass communication have evolved out of wartime contingency is Friedrich Kittler, who states " ...[computers] were not devised as communication tools, but as a means of planning and conducting total war. And yet, none of this is currently admitted by the cyberspace ideologists in the USA, Europe, or Japan." Quoted in Paul Virilio, Friedrich Kittler & John Armitage, "The Information Bomb: A Conversation." *Angelaki: Journal of the Theoretical Humanities,* Vol. 4 No. 2, pp. 81-90 (p. 83.)

[9] Genesis P. Orridge, review of *Resisting the Digital Life. Amok Fifth Dispatch,* ed. Stuart Sweezey, p. 16. Amok Books, Los Angeles, 1999.

[10] *Ibid.*

[11] Genesis P. Orridge, interview with *Budapest Pod,* 1998- unpublished.

[12] Keith Jones, "Music in Factories: A Twentieth Century Technique for Control of the Productive Self." *Social & Cultural Geography,* Vol. 6 No. 5, pp. 723-744 (p. 725.)

[13] Lanza enthusiastically agrees with and even pines for the standardizing methodology of Muzak, insisting that "There is something civically as well as aesthetically right about generic music complementing generic environments [Lanza has no critique for the generic environments themselves.]" Continuing, he claims that "This is one of the few examples in which a 'one size fits all' policy makes sense. When entering a public space such as a supermarket or mall, shoppers are entitled to an aural escape - a sound mark that delineates the safe retail environment from the more cacopohonous and unwieldy world outside." Joseph Lanza, *Elevator Music,* p. 285. University of Michigan Press, Ann Arbor, 2004.

[14] Marc Almond quoted in *Tape Delay,* p. 77. Ed. Charles Neal. SAF Publishing, Middlesex, 1987.

[15] Lanza, p. 228.

[16] Klaus Maeck quoted in *Naked Lens- Beat Cinema,* ed. Jack Sargeant, p. 204. Creation Books, London, 1997.

[17] Author uncredited, *Television Magick,* p.13. TOPY Heart, Birmingham / Denver, 1991/1988.

[18] Daniel Odier & William S. Burroughs, *The Job: Interviews with William S. Burroughs,* p. 180. Penguin Books, New York, 1989.

[19] *Ibid.*

[20] John Balance interviewed on VPRO Radio, Amsterdam, June 18, 2001.

[21] http://www.franciscolopez.net/aphorisms.html. Retrieved October 24, 2012.

[22] Email correspondence with the author, December 2007.

[23] Genesis P. Orridge, *Answering a Question: TG and Punk,* unpublished essay, 2000.

[24] http://library.nothingness.org/articles/all/all/display/314. Retrieved November 12, 2012.

[25] G.H. Hovagimyan, "Art in the Age of Spiritual Machines (With Apologies to Ray Kurzweil)." *Leonardo,* Vol. 34, No. 5 (2001), pp. 453-458 (p. 458.)

[26] Trevor Wishart, "Connections." *Contemporary Music Review,* Vol. 15 No. 3-4, pp. 89-97 (p. 90.)

[27] Moritz R quoted in *Verschwende deine Jugend,* Jürgen Tiepel, p. 87. Suhrkamp Verlag, Frankfurt am Main, 2001. Translated from the German by the author.

[28] Steven Grant and Ira Robbins, 'Throbbing Gristle' entry in *Trouser Press Record Guide* 4th edition, ed. Ira A. Robbins, p. 677. Collier Books, New York, 1991.

[29] Genesis P. Orridge (2000, 2).

[30] http://www.laibach.nsk.si/l22.htm. Retrieved November 12, 2012.

[31] http://www.nskstate.com/appendix/articles/xy_unsolved.php. Site now defunct.

[32] Alexei Monroe, *Interrogation Machine: Laibach and NSK,* p. 141. MIT Press, Cambridge MA., 2005.

[33] *Ibid.,* p. 244.

[34] Karen Collins, "Dead Channel Surfing: the Commonalities Between Cyberpunk Literature and Industrial Music." *Popular Music* Vol. 24. No. 2. (May 2005), pp. 165-178 (p. 169.)

[35] Laibach quoted in Monroe (2005), p. 256.

[36] Laibach quoted at http://www.nskstate.com/laibach/interviews/excerpts-86-90.php

[37] There seems to be more than a little stylistic kinship between the units within the NSK collective, and the Soviet Constructivism during the transitional years of the "New Economic Policy" (1921-1928). For a comprehensive overview of the latter, see Christina Kaier, *Imagine No Possessions: The Socialist Objects Of Soviet Constructivism* (MIT Press, Cambridge / London, 2005.)

[38] Monroe (2005), p. 53.

[39] Genesis P. Orridge interviewed by *MOJO* magazine 2001.

[40] This comes with the disclaimer that Rice and the Re/Search of V. Vale and Andrea Juno have quite publicly "fallen out" over issues of personal politics and claims of royalties owed: see Larry Wessel's 2011 film *Boyd Rice: Iconoclast* for more detail.

[41] Andrea Juno quoted in *Pranks!,* ed. Andrea Juno and V. Vale, p. 34. Re/Search, San Francisco, 1987.

[42] Ina Blom, "Boredom and Oblivion." *Fluxus Reader,* ed. Ken Friedman, p. 65. John Wiley & Sons, New York, 1998.

[43] Email correspondence with the author, February 2007.

[44] Marcel Duchamp & Pierre Cabanne, *Dialogues with Marcel Duchamp,* p. 77. Da Capo, London, 1971.

Chapter 2

[1] The New Blockaders, *Epater Les Bourgeois* 7" single, NOP Records Japan, 1992

[2] *Ibid.*

[3] *Ibid.*

[4] Generally put forth as an acronym for "Zealous Order of Candied Knights."

[5] Otto Mühl quoted in *Atlas Arkhive Documents of the Avant-Garde 7: Writings of the Viennese Aktionists*, p. 101. Ed. Malcolm Green. Atlas Press, London, 1999

[6] Otto Mühl quoted in "A Noisy Silence" by David Rush. *PAJ: A Journal of Performance and Art*, Vol. 21, No. 1 (Jan., 1999), pp. 2-10 (p. 5.)

[7] As David Rush recalls, "By 1971 he, in fact, abandoned art and actions to form a commune, which exists to this day, in which free sexual expression and uninhibited interactions are expected of all inhabitants. When some of these behaviors were discovered to include children, Muehl was imprisoned for seven years, from 1991-1998. His utopian practices had collided with the law, making transgressions intolerable to the society he saw himself as trying to liberate." *Ibid.,* p. 5-6.

[8] Rodney J. Payton, "The Music of Futurism: Concerts and Polemics." *The Musical Quarterly*, Vol. 62, No. 1 (Jan. 1976), pp. 25-45 (p. 25.)

[9] Luigi Russolo, *The Art Of Noise*, p. 6. Ubu Classics, New York, 2004.

[10] Jay Keister & Jeremy L. Smith, "Musical Ambition, Cultural Accreditation, and the Nasty Side of Progressive Rock." *Popular Music*, Vol. 27 No. 3. (October 2008), pp 433-455 (p. 437.)

[11] Genesis P. Orridge quoted in *Wreckers of Civilisation* p. 11.16, Simon Ford, Black Dog Press, London, 1999.

[12] Email correspondence with the author, December 2007

[13] Genesis P. Orridge quoted in Ford, p. 11.16.

[14] Charles Manson interviewed on KALX radio, Berkeley CA (date unknown.)

[15] Several of these have appeared either concurrently with the publication of this book's first edition, or shortly thereafter, and include *Sonic Warfare* by Steve Goodman (MIT Press, 2010) and *Noise:Music - A History* (Continuum, 2007.) Though it might be tempting to attribute this conspicuous omission to a 'politically correct' academic publishing environment, I cannot assume this to be the case for any or all of these publications. Art theorist Joseph Nechvatal, whose work mines a similar vein as the aforementioned authors, does include Whitehouse in his *Immersion Into Noise* (Mpublishing, 2007.)

[16] Jennifer Wicke, "Through a Gaze Darkly: Pornography's Academic Market." *Transition*, No. 54 (1991), pp. 68-89 (p. 82.)

[17] Email correspondence with the author, January 2008.

[18] Email correspondence with the author, February 2008.

[19] Email personal correspondence with the author, March 2006.

[20] *Ibid.*

[21] *Ibid.*

[22] *Ibid.*

[23] One example of this tendency (though it does not explicitly mention Whitehouse) is Nina Power's essay "Woman Machines: The Future of Female Noise," which largely revolves around the work of the instrument-builder and solo performer Jessica Rylan. I do not wish to imply that this egregious offender is representative of all such writing on the place of women within 'difficult' electronic music, though it does reveal some of the more embarrassing tropes within such 'identity politics' polemics. Power's claim that "there's nothing *nice* about [Rylan's] noise...no concessions to the cute, the lo-fi, the cuddly or the pretty" falsely presumes that the "noise" scene has already dismissed womens' input as being inextricably bound to the characteristics mentioned. See *Noise And Capitalism*, ed. Mattin & Anthony Iles, pp. 97-103. Arteleku, Madrid, 2009.

[24] William Bennett has not greeted this "backing" effort with great joy, saying "it's *really* disappointing [...] to hear about Thurston Moore showing old Come Organisation videos at last weekend's bash [the 2007 'All Tomorrow's Parties' festival] in without even asking for permission (which, by the way, wouldn't have been given)." See http://williambennett.blogspot.com/2006/12/all-yesterdays-teenage-bedroom-walls.html. Retrieved October 12, 2012.

[25] Bennett (2006.)

[26] http://www.franciscolopez.net/int_revue.html. Retrived October 15, 2012.

[27] Terre Thaemlitz, "Operating in Musical Economies of Compromise (Or . . . When do I Get Paid for Writing This?)" *Organised Sound*, Vol. 6 . No. 3 (December 2001), pp 177-184 (p. 182.)

[28] http://williambennett.blogspot.com/2007/07/nostalgie-de-la-boue.html. Retrieved October 12, 2012.

[29] William Bennett radio interview on Resonance FM, London, July 27 2003.

[30] Karen Green, "De Sade, De Beauvoir, and Dworkin." *Australian Feminist Studies*, Vol. 15 No. 31, pp. 69-80 (p. 69.)

[31] Sotos refers praisingly to Dworkin as "very vivid and lived in" (see http://hooverhog.typepad.com/hognotes/2008/10/instinct-drive-and-reality-an-interview-with-peter-sotos.html), while Bennett calls Dworkin "that most nakedly brutally honest of

feminists" (see http://williambennett.blogspot.com/2010/12/pornography.html.) Both retrieved October 15, 2012.

[32] Andrea Dworkin, *Pornography: Men Possessing Women,* p. 100. The Women's Press, London, 1991.

[33] John Gill quoted in liner notes to Whitehouse, *Great White Death Special Edition* CD. Susan Lawly, Edinburgh, 1997. Ironically, given Genesis P. Orridge's own long-term disdain for Whitehouse, Gill claims that "...Genesis P. Orridge might justify such confrontationism" within this review.

[34] http://www.susanlawly.freeuk.com/textfiles/wbinterview02.htm. Retrieved October 11, 2012.

[35] Marquis DeSade, *Justine, Philosophy In The Bedroom and Other Writings,* p. 253. Ed. and trans. Richard Seaver and Austryn Wainhouse. Arrow Books, New York, 1965.

[36] Camille Paglia, *Sexual Personae,* p. 247. Vintage Books, New York, 1990.

[37] Ruth Heyler, "Parodied To Death: The Postmodern Gothic of American Psycho." *MFS Modern Fiction Studies,* Vol. 46 No. 3 (Fall 2000), pp. 725-746 (p. 736.)

[38] See http://www.stewarthomesociety.org/white.htm. Retrieved October 15, 2012.

[39] Email correspondence with the author, August 8 2009.

[40] Georges Bataille, *Eroticism,* p. 188. Trans. Mary Dalwood. Penguin Classics, London, 2001.

[41] *Ibid.,* p. 190.

[42] Marquis de Sade quoted in Simone de Beauvoir, "Must We Burn Sade?" *The Marquis de Sade: An Essay by Simone de Beauvoir with Selections from his Writings,* p. 46. Trans. Annette Michelson. John Calder, London, 1962.

[43] Actually, in the case of Asahara, this is only partially correct. Much of the music made available for public consumption by his AUM Shinrikyo ['AUM Supreme Truth'] cult was fairly benign self-promotional material, though material circulating within AUM did directly reference their plans to accelerate Armageddon via the manufacture of sarin gas. In a particularly morbid parody, AUM members altered the lyrics of a popular *anime* program "Sally The Witch" or "*Mahoutsukai Sarii",* changing the choral chant of "Sal-ly!" to "Sa-rin!"

[44] See http://ubuweb.com/sound/whitehouse.html. Retrieved October 18, 2012.

[45] A word play on the acronym for "Erhard Seminar Training" and the Latin "it is."

[46] Heather Skinner & Paula Stephens, "Speaking the Same Language: The Relevance of Neuro-Linguistic Programming To Effective Marketing Communications." *Journal of Marketing Communications,* Vol. 9 No. 3, pp. 177-192 (p. 189.)

[47] Abhilasha Singh & A. Abraham, "Neuro Linguistic Programming: A Key To Business Excellence." *Total Quality Management & Business Excellence,* Vol. 19 No. 1-2, pp. 141-149 (p. 141.)

[48] Paul Tosey & Jane Mathison, "Neuro-Linguistic Programming and Learning Theory: A Response." *Curriculum Journal,* Vol. 14 No. 3, pp. 371-388 (p. 375.)

[49] The *Skeptical Dictionary* has pointed out the problems with this claims as follows: "One NLP guru, Dale Kirby, informs us that one of the presuppositions of NLP is "No one is wrong or broken." So why seek remedial change? See http://www.skepdic.com/neurolin.html. Retrieved October 16, 2012.

[50] Bennett (2006.)

[51] http://williambennett.blogspot.com/2007/11/fine-art-of-profanity.html. Retrieved October 15, 2012.

[52] http://www.susanlawly.freeuk.com/textfiles/wbinterview04.html. Retrieved October 14, 2012.

[53] Bennett (2006.)

[54] William Bennett, email correspondence with the author, February 22 2010.

[55] Willam Bennett, email correspondence with the author, February 12 2010.

Chapter 3

[1] http://www.desk.nl/~northam/oro/zk2.htm. Retrieved November 7, 2012.

[2] Jacques Attali, *Noise: The Political Economy of Music,* p. 12. University of Minnesota Press, Minneapolis, 2003.

[3] Hakim Bey, perf. *Temporary Autonomous Zone: A Night of Ontological Anarchy and Poetic Terrorism.* Videocassette, Sound Photosynthesis, 1994.

4 Brian Massumi, *Parables For The Virtual,* p. 257. Duke University Press, Durham / London, 2002.

[5] *Ibid.,* p. 258.

[6] *Ibid.,* p. 258.

[7] Spare was a member of Aleister Crowley's magical Order of the Silver Star, although Crowley would eventually dismiss him as a "black brother."

[8] Joseph Nechvatal, *Towards An Immersive Intelligence: Essays On The Work Of Art In The Age Of Computer Technology And Virtual Reality, 1993-2006,* p. 43. Edgewise Press, New York, 2009.

[9] *Ibid.,* p. 45.

[10] Lewis Mumford, *The City In History*, p. 7. Harvest Books, San Diego / London / New York, 1989.

[11] *Ibid.*, p. 8.

[12] Keith Jones, "Music in Factories: a Twentieth-Century Technique for Control of the Productive Self." *Social & Cultural Geography*, 6:5 (2005), pp. 723-744 (p. 724.)

[13] Email correspondence with the author, November 2007.

[14] Hugh B. Urban, "The Beast with Two Backs: Aleister Crowley, Sex Magic and the Exhaustion of Modernity." *Nova Religio: The Journal of Alternative and Emergent Religions*, Vol. 7 No. 3 (March 2004), pp. 7-25 (p. 11.)

[15] A 1987 police operation in Manchester, after which the resulting court case determined that consensual agreement to "bodily harm" (in this case, piercing) was not enough to deflect a charge of such.

[16] William Burroughs, *GYSIN/BURROUGHS/P-ORRIDGE - "Interviews & Readings"* cassette, Cold Spring, 1989.

[17] Nathan Moore, "Nova Law: William S. Burroughs and the Logic of Control." *Law and Literature*, Vol. 19, No. 3 (Fall 2007), pp. 435-470 (p.437.)

[18] *Ibid.*

[19] Brion Gysin quoted in *Re/Search #4/5*, p. 40. Ed. Andrea Juno & V. Vale. Re/Search Publications, San Francisco, 1982.

[20] Brion Gysin quoted in *Literary Outlaw* by Ted Morgan, p. 301. Avon Books, New York, 1988.

[21] Christopherson (2007.)

[22] Scott McDonald, "Against False Distinctions." *Film Quarterly*, Vol. 35, No. 1 (Autumn, 1981), pp. 58-60 (p. 59.)

[23] Gilles Deleuze, *Cinema 2: The Time-Image*, p. 215. Trans. Hugh Tomlinson and Robert Galeta. University of Minnesota Press, Minneapolis, 1989.

[24] Genesis P. Orridge quoted in *Love Sex Fear Death: The Inside Story of the Process Church of the Final Judgment* by Timothy Wylie (ed. Adam Parfrey), p. 178. Feral House, Port Townsend WA, 2009.

[25] John Balance, "AOS: Artist, Occultist, Sensualist." Essay from Austin Spare exhibition catalog.

[26] David Goodman, "New Japanese Theater." *The Drama Review: TDR*, Vol. 15, No. 2 (Spring 1971), pp. 154-168 (p. 166.)

[27] J.G. Ballard quoted in *Hans Ulrich Obrist Interviews, Vol. 1*, p. 67. Ed. Thomas Boutoux. Charta Books, Milan, 2003.

[28] Stephen L. Harris & Gloria Platzner, *Classical Mythology*, 2nd edition, p. 140. Mayfield Publishing Co., London / Toronto, 1995.

[29] Coil, liner notes, *Scatology* LP. Force and Form, 1984.

[30] Gilbert & George in conversation with Simon Dwyer, *Rapid Eye Vol.3*, ed. Simon Dwyer, p. 117. Creation Books, London, 1995.

[31] Ian Penman, "England's Dreaming." *The Wire* #194, April 2000, p.30.

[32] "Tainted Love" was featured as the b-side to "Panic" on the 1985 12" single on Force & Form, the proceeds of which were dedicated to the Terrence Higgins trust.

[33] Ben Neill, "Pleasure Beats: Rhythm and the Aesthetics of Current Electronic Music." *Leonardo Music Journal*, Vol. 12 (2002), pp. 3-6 (p. 5.)

[34] Stanislav Grof, *The Holotropic Mind*, p.15. Harper Collins, New York, 1990.

[35] John Balance, interviewed on VPRO radio 4/17/1991.

[36] Peter Christopherson interviewed on VPRO radio 4/17/1991.

[37] John Balance quoted in *Tyr* #2, p. 374. Ed. Joshua Buckley and Michael Moynihan. Ultra Publishing, Atlanta, 2004.

[38] *Ibid.*, p. 375.

[39] Christopherson (2007.)

[40] Quoted in *Haunted Weather: Music, Silence and Memory* by David Toop, p. 201. Serpents' Tail, London, 2004.

[41] LaMonte Young, "Ruminations on Radio." *Radiotext(e)*, ed. Neil Strauss and Dave Mandl, p.183. Semiotext(e), New York, 1993.

[42] Quoted in Paul Virilio, Friedrich Kittler & John Armitage, "The Information Bomb: A Conversation." *Angelaki: Journal of the Theoretical Humanities*, 4:2, pp. 81-90 (p. 82.)

[43] LaMonte Young & Marian Zazeela, *Selected Writings*, p. 13. UbuClassics, New York, 2004.

[44] As noted on the original release of the *How To Destroy Angels* EP (L.A.Y.L.A.H. Anti-Records, Belgium, 1984.)

[45] http://heathenharvest.com/article.php?story=20060901042847499. Retrieved November 19, 2012.

[46] Christopherson (2007).

[47] *Ibid.*

Chapter 4

[1] http://www.ashiya-web.or.jp/museum/10us/103education/nyumon_us/manifest_us.htm. Link defunct as of this printing.

[2] Reiko Tomii, "State v. (Anti-)Art: Model 1,000-Yen Note Incident by Akasegawa Genpei and Company." *Positions: East Asia Cultures Critique,* Vol. 10, No. 1, Spring 2002, pp. 141-172 (p. 152.)

[3] "Batzoutai" in fact refers to a fighting unit from this period, than a single individual.

[4] M. Behrens, "Merzbow." *SIAM Letter* Vol. 5. No. 1. (July 1992) pp 31-33 (p.31.) Translated from the German by the author.

[5] *Ibid.,* p. 32.

[6] Hisaaki Yamanouchi, "Yukio Mishima and his Suicide." *Modern Asian Studies,* Vol. 6, No. 1 (1972), pp. 1-16 (p. 1.)

[7] Sharon Kinsella, "Subculture in the 1990s: Otaku and the Amateur Manga Movement." *Journal of Japanese Studies,* Vol. 24, No. 2 (Summer 1998), pp. 289-316 (p. 291.)

[8] *Ibid.,* p. 308.

[9] A Japanese transliteration of the English term "Lolita complex." In both *manga* and fashion subcultures, this refers to an exagerratedly "girly" and naïve means of dressing or (in the case of *manga*) portraying central female characters.

[10] Kinsella, p. 309.

[11] Paul Hegarty, "Noise Threshold: Merzbow and the End of Natural Sound." *Organised Sound,* Vol.6. No. 3. (December 2001), pp 193-200 (p. 194.)

[12] David Novak, "2.5 x 6 Metres of Space: Japanese Music Coffeehouses and Experimental Practices of Listening." *Popular Music* Vol. 7, No. 1 (January 2008), pp. 15-34 (p. 24.)

[13] *Ibid.,* p. 26.

[14] Malise Ruthven, *A Fury for God: The Islamist Attack on America,* pp. 80-81. London / New York, Granta 2002.

[15] Michael Pedersen, "Transgressive Sound Surrogacy." *Organised Sound* #16, pp. 27-35 (p. 32.)

[16] Melle Jan Kromhout, "Over the Ruined Factory There's a Funny Noise": Throbbing Gristle and the Mediatized Roots of Noise in/as Music." *Popular Music and Society,* Vol. 34 No. 01 (2011), pp. 23-34 (p. 28-29.)

[17] John F. Szwed, *Space Is The Place: The Lives And Times of Sun Ra,* p.229. Da Capo Press, Cambridge MA, 1998.

[18] "Japan's Pornography Laws: Fleshing it Out", author uncredited. *The Economist* February 23rd-29th 2008, p. 60. London, UK.

[19] Masami Akita quoted in Behrens, p. 33.

[20] See, for example, the CCCC profile (in Japanese) at http://www.japanoise.net/j/cccc.htm. Retrieved October 13, 2012.

[21] A selection of which is available online at http://www.shocker.jp/SM/Sm24.htm. Retrieved October 12, 2012.

[22] http://www.esoterra.org/merzbow.htm. Retrieved October 12, 2012.

[23] Aniela Jaffe, "Symbolism in the Visual Arts." *Man And His Symbols,* ed. C.G. Jung, p. 291. Aldus Books Ltd., London,1964.

[24] Pedersen, p. 31.

[25] http://web.archive.org/web/20000902183436/http://www2.sbbs.se/hp/eerie/rcar.html. Archived from the original (http://www2.sbbs.se/hp/eerie/rcar.html). Retrieved October 14, 2012.

[26] Nick Smith, "The splinter in your ear: Noise as the Semblance of Critique." *Culture, Theory and Critique,* 46:1 (2005), pp. 43-59 (p. 54.)

[27] Clive Bell, review of *Rectal Anarchy* by Merzbow and Gore Beyond Necropsy. *The Wire* #163, (September 1997), p.59.

[28] http://www.allmusic.com/cg/amg.dll?p=amg&sql=10:7r6fmppj9f3o~T1. Retrieved October 6, 2012.

[29] Biba Kopf, review of *Space Metalizer* by Merzbow. *The Wire* #163, (September 1997), p. 67.

[30] Smith, p. 51.

[31] Hegarty, p. 199.

[32] John LaTartara, "Laptop Composition at the Turn of the Millennium: Repetition and Noise in the Music of Oval, Merzbow, and Kid 606." *Twentieth Century Music,* Vol. 7 No. 1 (March 2010), pp 91-115 (p. 103.)

[33] John Gray, *Straw Dogs: Thoughts on Humans and Other Animals*, p. 8. Granta Books, London, 2002.

[34] *Ibid.*

[35] Email correspondence with the author, June 2007.

[36] Clive Wynne quoted in "Animal Minds" by Virginia Morell. *National Geographic,* March 2008, p. 54.

[37] Frans de Waal, *Chimpanzee Politics,* p. 18. Johns Hopkins Press, Baltimore, 2000.

[38] Leopold von Sacher-Masoch ,*Venus in Furs*, p. 39. Belmont Books, New York, 1965.

Chapter 5

[1] Jussi Parikka, *Digital Contagions: A Media Archaeology Of Computer Viruses,* p. 104n. Peter Lang, New York, 2007.

[2] A better insight into what exactly is meant by a "Helvetica" culture - a sort of omnipresent commercial inoffensiveness - can be seen in the 2007 film *Helvetica.*

[3] Lloyd Dunn quoted in *Sonic Outlaws*, dir. Craig Baldwin. Other Cinema, 1995.

[4] Mark E. Cory, "Soundplay: The Polyphonous Tradition of German Radio Art." *Wireless Imagination: Sound, Radio and the Avant-Garde*, p.363. Ed. Douglas Kahn & Gregory Whitehead, MIT Press, Cambridge MA, 1992.

[5] Renato Poggioli, *Theory Of The Avant-Garde*, p. 161. Trans. Gerald Fitzgerald. Belknap/ Harvard, Cambridge / London, 1997.

[6] Max Ernst quoted in Robert Motherwell, *Max Ernst: Beyond Painting And Other Writings by the Artist and His Friends*, p. 9. Wittenborn & Schulz, New York, 1948.

[7] Tim Wu, *The Master Switch: The Rise And Fall Of Information Empires*, p. 154. Alfred A. Knopf, New York, 2010.)

[8] Mickey Vallee, "The Media Contingencies of Generation Mashup: A Žižekian Critique." *Popular Music and Society* iFirst (June 2012), pp. 1-22 (p. 2.)

[9] Uncredited actor, *Suite (242)*, dir. Douglas Davis & Nam Jun Paik, Electronic Arts Intermix, 1974.

[10] Negativland, "Teletours in Negativland." *Radiotext(e)*, ed. Neil Strauss, p. 310-311- Semiotext(e), New York, 1993

[11] Aniko Bodroghkozy, *Groove Tube: Sixties Television and the Youth Rebellion*, p. 126. Duke University Press, Durham / London, 2001.

[12] *Ibid.*, p. 238

[13] *Ibid.*, p. 240

[14] Mark Hosler quoted in Baldwin (1995.)

[15] http://csicop.org/si/9611/judas_priest.html. Retrieved November 4, 2012.

[16] *Ibid.*

[17] Don Joyce quoted in Baldwin (1995.)

[18] http://www.rogerebert.suntimes.com/apps/pbcs.dll/article?AID=/20040224/REVIEWS/40 2240301/1023. Retrieved November 4, 2012.

[19] http://www.negativland.com/edge.html. Link broken as of this printing.

[20] Prof. Lawrence Lessig, *Willful Infringement: Mickey & Me*, dir. Greg Hittelman. Fiat Lucre, 2007.

[21] Shervin Rezaie, "Play Your Part: Girl Talk's Indefinite Role in the Digital Sampling Saga." *Touro Law Review* No. 26 (2010), pp. 175-205 (p. 195.)

[22] John Oswald interviewed on 'Radio Radio', date unknown.

[23] Jacques Attali, *Noise*, p.119. Trans. Brian Massumi. University of Minnesota Press, Minneapolis, 2003.

[24] http://www.negativland.com/reviews/trip.html. Link broken as of this printing.

[25] http://www.rottentomatoes.com/m/meet_the_spartans. Retrieved November 4, 2012.

[26] http://www.avclub.com/articles/epic-movie,3609. Retrieved November 4, 2012.

[27] http://www.guardian.co.uk/commentisfree/2006/sep/22/arts.visualarts.
Retrieved November 4, 2012.

[28] Given the negative assessment of *Vice* magazine that appears here, it's only fair to mention the comparitively illuminating efforts of their "Vice Broadcasting System" film crews, which have gone on location in areas such as the Congo and Liberia to provide surprisingly concerned and un-ironic commentary on the plight of these nations.

[29] http://www.independent.co.uk/news/people/banksy-the-joker-417144.html.
Retrieved November 3, 2012.

[30] http://www.guardian.co.uk/commentisfree/2006/sep/22/arts.visualarts.
Retrieved November 4, 2012.

[31] Email correspondence with the author, August 3 2012.

[32] Vallee, p. 6.

[33] Reazaie, p. 182.

[34] Mark Hosler quoted in Baldwin (1995.)

[35] Vicki Bennett quoted in "Vicki Bennett: Everything I've Done has Just been by Accident" by Carl Abrahamsson. Unpublished interview transcript, January 2011.

[36] For example, Falco's "Rock Me Amadeus" is retitled as "Rock Me Ham-adeus," while the band has made occasional use of the pseudonym Notorious P.I.G.

[37] Philip Sherburne, "Donna Summer: He's a Rebel." *Wire,* April 2003, p. 14.

[38] Jason Forrest quoted in *Ibid.*

[39] Vicki Bennett quoted in Abrahamsson (2011.)

[40] Vallee, p. 2.

[41] Philip A. Gunderson "Danger Mouse's Grey Album, Mashups, and the Age of Composition." *Postmodern Culture* 15.1 (2004).

[42] Personal conversation with the author, January 2008.

[43] Mircea Eliade, *Shamanism: Archaic Techniques of Ecstasy,* p. 173. Princeton University Press, Princeton NJ, 1992.

[44] Genesis P. Orridge, "Thee Splinter Test." Unpublished / unedited manuscript, 1995.

[45] *Ibid.*

[46] Ken Sitz quoted in *Incredibly Strange Music Vol. II,* pp. 95-96. Ed. V. Vale & Andrea Juno. Re/Search, San Francisco, 1994.

[47] Jasper Johns, "Marcel Duchamp (1887-1968), An Appreciation." *Dialogues with Marcel Duchamp* by Pierre Cabanne, p. 110. Da Capo, London, 1971.

[48] *Neuromancer, Count Zero,* and *Mona Lisa Overdrive.*

Chapter 6

[1] With apologies to Fenn O' Berg, from whose 2002 Mego CD *the Return of Fenn O' Berg* this heading is taken from.

[2] Jim Green and Ira Robbins quoted in *Trouser Press Record Guide 4th Edition,* p. 243- ed. Ira Robbins, Coller Books, New York NY, 1991

[3] Lucien Roberts, "Profile: To Be Frank." *Design Week,* May 1 2003, p. 15.

[4] Herbert Blau, "From the Dreamwork of Secession to Orgies Mysteries Theatre." *Modern Drama,* Vol. 52 No. 3 (Fall 2009), pp. 263-282 (p. 277.)

[5] Hermann Nitsch, *Atlas Arkhiv Documents of the Avant-Garde 7: Writings of the Vienna Actionists,* p. 129. Ed. Malcolm Green. Atlas Press, London, 1999.

[6] Genesis P. Orridge, review of *Atlas Arkhiv Documents of the Avant-Garde 7: Writings of the Viennese Aktionists.* Unpublished essay, 2000.

[7] Caleb Stuart, "Glitching and Skipping Compact Discs in the Audio of Yasunao Tone, Nicolas Collins and Oval." *Leonardo Music Journal,* Vol. 13 (2003), pp. 47-52 (p. 50.)

[8] See http://www.heise.de/newsticker/meldung/Kommissar-Computer-Horst-Herold-zum-85-Geburtstag-212459.html. Retrieved October 28, 2012.

[9] Max V. Mathews quoted in *The C-Sound Book,* p. xxxi. Ed. Richard Boulanger. MIT Press, Cambridge MA, 2000.

[10] In my book *Unofficial Release* (2012), I have expanded on how the word "amateur" has evolved to mean not a "lover" or enthusiast of something (as is implied in the word's Latin root of *amare*), but a reckless trifler whose quickly-assembled works show more concern with public recognition than joy from engaging in the creative process.

[11] http://www.bobostertag.com/writings-articles-computer-music-sucks.htm. Retrieved October 25, 2012.

[12] *Ibid.*

[13] John Duncan quoted in liner notes to *Our Telluric Conversation* CD, p. 6 - 23five, San Francisco, 2006

[14] Janne VanHanen, "Virtual Sound: Examining Glitch and Production." *Contemporary Music Review,* Vol. 22 No. 4, pp. 45-52 (p. 45.)

[15] The duo in question has released a 2001 LP on the Tochnit Aleph label as P.O.P. ["Product of Power."]

[16] Tad Turner, "The Resonance of the Cubicle: Laptop Performance in Post-Digital Musics." *Contemporary Music Review,* Vol. 22 No. 4, pp. 81-92 (p. 83.) Since the performance venues I refer to in this chapter are generally clubs, bars, and concert halls, I recommend locating a copy of this article for further insight into the reception of "post-

digital" music as it is performed in art galleries and elsewhere. This topic will also be returned to in this book's chapter on Francisco López.

[17] Mark Harwood, review of "What is Music?" festival. *Wire* #194 (April 2000), p. 85.

[18] Turner, p. 85.

[19] Quoted in Bert Bongers, "Interview With Sensorband." *Computer Music Journal,* Vol. 22 No. 1, pp. 13-24 (p. 20.)

[20] Email correspondence with the author, February 2008.

[21] http://www.mego.at/mego032.html. Site no longer available.

[22] Personal conversation with the author, April 2006.

[23] Email correspondence with the author, July 2008.

[24] Andrew V. Uroskie, "Beyond the Black Box: The Lettrist Cinema of Disjunction." *October* #135 (Winter 2011), pp. 21-48 (p. 25.)

[25] Collins' method is described by Caleb Stuart as follows: "Without any real knowledge of the workings of the technology, Collins assumed correctly that the CD player's laser never left the disc's surface, reading not only audio information but 'hidden' information such as error-detection and information-coverage data, as well as data defining track locations, lengths and so on. Locating the player's control chip, Collins came across a 'mute' pin, which he removed, resulting in a constantly chattering playback." Stuart, p. 49.

[26] http://www.wfmu.org/~kennyg/popular/articles/glitchwerks.html. Retrieved October 24, 2012.

[27] Kim Cascone, "The Aesthetics of Failure: 'Post-Digital' Tendencies in Contemporary Computer Music." *Computer Music Journal,* Vol. 24, No. 4 (Winter, 2000), pp. 12-18 (p. 13.)

[28] *Ibid.,* p. 17.

[29] Zbigniew Karkowski quoted in *Substantials #01,* p. 8. Ed. Akiko Miyake. CCA KitaKyushu, KitaKyushu, 2003.

[30] Bongers, p. 13.

[31] Personal conversation with the author, April 2006.

[32] Email correspondence with the author, December 9 2010.

[33] Roberts, p. 15.

[34] Erik Morse, "Music Box." *Modern Painters,* March 2010, pp. 30-31 (p. 31.)

[35] Nicholas Negroponte, *Being Digital* p. 229, Alfred A Knopf, New York, 1995.

[36] Also an acronym for the unaffiliated *Groupe d'Etudes Sociotechniques pour les Télécommunications.*

[37] User 'tine' quoted at http://www.discogs.com/release/97472, July 12, 2006.

[38] Notes for E+ installation by Alku / Imbecil- part of the *rand()%lab* exhibition at Medialounge, The Media Centre, Huddersfield, UK, 04.11.04 - 07.01.05.

[39] Nick Collins & Andrew R. Brown, "Generative Music Editorial." *Contemporary Music Review,* Vol. 28 No. 1, pp. 1-4 (p. 2.)

[40] Email correspondence with the author, December 10 2010.

[41] Bob Ostertag, *Are Two Screens Enough? The Networked Screen and The Human Imagination,* p. 10. Unpublished manuscript, 2008.

[42] *Ibid.,* p. 7

[43] John Cage, *Silence,* p. 3. Wesleyan University Press, Middleton CT, 1973.

[44] Kim Ryrie quoted in *Vintage Synthesizers* by Mark Vail, p. 190. Miller Freeman, San Francisco, 1993.

[45] *Ibid.,* p. 196.

[46] Mel Gordon, "Songs From the Museum of the Future: Russian Sound Creation (1910-1930)." *Wireless Imagination: Sound, Radio, and the Avant Garde,* p. 212. Ed. Douglas Kahn and Gregory Whitehead, MIT Press, Cambridge MA., 1992

[47] Roman Jakobson, *Language in Literature,* pp. 369-370. Harvard University / Belknap Press, Cambridge MA, 1990.

[48] See http://www.vagueterrain.net/content/2011/09/new-high-low-adventures-low-bitrate-audio. Retrieved November 1, 2012.

[49] Davide Castelvechhi, "The Power of Induction: Cutting the Last Cord Could Resonate with Our Increasingly Gadget-Dependent Lives." *Science News,* Vol. 172, No. 3 (Jul. 21, 2007), pp. 40-41 (p. 40).

[50] VanHanen, p. 47.

[51] Terre Thaemlitz, "Operating in Musical Economies of Compromise (Or . . . When Do I Get Paid For Writing This?)" *Organised Sound,* Vol. 6 No. 3 (December 2001), pp 177-184 (p. 182.)

Chapter 7

[1] The title is borrowed from the track "Kick A King" on the Leif Elggren / Thomas Liljenberg CD *The Whole Wide World & The Codfish Suit* (Firework Edition, Stockholm, 1996.) The verbal content - a letter of consumer complaint read aloud by Elggren to an unidentified recipient - is as follows: "A while ago, I bought your new football 'Kick A King'. Now I want to complain. I want my money back! In the advertising, you say that it looks like the Swedish famous king, Carolus XII. But that's not true. It looks like Margaret Thatcher's ass! So I want my compensation. I don't want to kick an ass....I want to kick a *king*."

[2] Galia & Pil Kollectiv, "Birth of a State: A Distant Report on the First Congress of the NSK State in Berlin." *Art Papers* Vol. 35 No. 2 (March/April 2011), pp. 30-9 (p. 32.)

[3] "Nashi," which translates as "ours" in Russian, is officially a "youth anti-fascist democratic youth movement," but is often accused of having a more targeted mission, i.e. the intimidation and harrassment of the political rivals of Vladimir Putin and his United Russia political party. It is believed to have been formed as a reaction to the youth movement forming around the Ukraine's "pro-Western" presidential candidate Viktor Yuschenko during the Orange Revolution in 2004.

[4] John Gray, *Against Progress and Other Illusions*, p. 171. Granta, London, 2004.

[5] *Ibid.*, p. 175.

[6] George Michael's analysis of Mahler clarifies this as follows: "Mahler sees no contradiction between his leftist past and his current rightist orientation, as he explained, 'In the old days [1960s] our principal enemy was American imperialism. And today it still is: American policy is to balkanize Europe in order to render it non-competitive.' Furthermore, Mahler averred that the labels 'left' and 'right' no longer applied today. As he sees it, globalization is now the dominant issue and 'the only power that can stand up to globalization is the nation.'" George Michael, "The Ideological Evolution of Horst Mahler: The Far Left–Extreme Right Synthesis." *Studies in Conflict & Terrorism,* Vol. 32 No. 4, pp. 346-366 (p. 359.)

[7] Paul Virilio, *Unknown Quantity,* p. 132. Thames & Hudson, New York, 2003.

[8] *Ibid.*, p. 133

[9] Ken Friedman, "The Wealth and Poverty of Networks." Quoted in Annmarie Chandler and Norie Neumark, *At A Distance: Precursors To Art And Activism On The Internet,* p. 416. MIT Press, Cambridge MA, 2005.

[10] Slavoj Žižek, "The Ongoing 'Soft Revolution.'" *Critical Inquiry,* Vol. 30, No. 2 (Winter 2004). pp. 292-323 (p. 309.)

[11] *Ibid.*

[12] http://www.elgaland-vargaland.org/about/index.html. Retrieved October 25, 2012.

[13] Critical Art Ensemble, *Electronic Civil Disobedience and Other Unpopular Ideas,* p. 36. Autonomedia, New York, 1996.

[14] Leif Elggren, *Genealogy,* p. 73. Firework Edition, Stockholm, 2005.

[15] Email correspondence with the author, March 31 2006.

[16] Randy Yau quoted in *Parataxes* by Michael Gendreau, p. 189. Van Dieren Editeur, Lausanne, 2010. Translated from French by the author.

[17] http://www.cmvonhausswolff.net/curriculum_vitae.html. Retrieved October 25, 2012.

[18] Von Hausswolff (2006.)

[19] Branden W. Joseph, *Beyond The Dream Syndicate: Tony Conrad and the Arts after Cage*, p. 43. Zone Books, New York, 2008.

[20] Brandon LaBelle, "Sound as Space Creator: Frequency, Architecture, and Collaboration." *Soundscape: The Journal of Acoustic Ecology*, Vol 4 No. 2 (Fall / Winter 2003), pp. 48-49 (p. 48.)

[21] *Ibid.*

[22] Von Hausswolff (2006.)

[23] Torsten Ekborn quoted in booklet accompanying *Åke Hodell: Verbal Brainwash and Other Works* 3xCD, p. 8- Fylkingen Records, Stockholm, 2000.

[24] Von Hausswolff also founded the Friedrich Jürgenson Foundation in 2000, to coincide with an exhibition on Stockholm's Färgfabriken entitled " Friedrich Jürgenson: From the Studio for Audioscopic Research."

[25] Daniella Cascella, "Carl Michael von Hausswolff." *Organised Sound*, Vol. 13 No. 1. (April 2008), pp. 21-29 (p. 22.)

[26] *Ibid.*

[27] Mike Kelley, "An Academic Cut-Up, in Easily Digestible Paragraph-Size Chunks; Or, The New King of Pop: Dr. Konstantin Raudive." *Grey Room* #11 (Spring 2003), pp. 22-43 (p. 26.)

[28] *Ibid.*

[29] Thibaut de Ruyter, "CM von Hausswolff." *Art Press* No. 310 (March 2005), pp. 76-77.

[30] http://web.comhem.se/elggren/experiment.html. Retrieved October 24, 2012.

[31] http://web.comhem.se/elggren/bardot.html. Retrieved October 24, 2012.

[32] http://web.comhem.se/elggren/experiment.html. Retrieved October 24, 2012.

[33] *Ibid.*

[34] Leif Elggren, liner notes, *Virulent Images / Virulent Sound* CD. Firework Edition, Stockholm, 2004.

[35] *Ibid.*

[36] http://www.wfmu.org/~kennyg/popular/reviews/elggren.html. Retrieved October 24, 2012.

[37] http://epc.buffalo.edu/authors/goldsmith/goldsmith_boring.html. Retrieved October 24, 2012.

[38] Elggren (2005), p. 41.

[39] *Ibid.*

[40] Melvin Rader, "The Artist As Outsider." *The Journal of Aesthetics and Art Criticism*, Vol. 16 No. 3 (March 1958), pp. 306-318 (p. 310.)

[41] *Ibid.*, p. 29.

[42] Elggren (2005), p. 120.

[43] Rader, p. 316.

[44] Robert L. Heinbroner, *The Worldly Philosophers,* p. 125. Touchstone, New York,1992.

[45] Now performing as Cosmokinetic Cabinet Noordung.

[46] Galia & Pil Kollectiv, p. 30.

[47] One of the more notable examples here is the wave of applications for NSK passports that originated in Nigeria, and is described as follows: "In response to this situation, IRWIN traveled to Nigeria to interview applicants and find out why they were so interested in the project. It transpired that they had thought the passports would confer the right to travel to Europe, and despite being told of NSK's fictional status, insisted that friends had been to this country and found it lovely." Galia & Pil Kollectiv, p. 38.

[48] Alexei Monroe, *Interrogation Machine: Laibach And Nsk,* p. 250, MIT Press, Cambridge MA, 2005.

[49] *Ibid.,* p.227.

[50] It is worth reproducing the full quote here: "When we say that politics is the highest form of art, this politics, which is the most encompassing, comprehensive force in the whole social world, this politics is art that triggers senses by mental power, which changes images in our heads, gives meaning to life [...] Therefore we see ourselves as politicians, and in terms of its global character, the NSK state is the Internet of political subjects." Peter Mlakar quoted in Galia & Pil Kollectiv, p. 37.

[51] Dror Feiler, *Music, Noise & Politics.* Liner notes, *Sounds 99* triple CD. Blue Tower Records, Stockholm, 2000.

[52] *Ibid.*

[53] Žižek, p. 296.

[54] Elggren (2005), p. 67.

[55] Elggren (2005), p. 68.

[56] Hakim Bey, *Immediatism,* p. 2. AK Press, San Francisco, 1994.

[57] *Ibid.*

Chapter 8

[1] Brandon LaBelle, *Site Specific Sound,* p.62. Errant Bodies Press, New York, 2004.

[2] Javier Aguirre quoted in *La Mosca Tras La Oreja: de la música experimental al arte sonore en España,* ed. Llorenç Barber and Montserrat Palacois, p. 32-33. Translation from the Spanish by the author. Ediciones Autor, Madrid, 2009.

[3] Raymond Williams, *The Politics of Modernism: Against the New Conformists*, p. 52. Verso, London / New York, 2007.

[4] F.T. Marinetti quoted in *Futurist Manifestos*, p. 23. U. Apollonio, ed. London, 1973.

[5] Williams, p. 52.

[6] Jean Baudrillard, *Impossible Exchange*, p. 44. Verso, London / New York, 2001.

[7] Email correspondence with the author, March 2006.

[8] *Ibid.*

[9] Roman Jakobson, *Language In Literature*, p. 467. Ed. Krystyna Pomorska and Stephen Rudy. Belknap Press / Harvard University Press, London / Cambridge MA.,1987.

[10] Michael Gendreau, *Parataxes: Fragments Pour Une Architecture Des Espaces Sonores.* Lausanne: Van Dieren Editeur, 2010, p. 179. Translated from the French by the author.

[11] Francisco López, CD liner notes to *Buildings [New York].* V2_Archief, Asmterdam, 2001.

[12] Lionel Marchetti, "The Microphone and the Hand." Trans. Patrick McGinley & Matthew Marble. Reproduced in *Fo(a)rm* #5, p. 115.

[13] *Ibid.*, p. 109.

[14] Frank Dufour, "Pierre Schaeffer and the Invention of Musique Concrète." *Soundscape: The Journal of Acoustic Ecology,* Vol. 8 No. 1 (Fall / Winter 2008), pp. 17-19 (p. 17.)

[15] http://www.franciscolopez.net/cage.html. Retrieved October 15, 2012.

[16] López (2006.)

[17] Roland Barthes, *Image-Music-Text,* p. 152. Trans. Stephen Heath. Noonday, New York, 1977.

[18] López (2006.)

[19] http://www.franciscolopez.net/aphorisms.html. Retrieved October 15, 2012.

[20] Pierre Schaeffer, *Traité des Objets Musicaux*, p. 33. Éditions du Seuil, Paris, 2002.

[21] Francisco López quoted in "Francisco López: Belle Confusion" by Gregory Gangemi. *The Sound Projector,* No. 11 (2003), p. 32.

[22] Nick Prior, "OK COMPUTER: Mobility, Software and the Laptop Musician." *Information, Communication & Society,* Vol. 11 No. 7, pp. 912-932 (p. 926.)

[23] Roger T. Dean, Mitchell Whitelaw, Hazel Smith & David Worrall, "The Mirage of Real-Time Algorithmic Synaesthesia: Some Compositional Mechanisms and Research, Agendas in Computer Music and Sonification." *Contemporary Music Review,* Vol. 25 No. 4, pp. 311-326 (p. 315-316.)

[24] Francisco López quoted in Gangemi, p. 32.

[25] López (2006.)

[26] Atau Tanaka quoted in "Questionnaire" by Brandon LaBelle and Sabine Breitsameter *Soundscape: The Journal of Acoustic Ecology,* Vol. 3 No. 1 (July 2002), pp. 11-14 (p. 14.)

[27] *Ibid.*, p. 12.

[28] Fraqncsico López, CD liner notes to *Buildings [New York].*

[29] Sabine Breitsameter, "Acoustic Ecology and the New Electroacoustic Space of Digital Networks." *Soundscape: The Journal of Acoustic Ecology,* Vol. 4 No. 2 (Winter 2003), pp. 24-30 (p. 24.)

[30] *Ibid.*

[31] "The cellular phone, which the Germans appropriately called the 'Handy', is the latest installment in this drama. Answer when your master calls. Life without secrets, without privacy, without freedom. The latest shackle for the technological prisoner to carry about." R. Murray Schafer, "Open Ears." *Soundscape: The Journal of Acoustic Ecology,* Vol. 4. No. 2 (Winter 2003), pp. 14-18 (p. 18.)

[32] "If you can't name the birds, if you don't know how to recognize the leaves of the trees by the sounds they make, or hear a cataract down the river, or recognize when a winter wind is bringing in a storm, nature is anesthetized, and its survival will depend on forces other than human." *Ibid.*

[33] Dorion Sagan quoted in *A Foray into the Worlds of Human and Animals (With a Theory of Meaning)* by Jakob von Üexkull., p. 23. Trans. Joseph D. O'Neil. University of Minnesota Press, Minneapolis, 2010.

[34] *Ibid.*

[35] "The nature of life is to delight in all possible loopholes. It will break any rule it comes up with. Take these biological jaw-droppers: a female fish that is fertilized by the male mate who lives inside her, organisms that shrink as they grow, plants that never die. Biological life is a curiosity shop whose shelves never empty." Kevin Kelly, *Out of Control: The Rise of the Neo-Biological Civilization,* p. 340. Addison-Wesley, Reading MA., 1994.

[36] Francisco López quoted in *Substantials #01,* p. 140. Ed. Akiko Miyake. CCA Kita-Kyushu, Kita-Kyushu, 2003.

[37] López (2006.)

[38] Daniel Gasman quoted in *Ecofascism: Lessons from the German Experience,* by Janet Biehl & Peter Staudenmaier, p. 60. AK Press, San Francisco, 1995.

[39] *Ibid.*

[40] Jonathan Sterne, *The Audible Past: Cultural Origins of Sound Reproduction,* p. 343. Duke University Press, Durham / London, 2003.

[41] López (2003 [p. 114.])

[42] Adam Kadmon quoted in *Lords of Chaos: The Bloody Rise of the Satanic Metal Underground,* by Michael Moynihan and Didrik Søderlind, p. 339. Feral House, Los Angeles, 1998.

[43] *Ibid.*

[44] *Ibid.,* p. 340.

[45] See http://www.franciscolopez.net/int_revue.html. Retrieved October 15, 2012.

[46] Discogs.com user 'Peshehod' quoted at http://www.discogs.com/release/123683, March 8, 2005.

[47] http://www.franciscolopez.net/int_loop.html. Retrieved October 15, 2012.

[48] *Ibid.*

[49] Eugene Thacker,"Through The Looking Glass (review)". *Leonardo Music Journal,* Vol. 45 No. 3, (2012), pp. 300-301 (p. 300.)

Chapter 9

[1] Ed Pinsent, review of *Our Telluric Conversation* by John Duncan & CM von Hausswolff. *The Sound Projector* #15 (2007), p. 92.

[2] Mike Kelley, "John Duncan: Los Angeles, Late 1970s / Early 1980s." *John Duncan: Works 1975-2005,* p. 14. Errant Bodies Press, Copenhagen, 2006.

[3] Takuya Sakaguchi, "Woofer, Choir, Radio, Religion and DumDum Boys." *Ibid.,* p. 21.

[4] "Erwin Straus, in his classic book *The Primary World of the Senses* (1935), had established a fundamental distinction between perception and sensation. Perception, he argued, is a secondary rational organization of a primary, non-rational dimension of sensation (or 'sense experience', *le sentir.*) Earlier in the century, Marius von Senden had recorded the experiences of the congenitally blind people who were given sight after the operation to remove cataracts was developed. Initially such patients were afflicted by a chaos of forms and colors, a gaudy confusion of visual *sensations* within which they could distinguish neither shapes nor space. They would acquire a *perception* of the world only after an often-painful process of learning and apprenticeship, during which they developed the schemata and 'Gestalten' capable of providing this pre-reflective sense experience with the coordinates familiar to ordinary perception." Daniel W. Smith quoted in *Francis Bacon: The Logic of Sensation* by Gilles Deleuze, p. xiv. Trans. Daniel W. Smith. University of Minnesota Press, Minneapolis, 2005.

[5] Stephen Zepke, "The Concept of Art When Art is Not a Concept." *Angelaki: Journal of the Theoretical Humanities,* Vol. 11 No. 1 (2006), pp. 157-167 (p. 159.)

[6] *Ibid.,* p. 160.

[7] Personal conversation with the author, May 2006.

[8] John Duncan, booklet accompanying *Our Telluric Conversation* CD by John Duncan & CM von Hausswolff, p. 15. 23five, San Francisco, 2006.

[9] *Ibid.*

[10] Jerzy Grotowsky, *Towards a Poor Theater,* p. 16. Simon & Schuster, New York, 1969.

[11] *Ibid.*

[12] Annie Buckley, "Viewpoint." *Artweek* Vol. 38 No. 9 (2007), p. 4.

[13] http://www.johnduncan.org/abrahamsson.html. Retrieved November 24, 2012.

[14] *Ibid.*

[15] John Duncan, "Happy Homes". *Creed 7*", AQM, Los Angeles, 1981.

[16] Duncan (2006, 1.)

[17] *Ibid.*

[18] *Ibid.*

[19] http://www.johnduncan.org/interview.jp.html. Retrieved November 24, 2012. Translated from the Japanese by the author.

[20] http://www.nrk.no/nett-tv/indeks/247802. Retrieved January 25, 2011.

[21] It is interesting to note, with this in mind, Duncan's own self-reflection on *Blind Date* voiced during his mid-1980s period in Tokyo: "[it] made me think a lot more about the importance of myth and the importance of the belief in myth or religion; why these things are important. Not to me so much, but to people in general. It made me realize how blind people are to the fact that they need belief. They need it, they really need it. We need it. I need it." Quoted in "John Duncan Interview (author uncredited)". *ND #8* (1987), p. 33.

[22] http://www.nrk.no/nett-tv/indeks/247802. Retrieved January 25, 2011.

[23] Duncan (2006, 1.)

[24] *Ibid.*

[25] Harper Montgomery, "Teresa Margolles." *Art Nexus* Vol. 7 No. 71, pp. 139-140 (p. 139.)

[26] Pascal Beausse, "Teresa Margolles: Primordial Substances." Translated from the French by Anthony Allen. *Flash Art #38* (January 2005), p. 108.

[27] http://www.johnduncan.org/wlassoff.rc1.html. Retrieved November 24, 2012.

[28] John Duncan, *Toshiji Mikawa - Radio Code* cassette side A, AQM, Amsterdam, 1989.

[29] Tarou Amano quoted in Alexandra Munroe, *Scream Against The Sky: Japanese Art After 1945*, p. 70 (trans. Robert Reed.) Harry N. Abrams, New York, 1994.

[30] These involved, on separate occasions, the use of a backhoe to demolish a live venue, the on-stage dissection of a dead cat, and a performance that would have involved an entire venue catching fire had bandleader Yamatsuka Eye not been stopped from throwing a molotov cocktail onto a gas-drenched stage. Unsurprisingly, a nationwide ban on Hanatarash performances soon went into effect.

[31] Duncan (1989).

[32] Arthur Zich, "Japan's Sun Rises Over the Pacific." *National Geographic,* November 1981, p. 41.

[33] Duncan (1987), p. 33.

[34] Detlev Schauwecker, "Verbal Subversion and Satire in Japan, 1937-1945, as Documented by the Special High Police." *Japan Review,* No. 15 (2003), pp. 127-151 (p. 131.)

[35] Sakaguchi (2006.)

[36] Duncan (2006, 1.)

[37] Michael Prime, "Explorations in Bioelectronics." *Resonance* Vol. 9 No. 2 (2002), p. 17.

[38] *Ibid.*

[39] Rinus van Alebeek, "The Early Years." Unpublished manuscript, 2012.

[40] Erik Hobijn quoted in *Pranks!,* p. 207. Ed. Andrea Juno & V. Vale. Re/Search, San Francisco, 1987.

[41] Willem de Ridder, "Willem de Ridder." *Contemporary Music Review,* Vol. 25, Nos. 5/6, (October/December 2006,) pp. 397 – 402 (p. 401.)

[42] *Ibid.,* p. 400.

[43] Willem de Ridder and Andrew McKenzie, *This Glass is a Bicycle* promotional cassette. Unreleased / no label.

[44] *Ibid.*

[45] Carl Michael von Hausswolff, "A Palace in a Stack of Needles." *John Duncan: Works 1975-2005,* p. 20. Errant Bodies Press, Copenhagen, 2006.

[46] Email correspondence with the author, February 2008.

[47] Email correspondence with the author, June 2008.

[48] *Ibid.*

[49] Prime (2002.)

[50] Duncan (2006, 1.)

[51] Email correspondence with the author, January 2011.

[52] Email correspondence with the author, February 2011.

[53] *Ibid.*

Chapter 10

[1] Arthur Schopenhauer, *The World as Will and Idea,* p. 170-171. Tuttle Publishing, North Clarendon, 1995.

[2] Erik Davis, *TechGnosis: Myth, Magic and Mysticism in the Age of Information,* p. 291. Three Rivers Press, New York, 1999

[3] Richard E. Cytowic, M.D., *Synesthesia: A Union Of The Senses,* p. 46. MIT Press, Cambridge / London, 2002.

[4] See Cytowic pp. 101-103 for more detail on this subject.

[5] http://www.neurologyreviews.com/jul02/nr_jul02_mindseye.html

[6] http://barneygrant.tripod.com/synaes.htm. Retrieved October 24, 2012.

[7] György Ligeti, *Ligeti in Conversation*, p. 58. Eulenburg Books, London, 1983.

[8] Duke Ellington quoted in *Sweet Man: The Real Duke Ellington* by Don George, p. 191. G.P. Putnam's Sons, New York, 1981.

[9] Wassily Kandinsky, *Concerning The Spiritual In Art*, p. 42. Trans. by M.T.H. Sadler. Dover Publications, New York, 1977.

[10] Certain of the claims made in *Thought-Forms* are embarrassingly quaint relics of the Theosophist heyday- the author's preface boasts that telepathy and clairvoyance were entering the "Cinderella stage" of acceptance by non-esoteric researchers, or notes that a "Dr. Baraduc of Paris [...] is well on his way to photographing astro-mental images." (Annie Besant and C.W. Leadbetter, *Thought-Forms*, p. 12. Theosophical Publishing Society, London / Benares, 1905.) The "thoughtography" of the latter has become more widely associated with the disproven 20th century attempts of Ted Serios and Uri Geller.

[11] Email correspondence with the author, December 2007.

[12] One earlier reference point for this phenomenon is the performance of LaMonte Young's *Composition 1960 #4*, during which lights were turned off for the piece's duration (with the added performance instruction that no "intentional" actions were performed.)

[13] Z'ev quoted in *Acoustic Phenomenae* by Dmitry Koselnick. *The Egg and We #1*, March-June 1999 (unedited MS Word manuscript.)

[14] Email correspondence with the author, 1 August 2011.

[15] Errki Kurenniemi quoted in *The Future Is Not What It Used To Be,* dir. Mika Taanila. Kinotar, 2002.

[16] *Ibid.*

[17] *Ibid.*

[18] UPIC is an acronym for Unité Polygogique de CeMaMu, which is itself an acronym for Centre d'Etudes de Mathématique et Automatique Musicales, a cooperative research center formed in the 1960s by Xenakis.

[19] Henning Lohner and Iannis Xenakis, "Interview with Iannis Xenakis." *Computer Music Journal,* Vol. 10, No. 4 (Winter 1986), pp. 50-55 (p. 51.)

[20] *Ibid.,* p. 50.

[21] Jean-Baptiste Thiebaut and Patrick G. T. Healey, "Sketching Musical Composition." *Proceedings of the Cognitive Science Society Conference,* Nashville, USA, 2007.

[22] Roger T. Dean, Mitchell Whitelaw, Hazel Smith & David Worrall, "The Mirage of Real-Time Algorithmic Synaesthesia: Some Compositional Mechanisms and Research, Agendas

in Computer Music and Sonification, *Contemporary Music Review*, Vol. 25 No. 4, pp. 311-326 (p. 312.)

[23] " An array of computer musicians, DJs and VJs use algorithms to mediate sound or image production in performance with laptops and data projectors, though often with little interest in algorithmic synaesthesia, partly because different performer take responsibility for sound and image and work largely independently." *Ibid.*

[24] Messiaen's clinical synesthesia, extremely rare within adult humans to begin with, is made yet rarer by its "bi-directional" quality. Namely, his ability to perceive audible values in visuals, as well as the reverse, is limited to a minority of individuals diagnosed with synesthesia.

[25] Bert Bongers and Sensorband,"An Interview with Sensorband." *Computer Music Journal*, Vol. 22, No. 1 (Spring 1998), pp. 13-24 (p. 17.)

[26] *Ibid.*, p. 17.

[27] As of the 1998 interview / overview by Bert Bongers, each instrumentalist within Sensorband had been a soloist on their instrument for five years, suggesting a higher degree of patience with these instruments than with a keyboard synthesizer (Bongers, p. 13.)

[28] Bob Ostertag,*Creative Life*, p. 103. University of Illinois Press, 2008.

[29] Louise Provencher, "Atau Tanaka: Le Corps Sous Tension Ou De L'eloquence du Geste." Trans. Timothy Barnard. *Parachute* No. 121 (Spring 2006), pp. 62-77 (p. 65.)

[30] Zbigniew Karkowski quoted in Timothy Jaeger, "The Anti-Laptop Aesthetic." *Contemporary Music Review*, Vol. 22 No. 4, 53-57 (p. 57.)

[31] Morag Josephine Grant, "Experimental Music Semiotics." *International Review of the Aesthetics and Sociology of Music*, Vol. 34, No. 2 (December 2003), pp. 173-191 (p. 173-174.)

[32] *Ibid.*, p. 184.

[33] Schopenhauer, p. 165.

[34] *Ibid.*, p. 166.

[35] Christiaan Stuten quoted in *Cymatics: A Study of Wave Phenomena and Vibration*, Hans Jenny, p. 14. Macromedia Press, 2001.

[36] *Ibid.*

[37] Rob Young, "A Glitch In The System." *Modern Painters* June 2006, pp. 90-93 (p. 92.)

[38] Carsten Nicolai quoted in "The Perfect Strom" by Ben Borthwick. *The Wire* #283, December 2003, p. 42.

[39] *Ibid.* (Ben Borthwick.)

[40] http://www.carstennicolai.de/?c=biography. Retrieved October 24, 2012.

[41] See, for example, Nicolai's inclusion (alongside Carsten Höller, Keith Tyson and Mark Dion) in "Des Artistes ès Sciences" by Judicael Lavrador. *Beaux Arts* No. 207 (Summer 2007), pp. 97-99.

[42] *Ibid.*

[43] Le Corbusier, *Towards a New Architecture*, p. 110. Dover Publications, New York, 1986.

[44] Refer to 16 above.

[45] http://www.carstennicolai.de/?c=works&w=telefunken_wtc_version. Retrieved October 24, 2012.

[46] Carsten Nicolai, "The Responsive Eye: Beyond What We Call 'Art.'" *Flash Art*, March / April 2011, pp. 74-76.

[47] *Ibid.*

[48] Cytowic, p. 220.

[49] Cretien van Campen, *The Hidden Sense: Synesthesia in Art and Science*, p.31. MIT Press / Leonardo Books, Cambridge / London, 2010.

[50] Brian Massumi, *Parable For The Virtual: Movement, Affect, Sensation*, p. 188. Duke University Press, Durham NC, 2002.

[51] Refer to 3 above .

Chapter 11

[1] John Cage, *Silence*, p. 16. Wesleyan University Press, Middleton CT, 1973.

[2] *Ibid.*, p. 7.

[3] Christophe Charles, "Megalopolis Aborigines: The Tokyo-Osaka Action Art Ensemble's 1992 Tour." *Leonardo Music Journal*, Vol. 4 (1994), pp. 99-102 (p. 101.)

[4] Arata Isozaki, "As Witness To Postwar Japanese Art" (trans. Kohso Sabu.) *Scream Against The Sky: Japanese Art After 1945*, ed. Alexandra Munroe, p. 28. Harry N. Abrams, New York, 1994.

[5] Richard Chartier quoted in Philip Sherburne, "12K: Between Two Points." *Organized Sound*, Vol. 6 No. 3 (December 2001), pp 171 176 (p. 173.)

[6] See http://www.well.com/~demarini/kahn.html. Retrieved October 25, 2012.

[7] From all available evidence, this is one genre term that seems to have been decided upon by the artists themselves rather than the critical community. David Novak offers an interesting argument as to why the coining of a new genre term for this type of practice was more liberating than burdensome: " Seeking to avoid the detrimental effects of canon formation, many musicians rename their music in order to maintain authorial control over

their own history. For example, part of what led the Chicago-based collective Association for the Advancement of Creative Musicians (AACM) to choose the term 'creative music' in the late 1960s was to 'challenge the use of jazz-related images to police and limit the scope of black cultural expression and economic advancement."' David Novak, "Playing Off Site: The Untranslation of Onkyo." *Asian Music,* 41:1 (Winter/Spring 2010), pp. 36-59 (p. 42.)

[8] User "Namakemono," review of *Blank Tapes* by Reynols, June 16, 2008. Available online at http://www.discogs.com/release/325745.

[9] Taku Sugimoto, liner notes, *Off Site Composed Music Series In 2001.* A Bruit Secret, Paris, 2002.

[10] Steve Roden quoted in "Case Sensitive" by Christoph Cox, *The Wire,* # 229 March 2003, p. 30.

[11] Astro Twin quoted at http://www.japanimprov.com/astrotwin/profile.html

[12] *Ibid.*

[13] Alan Watts, *Tao: The Watercourse Way* p. 21. Pantheon Books, New York, 1975.

[14] Fritjof Capra, *The Tao of Physics,* p. 212. Shambala, Boston, 1991.

[15] Stefan Jaworzyn, review of "so delicate and strangely made" by in be tween noise. *Music From The Empty Quarter*, August/September 1995, p. 90.

[16] Novak, p. 55.

[17] Mattin, "Going Fragile." *Noise And Capitalism,* p. 21. Arteleku, Madrid, 2009.

[18] *Ibid.,* p. 22.

[19] Walter Benjamin quoted in *Ibid.*

[20] Terre Thaemlitz quoted in Timothy Jaeger, "The (Anti)-Laptop Aesthetic." *Contemporary Music Review,* 22:4, 53-57 (p. 55.)

[21] See Haino's see *Black Blues: Soft Version,* one of his penultimate expressions of strange evanescence, for a striking example of this.

[22] David Toop, *Haunted Weather: Music, Silence, and Memory,* p. 253. Serpents' Tail, London, 2004.

[23] Taku Sugimoto quoted in "Understatement of Intent" by Clive Bell. *The Wire,* # 237 November 2003, p. 30.

[24] Uplink Factory has relocated since the original draft of this article, though the new environs are only slightly removed from the ones already mentioned.

[25] Noriyuki Tajima, "Tokyo Catalyst: Shifting Situations of Urban Space." *Perspecta,* Vol. 38 (2006), pp. 79-90 (p. 89.)

[26] John C. Lilly, *Programming and Metaprogramming in the Human Biocomputer,* p. 76. The Julian Press, New York, 1972.

[27] Personal correspondence with the author, April 2008.

[28] *Ibid.*

[29] Samuel R. DeLany, *Dhalgren*, p. 610. Vintage Books, New York, 2001.

[30] *Ibid.*

Chapter 12

[1] Krzysztof Ziarek, "The Avant Garde and Power." *New Literary History* Vol. 33, No. 1 (Winter, 2002), pp. 89-107 (p. 89.)

[2] Nick Prior, "OK COMPUTER: Mobility, software and the laptop musician." *Information, Communication & Society,* Vol. 11 No. 7, pp. 912-932 (p. 925-926.)

[3] To wit: "When you hear a great moment in music, it is because there's a feeling of your eyes opening. That perhaps is why random sequencing, although surprising, is not musical in that is doesn't reveal as it surprises." Gareth Loy quoted in "Dartmouth Symposium on the Future of Computer Music Software: A Panel Discussion" by Eric Lyon, Max Mathews, James McCartney, David Zicarelli, Barry Vercoe, Gareth Loy and Miller Puckette. *Computer Music Journal*, Vol. 26, No. 4 (Winter 2002), pp. 13-30 (p. 19.)

[4] For a thorough analysis of 'progressive' eugenics in Tret'iakov, see pp. 247-254 of *Imagine No Possessions: The Socialist Objects of Soviet Constructivism.* MIT Press, Cambridge / London, 2005.

[5] Cedric Price & Joan Littlewood, "The Fun Palace." *The Drama Review: TDR,* Vol. 12, No. 3 (Spring, 1968), pp.127-134 (p. 129.)

[6] Mark Wigley, "Network Fever." *Grey Room,* No. 4 (Summer, 2001), pp. 82-122 (p. 106.)

[7] Stelarc interviewed by Carl Abrahamsson, 2002 (originally published at http://www.grounded-mag.net/stelarc.html. Link defunct as of this writing.)

[8] *Ibid.*

[9] Istvan Csicsery-Ronay, Jr., while reviewing Stelarc's posthumanist essay "From Psycho-Body to Cyber-Systems: Images as Post-Human Entities," makes a brief catalog of these worth repeating here: "[the manifesto] proposes to greet with delight the annihilation of individual will, at the same time that it calls for a technology that will give individuals the right to alter their own DNA. It calls for the complication of the body through prosthetics, and justifies this because the body has too many redundant systems. Stelarc calls for a conception of the body that will permit it to be used (involuntarily) by other minds, and to be subjected to surveillance at the cellular level. (Indeed, he discusses in the [*Digital Delirium*] interview a sculpture that is installed in his stomach; the object has no significance except as something to be scoped with some surveillance devices.)" Istvan Csicsery-Ronay, Jr., "Pre2K Post2K Virtualities: *Television, Media Art, and Cyberculture* by Margaret Morse; *Digital Delirium* by Arthur Kroker; Marilouise Kroker; *Virtual*

Futures: Cyberotics, Technology and Post-Human Pragmatism by Joan Broadhurst Dixon; Eric Cassidy - Review." *Science Fiction Studies,* Vol. 27 No. 3 (Nov. 2000), pp. 485-493 (p. 491.)

[10] John Gray, *The Immortalization Commission: Science and the Strange Quest to Cheat Death,* p. 217. Farrar, Strauss & Giroux, New York, 2011.

[11] Stelarc (2002.)

[12] Ziarek, p. 95.

[13] *Ibid.,* p. 91.

Made in the USA
Middletown, DE
13 November 2017